JOSEPHUS

JOSEPHUS

A Historical Romance

LION FEUCHTWANGER

*Translated from the German by
Willa and Edwin Muir*

A TEMPLE BOOK

NEW YORK   ATHENEUM   1985

Originally published in German under the title Der Jüdische Krieg
English translation Copyright 1932, © *1960 by Viking Press*
Published by Atheneum
Reprinted by arrangement with
The Jewish Publication Society of America
All rights reserved
Library of Congress catalog card number: 32-28823
ISBN 0-689-70345-7
Published simultaneously in Canada by Collier Macmillan Canada, Inc.
Manufactured in the United States of America by
Fairfield Graphics, Fairfield, Pennsylvania
First Atheneum Printing January 1973
Second Printing October 1981
Third Printing December 1985

CONTENTS

Book One
ROME

Book One

ROME

I

SIX bridges led across the river Tiber. On the right bank one was safe ; there the streets were full of men whose beards proclaimed them to be Jews ; everywhere Jewish and Aramaic inscriptions were to be seen, and with a little Greek one could easily make one's way. But as soon as one crossed any of the bridges and ventured on to the left bank of the Tiber, one was irretrievably in the great and turbulent city of Rome, a stranger hopelessly alone.

Nevertheless Joseph dismissed the boy Cornelius, his devoted little guide, at the Emilius Bridge ; he wanted to see how he could manage by himself, if only as a test of his confidence and adaptability. Little Cornelius would willingly have accompanied the stranger farther. Joseph gazed after him as he reluctantly walked back across the bridge, and suddenly with a kind smile he, the Jew Joseph, jestingly outstretched his arm with his hand open, and saluted the boy in the Roman fashion, and the Jewish boy Cornelius, likewise smiling, returned the Roman greeting, although it was strictly against his father's orders. Then he turned to the left at the corner of a tall building and was gone, and Joseph was alone, and now he would see how far he could depend on his Latin.

He knew that the place just in front of him was the cattle market, and that the Circus Maximus was to the right, and that over there on the Palatine and behind it, where there

3

were such crowds of people, the Emperor was building his new house, and that the street to the left led to the Forum, and that the Palatine and the Forum were the heart of the world.

He had read a great deal about Rome, but that did not help him much. The fire three months before had greatly changed the city. It had destroyed the four central districts, including over three hundred public buildings, some six hundred palaces and villas, and several thousand houses. It was astonishing how much these Romans had already rebuilt in the short time since. He could not endure them, these Romans ; indeed he hated them, but he was forced to admit that they had a talent for organisation ; they had their technique. Technique, he mused over the strange word, repeating it several times to himself in the foreign Latin tongue. He was not a dunce ; he would watch these Romans and learn something of their technique.

He strode on vigorously. He sniffed eagerly and with excitement the atmosphere of these strange houses and of these foreign people, in whose power it lay to raise him to power or to keep him where he was. At home, in Jerusalem, it was the month of Tishra now, and still very hot though the month was near its end ; but here in Rome it was called September, and to-day at any rate the air was fresh and pleasant. A light wind fluttered his hair, which he wore somewhat long for the Roman fashion. Besides, he should really have been wearing a hat ; for a Jew in his position, unlike the Romans, was supposed to go out with his head covered. But what did it matter ; here the overwhelming majority of the Jews went about bareheaded like the others, at least when they had the Tiber at their backs. His Jewish nationalism would not become more lukewarm, even if he did not wear a hat.

Now he found himself in front of the Circus Maximus. Everything lay in ruins ; the fire had begun here. Nevertheless the main lines of the masonry were intact. A gigantic business, this Circus Maximus. It took almost ten minutes to walk from one end of it to the other. The stadiums in Jerusalem and Caesarea were by no means small, but compared to this vast construction they seemed like toys.

Inside the Circus work was proceeding, stone was being laid on stone, carpenters were busy. A curious crowd of idlers and children strolled about. Joseph's clothes were not of the cut usually worn in the capital ; nevertheless as he strode along, young, slender, dignified, with eyes that took in everything, he looked elegant, not in the least common, a gentleman. Vendors thronged round him, offering him amulets, souvenirs, an effigy of the obelisk, which, alien and solemn, rose in the middle of the Circus. An authorised guide offered to show him all the sights, the imperial box, the model of the new Circus. But Joseph rejected his offer with an air of supercilious boredom. He clambered about among the stone tiers as if he had been a constant spectator of the races that had taken place here.

Those lower tiers were evidently the seats of the high aristocracy, the Senate. Nobody prevented him from sitting down on one of those enviously sought for places. It was nice to sit there in the sun. He squatted at his ease with his head on one hand, and gazed absently at the obelisk in the middle of the Circus. A better time for his plan than these months after the great fire he could not have wished ; the people were well disposed and receptive. The energy with which the Emperor had flung himself into the rebuilding of the city had communicated itself to every one. Everywhere there was bustle, confidence and activity ; the light, fresh air was very different from the brooding, sultry atmosphere of Jerusalem, where everything held one back.

In the Circus Maximus, sitting in the pleasant sunshine amid the hubbub of a new Rome being built, on one of the seats reserved for the Senators, Joseph weighed his chances passionately and yet coldly. He was twenty-six and had every quality that was needed for a great career ; he came of a noble house, possessed a wide culture, had ability in state matters, and a furious ambition. No, he did not intend to rot in Jerusalem. He was thankful to his father, who believed in him and had secured his being sent to Rome.

His mission here, nevertheless, was an extremely questionable one. Legally speaking the High Council in Jerusalem had neither any justification nor any authority to send a special emissary to Rome in this matter. And Joseph had had to scrape together all the arguments he could think of before the great gentlemen of Jerusalem had reluctantly capitulated.

The matter was as follows. Three members of the High Council whom the governor, Antonius Felix, had sent to Rome two years before as rebels to be tried by the imperial tribunal, had been unjustly sentenced to forced labour. It was true that the three men had been in Caesarea when in the course of the election disturbances the Jews had torn down and smashed the Imperial insignia before the Governor's residence : but they themselves had not taken part in the rebellious act. The Governor's selection of these three old men in high positions was an arbitrary act of injustice, a scandalous wrong, an insult to the whole Jewish people. Joseph saw in it a great and eagerly longed for opportunity to distinguish himself. He had hunted up new evidence for the innocence of the three prisoners ; he hoped to secure their rehabilitation or at least their reprieve at the Imperial court.

The Roman Jews, he had already noticed, would not put themselves to much trouble to help him in his mission. The furniture-maker Caius Barzaarone, president of the Agrippine Ward, with whom he was staying and to whom his father had given him a cordial letter of recommendation, had explained the situation to him slyly, benevolently and circumspectly, and mainly in hints. The hundred thousand Jews in Rome were not so very badly off. They lived in peace with the rest of the population. With discomfort they saw that the nationalist party in Jerusalem, which was hostile to Rome and called itself " The Avengers of Israel," was gaining more and more influence. They had no intention of endangering their comfortable situation by involving themselves in the perpetual squabbles that took place between the Jerusalem politicians and the Imperial Government. No, the real work Joseph would have to do himself.

Before him the building was going on, stone and wood were rising, bricks, columns in marble of every colour. He could almost see the edifice growing. When half an hour or an hour from now he should leave, it would have grown, not very much, it was true, perhaps to the extent of a thousandth part of its entire bulk ; but the prescribed stint would have been achieved. And he, too, had achieved something. His resolve to go forward had become more ardent, more burning, more irresistible. Every stroke of the hammers, every screech of the saws, that came across to him from where the masons and the carpenters were working, hammered and sawed on his mind, while, apparently at his ease, an idler among many other idlers, he lounged in the sunshine. He would have much to do before he got his three innocent men out of prison ; but he would bring it off.

Already his position seemed less hopeless and forlorn than during his first days here. His awe in front of the fleshy, impassive faces of these people had dwindled. He had noticed that these Romans were of smaller stature than himself. He walked among them, tall and slender, and the women turned their heads to look after him in Rome just as they had done in Jerusalem and Caesarea. Obviously Irene, the daughter of his host Caius, had remained behind in the room that morning simply because of him, Joseph, although it had displeased her father. He had a strong body, and a quick and supple mind. When he was twenty-one he had won his doctorate at the Temple High School in Jerusalem ; he had at his finger tips the entire complicated province of juristic and theological exegesis. And had he not also lived for two years as a hermit in the wilderness with the Essene Banus, so as to acquire the art of pure contemplation and concentration which in times of doubt gave one guidance and leading ? All that he demanded was the first rung of the ladder, the one favourable moment. It would come, it must come.

The young literatteur and statesman, Joseph Ben Matthias, set his teeth. You just wait, my fine gentlemen of the High Council, my high and mighty gentlemen of the Temple Court. You have snubbed me, you have kept me under. If my father hadn't given me something to eke out the grant you allowed me from the Temple Fund, I shouldn't have been able to come here at all. But now I'm here in Rome as your delegate. And mark my words, I'll make the most of the situation. I'll show you a trick or two, my learned doctors.

The people loitering in the Circus Maximus began to shout to one another and got up ; and all gazed in the same direction. From the Palatine was descending a brilliant

procession, heralds, pages, servitors, litters. Joseph, too, got
up to see what was happening. In a moment the guide who
had spoken to him before was at his side again, and this time
Joseph did not reject his services. No, it was neither the
Emperor, nor the captain of the Imperial Guard ; it was a
Senator or some other great man, who was being shown
round the new Circus by the architect Celerus.

The curious crowd drew nearer, but were held b⌐⌐k by
the police and the servants of the architect and the visitor.
The experienced guide managed to push his way with Joseph
into the front row. Yes, it was the Senator Marullus, as
he had already recognised from the liveries of the pages,
couriers and lackeys. Joseph knew something of this man ;
for as in all the other provinces, wild stories were told in
Jerusalem of this brilliant figure at the Imperial Court, by
whom, it was said, the Emperor was guided in all questions of
sophisticated enjoyment. Besides, it was whispered that
certain popular entertainments, for example the daring revues
which the great comedian, Demetrius Libanus, produced,
were written by Marullus. Joseph gazed greedily at this
much talked of gentleman, who while reclining languidly
in his litter was listening to the architect's explanations,
sometimes raising his jade lorgnette to his eye.

Joseph's glance caught another gentleman who also seemed
to enjoy the greatest esteem. But could that fellow be a
gentleman ? He had stepped out of his litter, and now in his
shabby and unkempt clothes was trailing about among the
building material lying everywhere. He was stoutish, with
an unshaven fleshy face and heavy sleepy eyes under a
projecting forehead. He gave only half an ear to the
architect's recitation, lifted up a piece of marble, turned it
about with his stubby fingers, brought it quite close to his
eyes, smelt it, threw it away again, snatched a tool out of a

mason's hand and fingered it, and at last seated himself on a block of stone and groaningly tied his shoe laces which had come undone, crossly rejecting the help of a lackey who had hastened up to him.   Yes, the guide knew him too ; it was Claudius Reginus.   " The publisher ? " asked Joseph.   It was possible that he sold books as well as other things, but the guide had not heard anything about that.   He knew him only as the Emperor's court jeweller.   A very influential gentleman, in any case, a great financier, although from his clothes you would think he was destitute and he laid so little importance on the number and splendour of his retinue. Very strange ; for he had been born a slave, son of a Sicilian father and a Jewish mother, and a self-made man usually liked to make a great display.   In any case this Claudius Reginus had achieved fabulous success during the forty-two years of his life ; that was certain.   Under the rule of the present Emperor, with his passion for getting things done, there were many plums to be had, and juicy ones too, and Claudius Reginus had his finger in all of them ; the most part of the Egyptian and Libyan grain fleet belonged to him, and his granaries in Puteoli and Ostia were show places.

The senator Marullus and the court jeweller Claudius Reginus conversed loudly and at their ease, so that in the first row of spectators, where Joseph stood, every word could be heard.   Joseph had expected these two men, whose names were mentioned with respect in literary circles all over the world—for Claudius Reginus was the chief publisher in Rome—to exchange interesting critical views upon the new Circus.   He listened intently.   He could not follow the speakers' fluent Latin, but one thing he could gather, that they were not conversing about aesthetic or philosophical matters at all, but about prices, rates of exchange and business deals. He could hear without difficulty the shrill, falsetto voice of the senator, who in a vein of complacent raillery enquired from his litter, so loudly that everybody around could hear : " Are you really making anything on the Circus Maximus, Claudius Reginus ? " The jeweller, who was sitting on a block of stone in the sunshine, his hands comfortably resting on his fat knees, replied without the slightest embarrassment : " Unfortunately no, Senator Marullus. I thought that our architect here had let you in on the business." Joseph heard a great deal more, but his defective knowledge of the language and of business terms prevented him from grasping it. The guide, who himself did not quite understand what it was all about, tried to help him. Evidently both Claudius Reginus and the senator Marullus had secured on cheap terms great areas of land in the outer suburbs that were still unbuilt on ; now, after the great fire, the Emperor was clearing the centre of the city for his public buildings, and forcing the population to house themselves in the outer suburbs ; so that the land on the outskirts of the city had appreciated fantastically in value.

" Yes, but isn't it forbidden by law for members of the Senate to take part in business ? " Joseph suddenly asked the guide. The guide, completely taken aback, gaped at his customer ; some of the people standing round had been listening ; they began to laugh, others laughed with them, the question of the man from the provinces was passed on from mouth to mouth, and finally the whole gigantic Circus rang with tumultuous laughter.

The senator Marullus enquired into the reason. A clear space was made round Joseph ; and suddenly he found himself face to face with the two great men. " So you disapprove of that, young man ? " asked the fat man aggressively and yet jocosely. He sat on his block of stone, his arms resting on his massive knees, like a statue of an Egyptian king. The hot sun was not oppressive, a light breeze was blowing, everyone was in a good humour. The numerous servants of the two gentlemen listened with delight to this entertainment at the expense of the man from the provinces.

Joseph stood his ground modestly and was not in the least put out. " I've only been three days in Rome," he said in his somewhat laborious Greek. " Is it very stupid of me not to have got used yet to the business customs of this great city ? "

" Where do you come from ? " the senator asked from his litter.

" From Egypt ? " asked Claudius Reginus.

" I come from Jerusalem," responded Joseph, and he gave his full name : Joseph Ben Matthias, priest of the first rank.

" That's a great deal, in Jerusalem," said the senator, and one could not make out whether he was joking or in earnest. The architect Celerus showed signs of impatience ; he wanted to explain his plans to these great men ; they were superb plans, full of ingenuity and daring, and he refused to be put out by this awkward provincial. But the financier Claudius Reginus was inquisitive by nature, and he sat at his ease on his warm block and questioned the young Jew. Joseph was perfectly ready to give information. But that was not very easy, in Greek. He talked away ; he tried to be original and interesting and show himself and his people in a favourable light. In Rome, he asked, was a house ever attacked by leprosy ? No, they told him, that had never happened. But in Judaea, Joseph went on, it was a frequent occurrence. At such times little reddish or greenish cavities appeared in the walls, and occasionally these were so bad that the house had to be demolished. Sometimes, however, the priest could be of help ; but the ceremony was by no means a simple one. The priest had first to scrape out the unsound part ; then he had to take two birds, some cedar wood, some wool dyed scarlet, and some hyssop. With the blood of one of the birds he sprinkled the house seven times, but the other bird he had to take outside the city and set it free. Then the house was cleansed and pure. The crowd standing round listened to this story with interest and for the most part without incredulity ; for they had a taste for the bizarre and loved the uncanny.

With his sleepy eyes the jeweller Claudius Reginus gravely regarded the lean, eager young man. " Are you here on business, Doctor Joseph ? " he asked. " Or have you merely come to see the rebuilding of our city ? "

" I am here on business," answered Joseph. " There are three innocent men whom I must set free. That is regarded among us as very urgent business."

" I am afraid," said the senator, yawning lazily, " that we're so busy at present rebuilding the city that we haven't much time for such trifles as the innocence of three prisoners."

The architect began impatiently : " For the balustrade of the imperial box I intend to employ this green and black veined serpentine. I have had a particularly fine block sent from Sparta."

" I saw on my way here the newly built streets in Alexandria," said Joseph, who did not intend to be thrust out of the conversation. " The streets there are broad, airy and straight."

The architect replied contemptuously : " Anybody could rebuild Alexandria. There's space there, and level ground."

" Be reassured, master," said Claudius Reginus in his high, unctuous voice, " A blind man can see that Rome is a different proposition from Alexandria."

"Let me instruct this young gentleman," said the senator Marullus with a smile. He was roused ; he felt a desire to dramatise himself, as the Emperor Nero loved to do, as well as many of the great men at the court.

He commanded the curtains of his litter to be drawn aside so that everyone might see him : the lean, well groomed head, the senatorial strip of purple on his robe. He contemplated the man from the provinces through his jade lorgnette. "Yes, young man," he said in his falsetto, ironical voice, "we are still in the midst of re-building, and not finished yet. All the same, without overstraining your imagination, you can already see what this city will be before the year is ended." He raised himself somewhat higher, advanced one foot, which was incased in the high-heeled, red shoe reserved for the highest aristocracy, and assumed, with a slight touch of parody, the tone of a market vendor. "I assert without fear of contradiction that no one can say he has really lived who has not seen the golden city of Rome. Wherever you may find yourself in Rome, young man, you are at the centre of things, for we have no frontiers, we swallow up more and more of the earth. You can listen here to a hundred languages. You can study here the peculiarities of all nations. There are more Greeks here than in Athens, more Africans than in Carthage. Without taking a single step you can find here all the products of the earth. You will find merchandise from India and Arabia in such abundance that you will be driven to the conclusion that the country-side there must be denuded for ever, and that if these peoples want to supply their own needs they must come to us. What do you lack, young man : Spanish wool, Chinese silks, cheese from the Alps, Arabian perfumes, medicinal drugs from the Sudan ? I offer you a prize if there is anything you cannot find

here.   Or do you want the latest news ?   The Forum and
the Campus Martius can tell you at a moment's notice when
the grain prices fall in Upper Egypt, or a general in the
Rhine makes an unwise speech, or our ambassador to the
court of the Parthian King excites unwelcome attention by
sneezing too loudly.   No scholar can labour without the
help of our libraries.   We have as many statues as citizens.
We pay the highest prices in the world for virtue and vice.
Whatever your imagination can conceive you will find in
this city.   But you will also find much more that your
imagination could never have conceived."

The senator had leant forward from his litter ; the whole
crowd standing round had been listening.   He had maintained his ironical tone to the very end, mimicking the
voice of a market vendor ; but a warmth rang through his
words, and everybody felt that this glowing eulogy of the city
was more than a parody.   They listened rapturously while
their city was being praised, their city with its consecrated
virtues and its consecrated vices, the city of the richest and
the poorest, the most living city in the world.

When Marullus had finished they tumultuously applauded
him as they might have applauded some famous actor in
the theatre.   But Marullus did not even listen, nor had he
a further glance for Joseph.   He vanished into his litter,
waved to the architect to approach, and commanded him to
explain the model of the new building.   Nor did the Jew
Claudius Reginus address another word to Joseph.   Nevertheless when Joseph was borne away by the dispersing crowd
he threw him a twinkling, ironical, encouraging smile which
changed his fleshy face and gave it a very sly look.   Without
a glance at his surroundings Joseph reflectively made his
way, frequently jostled, through the crowded city.   He had
not quite understood the Latin oration of the senator ; but

it had warmed his heart too, and set his thoughts flying.
He climbed up to the Capitol and drank in the view, feeding
his eyes on the temples, streets, monuments, palaces.   In
the golden house that was being erected over there the
Roman Emperor ruled the world ; and from the Capitol
the Senate and the people of Rome issued decrees that changed
the face of the world ; and in the archives, engraved in
bronze, lay the ordinances of the world, decreed by Rome.
Rome meant power ;   he pronounced the word, Rome,
Rome, and then he translated it into Hebrew, and there it
was called Gevurah and sounded far less formidable, and then
he translated it into Aramaic, where it was called Kochbah
and lost all its terrors.   No, he, Joseph, son of Matthias of
Jerusalem, priest of the first rank, had no fear of Rome.
He gazed down upon the city ;   it became more and more
animated ;   the afternoon bustle had begun.   Shouts, swarming crowds.   He drank in this picture of the city ;   but
behind it, more real than this real Rome, he saw his native
city, and the great hall in the Temple in which the High
Council sat, and, more real than the thunders of the Forum,
he heard the shrill piercing blast of the ram's horn by means
of which, on the great feast days, the priests of the Temple
called to Jehovah in the name of Zion's people.   He smiled.
Only a man born in Rome could become a senator.   This
man Marullus gazed proudly and arrogantly from his litter,
and his foot was encased in the red, high-heeled, black-laced
shoe of a senator.   But he, Joseph, preferred to have been
born in Jerusalem, although he did not possess even the ring
of an aristocrat of the second rank.   These Romans laughed
at him ;   but he laughed still more deeply at them.   What
they had to give, these men of the West, their technique,
their logic, could be learned.   But what could never be learned
was the East's clarity of vision and its holiness.   There

the nation and God, man and God, were one. But its God was an invisible God, who could neither be seen nor learned. One either possessed, or did not possess him. He, Joseph, possessed this thing that could not be learned. And that he would be able to learn the other things, the technique and the logic of the West, he did not doubt for a moment.

He descended from the Capitol. His large, piercing eyes burned in his pale, brown, lean face. It was known in Rome that many of the people from the East were possessed by their God. People esteemed them, some a little ironically, a few perhaps enviously, but the majority in good faith. And the women admired him as he passed them, glowing with his dreams, his ambition and his confidence in himself.

2

Caius Barzaarone, the president of the Agrippine Ward, with whom Joseph lodged, was the proprietor of the most flourishing art furniture factory in Rome. His main branch lay on the other bank of the Tiber, in the real city. He had a smaller shop in the Subura, and two great and luxurious establishments in the arcades of the Campus Martius ; and on workdays his roomy private house in the Jewish quarter near the Three Gates was crammed full of articles pertaining to his trade. But now on the Sabbath eve no trace of these was to be seen. The whole house, and especially the spacious dining-room, seemed transformed. Usually this room lay open to the courtyard ; to-day it was shut off by a heavy curtain, and Joseph, touched and moved, recognised the ancient custom, the usage of Jerusalem. He knew that so long as this curtain remained closed anyone who arrived would be welcomed as a guest. But when the curtain was drawn back to let the fresh air stream in, the meal would begin, and whoever came after that would be

too late.   Nor was the room lighted to-day in the Roman,
but in the Jewish fashion ;   silver lamps wreathed with
garlands of violets hung from the ceiling.   On everything,
on the table crockery, the beakers, salt cellars, oil, vinegar,
and essence flasks, glittered the emblem of Israel, a cluster
of grapes.   But amid all these things set out in preparation
Joseph's heart was touched most profoundly by a few chests
wrapped in straw ;   for on the Sabbath it was forbidden to
cook, and for that reason the food was kept warm in these
chests, and its odour filled the room.

Although these surroundings reminded him of his home,
Joseph felt dejected.   In his heart he had expected that, as
a priest of the first rank and the wearer of a Doctor's title,
he would be offered a place on one of the three banqueting
couches.

But the fact that after the great fire his furniture was
selling so well seemed to have gone to the head of this uppish
Roman, and it never occurred to him to lead Joseph to one
of the places of honour.   Instead he was evidently to sit
with the women and the less highly honoured guests at the
great common table.

But why were they all still standing about ?   Why did
they not draw aside the curtain and begin ?   Caius had long
ago laid his hand on his children's heads, blessing them with
the time honoured words ;   the boys with " God make thee
as Ephraim and Manasseh," and the girls with " God make
thee as Rachel and Leah."   Everybody was hungry and
impatient :   what were they waiting for ?

Then from behind the curtain came a voice that Joseph
recognised, and presently a stoutish gentleman shuffled in :
the financier Claudius Reginus.   He facetiously greeted
in the Roman fashion the master of the house and his ancient
father Aaron, then threw to the less esteemed guests a few

benevolent words, and Joseph suddenly became very proud ; for Claudius Reginus had recognised him. Reginus twinkled at him with his heavy, sleepy eyes, and said in his high, unctuous voice, so that everybody could hear : " Good day to you. Peace be with you, Joseph Ben Matthias, priest of the first rank." Then immediately the curtain was drawn up and Claudius Reginus reclined without further ceremony on the centre banqueting couch, the place of honour. Caius took his place on the first, old Aaron on the third. Then Caius uplifted his voice over a full beaker of Jewish wine, wine of Eskol, and recited the Sabbath prayer of consecration ; he blessed the wine, and the great beaker went from mouth to mouth, and then he blessed the bread, broke it, divided it, and everybody said Amen, and then at last the feast began.

Joseph sat between the plump housewife and Irene, the pretty sixteen-year-old daughter of the house, whose eyes were fixed on him with boundless devotion. There were many other people at the great table ; the boy Cornelius and another half-grown son of Caius, also two humble and insignificant theological students, who were looking forward to eating their fill this evening, and a young gentleman with a light brown, keen face, whom Joseph had already noticed returning from the synagogue, and who now sat opposite him looking him up and down very frankly. It came out that this man was about the same age as Joseph, that he, too, had been born in Judaea, though only in the semi-Greek city of Tiberias, that his name was Justus, Justus of Tiberias, and that his spiritual and secular development was curiously similar to Joseph's own. Like Joseph he had studied theology, jurisprudence and literature. Ostensibly he occupied himself with politics, and was in Rome as a representative of the titular king Agrippa ; and although his family was inferior to Joseph's, he had from his earliest years possessed a better knowledge of Greek and Latin ; also he had already been in Rome for three years.   The young men scrutinised each other inquisitively, not without good-will, but with considerable suspicion.

On the banqueting couches the conversation had become loud and unembarrassed.   The two splendid synagogues in Rome proper had been burnt down, while the three great prayer houses here on the right bank remained untouched. It was of course a painful visitation that the two houses of God had been destroyed, but nevertheless the president of the Jewish ward on the right bank was not entirely displeased. The five Jewish communities in Rome had each its own president and there was keen competition among them, above all between the very exclusive Velia Synagogue on the other side, and the many-headed and by no means fastidious Agrippine Ward presided over by Caius.   Old Aaron, Caius's father, toothlessly inveighed against the ambitious dunces on the other side of the river.   According to the ancient law of the nation, was it not ordained that synagogues must always be built on the highest point in the surroundings, just as the Temple in Jerusalem from its height commanded the city ?   But of course Julian Alf, the president of the Velia Ward, had to have his synagogue in the immediate vicinity of the Palatine, although to do so he had had to choose a lower site.   It was a punishment from God that his synagogue had been burnt down.   A punish-ment in particular for the iniquity of the Jews on the other side of the river in buying their salt from the Romans, when everybody knew that the Roman salt had been smeared with the fat of swine to give it a finer appearance.   So the old man went on grumbling over everything and everybody. As far as Joseph could gather from his vague and inconsecutive mumblings, he was now complaining about those who translated their sacred Hebrew names into Latin or Greek equivalents for fashionable or business reasons. His son Caius, who originally had been called Chajim, smiled good humouredly and sympathetically ; but really such things should not be said before the children. But Claudius Reginus laughed loudly, clapped the old man on the shoulder, and said that he had been called Reginus from his birth ; for he had been born a slave, and his master had given him that name. But really he should be called Melek ; his mother had often called him that, and he had no objection whatever if grandfather, too, should care to call him Melek.

Meanwhile Justus of Tiberias had been scrutinising Joseph, who felt his eyes upon him all the time. He had the impression that this Justus was secretly laughing at him, at his conversation, his pronunciation, his Jerusalem fashion of eating, as for instance when he took the perfumed sandal-wood tooth-pick between his thumb and third finger in raising it to his mouth. Now, without warning, this Justus fellow asked him, and it sounded again confoundedly super-cilious and condescending: " I presume you are here on political business, Doctor Joseph Ben Matthias ? " And then Joseph could no longer restrain himself ; he felt he really must show this sarcastic young Roman that he had been sent here on great and important affairs, and so he described the case of his three innocent men. He caught fire and spoke somewhat too melodramatically for the ears of these sceptical Romans ; nevertheless the whole room became still, silence fell on the banqueting couches and the long table, and all listened to the eloquent young man, carried away by his theme and his passion. Joseph was perfectly aware how rapturously Irene gazed up at him, how annoyed his rival

Justus was, and that Claudius himself was smiling as if he were pleased. This consciousness winged his words ; they became more lofty, his faith in his mission grew, he went on full sail. Until the old grandfather interrupted him crossly with the remark that on the Sabbath one should not speak of business matters. Joseph stopped at once, dismayed and humbled. But in his heart he was very well pleased ; he felt that his words had produced an effect.

At last the feast came to an end, Caius pronounced the long grace after food, the company left, and only the more serious male guests remained. Now Caius invited Joseph and Justus to the banqueting couches. The ceremonial wine-mixing apparatus was set on the table. After the austere old grandfather had left, the others took off their prescribed head coverings for the sake of coolness.

So there the four men reclined or sat at their wine, confections and fruits ; they were replete, comfortable, in a mood for talking. The room was filled with a pleasant subdued light ; the curtain was drawn, and from the dark courtyard came a welcome cool breeze. The two older men talked with Joseph about Judaea and asked him all sorts of questions. To his sorrow Caius had been only once in Judaea ; he had been a young man then ; it was a long time ago ; along with hundreds of thousands of other pilgrims he had led his sacrificial lamb to the Temple at the Paschal Feast. Since then he had seen many things, triumphal processions, sumptuous spectacles in the arena and the Circus Maximus ; but the sight of the white and golden Temple in Jerusalem and the rapturous multitudes who filled the vast hall still remained the greatest that he had ever beheld in his life. All the Jews in Rome were devoted to their native country. Had they not their own synagogue in Jerusalem ? Did they not send tribute and Temple offerings

there ? Did they not save up their money so that their
dead bodies might be sent to Judaea to be buried in the soil
of their fathers ? But these people in Jerusalem were doing
all they could to make their native country stink in their
nostrils. Why in God's name did they not live in peace
with the Roman administration ? One could easily get on
with the imperial officials ; they were tolerant people, that
had often been proved ; but no, these people in Judaea
always insisted on executing their private whims, the mania
for being in the right was in their blood, one fine day they
would spoil everything. They would be reduced yet to
eating locusts in the wilderness. Caius translated this last
prophecy into the Aramaic ; he smiled, but in reality he
was quite in earnest.

The jeweller Claudius Reginus noticed with a smile that
in accordance with strict Jerusalem etiquette Joseph did not
empty his beaker at one gulp, but set it down twice on the
table before the wine was finished. Claudius Reginus knew
very well the situation in Judaea ; he had been there only
two years before. It was not the Roman officials' fault that
Judaea was not at peace, nor that of the men at the head in
Jerusalem, but solely of those petty agitators, the Avengers
of Israel. Simply because they saw no other means of
making a career in politics, they were hounding the people
on to a hopeless armed revolt. Never had things gone
better with the Jews than under the rule of their beloved
Emperor Nero. They had influence in every sphere, and
their influence would grow if they were only wise enough
not to draw too much public attention to it. Which was
the more important : to possess power, or to show one
possessed it ? he concluded, rolling the tepid wine on his
tongue.

Joseph considered it high time to put in a word for the

Avengers of Israel.   The people in Rome, he said, should
not forget that cold reason was not the only thing that
counted in Judaea, but that men's hearts also insisted on
being heard.   At every step one took there, one ran up
against the insignia of Roman sovereignty.   Caius
Barzaarone still remembered the Paschal Feast in the
Temple with a glow at his heart.   But when you were
forced to see how brutally and cynically, for example, the
Roman police comported themselves in the Temple, men
who were actually stationed there to keep order during the
Paschal Feast, it was enough to make your blood boil, no
matter how peace-loving you might be.   It wasn't an easy
matter to celebrate the deliverance from Egypt when with
every word one felt the mailed fist of the Roman on one's
neck.   It didn't need much self-control to live quietly here
in Rome ; anybody could do that here ; but it was un-
endurably difficult in the land that God had chosen, the land
where God had had His dwelling place, the land of Israel.

" God is no longer in the land of Israel, God is in Italy
now," said a sharp voice.   They all looked at Justus, who
had spoken these words.   His hand tightly gripped his
beaker, he was not looking at anybody ; what he had said
was evidently intended for himself.   Nor was there any
trace of mockery or a desire to score in his voice ; he had
stated a fact, and now he was silent again.

They were all silent.   These words were unanswerable ;
even Joseph felt, and against his will, the truth in them.
" God is in Italy now," he translated the phrase into
Aramaic.   The words were like a blow.

" You may possibly be right there, young man," the
financier said after a pause.   " You must know," he turned
to Joseph, " that I'm not a Jew myself, but the son of a
Sicilian man slave and a Jewish mother.   My master refused

to have me circumcised, for which, to be frank, I am thankful to this day.   I am a business man, I avoid anything disadvantageous to me when I can, and seize my advantage wherever I find it.   Your God Jehovah appeals to me more than his rivals.   I sympathise with the Jews."

The great financier lay at his ease on his couch, the beaker filled with tepid wine in his hand, his sly sleepy eyes fixed on the dark courtyard.   On his third finger he wore a gigantic milky pearl from which Joseph could not tear his eyes.   "Yes, Doctor Joseph," said Caius Barzaarone. "That is the most beautiful pearl in the four seas."

"I only wear it on the Sabbath," said Claudius Reginus.

Joseph reflected that if he didn't exploit this opportunity, if he didn't take advantage out of the full-fed benevolence, the postprandial sentimentality of the great man, he would prove himself a fool and never manage to carry through to a successful issue this business of his three innocent men. "Seeing that you are one of the Jews' sympathizers, Claudius Reginus," he turned modestly and yet purposively to the financier, "won't you take up the case of the three innocent men from Caesarea ? "

The jeweller set down his beaker with a thump. "Caesarea," he said, and his eyes, usually so sleepy, became sharp, his high voice threatening.   "Caesarea is a fine city with a splendid harbour, the export trade is considerable, the fish market excellent.   Full of great possibilities.   You yourselves are to blame if it is wrested out of your hands. You with your silly aspirations.   It makes my wine sour when I hear of your Avengers of Israel."

Startled by the sudden violence of this placid man, Joseph replied with redoubled modesty that the setting free of the three innocent men was a purely ethical question, a matter of humanity, and had nothing to do with politics.   "We don't want to use political arguments," said he, " nor legal ones.   We know that nothing can be done except through personal influence at court," and he gazed humbly and imploringly at Claudius Reginus.

" Well, are your three innocent men innocent, at least ? " he asked at last with a twinkle.   Joseph responded at once with passionate assurances that, when the disturbances broke out, the three of them had been at the other end of the town. But Claudius interrupted him, saying that that was not what he wanted to know.   What he wanted to know was the political party the three belonged to.   " Did they hold forth in the Blue Hall ? " he asked.   The Blue Hall was the assembly place of the Avenger of Israel.   " Well, yes," Joseph had to admit.

" You see," said Claudius Reginus, and with that the affair was finished as far as he was concerned.

Justus of Tiberias gazed at Joseph's handsome, ardent, craving face. This man had suffered a public defeat, and Justus was elated.   Both repelled and attracted, he contemplated his young colleague.   This fellow had the same ambitions as himself : to be a great writer and to gain political influence. He had the same methods, the same way to go, the same object.   Insolent Rome was ripe for the more ancient culture of the East, as a hundred and fifty years before it had been ripe for the culture of Greece.   The thought that it could be undermined from within by the eastern culture was a tempting one, and to collaborate in that task a glorious vocation.   Divining this, he had come to Rome three years before, as Joseph had come now.   But he, Justus, had both a lighter and a heavier task.   He had a pure will, the keener talent.   But he was too fastidious in his methods, too dainty. He had seen deeply into the political and literary activities of the capital, and he was disgusted with compromises and

cheap effects. This Joseph fellow was evidently less
fastidious. He did not shrink from the coarsest means, he
was resolved to get to the top no matter how, he play-acted,
flattered, haggled, so that it was a pleasure for a connoisseur
to contemplate such boundless ambition. Justus's
nationalism was more intellectual than Joseph's ; they were
both fated to come to Rome. It would be a keen fight
between them, and it would not always be easy to remain
fair ; but he would be fair. He would allow his opponent
every advantage that came his way.

" I should advise you, Joseph Ben Matthias," he said, " to
approach the actor Demetrius Libanus about it." And
again they all gazed at the yellow faced young men. How
was it that this idea had not occurred to the rest of them ?
Demetrius Libanus, the most popular comedian in the
capital, the pampered darling of the court, a Jew who insisted
upon his nationality on every opportunity ; yes, he was the
right man for Joseph's business. The Empress liked him
and invited him every week to her receptions. Both the
other men agreed that Demetrius Libanus was the right man
for Joseph.

A little while later the company left. Joseph went up to
his room. He soon fell asleep, very content with himself.

Justus of Tiberias walked home wearily through the dark
streets. He smiled ; Caius Barzaarone had not considered
him important enough even to send a torch bearer to light
him on his way.

3

Soon after daybreak Joseph appeared at the Tibur Gate
accompanied by one of Caius Barzaarone's slaves. There a
driver from the overland transport company already awaited
him. The vehicle was small, confined, uncomfortable, and
dear as well ; it had only two wheels.

It was raining. The surly driver estimated that the journey would take about three hours. Joseph shivered with cold. The slave whom Caius had sent with him as an interpreter was not talkative and presently fell asleep. Joseph wrapped himself more closely in his cloak. In Judaea it would still be quite warm. But all the same he was glad that he was here. This time things must turn out all right ; he believed in his luck.

The Jews here in Rome always insisted on associating his three innocent men with the politics of the Avengers of Israel and with the Caesarean affair. Certainly it would be a matter involving the whole country's fate if Rome were by sharp practice to rob the Jews of their power in Caesarea ; but he refused to have that question mixed up with his three innocent men. He considered such an attitude cynical ; all that concerned him was the ethical principle. To help the prisoners was one of the chief moral commandments of the Jewish law.

Yet if he was to be quite honest the three innocent men had probably not been in Caesarea purely by chance at the time of the elections. From his own point of view the Governor Antonius Felix had had quite good grounds for seizing the three men. Nevertheless he, Joseph, was under no obligation to bother his head about the views of the Governor, who since then had fortunately been recalled. For him the three men were innocent ; his duty was to help the prisoners.

The carriage bumped along. The road was wretchedly bad. Presently they came in sight of the brick works, a yellowish grey waste, with everywhere piles and palisades, and behind these more piles and palisades. In front of the gate sentries lolled ; they gazed at him suspiciously and inquisitively, glad of the diversion. The slave harangued them, showing his papers. Joseph stood by uncomfortably.

They were conducted to the prison governor ; it was a discouraging and painful journey. Everywhere they could hear a dull, monotonous droning ; it was a law of the prison that the labourers should sing at their work. The overseers walked about with cudgels and scourges ; they gazed in astonishment at the strangers.

The governor seemed disagreeably surprised ; usually when visitors came he had been informed in good time. He suspected surveillance and all manner of unpleasant things, did not understand Joseph's Latin, or did not want to understand it ; his own Greek, he said, was poor. To make him understand Joseph had perpetually to call on the help of the interpreter. Then a subordinate official appeared and whispered with the governor, and immediately the governor's attitude changed. And he frankly explained why. The health of the three men was not of the best ; he had been afraid that they might have been put to work in spite of that ; now he had learned that they had been humanely allowed to remain in their cell. He was relieved at this gratifying fact, and thawed ; he now understood Joseph's Latin very much better ; his own Greek also improved ; he became loquacious.

He showed Joseph the records of the three men. They had been originally employed in Sardinia in the mines, but they had not been able to endure that for long. They had also been employed as road workers and scavengers, in the tread mills, and at the pumps in the public baths. The work in the brick works was the lightest of all. Factory foremen had not much love for Jewish forced labour. The Jews made all sorts of difficulties about the food, and refused to work on their Sabbaths. The governor, he could bear witness to that himself, had treated the three prisoners with especial humanity. But even humanity, unfortunately, had its limits. In consequence of the rebuilding of the city particularly heavy demands were being made on the state bricks works. So every man had to do his bit. The required stint of bricks had to be delivered whatever happened, and Joseph himself must know that the Roman architects were not modest in their demands. Fifteen hours a day was the official minimum at the moment. Among his eight hundred to a thousand workers there were four deaths on an average every week. He was delighted that the three Jewish prisoners had not been among these.

Then the governor entrusted Joseph to a subordinate official. Once more they went through the brick works, past overseers flourishing cudgels and whips, through the dull monotonous singing, through the shade and the glare, past bent or kneeling workmen panting under their burdens. A verse from the Scripture rose into Joseph's mind, telling how Pharaoh oppressed Israel in the land of Egypt. " And the Egyptians made the children of Israel to serve with rigour ; and they made their lives bitter with harsh bondage, in mortar, and in brick ; and they set over them taskmasters to afflict them with their burdens. And they built for Pharaoh treasure cities, Pithom and Raamses." For what did they celebrate the Paschal Feast with joy and great ostentation when here the children of Israel were still carrying bricks and helping to build the city of their enemies ? The clay clung heavily to his sandals and stuck between his toes. And all the time the dull monotonous singing.

At last they reached the cells of the forced labourers. A soldier fetched the head warder. Joseph waited in the ante-room and read the inscription on the door, an extract from the works of the celebrated contemporary writer

Seneca : " They are slaves ? But men too. They are slaves ? But also house-mates. They are slaves ? But also humble friends." A little book lay open, containing instructions drawn up by Columella, the great industrial expert. Joseph read : " There must be a roll call daily of the forced labourers. Also there must be a daily examination to see that the fetters are sound and the cells secure. The cells should be so arranged as to house fifteen convicts each."

He was conducted to the three men. The cell was under ground, the tiny windows were set very high up, so that the convicts could not reach them with their hands. The fifteen straw covered pallets stood ranged side by side, but the room was already unbearably crowded, though there were only five men in it, Joseph, the warder, and the three prisoners.

The three men were squatting side by side. They were half-naked, their clothes hung upon them in tatters, their faces were leaden. Round their ankles they wore rings to which chains were attached ; on their foreheads they were branded with the letter E. Their hair was shorn bare to their very skulls, so that their great beards, matted, straggling, and yellowish-white, looked grotesque. Joseph knew the names of the three men ; they were called Nathan, Gadia and Jehuda. He had met Gadia and Jehuda only once or twice, so it was no wonder if he did not recognise them now. But Doctor Nathan Ben Baruch, member of the High Council, had been his teacher ; for four years he had passed many hours with him daily ; so he should be able to dis-tinguish him from the others. But he was unable to do so. Nathan had been a somewhat corpulent man of medium height ; of the three whom Joseph saw crouching there two were middle sized skeletons, and the third was very tall.

And he simply could not make out which of the two middle
sized skeletons was his teacher Nathan.

He greeted the three of them. His healthy, solicitously
kind voice sounded strange in the wretched room : " Peace
be with you, my doctors and masters." The three glanced
up, and now he recognised his old teacher by his thick eyebrows. He remembered the fear and rage that the wild
eyes under those thick eyebrows had once inspired in him ;
for this man had flayed with his sarcasm, had humiliated with
his scorn the ten year old boy unable to follow the complicated methods of interpretation that he was being taught, had
broken down his self-confidence with bitter rebukes. At
that time—and how often !—he had wished the gloomy
morose man every misfortune ; but now that the dead glance
of those dulled eyes fell upon him his heart sank within
him and his pity took away his speech.

He had to speak long and cautiously before he managed
to break through the dull apathy of these three men and
arouse their interest. At last they replied to him, coughing
and mumbling. They were finished. For though their
tyrants had been unable to make them violate Jehovah's
decrees, yet they had been prevented from fulfilling His
commandments. So they had lost their share in this life
and in the next life as well. But even if they should be
scourged till they fell to the ground, even if they should be
nailed to the cross in the damnable fashion beloved by these
fiends of Romans : the law gave, and the law took away ;
the quicker the end came, the more welcome it would be,
the name of the Lord be praised.

The air in the small badly lit room was stifling ; through
the small window openings drove a cold rain ; an oppressive
stench filled the place ; from the distance came the dull
monotonous singing. Joseph felt ashamed that his body

was sound and his clothes whole, that he was young and full of vigour, that he could leave this place in an hour and get away from this region of clay and horror. The three men were unable to think of anything beyond the narrow circle of their wretched day-to-day existence. There was no point in speaking to them of his mission, of the steps that he intended to take for them, of political matters, of the more favourable situation at the court. For them the bitterest thing of all was that they were unable to observe the traditional rules of purification, the strict decrees of ritual cleansing. They had had all sorts of overseers and warders; some had been more harsh than others; these had taken away their phylacteries, so that they might not hang themselves; others were milder, they had left them their phylacteries; but whether harsh or mild, they were all uncircumcised blasphemers and villains. As for themselves, it was a matter of indifference to them whether forced labourers were well fed or not; for they refused to eat the flesh of beasts that had not been slaughtered according to the law. So all that remained to keep them alive was scraps of fruit and vegetables. They had debated among themselves whether they should accept the meat ration and exchange it with the other prisoners for bread and fruit. The debate had been a violent one, and Doctor Gadia had proved at the beginning with many arguments that this was permitted. But finally he, too, had had to agree with the others that it was permitted only to save one from imminent death; and who could tell whether the Lord, His name be praised, destined their death for this month or the next? So it appeared that it was not permitted, after all. When they were not too weary and apathetic, they debated on what was permitted and what was not permitted, using many theological arguments; and at those times their thoughts turned back to the great hall of the Temple. Joseph got the impression that these debates were often violent and developed into bitter squabbles, but obviously they were the only tie that held these three men to life. No, it was hopeless to talk to them reasonably. When he referred to the Empress's friendliness to the Jews, they replied that it was questionable whether it was permitted even to pray in this filthy underground hole ; and besides they never knew which day it was, so that probably they violated the Sabbath by putting on their phylacteries, and the working day by not putting them on.

Joseph gave it up. He listened to them, and when one of them quoted a passage of the Scripture he took him up and quoted a counter passage, and behold, they came to life and began to dispute, producing arguments with their feeble tongues, and so he disputed with them, and for them it was a great day. But they could not keep it up, and very soon they relapsed again into their apathy.

Joseph regarded them squatting in the wretched light of their cell. These three men, so miserable now in body, so filthy and forsaken, had been great in Israel ; their names had been glorious among the legislators in the great hall of the Temple. Set free the prisoners. No, he was not concerned whether the Jews held the whip-hand in Caesarea or not ; that did not matter to him. What mattered to him was these three men. The sight of them moved him profoundly, set him on fire ; he was filled with a religious pity that was almost unendurable. He was thrilled and uplifted when he saw them rigidly holding to the law in their misery, clinging desperately to the law, as if only the law breathed into them the courage to remain alive. He thought of the time he had spent in the wilderness in holy renunciation with his teacher Banus, the Essene, and re-

membered that illumination had come to him then in his
best moments, not through his reason, but through immersion
in himself, through contemplation, through God.

Set free the prisoners.   He compressed his lips, firmly
resolved not to think of himself until he had delivered these
three miserable men.   Above the melancholy song of the
forced labourers he heard the words of the sublime Hebrew
prayer.   No, he was not here out of vain self seeking ;
Jehovah had sent him here.   He strode back through the
grey rain, but he felt neither the rain nor the clay that clung
to his sandals.   Set free the prisoners.

4

IN Judaea a man with Joseph's political views could not
possibly go to the races or the theatre.   On one occasion he
had attended an entertainment, secretly and with a bad
conscience, in Caesarea.   But what a wretched affair that
had been compared with the spectacle he was watching now
in the Marcellus Theatre.   His head reeled with the
dancing, the ballet, the gigantic grandiose pantomime, the
splendour of the perpetual changes on the huge stage, which
during all those hours had never been left empty.   Justus,
who was sitting beside him, dismissed it all with a wave of
the hand.   The only item that he considered worth seeing
was the burlesque revue which the people loved so much and
with justice ; they had sat through all that had been presented
to them till now simply to be sure of a place for the revue, in
which the comedian Demetrius Libanus was to appear.

Yes, this man Demetrius Libanus, repellant though he
was in some ways, was a great artist and a human being.
Born as a slave in the imperial household and manumitted
by the Emperor Claudius, he had amassed immense wealth
and the title of the first comedian of the day.   The Emperor

Nero, whom he had instructed in the arts of acting and oratory, loved him.   A difficult fellow, this Libanus, exalted and humbled by his Jewish nationality.   Not even the prayers and commands of the Emperor could make him appear in public on the Sabbath or any of the Jewish holy days.   He was always debating with doctors in Jewish universities whether he was really rejected by God because he played on the stage.   When he had to appear in woman's clothing, thus violating the scriptural law, it cost him attacks of hysteria ; for the Bible said that a man must not wear woman's clothing.

Wearied by the long duration of the first part of the programme, which had lasted for several hours, the eleven thousand spectators in the Marcellus Theatre now noisily and tumultuously demanded that the burlesque should begin. The theatre manager hesitated, obviously because he was expecting the Emperor or the Empress, in whose box all the preparations had already been made.   But the public had now been waiting for five hours ; it was accustomed to stand up for its rights in the theatre even in the teeth of the court itself ; it threatened and shouted ; there was no choice but to begin.

The curtain was lowered, Demetrius Libanus's great act commenced.   It was entitled " The Fire," and people said that the senator Marullus was the author.   The hero, played by Libanus, was a slave called Isidor, belonging to the Egyptian city of Ptolemais, a fellow superior in ability to his master and everybody about him.   Libanus acted almost without any theatrical aids, wore no mask or expensive frippery, nor even the buskin.   He was simply the slave Isidor from the province of Egypt, a melancholy sly fellow whom nothing could put out, and who stood his ground in every difficulty.   He helped his slow-witted and unfortunate master out of countless embarrassments ; he secured money and property for him, and slept with his wife. Once, when his master gave him a buffet on the ear, he declared sadly and resolutely that now he must leave him, and that he would not return until a public apology had been made. The master put his slave Isidor in chains and informed the police, but of course Isidor succeeded in escaping, and to the tumultuous delight of the audience again and again led the police a dance. Unfortunately at the most exciting point, when it seemed inevitable that the police would at last secure their man, the play had to be interrupted ; for now the Empress appeared. The whole audience arose and with eleven thousand voices greeted the dainty fair lady, who with arm outstretched in the Roman fashion faced the audience and thanked them. Her appearance was a double sensation, for among those who accompanied her was the Abbess of the Vestals, and hitherto it had not been customary for the aristocratic nuns to attend the popular burlesques in the Marcellus Theatre.

The play had to be started anew. Joseph was very pleased by this, for the quite brazen realism of the performance was overwhelmingly new to him, and he understood it the second time far better. His burning eyes remained fixed on the actor Libanus, on his brazen and melancholy lips, on his eloquent hands, on his whole animated eloquent body. Now came the verse that everybody had been waiting for, the celebrated verse that Joseph in his short stay in Rome had already heard people singing, bawling and whistling a hundred times. The comedian stood on the stage surrounded by eleven clowns, cymbals crashed, trumpets blared, flutes shrilled, and he sang the verse : " Who is the master here ? Who pays for the butter ? Who pays for the girls ? And who pays for the Syrian perfumes ? " The audience had

leapt up and they sang too, even the yellow haired Empress
in her box moved her lips, and the dignified abbess laughed
heartily. But now at last the slave Isidor was surrounded ;
there was no escape ; the police were on every side of him.
He declared that he was not the slave Isidor, but how was
he to prove that to the policemen ? By a dance ; yes, that
was the idea, of course. And then came the dance. Isidor
was still wearing the fetters round his ankles. So what
he had to do was to dance and at the same time conceal his
fetters ; and that was terribly difficult, comic and pathetic
at the same time ; for this man was dancing for his freedom
and his life. Joseph was carried away, the audience were
carried away. Every movement of the comedian was
followed with breathless and sympathetic interest by the
audience. Joseph regarded himself as an aristocrat through
and through ; he had not the slightest scruple in having
the most menial services performed for him by slaves, nor
had most of the people who were sitting in the theatre ;
they had shown very clearly that they had no desire to
obliterate the distinction between the masters and the
slaves by having over ten thousand of the latter executed on
one occasion. But now that they watched the man in
fetters who passed himself off as a master, they were all for
him and against his employer, and they all shouted with joy,
these Romans and their Empress, when the impudent fellow
once more left the police standing and softly and slyly began
to hum again : " Who is the master ? Who pays for the
butter ? "

And now the acting became quite unashamed. The
master had published his apology and got back his slave.
But in the meantime he had committed many blunders ;
he had quarrelled with his tenants, and now they refused to
pay him his rent. Yet for very good reasons he dared not

evict them ; for his dear houses had depreciated greatly in value. Here nobody could help him but the sly Isidor, and he did. The assistance he provided, however, was of the same kind that, according to popular opinion, the Emperor and certain of the great courtiers had availed themselves of in a similar case ; he set fire to the district where the depreciated properties lay. Demetrius Libanus played his part impudently and with verve ; every sentence contained some allusion to the land speculators and the great financiers who were coining money over the rebuilding of the city. Nobody was spared, neither the architects Celerus and Severus, nor the celebrated old statesman and writer Seneca, with his philosophical praises of poverty and his actual life of luxury, nor the financier Claudius Reginus, who wore a gigantic pearl on his third finger, but unfortunately had not enough money to buy shoe laces ; nor even the Emperor himself. Every word found its target, the audience roared with delight and became breathless with laughter, and when at the end the comedian Libanus invited the audience to pillage the burning house on the stage there was a riot such as Joseph had never seen before. The alluring interior of the burning house was turned towards the audience by an ingenious device. Thousands of people made a rush for the stage, flung themselves on the furniture, the table decorations and the food. They trampled upon each other, shouting and screaming. And throughout the theatre and the square in front, throughout the gigantic, airy colonnades, over all the spacious Campus Martius, the air rang with the words, " Who is the master here ? Who pays for the butter ? "

5

WHEN, through the agency of Justus, Joseph received an invitation to supper from Demetrius Libanus, he suddenly felt timid. He was bold by nature. When he had been introduced to the High Priest, to King Agrippa, to the Roman Governor, he had not been embarrassed. But for the comedian he felt a deeper respect. Libanus's acting had carried him away. It had filled him with awed admiration to see a single man, this Jew Demetrius Libanus, compelling many thousands of people, high and low, Romans and foreigners, to think and feel as he did.

Joseph found the actor reclining on a couch in a comfortable green dressing-gown ; Libanus languidly stretched out his many ringed hand to his visitor. Joseph saw with embarrassment and surprise how mean of stature this man was who had filled the gigantic Marcellus Theatre.

It was a small and select banquet. Young Antonius Marullus, a son of the senator, was there, also another fledgling aristocrat, and a Jewish personage, one of the chief figures in the Velia synagogue, a certain Doctor Licinus, a very affected man to whom Joseph took an immediate dislike.

For the first time in a great and fashionable Roman house, Joseph accommodated himself with surprising ease to the many things new to him. The multifarious dishes and fish sauces, the diverse seasonings, confused him at first. But soon, by watching the antipathetic Doctor Licinus, who reclined on the banqueting couch opposite him, he had learned the most important points ; and in half-an-hour he was rejecting any dish that did not appeal to him with the same haughty and languid movement of the head as the other, while with a wave of the little finger he beckoned to the slaves to bring him whatever he desired.

Libanus himself ate very little. He complained about the diet which his accursed profession imposed upon him, extending, alas, to women as well, and he made a few wittily

obscene observations on the ingenious devices which certain
theatre managers affixed to the bodies of their slave actors
to keep them from throwing over the traces. But for hard
cash they sometimes agreed to free their poor actors for a
single night from this obstructing mechanism so as to gratify
certain high-placed ladies. Then, without transition, he
began to sneer at some of his colleagues, supporters of a
different style of acting, and at the absurdities of the traditional
mode, the mask, the buskin. He leapt up and caricatured
the actor Strathocles, strutting about the room so that his
dressing-gown billowed behind him; he was wearing
sandals without heels, but lo, the high heeled shoes and the
whole inflated bearing of the actor were there almost
physically before one's eyes.

Joseph took the plunge and said modestly but enthusiasti-
cally how discreet and yet unmistakable Demetrius Libanus's
allusions to the financier Reginus had been. The actor
glanced up. "What," he said, "so that passage pleased
you? I'm glad of that; for that part didn't get across as
I had hoped."

The ardent but modest Joseph described how the whole
performance had moved him. He had seen millions of
slaves; now for the first time he had learned and felt what
a slave was. The actor reached Joseph his beringed hand.
It was a great encouragement to him, he said, that someone
who had just come from Judaea should be so gripped by his
acting. Joseph must describe in detail how each stroke had
affected him. The actor listened reflectively, slowly
munching a salad prescribed for his health.

"You've just come from Judaea, Doctor Joseph,"
Demetrius Libanus at last changed the subject. "Oh, my
beloved Jews!" he went on in a lamenting and resigned
voice. "You're more bitter against me than all the others.

People curse my name in the Hebrew synagogues simply because I employ the gifts that God has given me, and they use me as a bogey for their children. Sometimes I see red, their narrowness makes me so furious. But when they have some affair to be settled at the Imperial court they come running to me quickly enough to pour their troubles into my ear. Then Demetrius Libanus is good enough for them."

"Good God," said young Antonius Marullus, "the Jews are always whining about something; everybody knows that."

"I forbid you to say such things," shouted the actor all at once, rising angrily to his feet. "I forbid you to say anything against the Jews in my house. I am a Jew."

The blood had rushed to Antonius Marullus's face, he tried to smile and stammered apologies. Demetrius Libanus did not even listen to them. "Judaea," he said, "Israel, Jerusalem. I have never been there, I have never seen the Temple. But sometime I will go there and lead my lamb to the altar." His melancholy grey eyes gazed full of yearning from his pale, slightly puffy face.

"I can do better things than you've seen me doing yet," he turned to Joseph, suddenly important and mysterious. "I have an idea. If it comes off, then I can tell you I'll really deserve the title of the greatest actor of the age. I know quite well how it must be done. It's purely a matter of courage. Pray for me, my dear doctor, that I may be able to summon the courage to do it." Antonius Marullus put his arm familiarly and coaxingly round the actor's neck. "Do tell us your idea, dear Demetrius," he said. "This the third time you've mentioned it to us." But Demetrius Libanus remained obdurate. "The Empress also has been pressing me," he said, "to tell her my idea. I fancy she would give a great deal to get me to carry it out," and he smiled with abysmal insolence. "But I don't intend to," he concluded.

"Tell me something about Judaea," he said, turning again to Joseph.

Joseph told him of the Paschal Feast, of the festival of wood bearing, of the day of expiation when the High Priest for the one time in the year called upon Jehovah by His real name, and the whole people, hearing that great and awful name, cast themselves down before the invisible God, and a hundred thousand knees knelt on the floor of the Temple. The actor listened with his eyes closed. "Yes, I shall hear the name sometime too," he said. "I have postponed my journey to Jerusalem from year to year, the working years of an actor are not many, he must economise in them. But sometime I shall take the ship. And when I am old I shall buy a house and a little property near Jerusalem."

While the actor spoke Joseph had been rapidly reflecting that the man was in a receptive mood, just in the right state of mind for his purpose. "May I tell you something more about Judaea, Demetrius Libanus?" he asked. And he told about his three innocent men. He thought of the brick works, and the damp and cold underground cell, and the three skeletons, and his pain at not having been able to recognise his old teacher Nathan. The actor listened with his eyes closed, his brow resting on his hand. Joseph went on, and his story was vivid and moving.

Everybody was silent when he finished. Then Doctor Licinus of the Velia synagogue said: "Very interesting." But the actor rebuked him sharply; he wanted to believe and be carried away. Licinus defended himself. Was there any proof that the three men were really innocent ? True, Doctor Joseph Ben Matthias himself was honestly convinced of it, but why should the evidence of his witnesses be any better than the evidence brought forward by the Governor Antonius Felix and found to be true by a Roman court ? But Joseph kept his eyes fixed trustfully and earnestly on the actor, and simply replied : " Have a look at these three men yourself. They are in the brick works at Tibur. Talk with them. If you believe in their guilt after that, not another word shall you hear from me about them."

The actor walked up and down ; his eyes were no longer weary ; all his lassitude was gone. " That's an excellent idea," he exclaimed. " I'm very glad, Doctor Joseph, that you came to see me. We shall go out to Tibur. I want to see these three innocent men of yours. I shall help them if I can, Doctor Joseph Ben Matthias." He stood in front of Joseph ; he was smaller than Joseph, but he seemed far taller. " Do you know this ? " he said mysteriously. " This journey is not altogether unconnected with that idea of mine."

He was animated, lively, attended to the mixing bowl himself, and had something pleasant to say to every-body.

The company drank a great deal. Later on someone suggested a little gamble. They played with four ivory dice. Demetrius Libanus had an inspiration. Somewhere or other he must have some Jewish dice that he had kept since his childhood ; they were very curious, with a sort of handle by which one could make them revolve like a top. Yes, Joseph knew of that kind of dice. They were sought for and found. The dice were rough hewn and primitive, and they revolved in a pleasantly quaint way. The play went on with much good nature. The stakes were not high,

but for Joseph they were enormous. He breathed freely
after he had won the first three games.

There were four dice in all. They were all inscribed
with the letters nun, gamel, he, shin ; shin was the worst
letter to turn up, nun the luckiest. Strictly orthodox Jews
regarded this game as wicked ; according to them the letter
shin was an ancient emblem of the god Saturn, the letter
nun an emblem of the goddess Noga' Istar, whom the
Romans called Venus. After the dice were spun they were
flung each time into the middle of the table, and the players
could select whichever of the four they preferred. In the
course of the play Joseph turned up again and again the
lucky letter nun. Being keen eyed he presently recognised
that it was one particular dice that invariably turned up this
letter ; the reason seemed to be that this dice was almost
imperceptibly chipped at one corner.

When Joseph saw this his blood ran cold. If the others
too noticed that it was the dice with the chipped corner that
had turned up all his nuns, would not all that he had gained
that evening, as well as the favour of this great man, be set at
hazard ? He became very cautious and lessened his stakes.
What remained was sufficient for him to live thenceforth in
Rome without having to scrape.

" Would you think it very forward of me, Demetrius
Libanus," he asked when the game was finished, " if I begged
you to give me this dice as a keep-sake ? " The actor
laughed. He roughly scratched his initials on one of the
dice.

" When shall we go to see your three innocent men ? "
he asked Joseph.

" In five days' time," Joseph suggested hesitatingly.

" The day after to-morrow," said the actor.

6

AT the brick works Demetrius Libanus was given a splendid reception. The soldiers and guards greeted the greatest actor of the age with clashing swords, and accorded him the salute of honour which was reserved only for men of the highest rank. The overseers and warders crowded to the gate and greeted the visitor in the Roman fashion, out-stretching the right arm with the hand open. From all sides came the shout : " Hail, Demetrius Libanus."

The sky was radiant, the clay and the bent forms of the forced labourers looked less comfortless, and from every side, amid the monotonous singing, came the well-known words : " Who is the master here ? Who pays for the butter ? "

Joseph walked awkwardly by the actor's side ; the spectacle of the homage which Demetrius Libanus enjoyed in this place of misery impressed him even more than the tumultuous applause of those thousands of people in the theatre.

But in the damp cold underground cell all the festive glow with which the brick works had been touched was gone at once. High narrow windows, stench, the monotonous singing. The three men crouched apathetically as before, the regulation iron ring round their ankles, the E branded on their foreheads, their matted beards sticking out grotesque-ly from their closely shorn heads.

Joseph tried to make them speak. With the same loving patience as the last time he extracted from them expressions of despair and of hopeless devotion to their faith.

Easily moved, the actor suddenly gave a sob. His eyes were immovably fixed upon the three old men, who sat there emaciated and broken, their throats painfully moving up and down while they brought out a few pitiable words. His ears drank in their rude and faltering speech. He would have liked to walk up and down, but that was impossible in the narrow low room, so he stood rigidly where he was, deeply moved. His quick imagination saw these men pacing solemnly in white garments in the great hall of the Temple, law-givers in Israel. Tears came to his eyes, he did not wipe them away, and they trickled down slowly over his slightly puffy cheeks. He stood with a strange motionless rigidity, then, clenching his teeth, raised quite slowly his hands with the beringed fingers and rent his garments as the Jews were accustomed to do in token of profound grief. Then he sat down beside the three prisoners without shrinking from their ill-smelling rags, sat so close to them that their bad breaths struck him in the face. And thereupon he began to talk to them in Aramaic ; it was a halting, rusty Aramaic ; he had not spoken it for a long time. But they understood the words he said, words more suitable to their mood and their situation than Joseph's had been ; words of sympathy for their petty daily round, very human words ; and they wept and blessed him when he left.

On the way back Demetrius Libanus remained silent for a long time ; then he gave voice to his thoughts. Compared to the slow gnawing misery of these three, which devoured heart and body, what was the great tragedy of a unique misfortune, that of Hercules in his Nessus shirt, or of Agamemnon in his fall ? What a long and dreadful way these three men, who had once been great in Zion, who had once borne the torch of the law, must have travelled before they had grown accustomed to such dull and impassive misery.

When they reached the city he said good-bye to Joseph at the Tibur gate, and then added : " Do you know what was the most dreadful thing about them ? Not what they

said, but the queer way they rocked their bodies to and fro
all the time.   Only people who crouch on the ground and
are accustomed to darkness can do that.   Words can lie,
but these movements are dreadfully true.   I'll have to think
that over.   There may be a possibility in it of securing new
effects."

That night Joseph did not go to bed, but sat in his room
and wrote a memorandum on the three men.   The oil in
his lamp ran dry and the wick grew too short ; so he renewed
the oil and the wick and wrote on.   He said very little about
the Caesarean affair, much about the misery of the three old
men, and a great deal about justice.   Justice, he wrote, had
been accounted by the Jews from the oldest times as the first
of virtues.   They could endure need and oppression, but not
injustice ; and they praised anyone who re-established justice
even if he should be one of their oppressors.   " The law
flows over the earth like a great stream," one of the prophets
had said, " and justice is a fount that will never dry up "
" The golden age will come," another had said, " when
justice shall dwell even in the wilderness."   Joseph caught
fire, and the wisdom of the ancients awoke again in him
He sat and wrote ; the wick of the lamp smoked ; he wrote
on.   From the direction of the city gates he heard the heavy
waggons rumbling in ; they were forbidden to drive through
the streets during the day.   He paid no attention ; he
wrote on and polished his essay.

7

THREE days later one of Demetrius Libanus's runners
brought Joseph a letter in which the actor curtly and drily
requested him to hold himself in readiness to wait upon the
Empress at ten o'clock on the day after next.

The Empress.   Joseph's heart stopped.   Her bust stood

everywhere in the streets and was worshipped as divine.
What should he say to her ?   How was he to find words that
would pierce to the heart of this strange woman, whose life
and thoughts were raised so high above those of other human
beings ?   While he was asking himself this question he already
knew that he would find the right words ; for she was a
woman, and he had a faint contempt for all women, and
simply because of that knew he would win her favour.

He read over his manuscript.   He read it aloud with
sweeping gestures, as he would have read it in Jerusalem.
He had written it in Aramaic ; now, laboriously, he
translated it into Greek.   His Greek was sprinkled with
vulgarisms and errors ; he knew that quite well.   Wouldn't
it be unwise to appear before the Empress with a badly
prepared manuscript full of errors ?   Or mightn't his very
errors seem naive and appealing ?

In the interval of waiting he avoided talking to people.
He wandered about the streets.   He turned the other way
when he saw an acquaintance, rushed to the barber, bought
himself a new perfume, and fell out of the most absolute
confidence into the deepest dejection.

The Empress's busts showed a head with a low, clear and
delicate brow, long eyes, and a mouth which was on the large
side.   Even her enemies admitted that she was beautiful and
said that on first seeing her everyone was dazzled.   How
would he, a petty provincial, be able to stand up to her ?   He
must find somebody with whom he could talk the whole
matter over.   He ran back to his lodgings and unburdened
his heart to the girl Irene.   Imposing strict secrecy on the
radiant, highly-flattered girl, he told her that he had something very important to divulge, and then everything came
out with a rush ; he described how he thought his interview
with the Empress would go and repeated what he intended

to say to her.   He rehearsed his speech before Irene and tried over the words and the gestures.

Next day, in his best clothes, he was borne in the splendid litter of Demetrius Libanus to the Imperial Palace. Couriers ran in front and a great train followed. Where the litter passed the crowd remained standing and cheered the actor. Joseph gazed at the Empress's busts in the streets ; some were of white marble, some were painted. Amber yellow hair, a pale delicate face, red lips. Poppaea, he thought. Poppaea meant a doll, Poppaea meant a baby. He thought of the Hebrew word : Jildi, or Janiki. He had himself been called that once. It could not be such a very great ordeal to face the Empress. From the descriptions which he had heard Joseph expected to find her dressed in exquisite robes and reclining on sumptuous cushions in the fashion of oriental princesses, surrounded by attendants fanning her and by female slaves bearing perfumes. Instead he found her sitting quite at ease on a comfortable chair ; she was very simply dressed, almost like a matron, in a long stola ; it was true that the stola consisted of a stuff which had a scandalous reputation in Judaea ; it was made of Coan silk, thin as a web. She was not heavily rouged, and her hair was merely parted in the middle and tied in a knot at the back of her head ; no trace of the piled up coiffure interwoven with jewels which was usually seen on the heads of ladies of the ruling class. The Empress sat on her chair like a pretty young girl and smiled with her red lips at the two gentlemen, stretching out her childish white hand to them. Yes, people were right to call her Poppaea, baby, Jildi ; but she was really dazzling too, and Joseph no longer knew what he should say to her.

She said : " Please be seated," and when the actor sat down Joseph sat down too, and a short silence followed.

The Empress's hair was really amber yellow, as the Emperor had called it in his verses ; but the eyelashes and eyebrows above her green eyes were dark. Joseph thought feverishly : she is quite different from her busts, she is a child, but a child who can have one executed at a moment's notice. What could one say to a child like that ? Besides she was supposed to be terribly clever.

The Empress gazed at him without concealment or embarrassment ; a light perspiration broke out on him, and he tried his utmost to maintain a humble and obsequious expression. Her mouth twitched almost interceptibly, and then she looked no longer childish, but an experienced and somewhat ironical woman. " You are fresh from Judaea ? " she asked Joseph. She spoke in Greek ; her voice was a little hard and unexpectedly deep. " Tell me," she said, " What do people think in Jerusalem about the Armenian question ? " It was a completely unexpected enquiry ; for even if the key of Roman oriental politics lay in Armenia, Joseph had considered his native country far too important to be considered only in relation to a land so barbarous as Armenia, and in actual fact people in Jerusalem did not think of Armenia at all, or at lest he himself never thought of it, and so he could find nothing to say in reply to the question. " The Jews in Armenia are quite well off," he said a little doltishly, after a long silence.

" Really ? " said the Empress, and now she smiled broadly, openly amused. She asked other questions of the same nature ; she had her jest at the expense of the young man with the long ardent eyes, who obviously had no idea what game was being played with his country.

" Thank you," she said at last, after Joseph had brought out a verbose sentence concerning the strategical position on the Parthenian frontier, " now I am considerably better

informed." She smiled appreciatively across at Demetrius
Libanus ; who was this comical specimen from the orient
that he had brought to her ? "I actually believe," she
exclaimed to the actor in surprised appreciation, "that he is
interesting himself for his three innocent men out of pure
goodness of heart ! " And she turned to Joseph with great
politeness and amiability : "Please tell me all about your
protegés." She sat comfortably in her chair ; her throat
was smooth and white, her arms and legs gleamed through
the thin silk of her severe dress.

Joseph drew out his memorandum, but when he began to
read in Greek she said at once : "But what are you thinking
of ? Read it in Aramaic."

"Yes, but then will you understand it all ? " Joseph asked
somewhat fatuously.

"And who told you that I wanted to understand it all ? "
replied the Empress.

Joseph shrugged his shoulders, more in defiance than
in pique, then he read on in the Aramaic in which he had
originally drawn up his speech ; and when he came to the
quotations from the ancient Scriptures he gave them un-
abashedly in the Hebrew. But he could not concentrate ;
he saw that his words were ineffective ; he gazed immovably
at the Empress, at first humbly, then a little stupidly, then
with interest, and finally almost with insolence. He could
not tell whether she was listening, far less whether she understood him. When he was finished she asked immediately :
"Do you know Cleo, the wife of my Governor in Judaea ? "
Joseph was struck dumb. What a queer sound it had :
"My governor in Judaea." He had imagined that such
words must sound as if they were engraved in marble,
monumental ; and now this child was sitting there and
saying with a smile : "My governor in Judaea," and it

sounded quite right, one knew that it was true : for
Gessius Florus was her governor in Judaea. Nevertheless
Joseph resolved not to be impressed. " I don't know the
governor's wife," he said, and then boldly : " May I expect
an answer to my petition ? " " I have taken a note of your
petition," said the Empress. How was one to know what
that signified ?

The actor thought it was high time to intervene.
" Doctor Joseph hasn't much leisure for social matters," he
said in defence of his protegé. " His vocation is literature."

" Oh," said Poppaea, and she became quite serious and
thoughtful. " Hebrew literature. I don't know much
about it. What I do know is beautiful, but very difficult."

Joseph gathered himself together for a supreme effort.
He must, he must succeed in breathing some warmth into
this woman who sat there so smilingly and ironically. He
said that it was his dearest ambition to open up the great
literature of the Jews to the Roman people. " You bring
back pearls and spices and gold and curious animals from the
East," he said. " But you leave its best treasures, its books,
lying where they are."

Poppaea asked how he thought of opening up the Jewish
literature to the Romans. " Open up a little of it to me,"
she said, gazing at him intently with her green eyes.

Joseph closed his eyes, as people did at home in Judaea
when they recited stories, and began. He took the first
theme that occurred to him, and told of Solomon, a king in
Israel, told of his wisdom, his power, his palaces, his Temple,
his wives and his idolatry, and how the Queen of Sheba had
visited him, and how wisely he had decided the quarrel of two
women over a child, and how he had written two very
profound books, one about wisdom, entitled *The Preacher*,
and one about love, called *The Song of Songs*. Joseph tried

to render a few verses from *The Song of Songs* in a mixture
of Greek and Aramaic. It was not easy. Now he no
longer kept his eyes closed, nor did he translate merely with
his lips, but tried to make clear the meaning of those burning
verses with gestures, with his whole body. The Empress
slid down from her chair. Her arms rested upon it ; her lips
were slightly parted.

" A beautiful poem," she said when Joseph paused,
exhausted by the effort. She turned to the actor. " Your
friend is a good young man," said she.

Demetrius Libanus, who felt himself being pushed a little
into the background, employed the opportunity to assert
himself again. The treasury of Jewish Literature was inexhaustible, he remarked. He himself often had recourse
to it when he felt he was becoming stale.

" You were splendidly vulgar, Demetrius," said the
Empress appreciatively, " as the slave Isidor. I laughed
until I was sore." Demetrius Libanus made a wry face.
The Empress must have known quite well that what she
said, coming from her in particular, was very mortifying to
him. This impudent young dolt from Jerusalem hadn't
brought him much luck. The audience has miscarried ;
he should never have arranged it. " Besides, you're still
due me an answer, Demetrius," the Empress continued.
" You're always talking of a great revolutionary idea that
you have in your head. Come, out with this idea, won't
you ? To be quite frank, I hardly believe in it by this time."

The actor sat, gloomy and irritated, in his chair. " I
have no need to keep back my idea any longer," he said at
last truculently. " It's on all fours with what we've been
talking about all this time." He made a short dramatic
pause, then added casually : " I want to play the Jew
Apella."

Joseph looked at the other in dismay. The Jew Apella was the caricature of the Jews manufactured by malicious popular Roman fancy, a repellent figure, superstitious, ill-smelling, scurrilous and disgusting ; the great poet Horace had introduced him into literature half a century before, and now Demetrius Libanus wanted—Joseph was horrified.

But the behaviour of the Empress alarmed him even more ; her pale face was slightly flushed. The variety of expression of which her face was capable filled him both with admiration and fear.

The actor savoured the effect of his words. "On our stage," he explained, "actors have presented Greeks and Romans, Egyptians and Barbarians ; but the Jews have not been presented yet."

"Yes," said the Empress softly, with excitement, "it's a splendid, a dangerous idea." All three sat for a while in thoughtful silence.

"Too dangerous an idea altogether," said the actor at last sadly, already regretting his words. "I fear I won't be able to carry it out. I shouldn't have divulged it at all. It would be splendid, all the same, to play the Jew Apella ; not the silly fool the people make him out to be, but the real Apella in his tragedy and his comedy, with his feasts and his invisible God. I'm probably the only man in the world who could do it. It would be marvellous. But it is too dangerous. Your Majesty understands us Jews : but how few other people do in Rome. The audience will only laugh, and the best that I have to give will be turned to ridicule. It would be a bad business for all us Jews." And after a pause he concluded : "And then I myself might be punished by my invisible God."

Joseph sat as if turned to stone. These were wild and equivocal matters that he had blundered into. He himself felt how immense might be the effect of such a dramatic presentation ; his quick imagination pictured the actor Demetrius Libanus standing on the stage and pouring all his uncanny life into the figure of the Jew Apella, dancing, leaping, praying, talking with the thousand tongues of his eloquent body. The whole world knew how arbitrary were the moods of the Roman public. Nobody could foresee what the after-effects of such a performance might be, effects which might spread as far as the Parthian border.

The Empress had risen. She lifted her hands to the back of her head, her sleeves slipping down, and walked up and down the room, the train of her stola trailing after her. The two men had jumped up when the Empress rose. " Be silent, be silent," she said to the actor ; she was on fire with enthusiasm. " Don't be a coward, now that you have got hold for once of a good idea." She paused beside the actor and almost tenderly laid her hand on his shoulder. " The Roman theatre is boring," she lamented. " It's either coarse, or obvious, or anchored to the old, withered, dry-as-dust tradition. Play the Jew Apella for my sake, dear Demetrius." She added, turning to Joseph : " Believe me, if he were to play the Jew Apella it would teach you all a great deal."

Joseph stood without speaking, in painful uncertainty. His face flushed and became pale again. Should he try to pursuade Demetrius ? He knew that the actor longed with his whole heart to present himself in the part of a Jew before the eyes of all Rome. Joseph need only say a word to set the ball rolling. Whither it would roll nobody knew.

" You're tiresome," said the Empress crossly. She had sat down again. The two men were still standing ; the actor, accustomed to retain control over his body, stood now in an awkward and helpless posture. "Speak to him, speak to him," the Empress kept urging Joseph

"God is in Italy now," said Joseph. The actor glanced up ; one could see that the phrase had struck him and blown away a whole load of scruples. The Empress too was struck by the phrase. "Excellently put," she said, clapping her hands, "you're a clever young man," she said, and she took a note of Joseph's name.

Joseph was filled with gratified embarrassment. He did not know how these words had come to his tongue. Had he really invented the phrase himself? Had he said it before some time? In any case it was the right phrase and had come at the right moment ; and it was quite immaterial whether he himself had invented it, or somebody else : the important thing was to say the right thing at the right moment. The phrase, "God is in Italy now," had only come to life now that it had produced such a great effect.

But had it really produced such a great effect? The actor still stood irresolute, or at least pretended that he was still irresolute. "Say yes, Demetrius," said the Empress. "If you manage to bring him to the point," she turned to Joseph, "then your three innocent men will get their freedom." Joseph's eyes glittered. He bent down gently, raised the Empress's white hand from the arm of the chair where it was lying, and imprinted a long kiss upon it.

"When will you play the Jew Apella?" the Empress asked the actor.

"I have made no promise," Demetrius replied quickly and apprehensively.

"Give him a written pledge for our three men," Joseph said in a wheedling voice. The Empress smiled appreciatively over the "him" and the "our." She summoned a secretary. "If the actor Demetrius Libanus," she dictated, "plays the Jew Apella, then I guarantee that the three Jewish labourers in the brickworks at Tibur shall be set free." She asked for the tablet and signed her initial P. at the bottom, and handed it to Joseph. Then she gazed at him with her clear, green, ironical eyes. And he returned her glance humbly, but so urgently and long that slowly the mockery vanished from her eyes and their clearness was troubled.

8

After the audience Joseph walked on air. Other people worshipped the busts of the Empress as those of a lofty, almost divine figure, who had had her powerful enemy, the Emperor's mother, done to death with a smile, and had brought the Senate and people of Rome to their knees. But he himself had spoken to this woman, the greatest in all the world, as he would have spoken to any ordinary woman of his acquaintance. Jildi, Janiki. He had merely had to gaze in her eyes for a little to make her promise to release these three men ; an achievement that the High Council in Jerusalem with all their wisdom and political cunning had not been able to bring off. With a light step he wandered about the Jewish quarter on the right bank of the Tiber. People gazed after him with awe. Behind him he could hear them whispering : That's Doctor Joseph Ben Matthias from Jerusalem, priest of the first rank, the Empress's favourite. Irene worshipped him as if he were a god. The time was past when he had to sit among the less highly honoured guests on the Sabbath eve. Now Caius Barzaarone felt honoured when Joseph reclined beside him on his banqueting couch. More than that. The sly old fellow became less taciturn and divulged to Joseph difficulties that he solicitously concealed from everybody else.

His great furniture factory was still as prosperous as ever,
But now a danger which he had forseen for years was becoming more and more imminent.   The fashion was growing
among the Romans of employing little sculptured animals
as ornaments ;   these figures were carved on the legs
of chairs or as bas reliefs, they were used in a hundred ways.
But it was written in the Scriptures :   " Thou shalt not
make any graven image," and the Jews were forbidden
to fashion effigies of living creatures.   So Caius Barzaarone
had until now refrained from producing those household
animals.   But his competitors were exploiting this refusal
of his more and more unscrupulously ;   they declared that
his products were obsolete ;   it was painful for him to reflect
how many of his customers were leaving him.   His policy,
now after the great fire, meant a great loss to Caius
Barzaarone.   He had looked round him for expedients,
for some way out.   He had tried to get out of the difficulty
by the argument that he himself did not use the things he
produced, but merely sold them to others.   He had obtained
the opinions of a whole row of theologians ;   well-known
doctors in Jerusalem, Alexandria and Babylon had declared
the production of the ornaments in question to be in his
case a venial sin, or even actually permissible.   Nevertheless Caius Barzaarone hesitated.   He did not mention
those decisions to anybody.   He knew quite well that if,
armed with them, he ignored the scruples of the orthodox, it
would seriously endanger his position in the Agrippine
Ward.   His old father Aaron might even die of grief over
such godless liberalism.   So this man, outwardly so self-
assured, was full of doubt and anxiety.

Joseph did not adhere strictly to the performance of all
the orthodox rites.   But " Thou shalt not make any graven
image " was more than a command ; it was one of the first

tenets of Jewish religion.   The word and the image mutually
excluded each other.   Joseph was a literary man to his very
marrow ; he put his faith in the invisible Word ; it was the
most miraculous thing in all the world ; though without
form, it had more power than anything endowed with form.
No one could possess God's Word in very truth, the sacred
invisible Word, who sullied it with sensual images, or did
not reject with all his heart all outward vain show.   He
listened to Caius Barzaarone's explanations with a stony and
impassive face, but his very impassivity inspired Caius
Barzaarone to renewed efforts.   Indeed Joseph had the
impression that the old man would not be displeased to have
him as a son-in-law.

Meanwhile the information had gradually trickled through
that a certain condition was attached to the setting free of
the three men.   When the Jews heard of that condition
their joy was suddenly turned to sorrow.   What !
Demetrius Libanus was to play the Jew Apella, in the
Pompeian Theatre too, before forty thousand people ?
The Jew Apella !   The Jews had a shiver down their
spines when they heard that spiteful nickname, into which
Rome had concentrated all its antipathy to the immigrants
on the right bank of the Tiber.   The Jew Apella ; the
word of scorn had played an evil role in the pogroms during
the reigns of Tiberius and Claudius ; it signified looting and
butchery.   Might not the Romans' hate, now happily
asleep, awaken again at any moment ?   Was it not both
stupid and blasphemous to stir that sleeping fury ?   There
were bad enough examples to show what the Roman theatre
public were capable of on occasion.   It would be a piece of
monstrous foolhardiness for Demetrius Libanus to conjure
up the figure of the Jew Apella on the stage.

The stricter among the Jewish doctors inveighed anew,

and with increased bitterness, against the actor. Was it not
a sin even to act on the stage, to slip into the shape and the
apparel of another human being ? Had not God, praised
be His name, given to every man his own face and his own
shape ? Was it not rebellion to wish to exchange them for
those of another human being ? But to act the part of a
Jew, to act the part of an heir of the seed of Abraham, one
of the chosen people, for the amusement of the uncircumcised;
that surely was mortal sin, blasphemous presumption, and
must bring calamity on everybody's head. And they
demanded that Demetrius Libanus should be excommunicated.

The more liberal among the doctors defended the actor
with warmth. What he planned doing was for the
redemption of three innocent men. It was the sole means
of saving them. And was not the commandment to help
the prisoners one of the chief commandments in the
Scriptures ? Could one say to the actor : Do not do it,
let the three die in prison, as thousands of their forefathers
died in the brick works of Egypt ?

The dispute was a violent one. In the theological
seminaries Biblical quotations were keenly bandied. The
interesting problem was put before scholars in all the Jewish
high schools, and it was debated in Jerusalem, in Alexandria,
among the great doctors of Babylon, and in the most remote
orient. It was a question providentially fashioned for
theologians and lawyers to practice their wits upon.

The actor himself went about as usual and showed
plainly, for anyone to see, the tragic conflict between his
religious and his artistic conscience. In his heart he had
long ago decided to play the Jew Apella no matter what it
cost him. He knew, too, exactly how he would do it.
Already his librettists, among them the subtle minded

Marullus, had composed an effective framework for him
with fertile situations.   And the strangely mechanical and
resigned rocking which he had noted in the three men in
their cell had given him many a grotesque and gruesome
inspiration.   The figure he wanted to present was a daring
mixture of the tragic and the comic.   In the popular taverns,
in the business quarter, and also in the barracks, he acted
single scenes to test their effect.   But then he would sink
into dejection at the thought that probably he would not be
able to give the play after all ; his conscience might forbid
him.   With gratification he became aware that gradually
all Rome was beginning to ask whether Demetrius Libanus
would really play the Jew Apella.   Wherever his litter
appeared he was greeted with acclamations.   The
people applauded him and shouted : " Hail, Demetrius
Libanus !   Play the Jew Apella to us."   He spoke to the
Empress about the matter, and complained what a wretchedly
risky business he had let himself in for, and how heavy his
scruples were.   The Empress laughed and gazed smilingly
at the irresolute actor.   Instructions had gone out to the
brick works in Tibur that the three Jewish forced labourers
were to be well treated, so that they might not die in the
interval.   Moreover Poppaea was waiting for a decision
from the Ministry of Appeal.   The setting free of the three
men was not a great affair ; nevertheless the oriental policy
of Rome was very complicated, and Poppaea was enough of
a Roman to be prepared to let the amnesty drop at once if
there was the slightest political objection to it.   She would
smilingly cancel her promise if it should be necessary.

In the meantime, however, it amused her to encourage
the actor in his original intention.   She told him that already
the aristocratic opposition in the Senate was working against
the amnesty.   So he would have to decide at once ; it was

cruel to protract the sufferings of the poor fellows un-
necessarily. She smiled : " When are you going to play the
Jew Apella, Demetrius ? "

9

PHILIP TALASSOS, head of the Imperial Ministry for the
Orient, summoned the masseur a second time to massage his
hands and feet. It was still early in the autumn, the sun
had only just set, and nobody felt cold except himself ; but
the minister could not get warm. Tightly packed in blankets
and cushions, the little vultured-nosed man lay on a couch ;
in front of him a charcoal burner warmed his hands, and
there was another at his feet. Standing at the other side
of the couch the masseur, a slave, apprehensively and diligent-
ly rubbed the old man's wrinkled skin, from which the veins
stood out, blue and shrivelled. The minister puffed and
threatened. The masseur did his best to avoid the scars
on the old man's shoulders ; these scars, he knew, dated
from the time when the minister, then a slave in Smyrna,
had been whipped by his master. The doctors had tried a
thousand remedies for removing those scars ; they had
operated, the great specialist Scribon Largus had tried all his
salves, but the ancient scars would not vanish.

It had been a bad day, a black day ; the whole staff in
the minister's house had already been made to feel that.
The secretary knew what was to blame for his master's
morose temper. It had descended upon him when he
received a letter from the Ministry of Appeal, a short informal
query. The people in that ministry, above all the stout and
sly Junius Thrax, would gladly have done without consulting
the minister, for whom they had no love ; but under the
present Emperor the Ministry for the Orient had become the
centre of the imperial policy, and they knew what a fuss

Philip Talassos was accustomed to make if his opinion was not requested on any subject even remotely related to his sphere. And so the Ministry of Appeal had postponed finally deciding a certain question sent to them by the Empress until they should first get his opinion.

In itself it concerned a matter of no great importance. It concerned a few old Jews, who had been condemned to forced labour several years before in connection with the disturbances in Caesarea. The Empress had evidently taken a whim into her head again, for the hundredth time. She wanted to have the offenders amnestied ; Her Majesty had a suspicious weakness for the Jewish rabble. "Whore ! Trollop ! " the minister thought, giving the masseur an angry push with his elbow. Probably she herself had a strain of the Jew in her, in spite of her old and noble name. From time immemorial these insolent Roman aristocrats had been infected with corruption to the very marrow.

Nevertheless there was not much that one could bring up against this whim of the Empress. Only very general objections ; the position in the Orient demanded the greatest severity even in apparently trifling matters, and so forth.

The little vulture-nosed man felt exasperated. He sent the masseur away ; the idiot wasn't of the slightest use to him. He turned on his side, drew his sharp knees up to his chin, and thought the whole matter over.

These confounded Jews ; they were always queering one's pitch.

Since the successes of Corbulo on the Parthian frontier Rome's oriental policy had been gratifyingly energetic. The Emperor dreamt of becoming a new Alexander and of extending the Empire's sphere of influence to the very Indus. A great and mysterious campaign to reach the distant East, of which Rome had dreamt for a century, and which for a

generation had dwindled into an empty fancy, was being
seriously discussed now in the Stadium.   The official heads
of the army had worked out plans ; the Finance Ministry
had after careful consideration decided that the money for
the campaign could be raised.

There was only one weak point in this daring plan for a
new Alexandrian campaign : the province of Judaea.   It
cut across the marching route, and one could not begin the
great work until this doubtful point was made safe and sure.
The other gentlemen in the Imperial Cabinet had smiled
when the minister Talassos drew their attention to this ;
they thought that his hatred of the Jews had become a fixed
idea.   But he, Philip Talassos, had known the Jews since
the days of his Asiatic youth.   He knew that one could not
live at peace with them ; that they were a fanatical, superstitious, insanely arrogant people, and that they would never
leave one in peace until they were taught a final lesson,
until their insolent capital was rased to the ground.   Again
and again the governors had been taken in by their ingratiating
promises, but again and again their assurances were discovered to be lies.   Never had this absurd little province
become a loyal part of the Empire, as so many other greater
and more powerful provinces had done.   Their God refused
to have anything to do with other gods.   In reality there
had been a state of war in Judaea ever since the death of the
last king who had resided in Jerusalem, and Judaea would
remain unsettled, there would be war in it, the projected
campaign would remain impossible, until Jerusalem had
been laid in ruins.

The minister knew that he was right.   But he knew
also that it was not entirely the Jews' fault, for as often as he
heard their name rage overmastered him.   He thought of
the past ; he had been presented along with an expensive

candelabra to a cultivated Greek ; while in his master's
service he had set himself obstinately to rise by means of
his intelligence and his talent for languages, so that at last
his master had agreed to provide him with a good education.
Finally he had entered into competition with candidates
for posts in the imperial service ; but when the secretary of
the Emperor Caius examined him the Jewish interpreter
Theodore Zachaeus laughed at his Aramaic, so that the
Imperial Board had just failed him and no more. And it had
been a trifling error ; indeed it was questionable whether it
had been an error at all. And the filthy Jew hadn't even
questioned his rendering ; he had merely bettered it. He
himself had said " Nablion," and the Jew had suggested
" Nabla " or alternatively " Nebel," but in no circumstances
" Nablion," and while doing so the low hound had smiled
contemptuously. And then, when after so many years of
sweat and expense, he had not been taken into the Roman
government service after all, what had his master done to
him ? He had had him whipped almost to death. When
the minister remembered how the Jew had smiled he became
cold with fear and rage.

Still it really was not personal resentment alone, it was his
keen political instinct that made him so bitter against the
Jews. The world was Roman, the world was pacified
through the harmonious Roman-Greek system. Only the
Jews held out and refused to recognise the blessings of this
all-powerful organisation which bound the peoples together.
The great trade routes to India, destined to carry Greek
culture to the distant Orient, could not be rendered secure
until this rebellious, stiff-necked people were humbled to
the dust.

At the court, unfortunately, they had no eye for this
Judaean peril. The atmosphere in the imperial palace was

far too friendly to the Jews.   His fat colleague Junius Thrax
acted as a patron to them.   They had crept into the Finance
Ministry too.   In the last three years alone twenty-two of
them had been raised to the nobility.   They were pushing
their way into the dramatic world and into literature.   One
could feel almost physically that they were disintegrating the
Empire with their silly, superstitious books.   That Claudius
Reginus fellow was throwing the stuff in ship loads on to the
market.   When the old minister thought of Reginus he
drew his knees still higher.   For the slyness of the man,
repellent as he was, he had respect.   And then Reginus had
a pearl in his possession, a flawless, gigantic, tenderly glowing
pearl.   Talassos would have liked to buy the pearl from
him.   He imagined that if he wore it on his finger it
would ease the dryness of his skin.   Probably the pearl
would have a good effect too on the scarred places on his
shoulders ; but the confounded Jew was rich, money did
not tempt him, and he refused to part with the pearl.

The minister Talassos thought of this and that, the
disturbances in Caesarea, Reginus and his ring.   Should one
summon the Senate ?   One could use the Parthian war as
an excuse.   And it was Nablion after all.

Suddenly he threw himself on his back, stretched himself,
and stared with his dry, reddened eyes at the ceiling.   The
pains in his stomach were gone, also the coldness in his feet.
He had an idea, a splendid idea.   No, he wouldn't wreak
any petty revenge.   What advantage would it be to him if
these three dogs perished in the brick works at Tibur ?
The Jews could get their darlings out if they wanted.   They
could pickle the three of them in garlic, or preserve them in
their Sabbath cooking chests.   He had something better up
his sleeve ; for the setting free of these three men he would
call the Jews to a reckoning such as no clerk in the Finance

Ministry would ever be able to work out. The edict, the edict concerning Caesarea. He would couple the Caesarean affair with the amnesty of the three men. To-morrow he would again lay the edict regarding Caesarea before the Emperor. For seven months he had been waiting for the signature ; on this occasion he would secure it, for one couldn't concede everything to the Jews, one couldn't grant them their three criminals and the city of Caesarea as well. It was either the one or the other. Seeing that the Empress desired it, her precious martyrs would be set free. But in return they must finally refuse the Jewish demands regarding Caesarea. He summoned a secretary and asked for his memorandum on Caesarea. As far as he could remember it was short and to the point ; that was how the Emperor liked things, for he hated to plague his head with politics ; his interests lay elsewhere. Besides, he was quick at grasping things, the Emperor, he had a quick keen mind. If one could only bring him to the point of carefully reading over the memorandum, one would soon have his signature for the edict as well. And this business of the three forced labourers simply could not be settled without finally deciding the whole Caesarean affair. Yes, this time the Emperor must come to a decision. It was a fortunate inspiration of the Empress to ask that these three men should be set free.

The secretary brought the memorandum. Talassos glanced over it. Yes, he had put the affair clearly and convincingly.

Apart from slaves, the population of Caesarea was composed of Jews, Greeks and Romans in the proportion of forty per cent of the first to sixty of the latter two. But in the town council the Jews held a majority. They were rich, and the election statutes based the franchise on economic principles. This franchise had remained intact in the provinces of Syria and Judaea. Why should not those who supplied the greater part of the common revenue decide how that revenue should be spent ? But in Caesarea those election regulations imposed extraordinary hardships on the majority of the population. For the Jews exploited their power in the town council quite unscrupulously. Instead of using the public monies for the needs of the people, they sent great sums of it to Jerusalem for the Temple and for religious purposes. So it was no wonder that there were bloody clashes again and again at the elections. The Greeks and Romans in Caesarea remembered with bitterness that they had been the original citizens when the city was founded in Herod's reign, and that they had built the harbour from whose revenues the city lived. Finally, the Roman Governor resided in Caesarea, and that the Greeks and Romans should be oppressed by the Jews in the official capital of the province was doubly unendurable. Surely one had given sufficient consideration to the touchiness of the Jews in conceding absolute autonomy to them in Jerusalem. It was not expedient to grant any further indulgence to this people who were never satisfied. Caesarea's history, the ancestry and religion of the greater part of the population, their blood and their powers, were Gentile. The city of Caesarea, on which the peace and security of the whole province depended, would not countenance it should the most loyal part of its population be permanently refused the electoral rights they so undeniably deserved.

In his adroit and skilful memorandum the minister had not tried in the lest to suppress the Jews' arguments. He had pointed out that in the event of an alteration in the franchise the Greek and Roman population would have control over the whole Jewish contribution to the city revenues, which in practice would amount to a comprehensive expropriation of the Jewish capitalists. But he very skilfully showed that that was a trifling evil compared with the monstrous injustice involved in the fact that the official capital of a province so important for the imperial policy in the East as Judaea, was actually controlled, under the existing franchise, by a small number of rich Jews.

He read the memorandum over again and carefully considered it : his arguments were irrefutable. He smiled ; his resolve was taken. Yes, he would renounce the smaller prize, the three prisoners, so as to wrest from the Jews the greater, the beautiful sea-port of Caesarea.

He summoned his servants and cursed them. He ordered the charcoal fires, the blankets and cushions to be carried out. What were the dunces thinking of ; did they want him to die of heat ? He walked up and down on his thin shanks ; life flowed back into his bony wrists. He sent an urgent demand to the Emperor for an audience next morning. He saw his way now ; his plan could not miscarry.

For he had no hurry ; he could enjoy his revenge at his leisure. Several decades had passed since the Jewish inter-preter had smiled at him. Nablion, yes, it was Nablion now, and it would continue to be Nablion. He could wait. Once the edict was signed, depriving the Jews in Caesarea of their insolent power, there would be no need for the fact to be announced at once ; the matter could rest for months or even for a year, until the plans for the great oriental campaign were ripe.

Yes, he would lay his suggestions regarding Caesarea before the Emperor to-morrow. He felt certain that in this form he would carry them through. He smiled. Before supper he dictated his reply to the query from the Ministry of Appeal regarding the amnesty of the three Jewish prisoners in the brick works at Tibur. Junius

Thrax would open his eyes when he learned that Talassos
had nothing, absolutely nothing, against the proposal.

At the supper table the jeweller Claudius Reginus noted
reflectively that the old morose minister was in strangely
high spirits.

10

DEMETRIUS LIBANUS liked Joseph better and better.   The
actor was no longer young, his life and his art demanded a
great deal of energy ; it seemed to him that he drew new
inspiration from the ardour of this youth from Jerusalem.
And had not Joseph also been the cause of his giving to the
world at long last his great and dangerous idea, the presentation of the Jew Apella ?   He asked Joseph more and
more often to his house.   Joseph laid aside his provincial
manners and with his quick brain soon learned the nimble
and adroit worldly wisdom of the capital, and became a man
of the world.   From the literary men whom he came to
know through the actor he learned something of their
technique and the jargon of their profession.   He had
political and philosophical talks with men of importance ;
he had love affairs with women, with girl slaves as well as
women of the aristocracy.

He lived very pleasantly amid the esteem of his friends.
Nevertheless when he was alone he was often overcome by a
gnawing feeling of dissatisfaction.   He knew of course that
the amnesty of the three men could not be secured in a day.
But now weeks and months had passed, and he still waited
and waited as he had done in Judaea.   The uncertainty
gnawed at him, and he had to put great constraint upon himself to retain his air of confidence.

Claudius Reginus had asked him to send the memorandum which had made such an impression on the
Empress.   Joseph sent it and waited with agitation for the

decision of the great publisher. But the publisher remained silent. Joseph waited for four long weeks ; Reginus still remained silent. Had he given the manuscript to Justus to read ? Joseph grew uncomfortable when he thought of the cool, keen face of his rival.

At last Reginus invited him to supper. The only other guest was Justus of Tiberias. Joseph was on his guard. He smelt a plot. He had not long to wait. After the first course his host remarked that he had read the memorandum. A remarkable gift for form, but the content, the argument, was feeble. Justus too had written, at the request of King Agrippa, his judgment on the case of the three men. Would Justus be kind enough to outline his views ? Joseph's knees trembled. Suddenly the opinion of all Rome seemed to him unimportant compared to that of this countryman of his, Justus of Tiberias.

Justus did not let himself be asked twice. The case of the three men, he said, could not be considered except in relation to the Caesarean affair. The Caesarean affair could not be considered except in relation to the whole imperial policy in the Orient. Ever since Corbulo had commanded in the East Rome had made concessions in appearance, but never in actual fact. With all respect to Joseph's gift for form, he did not think that his memorandum would have much effect on the imperial administration. Reports and suggestions from the Financial Ministry and the general staff would be more likely to do that. He, Justus, in the memorandum which, on the instructions of King Agrippa, he had sent in to the Ministry of the Orient, had insisted above all on the legal aspect of the Caesarean affair. He had referred to the example of Alexandria, where Rome had refused to yield to the intrigues of the antisemites. But he was afraid that the minister Talassos, who was in any case an antisemite and probably bribed by the Greeks in Caesarea, would in the present case yield to the intrigues of the Gentile population in spite of all legal arguments.   And from the point of view of the imperial policy in the Orient unfortunately with perfectly good reason.

Justus sat straight and erect on the banqueting couch ; he spoke sharply, logically, urgently.   Joseph listened lying on his back with his hands clasped behind his head. Suddenly he sat up, leant across the table towards Justus, and said with hostility : " It isn't true that the question of these men in the brick works has anything to do with politics. It's a matter of justice, of humanity.   It's simply for the sake of justice that I am here.   Justice !   That's what I've been shouting into people's faces ever since I've come to Italy.   I've gained the Empress over with my desire for justice."

Reginus turned his fleshy face from the one to the other, he gazed at Joseph's lean, pale brown face, and then at Justus's lean, golden brown face.   " Do you know, my friends," he said, " that you are very like each other ? "

They were both taken aback.   They scrutinised each other : the jeweller was right.   They hated each other.

" Besides, I'm in a position to tell you in confidence," Reginus went on, " that you're disputing about a case that's already settled.   Yes," he said, looking into their dazed faces, " the Caesarean affair is decided.   Some time may elapse before the edict is made public, but it is signed and despatched to the Governor General of Syria.   You are right, Doctor Justus.   The Caesarean affair has been decided against the Jews."

The two young men stared with blank eyes at Claudius Reginus, who sleepily gazed in front of him.   They were so downcast that they forgot themselves and their dispute.

" This is the worst blow to Judaea for more than a hundred years," said Joseph.

" I'm afraid blood will flow because of this edict," said Justus.

They drank in silence. " See to it, Doctor Joseph," said Reginus, " that your Jews remain reasonable."

" It's easy to say that here in Rome," replied Joseph, and his voice was full of anger. He sat humped up dejecte ' y, as if all the strength had run out of him. What this disgusting fat fellow had told him made him so sad that his heart had no room even for the humiliating feeling that he and his mission were equally ridiculous now. Of course his rival had been right ; he had foreseen everything, and he, Joseph, had been merely building castles in the air, and his success was empty.

Claudius Reginus spoke again. " In any case I intend," he said, " just now before the edict is known, to publish your memorandum, Doctor Justus. You must hear this treatise," he turned with unaccustomed enthusiasm to Joseph. " It is a little masterpiece," and he begged Justus to read a chapter. In spite of his hostility Joseph began to pay attention and soon was spellbound. Yes, compared with these clear, incisive sentences, his wretched melodramatic fulminations were not up to much.

He gave it up. He renounced the whole business. He resolved to return to Jerusalem and take a modest post in the service of the Temple. That night he slept badly, and next day he wandered about despondently. He ate little and without enjoyment, and he refrained from visiting the girl Lucilla, with whom he had made an appointment. He wished that he had never come to Rome, that he was in Jerusalem still, ignorant of the iniquitous and dreadful things that were being hatched here against Judaea. He told himself that probably what Reginus had said was mere rumour ; but in his heart he knew that it was true. He knew the city of Caesarea well, its harbour, its great warehouses, its shipping companies, its synagogues, its bazaars and brothels. Even the great buildings that the Romans had erected there, hated though they were, the residence of the Governor, the colossal statues of Juno and the first Emperor, the gymnasium ; even these enhanced the fame of Judaea so long as the city was governed by Jews. But should the government fall into the hands of the Greeks and the Romans the capital would become a Roman city and then everything would be reversed ; then the Jewish population in all Judaea, the population even of Jerusalem, would be only tolerated in their own country. When he realised this Joseph felt the ground sinking under his feet. Dejection and rage filled him from head to foot, so that he felt physically sick.

II

But when Demetrius Libanus solemnly and resolutely informed him that he had now made up his mind to play the Jew Apella, so that the three martyrs might be set free, Joseph once more glittered in the first undimmed radiance of his triumph. The Roman Jews accepted the actor's decision more calmly than one might have expected after their first agitation ; for it was winter now and the performance would not be a public one, but would be given in the little private theatre in the Emperor's gardens. There remained, it was true, one figure who still grumbled. The aged Aaron ; he continued to mutter curses against the godless behaviour of Libanus and the blasphemous newfangled generation in general.

"The Jew Apella" was the first popular operetta to be performed, in the Emperor's private theatre. The theatre seated only some thousand people, and the select society of Rome jealously sought invitations to this premiére. All the state ministers were there, the withered Talassos, the stout, good humoured Junius Thrax, Minister of Appeal, also the commander of the guard, Tigillinus. And of course the lively and inquisitive Abbess of the Vestals. Nor had Claudius Reginus been forgotten. Not many Jews were present ; the elegant Julian Alf, president of the Velia Ward, and his son ; with some difficulty Joseph had also managed to fish an invitation for Caius Barzaarone and the girl Irene.

The curtain was lowered. On the stage appeared the Jew Apella, a middle-aged man with a long pointed beard, which was beginning to turn grey. The scene is a country town in Judaea ; Apella's house is small ; he, his wife, and his many children live in one room. The great people in Jerusalem take from him half of his meagre earnings ; the Romans in Caesarea take half of the rest. When his wife dies he wanders out into the world. He takes with him the little scroll with his confession of faith, that he might fasten it to the door posts of his new house ; he takes also his phylacteries, his chest for keeping warm his Sabbath meals, his Sabbath candlesticks, his many children, and his invisible God. He goes towards the East, into the country of the Parthians. He builds a little house for himself, fastens to the door posts the little scroll with the confession of faith, binds the phylacteries round his head and his arm, and stands with his face towards the West, towards Jerusalem and the Temple, and prays. He makes a scanty livelihood, hardly enough to keep him alive, but he is thrifty, and he even manages to send something to Jerusalem for the Temple. But then appear the others, the eleven clowns ; they are the Parthians, and they mock him. They take away the little

scroll from his door post, and the phylacteries ; they examine
the phylacteries to discover what they contain ; they find
nothing but parchment with writing on it, and they laugh
at the absurd gods of this man.   They want to force him to
worship their gods, the bright Ormuzd and the dark Ahriman,
and when he refuses they pluck him by his beard and his
hair and pull at them until at last he has to kneel, and that
is very funny.   He refuses to recognise their visible gods,
and they refuse to recognise his invisible God.   But to make
matters safe they take away his little hoard of money that he
has managed to save ; they take it as an offering for the altar
of their gods, and they strike three of his seven children dead.
He buries the three children, he wanders about among the
three little graves, he sits down and sings an old song : By
the waters of Babylon we sat and wept, and his body rocks
in a curious fashion, grotesque and yet tragic.   Then he
washes his hands and wanders out again, this time to the
south, towards Egypt.   The little house that he has built
he leaves standing, but takes with him the scroll with the
confession of faith, the phylacteries, the warming chest,
the candlesticks, the remainder of his children, and his
invisible God.   He builds a new little house ; he takes to
himself a new wife ; years come and go ; he gathers together
a new hoard of money, and to replace the three children that
were killed he begets four new ones.   Now, when he prays,
he stands with his face towards the North, where lie
Jerusalem and the Temple, and he does not forget to send
every year his tribute to the land of Israel.   But even in the
south his enemies will not leave him in peace.   Again come
the eleven clowns ; this time they are Egyptians, and they
order him to pray to their gods, Isis and Osiris, the ox, the
ram, and the hawk.   But then comes the Roman Governor
and orders them to let him be.   The eleven clowns are very

funny as they retreat in disappointment. But he himself,
the Jew Apella, is still more comic in the exultation of
victory. Once more he rocks in the most curious way his
lean body ; but this time he is dancing before God ; he
dances before the chest containing the Holy Scriptures.
Grotesquely he lifts his legs till his knees reach his greying
beard ; his tattered garments flutter ; with a wrinkled and
dirty hand he beats a tambourine. He rocks, all his limbs
praise his invisible God ; so he dances before the chest where
the Scriptures are kept, as King David danced before the Ark
of the Covenant. The great Roman patricians in the
theatre laughed heartily ; but distinctly through the general
laughter could be heard the shrill snicker of the minister
Talassos. Most of the audience, however, were slightly ill
at ease, and the few Jews present stared with embarrassment,
almost with horror, at the hopping, skipping, swaying man
on the stage. They thought of the Levites who stood with
their sacred silver trumpets uplifted on the highest stairs of
the Temple, and of the High Priest, tall and dignified, as he
entered the presence of his God, splendid in fair raiment,
wearing the Temple jewels ; and was it not sacrilege, what
that man on the stage was doing ? But finally not even the
Roman Governor can protect the Jew any longer, for the
Egyptians are too many. The eleven clowns have grown
to eleven times eleven, and they drop poisoned accusations
into the Emperor's ear, and they dance comically, and they
prick the Jew Apella and pinch him and shoot at him with
little deadly arrows, and again they kill three of his children
and his wife as well. And at last the Jew Apella wanders
out once more with scroll and phylacteries and chest and
candlestick and children and his invisible God, and this
time he comes to Rome. But now the play becomes daring
and quite barefaced. The clowns no longer venture to

oppress him physically ; they keep to the farthest edge of
the stage. Nevertheless, leaping about like apes, they climb
on to the roof of his house, they even make their way into
his rooms, they look to see what is in the scroll or in the
cooking chest, they mimic him when he stands up to pray,
facing the East this time, where lie Jerusalem and the Temple.
The eleven chief clowns are now wearing very daring masks,
portrait masks ; without much difficulty the minister
Talassos can be recognised, Cassius Longinus the jurist of
the Senate, the philosopher Seneca, and other opulent
enemies of the Jews. But this time they can do nothing
against the Jew Apella ; he is protected by the Empress and
the Emperor. Yet they watch nevertheless for him to give
them an opening, and behold he provides it. He marries
a native Italian, a manumitted slave. Then they get behind
his wife and pour all their contempt for him into her ear.
A few extraordinarily spiteful couplets are sung on the
subject of the circumcised, his garlic, his stench, his fasts,
his cooking chests. Soon things get so bad that his wife
jeers at him in the presence of his children because he is
circumcised. Then he drives her out and remains alone
with his children and his invisible God, under the protection
of the Roman Emperor. He is resigned at last. He rocks
his body and sings with wild yearning his ancient song :
By the waters of Babylon we sat and wept ; in the distance,
quite softly, the eleven mimic him.

The audience looked at one another and did not quite
know whether to laugh or cry. Everybody glanced sur-
reptitiously at the imperial box ; the Empress said distinctly
in her clear, childish voice, so that everyone could hear,
that hardly any other contemporary play had interested her
so much. She complimented the senator Marullus, who
with false modesty declined responsibility for the text. The

Emperor was taciturn ; his teacher in literature, Seneca,
had inculcated tradition into him so assiduously that for the
moment he did not know what to make of the novel technique
of the play.   The Emperor was young and fair, his intelligent
face was slightly puffy, his eyes mustered busily and somewhat absently the audience, who dared not leave the theatre
before he set them an example.   The Jews in the audience
stood about awkwardly ; Claudius Reginus groaningly tied
his shoe laces and muttered incomprehensible things when
anyone asked what he thought of the play.   Joseph had
oscillated between exasperation and admiration.   The
harsh realism of the Jew Apella planted there on the stage
had almost shocked him.   That anyone should so recklessly
mix together all that was ridiculous and tragic in that figure
filled him with fascinated discomfort.   And with most of
the others it was the same.   They were impressed and
dissatisfied ; the Jews, indeed, actually disturbed.   The only
one who seemed really elated was the minister Talassos.

The Emperor commanded him and Junius Thrax to come
to his box, and said reflectively that he was keenly interested
to see how the Jews would respond to a certain decision.
Immediately before she left the Empress informed Joseph
that his three innocent men would be set free the very next
day.

12

NEXT day, immediately after sunrise, the three prisoners
were released.   In the country house of Julian Alf, president
of the Velia Ward, they were put under the supervision of
physicians, bathed, fed, clothed, and provided with rich
raiment.   Then they were seated in Julian Alf's fine
carriage.   Along all the road leading from Tibur to Rome
stood groups of Jews, and when the carriage passed, couriers
in front, a great train behind, they recited the blessing

that is prescribed after rescue from great danger, and cried
to the three men : " Blessed be ye that come. Peace be
with you, doctors and masters."

At the Tibur gate there was an immense throng.   Here,
in a space guarded by police and soldiers, the presidents of
the five Jewish wards awaited the prisoners, also the state
secretary Polybius from the Ministry of Appeal, one of the
Empress's masters of ceremony, and conspicuous above all,
the writer Joseph Ben Matthias, delegate from the High
Council in Jerusalem, and the actor Demetrius Libanus.
Naturally here, too, the great actor excited the most interest ;
but without exception Romans and Jews alike pointed out
to each other the slender young man with the lean fanatical
face, the salient nose and the ardent eyes : that was Doctor
Joseph Ben Matthias, who had secured the deliverance of
the three men.   It was a great hour for Joseph.   He looked
young, grave, exalted and dignified ; he made a good figure
even by the side of the great actor.

At last the chariot with the three prisoners arrived.   They
were carried out of it.   They were very feeble, and their
bodies swayed to and fro with a curious mechanical motion.
With dead eyes they gazed at all those faces, all those solemn
white robes, and listened dully to the speeches in their
praise.   The spectators pointed with deep indignation at
their half-shorn skulls, and the E branded on their brows,
and the marks of the fetters above their ankles.   From
every side the cry rose again and again : " Hail, ye that come.
Peace be with you, learned doctors," and many people wept.
But the actor Demetrius Libanus knelt down, he bowed his
head in the dust of the road and kissed the feet of those men
who had suffered for Jehovah and the land of Israel.   People
were accustomed to see him in the role of a clown ; and the
people laughed wherever he showed himself.   But nobody

thought him funny as he lay in the dust before the three men and kissed their feet and wept.

Next Sabbath the great service of thanksgiving took place in the Agrippine Synagogue. The oldest of the three men read the first verse of the text chosen : he brought the words rumblingly and with difficulty from his chest, the great house was filled with people to the last corner ; a dense crowd, silent and intent, filled the whole street. Then Joseph was summoned after the end of the reading to lift up the Thora Scroll. Slender and serious he stood on the elevated place, with both hands he lifted the scroll, turned round so that everyone should be able to see it, and with his ardent eyes gazed over the great assembly. And the eyes of the Roman Jews hung on this young, enthusiastic man as he uplifted for them the sacred scroll of the Scriptures.

That winter the three martyrs were greatly feted. Slowly they recovered their strength, their emaciated bodies filled out, their shorn skulls were covered sparsely with new hair ; under the supervision of Scribon Largus the scars made by the fetters above their ankles gradually healed. One ward after another, one influential Jewish merchant after another, took them up ; they accepted the honour shown them somewhat dully, as a tribute which they deserved.

Gradually, as their powers increased, they began to talk more. It was presently clear that these martyrs were quarrelsome, disputative, irascible old fellows. Nothing was pious enough for them, or sufficiently in conformance with the law. They squabbled among themselves and with everybody else ; they went about among the Jews in Rome as if they were in Jerusalem and everybody was under their authority ; they ordained and they prohibited. Until finally Julian Alf politely but firmly drew their attention to the fact that his Velia synagogue did not lie within their

Temple jurisdiction. Thereupon they cursed him and demanded to have him excommunicated. Everybody was glad when the sailing season began again and the three men could be sent to Puteoli to be shipped from there to Judaea.

13

Joseph's task in Rome was ended. Yet he stayed on. Once more he saw in vast outline the goal that he had had before him in coming to Rome : to conquer the city. More and more clearly he saw that if he were to do this there was only one path for him : literature. A great subject out of the history of his country tempted him. From his earliest days the episode that had attracted him most in the ancient books of his people was the war of freedom of the Maccabees against the Greeks. The deliverance of the three learned doctors had not been the real aim of his journey to Rome. Only now did he recognise why everything had driven him here. Rome was ripe to receive the wisdom and the mysteries of the East. His task was to describe to the Roman world that tragic and heroic excerpt from the earlier days of Israel, so that everyone might see that this land was a chosen land, and that God dwelt in it.

He spoke to no one of his intentions. Outwardly he led the life of a young society man. But everything that he saw, heard, experienced, took on some relevance to his work. It must be possible to understand both, the East and the West. It must be possible to give the hard and clear form which the theories of the young prose writers demanded to the story of the Maccabees with its faith and its marvels. In the ancient books he lived with these martyrs of a former time who had taken upon themselves a tragic fate so as not to offend the law of Jehovah ; and in the Forum, in the colonnades of Libia, in the Campus Martius, in the public

baths, in the theatre, he made himself at home amid the life
and the " technique " of this city of Rome, which enthralled
its inhabitants, so that everyone cursed it and everyone
loved it.

He felt to the full the tremendous seduction of the city,
when the opportunity was offered him to remain in it
permanently.   For Caius Barzaarone wished to find a
husband for Irene.   At the wish of the mother he had kept
young Doctor Licinus of the Velia synagogue in view as a
son-in-law, but in his heart he did not desire the connection,
and the girl Irene's eyes still hung with the same rapturous
admiration as at first on Joseph's fanatical face.   The
wedding was put off ; it would have cost Joseph only a word
to become for all time a rich man as the son-in-law of his
host.   It was tempting ; it meant quiet, a spacious life,
esteem and wealth.   But it meant also stagnation and an end
to his ambitions.   Was the goal not too petty for him ?

He flung himself with redoubled ardour into his books.
He prepared with infinite care his " History of the Maccabees."   He was not ashamed to con like a schoolboy Latin and
Greek grammar. He practiced his skill on difficult episodes.
So, in this humble and laborious way, he kept at work
through the whole spring, until at last he felt himself fit to
begin his book.

Then an event occurred that shook the foundations of his
life.   Early that summer the Empress Poppaea, still very
young, died quite suddenly.   She had desired to die young
and unwithered ; she had often spoken of death ; now her
wish was fulfilled. Even after her death she still gave proof
of her love for the East ; for in her will she had decreed that
her body should not be burnt, but embalmed after the eastern
custom.

The Emperor made his grief and his love the occasion for

a prodigious celebration. The gigantic funeral procession
went through the city, with choirs of singers, lamenting
women, and the chorus. Endlessly the train of ancestors
defiled through the streets, including now, as the last among
them, the Empress herself. The waxen masks of the long
dead first fathers of the royal line had been taken out of their
sacred caskets for this public spectacle. They were worn
by actors dressed in the pompous official robes of these dead
consuls, presidents, and ministers, and each was preceded by
his lictors with the battle axe and the fasces. Then the
whole procession was repeated again, composed this time of
dancers and comedians who gave a grotesque parody of the
train which had preceded them. The dead Empress herself
was caricatured in this second procession ; Demetrius
Libanus had not been able to avoid according his protectress
this last gruesome service of love ; and when the jumping,
hopping, painfully absurd caricature of their mighty patroness
went past the Jews wept with laughter and grief. Then
followed all the servants of the deceased, a long train of
officials, slaves, free men, then the officers of her bodyguard, and finally, borne by four senators, the dead Empress
herself, artistically embalmed by Jewish physicians and
surrounded by a cloud of incense, sitting on a chair as she
had always preferred to do, and clothed in one of those
severely cut, yet enigmatically transparent robes that she had
loved. Behind her came the Emperor in simple black garb
without any of the insignia of his power, his face covered.
And behind him the Senate and the people of Rome. Before
the tribune of the Forum the procession halted. The
ancestors descended from their chariots and seated themselves
in the ivory chairs, and the Emperor made the funeral
oration. Joseph saw Poppaea ; she sat in her chair as she
had sat when he had spoken to her, her hair the colour of

amber and her face a little ironical ; and then the Emperor concluded his speech and Rome greeted the Empress for the last time. The multitude stood with arms outstretched, the ancestors also arose from their chairs and stretched out their arms, and so they remained for a moment, all standing, and only the dead woman sat.

14

JOSEPH had avoided Justus all this time. Now he sought him out. The two young men strolled through the colonnades of the Campus Martius. Justus was of the opinion that now that Poppaea was dead Talassos and his friends would not delay much longer the publication of the edict. Joseph shrugged his shoulders in silence. They walked on amid the crowd of elegant idlers who thronged the colonnades. Then, just in front of Caius Barzaarone's beautiful warehouse, Justus stopped and said : " And if the Jews of Caesarea have their rights stolen from them now, nobody can have any complaint. In this affair the Jews will be forced to appear in the wrong. If they can bring forward objections that seem even half justified, then Rome is bound to listen to them, isn't it ? Hasn't Rome pardoned your three innocent men ? Oh, Rome is great of heart ! Rome treats Judaea mildly, more mildly than other provinces."

Joseph turned pale. Was this man right ? Was his success, was the deliverance of the three men, a disaster for the general policy of the Jews, seeing that Rome could treacherously sugar over the severity of its main decision by showing mildness in an affair that did not matter ? With unseeing eyes he gazed at the furniture that stood idly in front of Caius Barzaarone's warehouse.

He did not reply and presently said good-bye. He felt

sick at Justus's words ; they must not be true. He had his
hours of vanity : who had not ? But in the affair of the
three innocent men he had acted with a clean heart ; he had
not worsened the position of his people to gain a petty
personal success.

With new and burning ardour he threw himself into his
work. He fasted, scourged himself, and made a vow not to
touch a woman until he had finished his task. He worked.
He closed his eyes to see more clearly the figures in his book,
and opened them to set those figures in a true light. He
told for the whole world the story of the wonderful war of
freedom waged by his people. He suffered and triumphed
with the martyrs whose story he was telling ; with Judas
Maccabaeus he consecrated the Temple anew ; his faith
surrounded him like a great cloud. Faith, deliverance,
triumph ; all the sublime feelings he had divined in the
ancient books he poured into his work. While he wrote
he was the chosen warrior of Jehovah. He forgot Caesarea ;
he read his book to a select circle of young literary men.
They congratulated him. He sent the manuscript to the
publisher Claudius Reginus. Reginus declared at once
that he would undertake its publication.

But simultaneously, under the same imprint, appeared a
book by Justus : " On the Jewish Idea." Joseph regarded it
as a mean trick that neither Reginus nor Justus had mentioned
it to him beforehand. He found fault with Justus's book ;
it was dry and lifeless. But in his heart he thought his own
book vapid bombast compared with the new, condensed and
forceful arguments of his rival. He read the little work a
second, a third time. His own attempts seemed puerile and
hopeless.

But, behold, the girl Irene, now the wife of Doctor Licinus,
was not the only one who thought Joseph's book splendid ;

it found appreciative readers on the right bank of the Tiber, not to speak of the elegant literati on the left bank. Joseph's fame spread. His history of the Jewish war was acclaimed as an interesting and novel revival of the heroic epic. Young literary aspirants approached him for advice; already he was being imitated and regarded as the head of a school. The great families invited him to give readings to private parties. On the right bank of the Tiber his history was used as a school book. But Justus's book was neither known nor read. Claudius Reginus's book-keeper told Joseph that one hundred and fifty copies of Justus's book, and four thousand copies of Joseph's had been sold, and the enquiries for the latter from all the provinces, particularly from the Orient, were increasing steadily. Justus himself seemed to have withdrawn from Rome; in any case Joseph never met him during those months of literary success.

15

THE winter passed, and early spring brought an impressive demonstration of the power of Rome; the long prepared for triumph of the Empire over the East. It was the magnificent prelude to the new campaign which was to rival that of Alexander the Great. Rome's neighbouring rival in the East, the Parthian Empire ruled by King Vologas, the only great power in the known world outside of Rome, was weary of the long war, and had renounced its claim to Armenia, the territory in dispute. The Emperor himself solemnly closed the Temple of Janus as a sign that peace ruled on the earth. Then in a magnificent spectacle he prepared to celebrate this first victory over an Orient that was to be conquered anew. The Armenian King Tiridates was to appear in person before him to receive from his hands the crown which he would wear now only as a vassal. For

months the eastern ruler rode with a mighty following, with
horses and splendid gifts, gold and myrrh, towards the West,
to pay his homage to the Roman Emperor. Through the
whole Orient ran stories of three Kings of the East who had
set out that they might worship the uprising star in the West.
The Finance Ministry in Rome, however, had heavy
anxieties in devising how they were to pay for the whole
business, which of course would be at the cost of the Imperial
Exchequer.

When at last King Tiridates and his train reached Italian
soil the Senate and people of Rome were summoned by
proclamation to be present to behold the submission of the
East to the Emperor. The streets were thronged with inquisitive crowds ; the Imperial Guards had to be ordered out
to keep them back. Between their ranks advanced the
eastern king in the rich garb of his country, a tiara on his
head, the short Persian sword at his side ; but it was harmless,
for it was nailed to the sheath. So he proceeded to the
Forum, ascended the dais on which the Roman Emperor
was seated on his throne, and bowed his forehead to the
ground ; but the Emperor took the tiara from his head and
set in its place the diadem. And then the soldiers clashed
their shields and spears together and shouted in a mighty
chorus which they had rehearsed for many days : " Hail,
Caesar, Imperator, God ! "

On a raised platform in the Street of the Gods that ran
past the Forum were sitting guests of honour to watch the
spectacle, and among them was Joseph. With profound
agitation he witnessed the humiliation of Tiridates. The
struggle between the East and the West was an ancient one.
In their time the Persians had provided a dam against the
West, but then Alexander had flung the East back for
centuries. But in the last few centuries, and particularly

since, about a hundred years before, the Parthians had destroyed a great Roman army, the East again seemed to be pressing forward. In any case the East felt itself intellectually superior, and a new hope filled the Jews that in the East a Redeemer would appear and Jerusalem would become the capital of the world, as the ancient prophecies had foretold. And now Joseph had to see with his own eyes Tiridates, the brother of the mightiest ruler in the East, abasing his brow in the dust before Rome. The Parthian Kingdom was far away, a campaign there involved tremendous difficulties, and the grandson of the man who had defeated the great Roman general Crassus with all his cavalry and infantry was still living there. And yet the Parthians had submitted to this wretched compromise. This Parthian prince had suffered his sword to be nailed to its sheath. By such means he still retained at least a certain autonomy and also his diadem, even if he wore it only on sufferance. When the mighty Parthian was content to do that, was it not madness for a few ambitious fools in the little country of Judaea to imagine that they could challenge the power of Rome ? Judaea was easy to reach and surrounded by Romanised provinces ; more than a century before Rome had introduced there its administration and its military technique. The things the Avengers of Israel spouted in the Blue Hall in Jerusalem was crazy nonsense. Judaea would have to accept its place in the world like the other nations ; God was in Italy, and the world was Roman.

Suddenly he found Justus beside him. " King Tiridates cuts a poor figure beside your Maccabees, Doctor Joseph," he said.

Joseph glanced at him ; he looked bilious, sceptical, a little bitter and far older than Joseph, although he was not really older. " Is he laughing at me, or what does he

mean ? " Joseph wondered. " I certainly admit," he said,
" that a sword nailed to its sheath appeals less to me than a
drawn sword."

" Yet in certain cases it may be wiser, and perhaps in
some actually more heroic," replied Justus. " Seriously,"
he added, " it's a pity that such a talented man as you should
develop into such a pernicious fool."

" You dare to say that ! " Joseph exclaimed angrily. It
made him furious that anyone should formulate so clearly
and bluntly the nebulous reproaches which sometimes
tormented him at nights. " My book on the Maccabees,"
he said, " has shown Rome that we Jews are still Jews and
not Romans. Is that pernicious ? "

" I suppose the Emperor will withdraw his signature to
the Caesarean edict now, what ? " asked Justus mildly.

" The edict hasn't been made public yet," replied Joseph
stubbornly. " There are people," he quoted, " who pretend
to know what Jupiter whispers into Juno's ear."

" I'm afraid," said Justus, " that after Rome has finished
its business with the Parthians it won't delay much longer
with the publication of the edict."

They sat on the platform ; beneath them the cavalry rode
past, the horsemen sitting lazily and comfortably on their
saddles ; the crowd cheered, the officers gazed haughtily
in front of them, glancing neither to the right nor to the
left.

" You should not try to shut your eyes to things," said
Justus, almost contemptuously. " I know," he added,
" that you have written the classical account of our war of
freedom ; you're the Jewish Titus Livius. But, you see,
when our living Greeks read to-day of dead Leonidas, it's
only a harmless academic pleasure after all ; but when our
Avengers of Israel in Jerusalem read your history of Judas

Maccabaeus the blood rushes to their heads and they look round for their swords.   Do you consider that desirable ? "

Below them the man with his sword nailed to his sheath was riding past now.   Everybody on the platform got up. The crowd shouted in a frenzy at the man passing by.

" Caesarea," said Justus, " is finally wrested from us. You have made that in a certain sense easier for the Romans. Do you want to give them still further pretexts, so that they may be able to make Jerusalem a Roman city too ? "

" What can a Jewish writer do to-day ?   I have no desire for Judaea to be swallowed up by Rome," said Joseph.

" A Jewish writer," responded Justus, " must recognise at least that the world to-day cannot be saved by iron and gold."

" Even iron and gold become spiritual things when they are employed for spiritual ends," said Joseph.

" A fine phrase for your books, Titus Livius, when you don't happen to have any facts to bring forward," Justus jeered.

" What must Judaea do so as not to go under ? " Joseph asked in reply.   " The Maccabees were victorious because they were ready to die for their convictions and their faith."

" I can see no sense," replied Justus, "in dying for one's faith.   To die for one's convictions is a soldier's virtue.   The task of the writer is to record the soldier's death and hand it on. I don't think," he went on, " that the invisible God of Jerusalem is as easy to grasp to-day as the God of your Maccabees.   I don't believe that much is effected by dying for Him.   He is in Italy.   His house in Jerusalem is no longer big enough for Him.   It's a fearfully hard task to build an invisible house for the invisible God.   At any rate, Doctor Joseph, it certainly isn't as simple as you think. Your book may bring a little of the Roman spirit into

Judaea, but it certainly won't bring any of the Jewish spirit into Rome."

Joseph was more impressed by this conversation than he was prepared to admit. In vain he told himself that Justus had spoken out of envy, because his own book had been unsuccessful. Justus's accusations stuck ; he could not drive them out of his mind. He read over his book on the Maccabees ; he summoned to his aid all the sublime feelings he had felt in the lonely nights when he had written it. In vain. He must settle with this fellow Justus. He could not live on as he was doing.

He decided to accept the Caesarean decision as a sign. For a year now they had been brandishing that silly edict under his nose ; this Caesarean business was the sole thing that justified Justus's thoughts of him. Very good. If the matter was really decided to the disadvantage of the Jews, then he would confess himself beaten. Then he was wrong, then his book on the Maccabees was not in the genuine Jewish spirit ; then Justus was the great man and he himself a petty, conceited place-hunter.

For several endless days he went about in tortured expectation. At last he could no longer endure the tension. He fetched out his dice. If they turned up luckily, then the decision would be lucky for the Jews. He spun the revolving dice. Turned up an unlucky number. Spun again. Turned up another unlucky number. He spun a third time ; this time he was lucky. He felt alarmed. Without intending it he had selected the chipped dice.

He longed to be back in Judaea again. During those eighteen months in Rome he had forgotten a great many things in Judaea ; he could no longer envisage it ; he must go back and gather new strength from it.

In great haste he prepared for his departure. Half the

Jewish population were standing at the Gate of the Three Streets where the car was awaiting him which was to take him to Ostia and his ship. Three people accompanied him : Irene, the wife of Doctor Licinus, the actor Demetrius Libanus, and the writer Justus of Tiberias.

On the way Demetrius told him once more that he, too, intended sometime to journey to Zion, and then it would be for good. He did not mean to wait very much longer. He did not think that his acting life would last for more than seven or eight years now. Then, at last, he would see Jerusalem. He dreamt of the Temple, he said, hanging radiantly with its huge terraces over the city ; he dreamt of its white and golden halls. He dreamt of the softly shimmering curtain that veiled the Holy of Holies ; it was the most delicate fabric in the known world. He knew everything about the holy place, better probably then many who had seen it with their own eyes ; so often had he asked people to tell him about it.

They reached the harbour of Ostia. The sundial pointed to the eighth hour. Laboriously and with childish persistance Joseph reckoned up the time he had been away from Judaea. It was now one year, seven months, twelve days and four hours. Suddenly he was overcome by a simple physical longing for Jerusalem ; he wished he could have hurried on the ship with his own breath, so that it might speed the faster.

His three friends stood on the quay ; Irene grave and quiet, Justus mocking and sad ; but Demetrius Libanus with a large gesture outstretched his arm with the hand open, his body bent forward. It was more than a farewell greeting to Joseph ; it was a greeting to all that distant and ardently yearned for land.

His three friends disappeared   Ostia, Rome, Italy disappeared.   Joseph was on the open sea.   He was on his way to Judaea.

On the same ship sailed the secret courier bringing to the Governor of Judaea orders to publish the imperial decision on the franchise question in Caesarea.

Book Two
GALILEE

Book Two

GALILEE

I

On the thirteenth of May, at nine o'clock in the morning, the Roman Governor, Gessius Florus, received a deputation from the magistrates of Caesarea and had the imperial decision regarding the franchise read to them, a decision by means of which the Jews lost their power in the official capital of the country. At ten o'clock the edict was publicly proclaimed by the herald of the Government from the tribune of the Forum. In the workshop of the brothers Zacynth artificers were already busy in casting the words of the edict in bronze, that it might be preserved in the archives of the city for all time.

Immense rejoicings broke out among the Greek and Roman population. The colossal statues at the entry to the harbour, the commemorative columns raised to the goddess of Rome and the founder of the imperial line, the portly busts of the ruling Emperor at the street corners, were solemnly decked with garlands. Choirs of musicians march-ed through the streets ; in the harbour wine was to be had free ; the slaves were given a holiday.

But in the Jewish quarter the houses, usually so full of noise and bustle, stared out white and deserted ; the shops were closed ; the terror of a pogrom lay oppressively over the hot streets. Next day, a Sabbath, the Jews found, when they visited their chief synagogue, a Greek troop before the door just preparing to sacrifice a cock. Lepers were

accustomed to make such sacrifices ; and the favourite way
of insulting the Jews in Asia Minor was to declare that they
were descendants of Egyptian lepers.   The synagogue
attendant requested the Greeks to seek some other place
for their sacrifice.   The Greeks jeered at him, saying that
the time was past when Jews could afford to raise their voices
in Caesarea.   The officials of the synagogue appealed to the
police ;   the police declared that they must first get
instructions from their superiors.   A few hot-heads among
the Jews refused any longer to witness the insulting ceremony
and attempted to remove the sacrificial basin by violence.
Daggers and knives flashed out.   Finally, when the dead and
wounded were already lying about, Roman troops intervened.
They arrested a number of Jews as the originators of
the breach of the peace.   They confiscated the Greeks'
sacrificial basin.   Those of the Jews who could now fled
from Caesarea with their portable property ;   the sacred
scrolls of the Scriptures were hidden in a safe place.

The result of these events in Caesarea caused by the edict
was that the guerilla war which Judaea had for more than a
hundred years waged against the Roman power flamed out
over all the land with new and savage bitterness.   Hitherto,
at least in Jerusalem, the chief parties in the Administration,
the aristocratic Strict Constitutionalists and the middle-class
Scriptural Believers, had been able to prevent acts of violence
against the Romans ;   now, after the edict of Caesarea, the
third party, the Avengers of Israel, got the upper hand.

More and more adherents of the Scriptural Believers
went over to them, including even the head of the Temple
Administration, Doctor Eleasar Ben Simon.   Everywhere
their watchword could be seen, the word Makkabi, consisting
of the initials of the Hebrew sentence : Who is like thee,
O Lord ? the watchword of rebellion.   In Galilee the

agitator Nahum suddenly appeared : he was the son of the
patriotic leader Juda, who had been executed by the Romans.
He had been forgotten almost for a decade ; people thought
that he was dead ; now suddenly he took his way through
the towns and villages of the provinces in the North, and
everywhere the people flocked to him. " What are you
waiting for ? " he shouted fanatically to his sullen and
indignant listeners. " The very presence of the uncircumcised defiles your land, the soil chosen by Jehovah.
Their soldiers trample the pavement of the Temple ; their
trumpets break blasphemously into the sacred music. You
are chosen to serve Jehovah : you cannot pray to the
Emperor, the eater of swine's flesh. Think of the great
servants of the law, of Pinchas, of Eli, of Judas the
Maccabee. Do not your own tyrants oppress you enough ?
Must you let your blessing be stolen from you by strangers
as well, the blessing that Jehovah intended for you ? Do
not let yourselves be daunted by the cowardice of the
Scriptural Believers. Do not submit to the exactions of the
greedy Constitutionalists, who kiss the hand of the oppressor
because he protects their money bags. The time is fulfilled.
The Kingdom of Heaven is nigh. In it the poor shall have
as much as the rich. The Messiah is born ; he only waits
for you to rise ; then he will show himself. Throw off
your servile cowardice ! Slay those cowards in the High
Council in Jerusalem ! Down with the Romans ! "

The enthusiastic bands of the Avengers of Israel, which
the Romans had thought they had exterminated, suddenly
appeared again all over the country. Romans who ventured
on the roads without military escort were seized and dragged
away as hostages. In Jerusalem there were riots and wild
prophecies. Though the Roman financial administration
was just then extorting with the utmost severity old out-

standing taxes, young adherents of the Avengers of Israel appeared with collection boxes in the streets and begged from the passers by : " Be kind and give something for the poor unfortunate Governor."   Gessius Florus decided to intervene drastically and demanded that the ringleaders should be delivered up.   The Jewish authorities declared that they could not lay their hands on them.   The Governor commanded his troops to search all the houses in the vicinity of the upper market and the neighbouring streets, which were regarded as the head quarters of the Avengers of Israel. The house to house search developed into pillage.   The Jews defended themselves, and arrows were shot from the roofs of one or two houses.   Among the Romans, too, there were casualties.   The Governor proclaimed a state of martial law.   The enraged soldiers dragged innocent and guilty alike before justice ; the mere charge that a man belonged to the Avengers of Israel was sufficient.   Death sentences rained from the sky.   The law forbade Roman citizens to be executed except by the sword.   Gessius Florus commanded Jewish men, some even who possessed the noble title and the golden ring of the second Roman aristocracy, to be shamefully nailed to the cross.

When two members of the High Council were on the point of being executed, Princess Berenice, the sister of the titular king Agrippa, appeared before the officers of the court martial escorted by a silent, reverential and deeply moved crowd.   In thanksgiving for her recovery from sickness she had made a vow, and now appeared without ornament and with her hair cut short.   She was very beautiful, much beloved in Jerusalem, and a welcome visitor at the Roman court.   The grace with which she moved was famous.   From the German frontier to the Sudan, from the coast of Britain to the Indus, no one could pay a

woman a more treasured compliment than to tell her that
she walked like Princess Berenice. Now this great lady
appeared barefoot in the guise of a suppliant, wearing a
black robe fastened only by a cord round her waist, and
bowed her shorn head. She made an obeisance to the
judges of the court and begged them to pardon the two
priests. The officers were courteous at first and jested
gallantly with her. But when the Princess refused to be
put off they became distant and curt, finally almost rude,
and Berenice had to withdraw in humiliation.

In these five days from the twenty-first to the twenty-
sixth of May over three thousand people lost their lives,
among them a thousand women and children.

The city seethed with sullen rage. Hitherto it had been
mostly peasants and workmen who had flocked to the
Avengers of Israel ; now more and more well-to-do
citizens followed them. Everywhere it was rumoured or
shouted that the day after to-morrow or actually to-morrow
the land would rise against the Roman tyranny. The
Jewish Administration, consisting of the College of Priests
and the High Council, awaited with apprehension the course
that things would take. All the Jewish aristocracy wished
for an understanding with Rome and dreaded a war. The
Strict Constitutionalists, mostly aristocrats and rich people,
occupied the most important state offices, and feared that a
war against Rome would unavoidably develop into a
revolution against their own authority ; for they had always
inexorably and haughtily rejected the modest demands of
the small farmers, the middle-class and the working people.
But the Scriptural Believers, composed of doctors of the
Temple of Jerusalem, scholars, democrats, and the great
mass of the people, believed that the restoration of the
ancient freedom of the nation must be left in God's hands,

and warned the people against any violence so long as the Romans did not lay their hands upon the law and the commandments of Moses.

The leaders of both parties appealed urgently to King Agrippa, who resided in Egypt, and implored him to mediate between the rebels and the Roman government. The Romans, it was true, had left this prince effective authority only in Transjordania and a few Galilean towns ; in Judaea they had confined his powers to the superintendence of the administration of the Temple. Nevertheless he possessed a king's title, was accounted the chief man among the Jews, and was much beloved. At the request of the Jewish Administration he rode post haste to Jerusalem, resolved to address the people in person.

A great multitude came to hear him. They greeted the King somewhat suspiciously, and with profound anxiety. Then between rows of bowing officers Princess Berenice issued from the gate of her palace, once more robed in black, but not this time in the garb of a suppliant, but in heavy brocade. Beneath her short hair her long noble face looked doubly venturesome. Everybody fell silent when she appeared, as the worshippers cease to pray when the new moon appears on the evening dedicated to it : it was hidden behind the clouds and now it emerges, and everyone is glad. Slowly the Princess descended the steps before the palace and went to meet her brother ; the brocade billowed heavily as she advanced. And now that she raised both hands with the palms open in greeting to the people, they returned her salute, wildly and tempestuously : Hail, Berenice, Princess you too come in the name of the Lord.

Then the King began his speech. Forcibly he pointed out how hopeless any rising against the Roman power must be. The elegant prince raised his shoulders and let them fall again and indicated with his whole body the senselessness of such an enterprise. Had not all the nations in the world accepted the accomplished fact ? The Greeks, who once had been able to resist all Asia ; the Macedonians, whose King Alexander had in former times sowed the seed of a world empire. And now was not an army of two thousand Roman soldiers sufficient to maintain order in these countries? Gaul contained three hundred and five different tribes, possessed excellent natural fortresses, produced within its own frontiers all the raw materials it needed : and was not an army of twelve hundred men, a man for every town in the land, enough to crush the faintest thought of rebellion ? Two legions were sufficient to maintain Roman order in the huge, rich, ancient civilisation of Egypt. Against the Germans, well known to be more violent by nature than the most savage beasts, four legions sufficed, and in the whole tract beyond the Rhine and the Danube travelling was as safe as in Italy itself. " Have you no measure," the King shook his head sorrowfully, " for your own weakness and Rome's strength ? Tell me, where is your fleet, your artillery, your sources of revenue ? The whole world is Roman : where are you to find allies and assistance ? Perhaps in the uninhabited wastes ? "

King Agrippa spoke to his Jews as if they were ignorant children. Regarded objectively, the taxes that Rome demanded were not excessive. " Reflect that the city of Alexandria alone brings in more taxes in a month than all Judaea in a year. And does not Rome provide all sorts of services in return for those taxes ? Has it not given you excellent roads, modern water supplies, and an expeditious and efficient administration ? "

With sweeping and urgent gestures he addressed the crowd. " The ship is still lying safe in harbour. Be wise. Do not sail out into the dreadful tempest and certain destruction."

The King's speech made a considerable impression. From the crowd came shouts that they were not against Rome ; they were only against its Governor, Gessius Florus. But here the Avengers of Israel struck in skilfully. The young and elegant Doctor Eleasar, who had deserted the Strict Constitutionalists for the Avengers of Israel, now demanded in an incisive speech that the King as the chief man in the land should set his name to an ultimatum to Rome demanding the immediate recall of the Governor. Agrippa started back, tried to shuffle and hedge. Eleasar pressed for a clear answer ; the King declined his proposal. There was a louder and louder cry of " The signature ! The ultimatum ! Down with Gessius Florus ! " The temper of the crowd changed. They shouted that the King was on the side of the Governor ; everybody was out simply to exploit the people. Already a few resolute young men were pushing their way towards the King.

He was just able to withdraw into the palace in safety under the cover of his men. Next day he left the city in a very bitter mood and betook himself to his safe Transjordanian provinces.

After this defeat of the feudal lords and the Government the radicals used all the means in their power to push matters to extremes. Since the foundation of the Empire a century or so before, the Emperor and the Senate of Rome had sent every week an offering for Jehovah and his Temple. Now Doctor Eleasar as head of the Temple Administration gave instructions to refuse this offering in future. In vain did the High Priest and his colleagues implore him not to provoke the power of Rome in such an unheard of fashion.

Doctor Eleasar sent back with contumely the state officials who brought the Emperor's offering.

This was the signal for the Jewish petty burghers, peasants and workmen to rise openly against the Romans and their own feudal lords. The Roman garrison was small in numbers. The Avengers of Israel were soon in possession of the strategically important points in the city. They set fire to the Ministry of Finance, and destroyed with shouts of joy the tax lists and mortgage contracts. They destroyed and looted the houses of many of the more unpopular aristocrats. They laid siege to the Roman troops in the Palace of the Maccabees. The Romans held this last, strongly fortified defence with great heroism. But their position was hopeless, and when the Jews guaranteed them a safe retreat in return for delivering up their arms they accepted the offer with joy. Both parties confirmed the agreement by oath and by shaking hands. But as soon as the besieged had laid down their arms the Avengers of Israel flung themselves on the defenceless men and set about butchering them. The Romans put up no resistance ; they did not even beg for their lives ; but they shouted : " The oath ! The agreement ! " They shouted it in chorus ; fewer and fewer of them shouted it ; the chorus became feebler and feebler ; and at last only one man cried : " The oath ! The agreement ! " and then he, too, was silenced. This occurred on the seventh of September, or the twentieth of Elul by Jewish reckoning, a Sabbath.

The intoxication of the deed was hardly over when the whole city was plunged into deep dejection. As if in confirmation of this mood, news very soon came in that in countless cities with a mixed population the Greeks had fallen upon the Jews. In Caesarea alone twenty thousand Jews were slaughtered on that Black Sabbath ; the remainder were driven into the docks by the Governor and declared slaves. The Jews replied to these pogroms by exterminating the Greeks in towns where they were in a majority. For centuries the Greeks and the Jews who lived together on the coast, in Samaria, and on the borders of Galilee, had hated and scorned one another. The Jews were proud o their invisible God Jehovah ; they were convinced that the Messiah would come for them alone ; they walked proudly in the conviction that they were a chosen people. The Greeks made merry over the fixed ideas, the stupid super-stition, the ridiculous and barbarous customs of the Jews, and treated their Jewish neighbours like dirt. There had repeatedly been bloody encounters between them. Now a fury of pillage, murder and arson raged far beyond the borders of Judaea, and the land was filled with unburied corpses.

When things had reached this stage Gessius Florus's superior, Cestius Gallus, Governor General of Syria, decided at last to intervene. He was a sceptical old gentleman, convinced that one generally regretted more bitterly what one did than what one left undone. But seeing that things had definitely grown so bad, he decided that he could not show any false mildness : Jerusalem must be sharply chastised.

Cestius Gallus mobilised the whole twelfth legion, also eight additional regiments of Syrian infantry. He likewise demanded substantial contingents from the vassal states. The Jewish titular king Agrippa, anxious to show his fidelity to Rome, alone assembled two thousand cavalry, as well as three regiments of guards, and set himself in person at their head. Cestius Gallus planned circumstantially, to the smallest detail, his punitive expedition. He did not even forget the signal fires which were to carry to Italy the news of victory. Rome would learn that he had entered Jerusalem as judge and avenger on the very day that it happened.

From the north he burst irresistibly into the rebellious land. According to programme he took the beautiful town of Zabulon, looted it, and burnt it to the ground. Next he took the seaport Joppa, looted it, and burnt it to the ground. Pillage and smoking cities and slaughtered men marked his route, until at last, according to programme, he appeared on the twenty-seventh of September before Jerusalem.

But there he was held up. He had calculated that he would be in possession of Fort Antonia on the ninth of October, in possession of the Temple on the tenth. The fourteenth had already arrived, and Fort Antonia still held out. The Avengers of Israel had not hesitated to arm the countless pilgrims who had come for the feast of the vine grapes ; the city was crammed with voluntary troops. The twenty-seventh of October arrived, Cestius Gallus had now been waiting for a whole month before Jerusalem, and the carefully prepared signal fires were still waiting. Their attendants were beginning to fear that the apparatus would fail and that they would be punished for it. Cestius gave orders for new reinforcements, with great labour planted all his battering engines in readiness before the walls, and prepared for the second of November a final attack with means which according to human calculation, could not miscarry.

The Jews behaved gallantly. But what could individual bravery avail against the superior organisation of the Romans ? What for instance could the touching exploit of three old men do, three old men who, on the first of November, the day before the attack, appeared before the walls to set the Roman besieging engines on fire ? In clear noonday they appeared suddenly in front of the Roman posts, three ancient Jews wearing the badge of the Avengers of Israel, the letters Makkabi, consisting of the initials of the Hebrew sentence : Who is like thee, O Lord ?

At first the Romans thought these men were messengers bringing a proposal from the besieged ; but they were by no means messengers, for they began to shoot burning arrows with their trembling hands at the besieging engines. It was sheer madness, and the Romans—what else could they do with these old madmen ?—gazed at them with astonishment and jokingly, good humouredly, almost regretfully cut them down. On the same day it came out that these three men were members of the High Council, Gadia, Jehuda, and Nathan, once sentenced to forced labour by the court of the Emperor, and since as an act of great mercy set free. The Romans had again and again appealed to this amnesty as a striking example of their own goodwill, and had tried to prove that the chief blame for the present disturbances was not due to Roman harshness, but to the stiff-necked obstinacy of the Jews. Even in the speeches of the Strict Constitutionalists and the Scriptural Believers this amnesty had played an important role as a proof of Roman magnanimity. The three martyrs had refused to go about in their own city as living examples of the noble temper of their arch enemies. In their hearts they belonged to the Avengers of Israel. So they had resolved as fanatical believers to enact this exemplary, pious and heroic deed.

But the leaders of the Avengers of Israel knew very well that with faith alone they could do little against the besieging engines of the Romans. Resolved not to surrender the city, yet without hope of holding it, they watched the preparations for the final attack which must follow next day.

It did not follow. During the night Cestius Gallus ordered the siege to be raised and the army to withdraw. He looked ill and harassed. What had happened ? Nobody knew. The men crowded round Paulinus, the Commander's

adjutant.   He shrugged his shoulders.   The generals shook
their heads.   Cestius gave no reason for his surprising order
and forbade anyone to ask him about it.   The army set
itself in motion and began its retreat.

At first with incredulous and thunderstruck amazement,
then with a sigh of immense relief, then with tremendous
rejoicings, the Jews watched the departure of the besieging
army.   Hesitatingly, for they still feared that the Romans'
withdrawal might be a tactical manoeuvre, but presently
with mounting confidence, they set out in pursuit.   The
Romans found their retreat a difficult business.   The rebels
from Jerusalem pressed hard at their heels.   In the northern
province through which they had to pass a certain Simon
Bar Giora, a Galilean and the leader of a troop of armed
volunteers, had organised a relentless guerilla warfare.
Now, after a quick flanking march, he occupied with all the
men at his disposal the ravine of Beth Horon.   The name of
this ravine sounded sweet in the ears of the Jewish volunteers.
Here the Lord had commanded the sun to stand still so that
General Joshua might win a victory for Israel ; here Judas
Maccabaeus had triumphantly defeated the Greeks.   The
manoeuvre of Simon Bar Giora also succeeded ; the Romans
suffered a blow such as they had not experienced in Asia
since the Parthian wars.   The Jews did not lose more than a
thousand men ; of the Romans five thousand six hundred
and eighty footmen were killed, and three hundred and
eighty cavalry.   Among the slain was the Governor Gessius
Florus.   All the artillery, all the war material, also the
golden eagle of the legion, in addition to a great sum of
money, fell into the hands of the Jews.

This happened on the third of November in the Roman,
the eighth Dios in the Greek, the tenth Marcheshvan in the
Jewish calender, in the twelfth year of Emperor Nerò's reign.

2

WITH trumpets solemnly uplifted the Levites stood on the steps of the holy Temple, behind them in the Temple itself the priests of all the twenty-four ranks. After the un-expected victory over Cestius Gallus the High Priest Anan had been forced, although he led the party of the Strict Constitutionalists, to institute a service of thanksgiving, and now the great Hallel was being celebrated. The events of the past days had brought hosts of visitors into the city ; they stared with dazed eyes at the austere splendours of the Temple. From the crowds lining the white and golden steps rose like the thunder of a sea : " This is the day of the Lord. Let us be glad and rejoice." And again and again, through all the hundred and twenty-three prescribed variations ; " Praise be to the Lord ! "

Joseph stood well in front in his white sacerdotal robes, the blue sash with the embroidered flowers round his waist. Carried away like the others he swayed his body to the prescribed rhythm. Yes, he was rejoiced in his very heart ; nobody felt more deeply than he how marvellous was the victory which the unschooled volunteers had won over a Roman legion, over that masterpiece of technique and precision which, although consisting of many thousand men, moved like a single body directed by one brain. Beth Horon, Joshua, now this miracle. It was a splendid confirmation of his feeling that for the plight of Jerusalem reason alone was not enough. Great deeds were not achieved by reason ; they were born of pure divine inspiration. The crowds in front of the Temple stairs saw with emotion how enthusiasti-cally this young and glowing priest joined in the singing of the hymn of thanks.

But in spite of his pious ardour he could not prevent his

thoughts from occupying themselves with the consequences which this unforeseen victory of the Avengers of Israel might have for himself personally.

Jerusalem had not had much opportunity to honour him for his success in the matter of the three innocent men. Less than a week after his return the disturbances had broken out. Nevertheless his Roman success had made him popular. The moderate members of the Government could no longer cold shoulder this young aristocrat, although he was seen so often in the Blue Hall with the Avengers of Israel : he was given the office and title of a private secretary in the service of the Temple. Far too small a reward. Now, after the great victory, his chances had improved enormously. The Government would be forced in spite of itself to include a few of the Avengers of Israel in its ranks ; the pressure of popular opinion was too strong to be flouted. That very afternoon a meeting of the three legislative bodies was to be held. Power would have to be redistributed. They would never dare, in the course of the redistribution, to pass him over.

Praise be to the Lord ! The song went on ; praise be to the Lord ! He could quite well understand why the Government had until now sought by all the means in their power to avoid war with Rome. Even the day before, after the great victory, several very prudent people in the city had fled in the greatest haste to the Governor-General Cestius Gallus to assure him, in spite of his defeat, that they had had nothing to do with the treacherous attack of the rebels on the imperial army. Rich old Chanania had vanished from the city ; the Secretary of State Zebulon had left his house empty and disappeared ; the priests Zefania and Herod had fled beyond the Jordan into the country of King Agrippa. Many Essenes, too, had left after the victory over Cestius, and the sectaries who called themselves Christians had all departed. Joseph had little sympathy to spare for the insipid piety of the one party, or the cold calculation of the other.

The sacred ceremony came to an end. Joseph pushed his way through the crowds that filled the spacious Temple precinct. Most of them wore bands with the badge of the Avengers of Israel, the word Makkabi. In dense crowds they stood round the captured engines of war, touched with their hands the battering rams for demolishing walls, the lighter catapults, the heavier ballistas, which could fling their heavy projectiles for many hundred yards. Everywhere in the pleasant November sunshine there was merry, good-humoured competition for the Roman booty, for clothes, arms, tents, horses, mules, furniture, ornaments, souvenirs of every kind, the fasces and axes of the lictors. With malicious enjoyment they pointed out to each other the straps that every Roman soldier carried with him to bind his prisoners. The bankers of the Temple were kept very busy changing foreign currency which had been taken from the dead soldiers.

Joseph found himself in an excited group of soldiers, burghers and priests, who were disputing violently. The subject of the debate was a golden eagle embellished with a portrait of the Emperor ; it had once been the possession of the twelfth legion. The officers of the voluntary troops wished to have the eagle fixed in a prominent position on the outer walls of the Temple, beside the trophies of Judas Maccabaeus and Herod, as a heartening signal to Jerusalem and Judaea. But the Scriptural Believers would not hear of that ; images of animals were not allowed by the law, no matter under what pretext. A middle way was suggested ; the eagle should be put at the disposal of Doctor

Eleasar for the Temple treasury, Doctor Eleasar being head
of the Temple Administration and himself an adherent of
the Avengers of Israel. But no, the officers would not
agree to that. The men who were carrying the eagle stopped
in hesitation ; they, too, would have preferred not to see
the trophy vanishing into the Temple treasury. They had
laid down the thick pole which upbore the eagle. Seen
close at hand, this dreaded emblem of the Roman army
looked rough and clumsy ; the portrait of the Emperor on
the medallion below it was rude and coarse, and not in the
least terrible. The men argued violently. Then the spirit
descended upon Joseph, and his young full voice rang
imperiously through the confusion. The eagle should
neither be fastened to the Temple wall, nor added to the
Temple treasury. It should be destroyed, hacked to pieces.
It should disappear. This was a proposal after everybody's
heart. But it was not very easy to carry out. The eagle
was extremely solid, and it took a good hour to reduce it to
bits, so that every one could carry away his little scrap of
gold. Joseph, the hero in the episode of the three innocent
men of Caesarea, had won new sympathies.

He was tired by now, but he felt that he could not go
home, and continued to wander through the Temple quarter.
Who was that man for whom the crowd were eagerly making
way ? A young officer, not very tall ; above his short
well-groomed beard rose a strong straight nose ; his eyes
were small and brown. It was Simon Bar Giora, the leader
of the Galilean free troops, the victor. In front of him a
snow white lamb without blemish was being led, obviously
a thanksoffering. But, Joseph noted with disagreeable
surprise, Simon Bar Giora was armed. Did he intend to go
to the altar, which had never been defiled with steel, neither
during the time it was built nor later ; did he intend to go

to the altar with a sword at his side ?   He must not.   Joseph
stepped in front of him.   " I am Joseph Ben Matthias," he
said.   The young officer knew at once to whom he was
speaking, and greeted Joseph respectfully and cordially.
" You are going to make an offering ? " asked Joseph.
Simon admitted that it was so.   He smiled gravely, a deep
happiness and confidence went out from him.   But then
Joseph asked :   " With your sword ? "   Simon flushed.
" You are right," he said.   He asked his men who were
leading the lamb to wait :   he would put off his sword.   But
then he turned again to Joseph.   He said cordially and
frankly, so that everyone could hear :   " You, Doctor Joseph,
were the first of us.   When you got the three innocent men
out of the prison of the Romans I felt that the impossible was
possible.   God is with us, Doctor Joseph."   He saluted
Joseph, his hand lifted to his brow ;   from his eyes beamed
piety, daring, and good fortune.

3

JOSEPH walked through the gently rising streets of the new
town, through the clothiers' bazaars, the Square of the Smiths
and the Street of the Potters.   Again he noticed with
satisfaction that the new town was developing into a business
quarter full of bustle and life.   He owned land here which
the glass-manufacturer Nachum Ben Nachum was very
eager to buy.   Joseph had already decided to let him have it.
Now, after the great victory, he resolved not to do so.   The
glass-blower Nachum was waiting for his decision.   Joseph
resolved to call upon him at once and tell him that he would
not sell.   He would build a house for himself here in the
new town.

Nachum Ben Nachum was sitting cross-legged on
cushions before his workshop.   Over his head above the

entry hung a great cluster of grapes made of coloured
glass.   Nachum stood up to welcome Joseph, and then
invited him to be seated.   Joseph sat down on the
cushions a little awkwardly, for he had become accustomed
to sitting on chairs.

Nachum Ben Nachum was a stately full-bodied man of
some fifty years.   He had the beautiful animated eyes for
which the Jerusalem people were famed, and his ruddy face
was framed in a thick, square, black beard, sprinkled here and
there with a few grey hairs.   He was eager to hear Joseph's
decision, but he did not let any sign of that appear, and began
a casual conversation about politics.   It would probably be
a good thing, he said, if the young people were given a chance
for once to show what they could do.   True, he said, one
should stand up in the presence of the old ; but, he quoted
another popular saw, to eat of youth is to eat new life.   The
ruling gentlemen in the Quadern Hall must, now that they
had eaten of youth, unite with the Avengers of Israel.
He spoke with animation, yet not without dignity and
authority.

Joseph listened attentively.   It was interesting to hear what
Nachum Ben Nachum thought of the situation after the
great victory at Beth Horon.   What he said was probably
the opinion of most respectable citizens in Jerusalem.   Only
eight days before they had all been against the Avengers
of Israel ; now they had forgotten that ; now they were
convinced that the Avengers of Israel should have been
given a share of the power long ago.

Doctor Nittai, an elderly morose gentleman, appeared in
the door-way.   He was distantly related to the glass-blower,
who had taken him into partnership.   Doctor Nittai, it
was true, knew nothing about business ; but it raised the tone
of the firm to co-opt a scholar and let him share in the profits.

So the Doctor and Master Nittai lived somewhat silently and ungraciously in the house of the glass-blower. He regarded it as a great favour on his part to allow the manufacturer to carry on the firm under the names of Doctor Nittai and Nachum, and to pay him a share of the profits. When he was not disputing in the Temple University he sat before the house in the sun with a roll of the Holy Scriptures before him, muttering to himself and weighing against each other the various interpretations. Nobody dared interrupt him at such moments ; for anyone who broke into the study of the Scripture by saying : " Look, what a lovely tree ! " was liable to excommunication.

But this time he was not engaged in study, and so Nachum asked him if he too was not in favour of the Avengers of Israel being taken into the government. Doctor Nittai wrinkled his brow. " Do not make the Scripture into a spade," he said harshly, " to dig with. The Scripture does not exist to be a hand-book for politicians."

There was great bustle in Nachum's factory and store rooms. The Roman booty had brought money into the city, and there were many purchasers for Nachum's widely famed glasses. Nachum greeted the buyers with dignity, offered them iced drinks and confections. A great and glorious victory, wasn't it ? Business was going splendidly, God be praised. If it went on, he would soon be able to set up a new wing as big as the shop of the Brothers Chanan under the cedars of the Mount of Olives. The man, he quoted somewhat inappositely, who lives by the labour of his own hands is more admirable than the man who fears God. But he had achieved his aim : the Doctor became annoyed.

Doctor Nittai knew of many counter quotations, but he swallowed them down. For when he grew excited his Babylonian accent came to the top, and people used to chaff

him, in all reverence, on account of this accent. "You
Babylonians destroyed the Temple," people would say to
him, and Doctor Nittai could not stand chaffing. So he
took no part in the conversation, he did not even study the
Scripture ; he sat in the pleasant sunshine in a vague day-
dream. Often, since he had come to Jerusalem from his
Babylonian home town, Nehardea, the priests of the eighth
rank, the Abija rank, to which he belonged, had been
employed in the Temple service. Often he had succeeded
in being allowed to bear parts of the sacrificial lamb to the
altar. But his highest dream, that of serving the golden
censer with incense before the altar, had never been fulfilled. Always, when the Magrepha sounded to show that
the burnt offering was being celebrated, he was seized with
a deep envy of the priests who were privileged to officiate.
He had all the capabilities required, he had none of the 147
physical defects which debarred a priest from such service.
But he was no longer young. Would Jehovah allow him
some time yet to celebrate the burnt sacrifice ?

Meanwhile Joseph had informed the glass-blower of his
decision to keep the land to himself. Nachum listened to
the news without the slightest sign of annoyance. "May
your decision be lucky for us both, my Doctor and Master,"
he said courteously.

Nachum's youngest son appeared, the fourteen-year-old
Ephraim. He was wearing the arm band with the initials
Makkabi. He was a beautiful, vigorous lad, and to-day he
was glowing with added life. He had seen the hero
Simon Bar Giora. His large eyes beamed with rapture in
his dark, glowing face. He put his arm through his father's.
Perhaps he had been wrong in rushing out of the workshop.
But he simply couldn't miss the great Hallel in the Temple.
And he had been rewarded too, he had seen Simon Bar Giora.

Joseph was on the point of leaving when Nachum's elder son Alexas appeared. Alexas was stately and full-bodied like his father, and he had the same thick, square beard and ruddy complexion. But his eyes were troubled, he shook his head doubtfully, and often tugged at his beard with his roughened hand, which was all cracked with handling the hot glass. He was not calm and composed like his father ; he looked as if something was worrying him. He grew animated when he saw Joseph. Joseph must not go. He must help him to convince his father that they must leave Jerusalem while it was still possible. " You were in Rome," he said to Joseph. "You know Rome. Tell me yourself, isn't what the Avengers of Israel are doing bound to lead to a clash ? I have the best connections, I have business friends in Nehardea, in Antiochia, in Batna. I swear by the life of my children that within three years I can build up in any city you like to mention a business as good as this one here. Try to persuade my father to leave this dangerous place."

The boy Ephraim screamed at his brother, and his fine eyes became black with rage. " You don't deserve to live in these times. Everybody looks askance at me because I have such a brother. Go among the pig-eaters, if you want ! Jehovah has spewed you out of his mouth." Nachum reproved the boy, but only half-heartedly. He himself did not like Alexas's words. Certainly the wild doings of the Avengers of Israel had sometimes alarmed him, and he had been against them once, like all the other strictly orthodox people ; but now that almost all Jerusalem was on the side of the Makkabi men one did not make such remarks as Alexas had just done. " Don't you listen to my son Alexas, Doctor Joseph," he said. " He is a good son, but he must always think differently from the others. His head is always full of odd ideas."

Joseph knew that it was precisely to these odd ideas of
Alexas that Nachum's factory owed its success. Nachum
Ben Nachum had run his workshop like his father and
grandfather before him. He had turned out the same things
and sold the same things. He had confined himself to the
Jerusalem market, had gone daily to the Exchange, and with
the help of the notaries had drawn up his ceremonious,
circumstantial contracts, and seen to it that they were
deposited in the city archives. To do more than that seemed
to him wrong. When a second glass factory was set up in
Jerusalem he had not been able to hold out against the
keen competition with such simple principles. Then Alexas
had stepped in. Previously everything had been done by
hand in the workshop, but Alexas modernised the whole
business, so that now the long, glass-blowing pipe was
exclusively employed, and by means of it the workmen blew
beautiful oval vessels as God blew breath into the human
body. Moreover Alexas had set up a very profitable
branch in the upper town, in which only expensive glass
wares were sold. Also he had sent the firms' goods
to the great markets of Gaza, Caesarea, and Batna in
Mesopotamia. All these innovations had had to be carried
out by Alexas, who was still under thirty, against the persistent obstruction of his father. Seconded by Doctor
Nittai, Nachum had resisted with particular stubbornness
the sending of goods to the foreign fairs ; for these fairs
were held in connection with annual festivals in honour of
strange gods. But young Alexas was a hard-headed fellow
and his father had not been able to do anything to stop him.
So at first the father had grumbled ; but when Alexas's
measures were successful he behaved as if it were all his own
doing, and his son had been in the wrong.

To-day, too, he was all against his son and his over prudent and too clever talk. After this calamity the Romans would never march on Jerusalem again. And if they did come the Jews would drive them back across the sea. In any case he, Nachum Ben Nachum, the great merchant, would never leave his glass factory or Jerusalem. When there had been nothing in the neighbourhood but gardens and fields, the glass factory had stood there. And it would continue to stand there. The man who departed from the ways of his fathers would come to grief. And to what could one compare a man who learned from his juniors ? To one who ate unripe grapes and drank wine from the wine press. They had formed glasses by hand and blown glasses through the blow pipe, and Jehovah had blessed their work. For centuries they had been glass-blowers in Jerusalem, and glass-blowers in Jerusalem they would remain.

Father and son sat on their cushions, outwardly calm, but both of them agitated, and both tugged violently at their square, black beards. The boy Ephraim gazed with wild eyes at his brother ; it was obvious that only his respect for his father kept him from letting fly with his fists at Alexas. Joseph glanced from the one to the other. Alexas seemed quiet and composed, and there was a smile on his face ; but Joseph could see quite well how bitter and troubled he was. Of course Alexas was right, but his prudence seemed mean compared with the resolution of the father and the confidence of the younger brother.

Alexas once more insisted upon being reasonable. " If the Romans refuse to let through our sand transports on the river Belus, then we can close down our factory. Of course you, Doctor Joseph, are a statesman, and so you must stay in Jerusalem. But simple tradesmen like us—(" merchants,") Nachum corrected mildly, stroking his beard)—wouldn't it be the best thing for us to leave Jerusalem as soon as we can ? "

But Nachum did not want to listen to such arguments any longer. He abruptly changed the subject. " Our family," he explained to Joseph, " has always been obstinate. When my grandfather, his memory be blessed, died, he had twenty-eight teeth left, and when my father, his memory be blessed, died, he had thirty teeth left. I'm fifty to-day, and I have still all my thirty-two teeth, and my hair is still almost black and as thick as ever it was."

When Joseph was about to go Nachum invited him to visit the workshop and carry away a present. For the festival for the victory of Beth Horon was not yet over and there must be presents at a festival.

The oven sent out an unendurable heat, and the workshop was filled with smoke. Nachum wanted to press a very beautiful glass vessel upon Joseph, a great oval beaker, covered on the outside with delicate net-work. Nachum sang a verse of the old song ; " Give me just for once my lovely beaker, let me have it to-day, and to-morrow it can be broken." But Joseph, as polite custom demanded, refused the precious gift, and contented himself with a simpler one.

Ephraim could not resist the temptation of entering into a new and bitter political argument with his elder brother in the heat and smoke of the work room. " Were you at the great Hallel ? " he shouted at him, " of course you weren't. Jehovah has struck you with blindness. But I'm not going to listen to your arguments any longer. I'm going to join the citizen army."

Alexas's mouth was wry. All that he could return to the burning words of his young brother was a silent and embarrassed smile. He would dearly have loved to leave Jerusalem with his wife and his two young children. But he was devoted with all his heart to his family, to his hand-some foolish father Nachum, and his handsome foolish brother Ephraim. He was the only one in the place who could think reasonably. He would have to stay to protect the others from the worst.

At last Joseph was able to go. He stepped out through the door over which hung the great glass cluster of grapes, and after the heat and smoke of the work-room breathed in the lovely fresh air. Alexas accompanied him for a little way. "You see," he said, "how madness is growing in the city. Only a week ago my father was a convinced enemy of the Makkabi crowd. You, at least, must remain reasonable, Doctor Joseph. You have the peoples' sympathies. Risk a part of their sympathies, and stick to what you think reasonable. You are our great hope. I hope with all my heart that they'll include you in the government in the Quadern Hall to-morrow."

Joseph thought to himself : He wants to make me as unpopular as he is himself. When they were saying good-bye, Alexas said sadly ; "I wish that this victory had been spared us."

4

HALF an hour before the specified beginning of the assembly Joseph arrived in the Quadern Hall. But already almost all the delegates from the legislative bodies were there. The members of the priests' college in their blue official robes, the representatives of the High Council in their white and blue regalia, the legal dignitaries from the high court of justice in white and red. Among them stood Simon Bar Giora and a few of his officers with their swords at their sides, cutting a somewhat incongruous figure.

Hardly had Joseph arrived when his friend Amram Bar Illai rushed up to him. Doctor Amram Bar Illai was an

old schoolmate of Joseph's ; he was regarded as a very
gifted man, but he came of a humble family, had few connections and no luck.   A fanatical adherent of the Scriptural Believers, the young doctor, embittered by disappointment had become transformed into an equally fanatical
supporter of the Avengers of Israel.   Formerly he had
been suspicious of Joseph, but after Joseph's return from
Rome he had flung himself with wild affection on his old
schoolmate's neck.

The news he had to confide to Joseph now was bound to
please his friend.   One of the volunteer bands in Galilee
had captured a Roman courier and seized an important
dispatch that he was carrying.   Simon Bar Giora had shown
the letter to Doctor Amram Bar Illai, of whom he had a
great opinion.   In it Paulinus, Cestius's adjutant, reported
confidentially on the defeat of the twelfth legion.   There
appeared to have been no reasonable grounds for the
unfortunate order to retreat.   Cestius had simply lost
his nerve.   And the cause of his nervous crisis, a strange
and bitter trick of fate, had been a trifle : the suicidal deed
of the three mad forced labourers of Tibur.   All his life
the old fellow had believed in nothing but reason.   The
insane and heroic death of the three men had upset him.
To employ a regular army against a people of fanatics and
madmen was senseless.   So he had given up the fight.   He
had surrendered.

Joseph read the letter ; his head felt hot under his priests
hat, although it was a cool November day.   This letter
was a great and marvellous confirmation.   Often during
those last days he had doubted whether his policy in Rome
had been a good one.   When the Romans, when the very
Strict Constitutionalists themselves, brought up the amnesty
again and again as a proof of the mildness of the Imperial

Administration, it really had seemed that Justus would turn out to be right after all with his cold logical reasoning. But now it became manifest that his, Joseph's, deed had worked out for good after all. Yes, my Doctor Justus of Tiberias, my policy was perhaps unreasonable, but has it not been splendidly justified by the results? Cold calculation is not the most essential thing, but faith and grace, intuition, my dear Doctor Justus. Joseph was filled with a great security.

The High Priest Anan opened the assembly. To-day his task was not a light one. He stood at the head of the Strict Constitutionalists, led the right wing of extreme aristocrats who, protected by Roman power, had harshly and haughtily refused any alleviation to the lot of the petty burghers, peasants and workmen. His father and three of his brothers had, one after the other, occupied the post of High Priest, the supreme position in the Temple and the state. Clear minded, cool and just, he had been the right man to treat with the Romans; now his policy of mutual understanding had ignominiously come to grief, war was imminent, if indeed the country was not already involved in it. What would the High Priest do and say now? Calm as ever, he rose in his hyacinth-coloured robe; he did not even raise his deep powerful voice, and the audience became quiet as soon as he began. He was indeed a brave man; as though nothing had happened he said: "I am astonished to see Simon Bar Giora here in the Quadern Hall. It seems to me that the soldier is competent to decide issues only in the field. The future fate of this Temple and this land of Israel still lies for the time being with the college of high priests, the High Council, and the high court of law. Therefore, I request, Simon Bar Giora and his officers to withdraw." From all sides rose cries of rage against the High Priest. The leader of the volunteer troops looked round him dazedly as though he had not understood. But Anan went on, still in the same voice, not loud, but deep : " As Simon Bar Giora is here, I should like to ask him to what authority he has delivered the money captured from the Romans." The incisiveness of this question had a cooling effect. The officer, his face flushing a dark red, replied curtly : " The money is in the hands of the head of the Temple Administration." All faces were turned towards elegant, young Doctor Eleasar, who stared straight in front of him. Then, with a brief salute, Simon Bar Giora left the meeting.

Hardly had he gone when Doctor Eleasar leapt to his feet. The Jewish people, he said, would want to know why the hero of Beth Horon had been excluded so insolently from the meeting by the High Priest. The Avengers of Israel were no longer disposed to endure the vapid rationalism of the gentlemen present here. In their little faith and their dependence in reason they had always maintained that it was impossible to make a stand against Roman troops. But where was the twelfth legion now ? God had visibly declared Himself for those who refused to wait any longer ; He had wrought a miracle. " Rome has twenty-six legions," cried one of the young aristocrats. " Do you fancy that God will work twenty-five more miracles ? "

" Take care that you don't say such things outside those walls," Eleasar replied threateningly. " The people are in no mood just now for such wretched witticisms. The position demands a re-distribution of power. You will all be swept away, all of you who are sitting here, except for the Avengers of Israel, if you do not offer Simon Bar Giora a seat and a voice in the government of national defence which will have to be formed."

" I do not intend to offer Simon Bar Giora a seat in the

Government," said the High Priest Anan. "Do any of my colleagues suggest it?" Slowly his grey eyes swept the circle of listeners; his long, narrow face under the blue and gold fillet seemed quite unconcerned. No one spoke. "What do you think of doing with the monies which Simon Bar Giora confided to you?" Anan asked, turning to the head of the Temple Administration.

"The monies are intended exclusively for purposes of national defence," replied Doctor Eleasar.

"Not for other purposes of government as well?" enquired Anan.

"I know of no other task before the Government," responded Doctor Eleasar.

"This rash stroke of your friend," said the High Priest, "has created a situation which makes it advisable that the Executive should call upon the Temple Administration for assistance. But you must understand that if you take such a narrow view of our task we cannot share our powers with you."

"The people demand a government of national defence," said young Doctor Eleasar stubbornly.

"There shall be such a government, Doctor Eleasar," replied the High Priest, "but I fear that it will have to dispense with the collaboration of Doctor Eleasar Ben Simon. In Israel, in times of need, there have been governments," he went on, "in which there was neither financier nor soldier, but only priests and statesmen. Nor were these the worst governments that have ruled in Israel." He turned to the assembly: "The law concedes Doctor Eleasar Ben Simon autonomous control over the revenues of the Temple Administration. The coffers of the Government are empty, the revenue at Doctor Eleasar's disposal has been increased to the extent of at least ten million sesterces by the booty captured at Beth Horon. Do you wish, my learned doctors, that Doctor Eleasar should be included in the executive ? " Many rose to their feet, appealed for peace, and tried to intercede. " I have nothing to add and nothing to withdraw." said the High Priest in a voice not loud but deep. " Money is necessary in these difficult times ; the inclusion of the temperamental Doctor in the Government I look upon as a disadvantage. The pros and cons, are perfectly clear. I move we put it to the vote."

" There is no need to put it to the vote," said Doctor Eleasar with a white face. " I would refuse to enter such a government." He got up and without ceremony left the silent assembly. " We have neither money nor soldiers," said Doctor Jannai, the Treasurer of the High Council, reflectively.

" We have on our side," said the High Priest, " God, justice and reason."

The Government's plan of action for the next few weeks was decided upon. The college of priests, the High Council, and the high court of law came after careful examination of the situation to the conclusion that Judaea was not in a state of war with Rome. The rebellious actions had been committed by individuals ; the authorities bore no responsibility. As things stood now the Jewish central government in Jerusalem must give orders for mobilisation. But they would respect the neutrality of Samaria and the coastal provinces, which were directly under Roman administration. They strictly forbade any act that could be interpreted as an attack on Rome. Their programme was one of armed peace.

There was no headway to be made against the cool and calm stand of these old gentlemen. It was immediately evident that in spite of the victory at Beth Horon the

Strict Constitutionalists and the Scriptural Believers would
remain in power. Joseph had come to the meeting with
high confidence. He was convinced that the administration
of the land would be redistributed ; a share of it was certain to
fall to him ; this time he felt certain that he would have an
equal chance with those who were already satiated with
power, and yet still greedy for it, and snatch a province for
himself. His furious ambition justified him if nothing else
did. But during these debates on the plan of action all his
hopes had run out like wine from a flask full of holes. His
brain felt empty. When he arrived he had felt certain that
he would have something of importance to say, something
that would move these men to give him a leading position.
Now he recognised that this moment too, this great opportunity too, would pass, and that he would have to remain
at the bottom of the ladder as before, an insignificant busy
place-hunter. To secure the maintenance of armed peace
in the seven provinces of the country there were to be
for each province two people's commissaries with dictatorial
powers. Joseph lolled in his seat near the back of the hall.
What had it all to do with him ? No one would ever think
of proposing him.

The city and province of Jerusalem was disposed of,
Idumaea was disposed of, Tamna and Gophna were disposed
of. Now the northern frontier province, the rich agricultural province of Galilee, was in the scales. Here the
Avengers of Israel had the most of their adherents.
Here the movement for freedom had originated. Here the
strongest volunteer bands were to be found. Someone
proposed that to this province old Doctor Jannai should be
sent ; he was a prudent sober gentleman, the best financial
expert in the High Council. Joseph was roused from his
apathy. That beautiful land with all its riches, its slow,

reflective people. That wonderful, difficult and complicated province. And they intended to hand it over to old Jannai? An excellent theorist, certainly, an admirable political economist; but all the same not the man for Galilee. Joseph felt a desire to shout no; he half rose to his feet, he bent forward, the people sitting round stared at him; but he said nothing, it would have been of no use; so he only sighed heavily, like a man who had much to say and must swallow it down again.

Those sitting near him smiled at the uncontrolled young gentleman. But one man had seen him, had seen his anger and his resignation. And he did not smile. It was by pure chance that he had observed the young man's furious gesture; for from long habit he usually sat with his yellow, creased eyelids closed. He was a little gentleman, withered and very old, the supreme priest in the country, the very learned Doctor Jochanan Ben Sakkai, Rector of the Temple University. When, after Jannai had been unanimously elected, the meeting was waiting somewhat undecidedly for a second proposal, the old man got to his feet. His eyes looked strangely bright and lively in his little face covered with a thousand wrinkles, and he said: "As second commissary for Galilee I propose Doctor Joseph Ben Matthias.'

Now that everybody was gazing at him, Joseph sat in a curious immobility. That day he had savoured hope and renunciation over and over again, had in imagination drunk fulfilment and disappointment to the lees: now that his name was called he was incapable of any emotion. He sat in vacancy, as if they were speaking of someone else.

The proposal came as a great surprise to the meeting. Why had the mild and sober Doctor Jochanan Ben Sakkai, the eminent legislator, proposed this young man? He had not proved himself until now in any responsible post, but instead, ever since he had won the popularity of the people through his trifling success in the matter of the three innocent men, had been coquetting romantically with the Blue Hall. But perhaps the venerable Doctor considered it advisable that old Jannai should be given a collaborator who was in good odour with the Avengers of Israel? Yes, that must be the explanation ; the proposal was quite a clever one.   The ardour of Avengers of Israel was accustomed to cool pretty quickly once they were in enjoyment of dignified offices ; Doctor Joseph would presumably be more docile in Galilee than in Rome and Jerusalem, and the sober wisdom of the old financial theorist Jannai could quite well stand a slight dash of the new wine that would be provided by this ardent young man.

Meanwhile Joseph had awakened out of his frozen apathy. Had not someone mentioned his name? Someone? Jochanan Ben Sakkai, the great doctor ! Often, as a child, Joseph had felt the light hand of the mild old man laid in blessing upon his head.   In Rome he had learned that the aged doctor was accounted there as one of the wisest men in the world.   Jochanan had achieved this result entirely without any effort of his own, and simply through the operation of his nature.   The man's quietism and total lack of ambition made him incomprehensible, almost uncanny to Joseph ; it exacerbated and dejected him ; he preferred to avoid the great doctor.   And now this man had proposed his name.

He was deeply moved when the meeting confirmed the proposal.   These men who had given him power were wise and good.   He, too, would be wise and good.   He would not go to Galilee as one of the Avengers of Israel : nor would he give rein there to his ambition.   He would be quiet and humble and have faith that the right spirit would be granted him.

Along with old Jannai he took his leave of the High Priest. Anan stood before him, cool and clear sighted as ever. His main instructions were unequivocal. Galilee was the most threatened province in the country. It was essential that peace should be maintained there at all costs. " If you are in a difficult situation, do nothing at all rather than anything rash. Wait until you get instructions from Jerusalem. Keep your eyes continually on Jerusalem. Galilee has strong volunteer bands. On you, my learned doctors, is laid the task of holding these forces at the disposal of Jerusalem." And to Joseph he added, mustering him without good will : " A responsible post has been entrusted to you. I hope that we have not erred."

Joseph listened to the High Priest's instructions courteously, almost humbly. But they only reached his ear. Certainly he must obey the High Priest while he was in Jerusalem. But as soon as he crossed the Galilean border he would be responsible only to one man, himself.

That evening Anan said to Jochanan Ben Sakkai : " I hope we were not too hasty in sending Joseph Ben Matthias to Galilee ; he cares for nothing but his own ambition."

" It may be," replied Jochanan Ben Sakkai, " that there are more reliable men than this particular one. It may be that for many years to come he will seem to act merely for his own advantage ; but as long as he lives I will continue to believe that in the end he will have acted for us."

5

THE new commissary Joseph Ben Matthias travelled through his province from end to end. There had been a good rainy season that year, Jehovah was merciful, the cisterns were filling ; on the mountains of Upper Galilee snow was lying, and the hill streams made a cheerful noise. On the plains the peasants bent over the earth, drinking in the smell of the soil after rain. Yes, it was a rich land, fertile and various, with its valleys, hills, mountains, its Lake of Genezareth, its river Jordan, its sea coast, and its two hundred towns. In its magically clear air it lay like the Garden of God. Joseph expanded his chest. He had managed it ; he had risen very high ; it was splendid to be the ruler of this province. Anyone coming into this country with full powers as he had done must succeed in gaining a great name for himself, a name that would be remembered. If he was not an incapable fool.

But after a few days a deep despondency began to gnaw him, and it ate further into him with every day. He studied the state papers, the archives ; he summoned the district superintendents to him, interviewed the local authorities, the priests, and the heads of the synagogues and schools. He tried to organise the affairs of the province, gave instructions, found agreement on every hand and willingness to obey ; yet he recognised quite clearly that all this readiness was lukewarm, and his measures remained ineffective. Things had a different look in Galilee from what they had had in Jerusalem. When complaint after complaint had reached Jerusalem that the land was groaning under the oppressive taxes, the people there had shrugged their shoulders, sent back figures, dismissed the lamentations of Galilee as the usual protests of a rich people, and, under the protection of the Roman arms, had gone on extorting the taxes as before. Now, with tightly compressed lips, Joseph compared the Galilean reality with the statistics in Jerusalem. He recognised gloomily that the complaints of these Galilean peasants, fishermen, handworkers, harbour and factory

labourers, were not mere hot air.   There they were in the
promised land ; but their vines did not grow for them, the
fat of the land went to the Romans in Caesarea, its oil to the
great gentlemen in Jerusalem.   The fruits of the soil were
filched from them in the following proportions :   A third
part of the agricultural produce, half of the wine and oil, a
quarter of the fruit.   Then there were the Temple tithes,
the yearly poll tax for the Temple, the tax for the upkeep of
holy places.   And after that the salt tax, and the dues for
the upkeep of roads and bridges.   Taxes here, taxes there,
taxes everywhere.

Well, these financial matters were Doctor Jannai's
concern.   Nevertheless Joseph could not blame the people
of Galilee when they turned black looks on the doctors of
the Temple, who by cunning and complicated interpretations
of the Scripture filched the best of their wealth away ; or
when they cast ill glances at him, the representative of these
men.   In Rome and Jerusalem he had learned how discontented people could be soothed by slight alleviations of
their lot, by severe or mild speeches, by solemn proclamations
and cheap flattery.   But by such means as these he would
not advance any further here.

The people in Jerusalem compressed their lips haughtily
when the people of Galilee were mentioned ;   they were
yokels, provincials, without culture, and of rude manners.
In the very first week Joseph had to lay aside that cheap
superiority.   True, the people here were lax in the fulfilment of the law, and learned interpretations of the Scripture
did not count for much with them.   But then on the other
hand they were strangely austere and fanatical.   They
refused violently to be content with things as they were.
They maintained that the State and the daily life of the
people must be radically altered ;   only then could the words

of the Scripture be fulfilled. Everybody in this country
knew the book of the prophet Isaiah by heart. The cattle-
dealers talked of eternal peace, the dock labourers of the
Kingdom of God on earth. Not long ago a weaver had
corrected him when he quoted incorrectly a passage from
Ezekiel. They were slow people, difficult to get on with,
quiet and peaceful in outward bearing, but by no means
peaceful in their hearts ; there they were violent, looking
for great events and ready for anything. Joseph felt that
these were people after his heart. Their sullen and savage
faith was a firmer basis for a great enterprise than the empty
erudition, the smooth scepticism of Jerusalem. Zealously
and eagerly he sought to make himself understood to these
people of Galilee. He did not want to serve Jerusalem, but
those people. His fellow commissary, old Doctor Jannai,
left him alone and never interfered with him. Nothing
interested the old doctor but his finances. He had planted
himself in Sepphoris with a prodigious pile of documents.
Sepphoris was the comfortable and quiet capital of the
country. There Jannai occupied himself benevolently, but
stubbornly and persistently, with the reorganisation of the
finances. Everything else he left to his younger colleague.
But although Joseph was allowed to arrange and plan whatever he liked, he found that he was not advancing. He put
away all his professorial arrogance, all his aristocratic and
priestly pride ; he talked with fishermen, wharf labourers,
peasants and handworkers as with equals. The people were
friendly and flattered, but behind their words and bearing
he felt an inner reserve.

The country of Galilee had other leaders. Joseph did not
want to admit this ; he wished to have nothing to do with
these men, but he knew their names quite well. They
were leaders of voluntary bands which were not recognised

in Jerusalem ; the peasant leader John of Gishala, and a
certain Sapita from Tiberias. Joseph saw that the eyes
of the people lit up when the names of these men were
mentioned. He would have liked to meet the two men,
hear what they had to say, and find out what they were after.
But he felt inexperienced, ineffectual, uninventive. He had
his office and his high title, perhaps also the ability to use
them ; but the others possessed the power.

He worked very hard. He was seized more and more
completely by the desire to win over this country of Galilee.
But the land barred itself against him. For five weeks now
he had been there, but he was no further forward than on
the first day.

6

ON one of those winter evenings Joseph passed through the
streets of the little town of Capernaum, one of the centres of
the Avengers of Israel. A flag hung from an old house,
signifying that it was an inn which had new wine to sell.
Joseph had seen his Galileans often enough at council meetings and commissions, in synagogues and schools. He
wanted to see them now over their wine ; so he entered.

It was a low room, primitively furnished, and poorly
heated by a single brazier in which dung was burning.
Through the evil smelling smoke Joseph caught sight of
over a dozen men. They looked up when the well-dressed
gentleman entered and mustered him with reserve, but
without enmity. The innkeeper came, asked what he
desired, and declared that the gentleman was in good luck
to-day. A merchant with a caravan had passed through
and had ordered a sumptuous repast ; there was still a good
portion left of chicken boiled in milk. To eat flesh with
milk was strictly forbidden ; but the country population of
Galilee were of the opinion that fowl was not flesh, and

refused to renounce their custom of boiling or stewing it in milk.   When Joseph politely declined this dainty the others made good-humoured witticisms at his expense.   They asked him who he was, where he intended to pass the night, and discovered by his speech that he was from Jerusalem. Joseph replied affably but somewhat vaguely to their questions ; he could not tell whether they had recognised him or not.

The innkeeper sat down beside him and began to talk volubly.   His name was Theophilus, but he called himself Giora, the stranger, for he was a sympathiser with the Jews and had the intention of going over to the Jewish faith. In Galilee there was a strong mixture of Gentiles ; and many of these were sympathetic to the Jews, and felt strongly attracted by their invisible God Jehovah.   Theophilus Giora had been categorically counselled by the doctors not to go over to the Jewish religion ; for as long as he was a Gentile he would not risk his eternal salvation even if he did not keep the six hundred and thirteen commandments.   But if he once accepted the responsibility, his soul would be imperilled if he failed to fulfil the law, and the law was difficult and strict.   Theophilus Giora was not yet circumcised ; the words of the doctors had made an impression upon him ; yet their very austerity attracted him.

The other men, broad, slow, somewhat awkward fellows, began once more, excited by the presence of the gentleman from Jerusalem, to talk of their favourite theme, the heavy oppressions of the Government.   The joiner Chalafta had had to sell his last vineyard.   He had introduced goats from beyond the Jordan ; the Romans laid a high customs duty on these beasts ; he had tried to smuggle them through, but he had been caught.   Whatever one did was wrong in the eyes of the customs officers.   They came down upon you

if you declared your goods ; they came down upon you if
you did not declare them. They had imposed a very heavy
fine upon him, for this was his second offence, and he had
had to sell his vineyard. The cloth weaver Asaria had had
to give up his third weaving loom as a pledge to the market
overseer of Magdala, because he was behind with his taxes.
All the men in this rich land looked poor and ragged ; they
lived wretchedly. There was much game in Galilee, and
goat's milk was cheap ; yet they smacked their lips greedily
when the innkeeper Giora spoke of his chicken boiled in
milk. They enjoyed such dainties only on the great feast
days. They could not fill their own bellies, though they
filled those of the gentlemen in Caesarea and Jerusalem.
The times were hard. Their fathers and forefathers had
dwelt in the land before them. They, too, had said that
things could not be worse ; but now they had grown worse
for all that.

Was the time fulfilled ? Long before the agitator Juda
had announced this message in Galilee and founded the
Avengers of Israel ; but he had been crucified by the Romans.
Now his son Nachum wandered through the land
announcing it. Theuda, too, had come from Galilee, had
worked miracles and then departed for Jerusalem, declaring
that the river Jordan would divide before him. But the
Romans had crucified him, and the gentlemen of the High
Council had given their consent.

The olive-grower Teradion remarked that perhaps this
Theuda had been a mere swindler. The joiner Chalafta
shook his head heavily and doubtfully : " A swindler ! A
swindler ! Well, perhaps the Jordan didn't divide after
all at the man's command. But even if it didn't, that
doesn't prove he was a swindler. He was a forerunner.
For when will the time be fulfilled if not now, when Gog

and Magog are threatening to fall on Israel again, as it is written in Ezekiel and Targum Jonathan ? "

The cloth-weaver Asaria put in knowingly that this Theuda certainly couldn't have been the real Messiah ; for he had it from reliable sources that Theuda had been an Egyptian, and it was impossible for an Egyptian to be the Messiah.

The wine was good and plentiful. The men forgot the gentleman from Jerusalem, and, sitting in a cloud of stinking smoke from the dung in the brazier, they talked piously and importantly of the Messiah who must come, it might be to-day or to-morrow, but most certainly some time that year. Of course the Messiah could be an Egyptian, the joiner Chalafta maintained doggedly and monotonously. For did not the Scriptures speak of the iron broom that would sweep the corruption from Israel and the world. And was not the Redeemer that iron broom ? But if he was, would Jehovah send a Jew to smite the Jews ? Would He not rather send one of the uncircumcised ? But the shopkeeper Tarfon complained in his dark, heavy, guttural dialect : " Of course he will be a Jew. For doesn't the great doctor Dossa Ben Nathan teach that he will gather together all those who are scattered, and that afterwards he will lie dead and unburied in the streets of Jerusalem, and that his name will be Messiah Ben Joseph ? But how can the name of a Gentile be Messiah Ben Joseph ? " But now the innkeeper Theophilus Giora intervened, and he took the side of the joiner Chalafta ; for he felt offended at the thought that a foreigner could not be the Messiah. Gloomily and obstinately he insisted that only a Gentile could be the Redeemer. For did not the Scriptures say that he would roll the heavens up like a scroll, and that only then would the day of reckoning begin with great slaughter and fire in

the corrupt city ?   Several of the men agreed with him,
others disagreed.   They were all deeply stirred ; slowly,
complainingly, indignantly, they argued with one another,
debating fervently those dark and contradictory prophecies.
They were firmly persuaded, these Galilean men, that the
Redeemer would come.   But each had a different picture
of him, and each defended his own picture ; each saw it so
clearly, each knew that he was right and the others wrong,
and sought to justify his picture by passages from the
Scriptures.

Joseph listened intently.   His eyes and nose were smarting
with the biting, evil-smelling smoke, but that did not trouble
him ; he gazed at the men whose hard skulls were seething
with arguments.   He could literally see their minds at work,
saw the labour it gave them to translate their thoughts into
words.   At the time when he was living with Banus in the
wilderness the prophecies of the Scriptures had been a
sublime and perpetual presence to him ; they had been like
the air he breathed.   But in Jerusalem the prophecies had
faded, and of all the passages in the Scriptures those which
spoke of the Redeemer had become the thinnest and most
remote.   The doctors in the Temple were not too well
pleased when one applied those auguries to the present ;
many supported the opinion of the great doctor of law,
Hillel, that the Messiah had appeared long since in the
shape of King Hiskia ; they struck out of the eighteen
petitions the prayer for the appearance of the Redeemer,
and when Joseph sat his examination the hope of the coming
of the Messiah had for many years held no place either in
his thoughts or his life.   Now, this evening, in the dark
and smoky tavern, he was given back again his faith that
the Redeemer would come, and it became an inner joy and
torment, the corner stone of his life.   With an open mind

and a full heart he listened to these men ; and the opinions
of these cloth weavers, joiners, olive growers, seemed of more
importance to him than the subtle commentaries of the
Jerusalem doctors. Forgetting the superiority of the scholar,
he listened intently, swayed this way and that by their
rough and ready arguments. Would the Redeemer bring
the olive leaf, or the sword ? He saw that these men were
becoming more and more heated by the clash between their
violent faiths and in spite of all their piety were shouting
almost threateningly at one another.

At last things came to a head ; the joiner Chalafta
prepared to attack the shopkeeper Tarfon with his fists.
Then suddenly one of the younger men said, hastily and
urgently : " Stop. Wait a bit. Look over there. The
second sight has come on him." They all stared across at
the stool standing beside the brazier, where a pale-faced
humpback was sitting. There was nothing very remarkable
about him ; and until now he had hardly opened his mouth.
He was a dried, withered fellow, and, as it appeared, short-
sighted as well. He stared intently through the smoke,
narrowed his eyes as though he were trying to catch sight
of something on the very verge of his range of vision, opened
them widely again, and blinked rapidly. The men asked
him eagerly : " Do you see anything, Akavia ? Tell us
what you see." But, still tensely gazing, the sandal-maker
Akavia said matter-of-factly in broad dialect, his voice
hoarse with the wine and the smoke : " Yes, I see him."

" What does he look like ? " asked the men.

" He is not tall," said the gazer, " but he is broad."

" Is he a Jew ? " they asked.

" I don't think so. He has no beard. But who can
tell from a man's face whether he is a Jew or not ? "

" Is he armed ? "

" I can't see a sword," responded the gazer, " but I think he is in armour."

" What does he say ? " asked Joseph.

" He opens his mouth," replied the sandal-maker Akavia, " but I can't hear him. I think he's laughing," he added importantly.

" How can he laugh if he is the Messiah ? " asked the joiner Chalafta with displeasure. The gazer replied : " He is laughing and yet he is awful."

Then he wiped his eyes with his hand, and declared that he could see no more. He seemed very tired and hungry all at once ; he became morose, began to drink a great deal of wine, and demanded also some of the chicken boiled in milk. The innkeeper told Joseph about the sandal-maker Akavia. He was very poor, but nevertheless he made every year his pilgrimage to Jerusalem and brought his lamb to the Temple. He dared not set forth in the inner courts, for he was a humpback. But he was very devoted to the Temple and prepared to give all he had to it, and also knew far more about the inner courts than many who had entered them. Perhaps it was because he could never see the inner courts of the Temple that Jehovah had given him the power to see other things.

The men stayed on for a long time, but they did not talk again of the Redeemer. Instead they spoke of the great increase in the numbers of the Avengers of Israel, and of their organisation and equipment. The day for action would soon be coming. The sandal-maker Akavia, once more cheerful, rallied the uncircumcised innkeeper, saying that when that day came he would have to believe. Then they turned round and began to talk to the gentleman from Jerusalem, chaffing him in their rude but not unfriendly way. Joseph replied amicably and laughed with them ; finally

they asked him to be their guest and eat of the chicken
cooked in milk.   The sandal-maker Akavia, in particular,
insisted upon this.   Capriciously and persistently he bawled :
" Eat, man.   You must eat, man."   Joseph had not shown
much scruple in Rome about observing the Jewish customs ;
in Jerusalem he had observed them strictly.   This was
Galilee.   He reflected for a little.   Then he ate.

7

As his headquarters Joseph had chosen Magdala, a fine large
town on the Lake of Genezareth.   If he sailed out a little
distance into the lake he could see to the south a white and
splendid city, the most beautiful city in the country, but it
did not belong to his province ; it was under King Agrippa's
jurisdiction and was called Tiberias.   And in it, as the
King's viceroy, resided Justus.   The city was not easy
to govern ; more than a third of its population were Greeks
and Romans who were pampered by the King ; but Doctor
Justus, it could not be gainsaid, kept good order.   When
Joseph came to Galilee Justus had courteously responded
to his visit of ceremony, but he had not dropped a single
word about politics.   It was obvious that he did not regard
the powers that Joseph had been granted by Jerusalem as
important.   That wounded Joseph to the heart.   A bitter
desire filled him to teach the other a lesson.

On the heights above Tiberias gleamed the spacious and
stately palace of King Agrippa, where Justus resided.
Along the quays there were fine villas and warehouses.
But there were also many poor people in Tiberias, fishermen
and dockers, carriers and factory workers.   In Tiberias the
Greeks and Romans were the rich people ; the Jews the
proletarians.   The work was heavy, the taxes were high ;
in the city the poor felt still more bitterly than on the land

all that they had to renounce. There were many discontented men in Tiberias. In all the taverns one could
hear seditious talk against the Romans and King Agrippa,
who depended on their support. The ringleader of these
discontented men was Sapita, the secretary of the fishermen's union. He appealed to the words of Isaiah : " Woe
to them that add house to house, and field to field." With
all the means in his power Justus had tried to repress this
movement ; but his power ended at the city frontier of
Tiberias, and he could not prevent Sapita's voluntary bands
from establishing rallying points in the rest of Galilee
and gaining fresh support there.

Not without pleasure Joseph saw that Sapita's adherents
were growing in number, and that his bands were spreading
everywhere, even in this province under the government of
Jerusalem. Sapita's men demanded from the communes
under Joseph's jurisdiction contributions for the national
cause, organised punitive expeditions in case of refusal,
expeditions which looked very like robbery and pillage.
Joseph's police seldom intervened ; his courts treated the
prisoners with lenience.

Joseph was intensely pleased when Sapita came to see
him. Galilee was beginning to trust him ; Galilee was
coming to him. Now he felt that it would not take long
to goad the haughty Justus out of his dignified reserve.
But he wisely concealed his joy. He gazed across at Sapita.
Sapita was a powerful, thick-set man ; one of his shoulders
was lower than the other. He had a ragged, two pointed
beard, and small fanatical eyes. Joseph talked to him and
came to an understanding, all, however, in half hints. It
was easier to treat with him than with Justus. Nothing
was set down in writing ; but when Sapita left they both
knew that an understanding had been come to more effective

than any formal contract.   Any of Sapita's men who did
not feel safe in Tiberias could with safety seek refuge in
Joseph's province.   There they would be indulgently
treated.   And Joseph would not have to expend so much
breath in future in squeezing money for his war fund out
of the miserly Doctor Jannai ; if it was refused him, Sapita
would come to his aid.

This agreement was kept.   And now at last Joseph had
got Justus to the point where he actually mentioned politics.
In a letter Justus urgently requested the Jerusalem delegate
not to sabotage any longer his efforts to crush these illegal
bands.   Old Doctor Jannai put a few uncomfortable
questions to Joseph.   But Joseph looked astonished ;
Justus must evidently be labouring under hallucinations.
When he was alone he smiled with satisfaction.   He looked
forward to the combat.

It was agreed that he should talk the matter over personally
with Justus.   By the side of Jannai Joseph rode on his
beautiful Arabian horse, Arrow, through the well-kept
streets of Tiberias ; the crowds stared at him curiously.
He knew that he looked well on horseback ; so he gazed in
front of him immovably and a little haughtily as he rode up
the hill to the palace of King Agrippa.   In front of the
gate stood the colossal and magnificent statue of Tiberius,
the emperor after whom the city was named.   The arcades
in front of the palace were lined with statues.   They were
a thorn in Joseph's flesh.   He was not devoted to the ancient
beliefs, but his heart was filled with his invisible God Jehovah, and he was deeply indignant that in the country of
Jehovah his eyes should be forced to gaze on blasphemous
idols.   To fashion the human form was the privilege of the
Creator.   He had permitted men to give names to the shapes
He had created ; to fashion them themselves was blas-

phemous presumption. These statues standing about were
an insult to the invisible God. The faintly guilty uneasiness
with which Joseph had begun his journey was gone ; now
he was filled with pure exaltation and felt superior to Justus.
Justus stood for a cautious and grovelling policy ; he,
Joseph, came as the soldier of Jehovah.

Justus, the sworn enemy of all ceremony, endeavoured
to make the interview as unofficial as possible. The three
gentlemen ate, lying on their banqueting couches. Justus
had begun by talking in Greek, but then politely changed
over to Aramaic, though that language obviously gave
him difficulty. Joseph had by now given up his Roman
table manners ; after the most strict Jerusalem ritual he
took the perfumed sandalwood toothpick between his thumb
and third finger when he raised it to his mouth, and he did
not empty his beaker at one draught, but invariably set it
down twice on the table before the wine was finished. Did
Justus remark that ? Probably he did. But he did not
venture to smile, all the same.

The conversation gradually converged on politics. Doctor Jannai was zealous and genial as ever. Joseph defended
his own policy ; he defended it more violently than he had
intended. If one wanted to keep the war party from
injudicious aggression, one would have to meet them half
way. " You mean that we must have an aggressive
peace ? " asked Justus, and the words sounded disagreeably
ironical. " I really must assure the author of the history
of the Maccabees that to-day any Maccabaean gesture what-
soever seems to me ill-timed and out of place."

" Aren't some of the most violent Maccabaeans actually
here in Tiberias ? " asked Doctor Jannai sympathetically.

" Unfortunately I haven't enough authority," Justus
frankly admitted, " to arrest Sapita. But you, gentlemen,

could do it quite easily.   And, as I've informed you already,
it's really the mildness of your law courts that makes my
Avengers of Israel so proud and unruly."

" It isn't so simple for us either," replied Doctor Jannai
apologetically.   " After all, these people aren't common
robbers."

Joseph put his word in : " These people appeal to Isaiah
for justification.   They believe," he added aggressively,
" that the time is fulfilled and that the Messiah will soon
appear."

" Isaiah says," responded Justus, not loudly, but stubbornly, " that one should not resist force.   Resist not, and
trust in God ; that is what Isaiah teaches."   Joseph was
annoyed by the citation.   Was this fellow trying to teach
him ?   " The seat of the trouble is your city of Tiberias,"
he said sharply.

" The seat of the trouble is Magdala, Doctor Joseph,"
replied Justus politely.   " I can do nothing when your
courts let my riff-raff go free.   But when, in addition to
that, you fatten your war funds out of the booty of these
robbers, Doctor Joseph," he spoke now with particular
politeness, " then I cannot give you any assurance that my
King will not reclaim these sums again by force."

Doctor Jannai jumped to his feet.   " Have you any of
Sapita's money in your exchequer, Doctor Joseph ? "
Joseph was furious.   This confounded fellow Justus must
have a very clever secret service ; great pains had been
taken to disguise these contributions.   He tried to evade
the question, and said that certainly he had received money
from Tiberias for the Galilean militia ; but it was inconceivable to him that it should emanate from Sapita's band.

" Believe me, that's where it came from," declared
Justus amicably.   " I must really ask you not to counte-

nance such riff-raff any longer. I consider it incompatible
with my duty to the King to look on while the city under
my jurisdiction is stirred up against me by you."

He still spoke in a very polite tone ; and only by the
fact that he had once more reverted to Greek did he show
his agitation. But in a clap Doctor Jannai had lost all his
amiability ; he jumped up and began to gesticulate in
Joseph's face : " Have you accepted money from Sapita ? "
he screamed. " Have you accepted money from Sapita ? "
And without even waiting for Joseph's answer he turned to
Justus. " If any money has been sent to us from Tiberias
it shall be returned to you," he promised.

Hardly were they out of the city when the two commissaries parted company. " I beg to draw your attention
to the fact," said Jannai, and his voice was icy, " that you
are not in Magdala as one of the Avengers of Israel, but
as a commissary appointed by Jerusalem. I refuse to
countenance your romantic filibustering adventures," he
shouted. Pale with rage, Joseph could find nothing to
reply. He saw clearly that he had overestimated his power.
Doctor Jannai had a good sense of what was and what was
not permissible. If this man dared to dress him down like
a schoolboy, then his position must be confoundedly shaky.
He should have waited a little longer ; he should not have
ventured on this struggle with Justus so soon. At the first
excuse he gave it, Jerusalem would recall him, and Justus
would smile, would put on that infamous smile that Joseph
knew so well.

Justus wouldn't smile. Joseph would take care that did
not happen. What did this Justus fellow know about
Galilee ? By now Joseph felt that he himself knew it
thoroughly. He had no longer any fear or shyness of the
Galilean leaders. Sapita had come to him of his own will ;

he would himself summon John of Gishala.　He would prove that it was not Jerusalem, but the triumvirate John, Sapita and Joseph, who possessed the true power in the country.　Would people call them robber bands then or riff-raff?　He had no intention of dropping his connection with Sapita.　On the contrary he would organise into a single unit all the armed bands, recognised or not, which existed under the jurisdiction of Jerusalem and beyond that jurisdiction.　And not as a commissary from Jerusalem, but as the party leader of the Avengers of Israel.

8

JOHN OF GISHALA, the leader of the well-armed Galilean peasant troops, was obviously gratified when Joseph summoned him.　John belonged to the small gentry.　He was broad, slow, good-humoured, sly, a man entirely after the hearts of the Galileans.　During the campaign of Cestius he had organised a crafty and bitter guerilla war against the Romans.　He was always on the move, and knew every nook and corner of the land.　When John at last arrived Joseph could not understand why he had not made this man's acquaintance long before.　Not very tall, but strongly and vigorously made, John sat before him with his brown peasant face, clipped moustache, flattened nose and crafty blue eyes.　In spite of all his slyness, a courageous and frank fellow.

He came out at once with a bold proposal.　Everywhere in the country King Agrippa had been collecting grain, doubtless for the Romans.　John wanted to requisition this grain for his defence troops, and requested Joseph's consent to that necessary measure.　At the instigation of the rich men and the aristocrats, he complained, Jerusalem was denying all connection with its defence troops.　He had

the impression that Joseph was different from the soft-
stepping gentlemen in the Temple. " You, Doctor Joseph,
belong in your heart to the Avengers of Israel ; one can see
that three miles off. I would like to put my defence troops
under your command," he went on trustfully, and he gave
Joseph an exact account of his organisation. He commanded eighteen thousand men. Joseph gave his consent
that the grain should be requisitioned.

He did not fear the tempest that the measure was bound
to arouse. If he exploited his power to the utmost, if he
got the real power of Galilee into his hands, perhaps the
people in Jerusalem would not be able to recall him. And
he would be in a position, in any case, to decide whether
he would allow himself to be recalled. With almost
pleasurable excitement he waited to see what would happen.

John of Gishala was also pleased with his interview.
He was a brave man, and had a sense of humour. All
Galilee knew that it was he who confiscated King Agrippa's
grain ; but when asked he put on an innocent air and said
he knew nothing about it. What had been done had been
done at the command of the commissary from Jerusalem.
Quite publicly he journeyed into Tiberias, into the territory
of his enemy, to cure his rheumatism at the hot springs
there. He knew that if Justus did anything against him
his men would sack Tiberias. Justus laughed. Pernicious as the actions of the peasant leader might appear to
him, he liked his style.

But he sent indignant letters to Jerusalem and Sepphoris.
Quite beyond himself, panting with fury, old Doctor Jannai
came to Joseph. The grain must be returned immediately.
Joseph received the furious old man very politely. The
grain unfortunately could not be returned, for he had sold
it. With nothing achieved, Jannai had to take leave of

the polite and regretful Joseph.   A small comfort remained :
Joseph sent a considerable part of the proceeds to Jerusalem.

9

ONE of the favourite weapons of the Avengers of Israel
in Tiberias was to point out the godlessness of the
ruling class, and their habit of imitating the Romans
and Greeks.   When Sapita visited Joseph for the second
time he said that he, too, saw with the deepest indignation
the statues that flaunted themselves so provocatively in the
sun in front of the King's palace.   The gloomy and fanatical
fellow drew up his right shoulder higher than ever, shot a
glance at Joseph from his tiny eyes and lowered them again,
and tugged nervously at the two points of his beard.   Joseph
encouraged him.   He quoted the prophet : " Thy calf,
O Samaria, hath cast thee off ; the workman made it ;
therefore it is not God."   He waited for Sapita to complete
the celebrated passage : " The calf of Samaria shall be
broken to pieces."   But Sapita merely smiled.   He ignored
the invitation and quoted very softly, more to himself than
to Joseph, the later sentence : " They have sown the
wind, and they shall reap the whirlwind."   Then he
remarked soberly : " We have always protested against
this blasphemous nuisance.   We would be grateful to the
commissary of Jerusalem if he would also send a remon-
strance to Tiberias."

Sapita was not so frank as John of Gishala, but when he
gave a hint it could be relied upon.   Whoso sowed the
wind would reap the whirlwind.   Without consulting
Doctor Jannai Joseph asked Justus for a second interview.
Joseph journeyed to Tiberias with only a single attendant.
This time Justus greeted him in the Roman fashion, stretching out his arm with the hand open and letting it fall again,

smiling almost apologetically. He pronounced the Hebrew greeting : " Peace." Then the two gentlemen sat down opposite each other without any third part to embarrass them ; they gazed at each other in cordial enmity ; they both knew a great deal about each other. They had both achieved something since they had disputed together in Rome ; they possessed power over events ; they had grown older, and their features were harder ; but they still resembled each other, Joseph with his pale brown, and Justus with his golden brown face.

" You quoted the prophet Isaiah," said Joseph, " the last time I saw you."

" Yes," said Justus, " Isaiah taught that Judaea should not enter into conflict with its powerful enemies."

" He taught that," said Joseph, " and at the end of his life he took refuge in a hollow cedar and was sawn in two."

" Better for one man to be sawn in two than a whole land," said Justus. " What are you really after, Doctor Joseph ? I've tried to discover some coherent connection between your actions. But either I am too stupid to understand them, or else they are all intended for one purpose : to get Judaea to declare war on Rome under the leadership of the new Maccabee, Joseph Ben Matthias."

Joseph curbed himself. Since his Roman days he had, of course, been aware of this fixed idea of Justus that he was a fire eater. But he wasn't. He didn't want a war. But he wasn't afraid of one either. Besides, he held Justus's methods to be wrong even from Justus's own standpoint. Incessant insistence on peace led just as inevitably to war as perpetual insistence on war. Instead of pursuing such a policy one should on the contrary, by adroit concessions, deprive the war party of all pretext for aggression.

" And don't we in Tiberias do that ? " asked Justus.

"No," replied Joseph.   "You do not do that."

"I'm listening," said Justus politely.

"In Tiberias," said Joseph, "you maintain, for instance, this royal palace of yours with all those images of men and beasts, which is a perpetual irritation to the whole province, a standing challenge to war."

Justus gazed at him, then smiled broadly.   "Have you come to tell me that?" he asked.   Joseph allowed all his hatred of those brazen images to fill him.   "Yes," he said.

Then Justus rose and asked Joseph to follow him.   He led him through the palace.   The palace was with justice celebrated as the most beautiful edifice in Galilee.   Justus led him through the halls, courts and gardens.   There were statues everywhere; they were an organic part of the building.   King Agrippa and his two predecessors had with much labour gathered together beautiful and costly things from every corner of the world and found a place for them here; among them were ancient and celebrated works of art.   In a courtyard of brown ashlar Justus remained standing before a little piece of statuary, faded old Egyptian work; it showed a branch on which was perched a bird.   It was very severe, even angular in style, but although the little bird rested on the branch one could divine in it the blissful lightness of the flight for which it was preening its wings.   Justus stood for a little while, quite absorbed by the bird on the branch.   Then, as if awakening, he asked gently: "Must I destroy that?" and pointing all round: "And that?   And that?   Then the whole building would be without any meaning."

"Then pull the building down," said Joseph, and there was such measureless hate in his voice that Justus said no more.

Joseph sent a message to Sapita asking him to come the

very next day. Sapita asked him if he had managed to
effect anything in Tiberias. No, replied Joseph, they had
hardened their hearts, but his power unfortunately stopped
at the walls of the city. Sapita pulled violently at one
point of his beard. This time he uttered the sentence
that he had passed over last time : " The calf of Samaria
shall be broken to pieces."

If the people of Tiberias, replied Joseph, should sweep
away the abomination, he could find it in his heart to forgive
them.

" And provide an asylum as well ? " asked Sapita.

" Perhaps an asylum as well," said Joseph.

When Sapita had gone Joseph found himself with a
divided mind. In spite of his one shoulder being higher
than the other, this Sapita was a powerful fellow ; he would
not be unduly gentle in such matters. If he and his men
invaded the palace it would not be statues only that would
be broken. It was a beautiful building ; its ceilings were
of cedar and gold ; it was full of rare things. It belonged
unquestionably to King Agrippa, and stood unquestionably
under Roman protection. For some time now the land
had been peaceful, and in Jerusalem people hoped that
they would be able to come to an understanding with Rome.
The sandal-maker Akavia had seen the Messiah in the
smoky tavern in Capernaum ; and the Messiah had not
worn a sword. Certain people in Rome were simply
waiting for the Government in Jerusalem to do something
that might be construed as an act of aggression. The
words he had said just now might set rolling a stone that
had hitherto been held in its place only by a supreme effort.

On the following night King Agrippa's palace was
taken by storm. It was a large building, very strongly
built, and not easy to rase to the ground. Nor did the

attackers quite succeed in their purpose. Everything was done by feeble moonlight, and, remarkably enough, without any great noise. The crowd flung themselves stubbornly on the firmly masoned stones, tugged at them with their hands, kicked them and trampled upon them. Trampled also the flower plots in the gardens. But they wreaked their bitterest fury on the fountains. They rushed about busily securing the costly carpets and tapestries, the gold mountings on the ceiling, the rare crockery; all in silence. Justus soon recognised that his troops were too small in number to intervene with success, and forbade any resistance. But the Avengers of Israel had already cut down a hundred soldiers and Greek citizens, who at the start had tried to prevent the looting. The palace itself burned for almost all next day. All Galilee was frozen with horror at the news of the destruction of the palace at Tiberias. In Magdala the authorities pressed Joseph urgently for instructions as to how they should act. Joseph remained stubbornly silent. Then suddenly, the very day after the fire, he set out for Tiberias in great haste to express to Justus the condolences of the Jerusalem Government and to put his resources at Justus's disposal. He found Justus wandering dully and restlessly among the ruins. Justus had not sent to his king for troops and had attempted nothing against Sapita and his men. Usually so capable, he had let his hands fall helplessly and despairingly by his side. Even now that Joseph appeared, he did not greet him with taunts, nor did he address a single bitter word to him. With a very pale face he said, and his voice was hoarse with agitation and misery : " You have no idea what you have done. The refusal of the Temple offering was bad ; so was the attack on Cestius ; and so was the edict of Caesarea. But none of those was fatal. This, this that you have done, means war." He had tears of rage and grief in his eyes. "You are blind with ambition," he said to Joseph.

A great part of the booty from the palace Sapita put at Joseph's disposal ; gold, ornaments of fine wood, fragments of statuary. Involuntarily Joseph looked to see if he could find the branch with the bird on it. But he could not find it ; it had evidently been made of fragile material, easy to destroy.

10

THE news from Tiberias struck the Jerusalem Government to the heart. Already, through the mediation of the peace-loving Paulinus, they had received a half promise from the Imperial Government that if Judaea remained quiet Rome was prepared to content itself with the surrender of a few of the leaders, such as Simon Bar Giora and Eleasar. In Jerusalem they were very relieved at the thought of getting rid of such firebrands. Now this senseless piece of folly in Tiberias had ruined everything.

The Avengers of Israel, who had been fighting with their backs to the wall, obtained a breathing space. Their assembly place, the Blue Hall, became the centre of politics in Judaea. They succeeded in getting their leader Eleasar included in the cabinet. Grown insolent, resolved to savour to the utmost his opponents' humiliation, the young and elegant Eleasar refused to accept until they begged him on their knees. But not even the Blue Hall could maintain in office the rebellious governor of Galilee who had acted in such a flagrant manner against the instructions of his government. Doctor Jannai had reported personally to the High Council and stubbornly demanded the deposition and chastisement of the criminal fool, Joseph Ben Matthias. The Avengers of Israel did not dare to defend him ; they merely abstained from voting. Among the members of the Government there was only one who had a word to say for Joseph : the mild old doctor, Jochanan Ben Sakkai. He said : " Condemn no one until he is dead."

Joseph's old father, the wrinkled, sanguine Matthias, was filled with despair, as he had been with delight when his son was appointed. He urgently implored Joseph to come to Jerusalem before the decree recalling him reached Galilee ; to appear before his judges and justify himself. If he remained in Galilee it would mean certain ruin. His heart, Matthias said, was troubled to death. He did not want to go to his grave without seeing his son once more.

Joseph smiled when he received the letter. He loved the old man, but knew that he looked on things far too apprehensively and gloomily. Joseph's own heart was full of confidence. And in Galilee things looked quite different from what they did in Jerusalem. Since the image breaking at Tiberias Galilee had acclaimed him ; it was known throughout the whole land that without his consent that deed would have been impossible. He had torn down the wall that stood between him and the people of Galilee ; they regarded him now as a second Judas Maccabaeus, the name with which Justus had jeeringly dubbed him. The armed bands listened to his advice ; he was no longer dependent on Jerusalem ; Jerusalem was dependent on him. He could if he liked simply tear up the decree deposing him.

That night he had a bad dream. By all the roads the Roman legions were marching on Judaea. He saw them approaching, slowly, inexorably, in strict order in rows of six men ; many thousands of them, and yet like a single entity. It was war incarnate that was marching on him ; "technique," a monstrous omnipotent machine of blind efficiency ; it was senseless to resist it. He saw the legions marching on rhythmically ; he saw them quite distinctly ; but, and that was the most horrible thing, he could hear nothing. He groaned. It was one gigantic foot encased in a monstrous military boot, that rose and fell, rose and fell ; he could not escape it ; in five minutes, in three minutes, it would trample him into the dust. Joseph sat on his horse Arrow ; Sapita, John of Gishala, everybody gazed at him gloomily and expectantly, and waited for him to draw his sword from his sheath. He tore at his sword, but it would not move, it was firmly nailed to the sheath ; he groaned, Justus of Tiberias smiled, Sapita tugged furiously and savagely at his two-pointed beard, the joiner Chalafta raised his mighty fists ; Joseph pulled at his sword, an eternity passed, he pulled and pulled and could not get it out of the sheath. The sandal-maker Akavia shouted raucously : " Eat, man ! You must eat ! " And the foot in the gigantic military boot rose and fell, and came nearer and nearer.

But when Joseph awoke it was a radiantly clear winter morning, and the horrible suspended eternity in which he had watched the boot rising and falling was wiped from his mind. Everything had worked out for good. It was not Jerusalem, but God Himself who had put him where he was. God had decided for war.

With wild ardour he set about preparing for the holy war. How could he have sat in Rome at the same table with these foreigners, slept in the same bed with them ? Now like the others he loathed their very smell ; they infected the land. It was possible that the Romans' administration was good, also their roads and their water supplies ; but it was as if this holy land of Judaea became afflicted with leprosy when people did not live in it in the Jewish fashion. The same burning ardour descended upon

him as in those months when he had written his book on
the Maccabees.   With a prophetic soul he had described
his own future.   His strength grew.   Day and night he
laboured indefatigably.   He tightened his administration,
accumulated supplies, drilled his defence troops, strengthened
his fortresses.   He travelled through the towns of Galilee,
through its peaceful and spacious countrysides, passed mountains and valleys, the banks of rivers, lake and sea coast,
vineyards, olive and sycamore groves.   Young and vigorous,
he rode on his horse Arrow ; confidence and cheerfulness
radiated from him ; before him waved the standard with
the letters Makkabi, Who is like thee, O Lord ?   And his
bearing, his words, his banner, set the youth of Galilee on
fire.

Many, when they listened to Joseph's words confidently
prophesying that Edom would be destroyed, words that
broke out of him like lava and flame from a volcano, exclaimed that a new prophet had arisen in Israel.   " Marin,
Marin, our Lord, our Lord," they cried with passionate
devotion wherever he went, and they kissed his hands and
his cloak.

He rode to Meron in Upper Galilee.   It was an insignificant little town, noted only for its olives, its university and
its ancient tombs.   Here rested the bones of two ancient
law givers, the venerable Doctor Shammai and the venerable
Doctor Hillel, the first famed for his severity, the second
for his mildness.   The people of Meron were regarded as
particularly fanatical in their religion.   It was said that out
of the graves of these two teachers a deeper and diviner
wisdom grew.   Perhaps that was the reason why Joseph
went to Meron.   He spoke in the old synagogue ; the
people listened to him in silence ; they were mostly doctors
and students ; it was a more attentive audience than any

other he had addressed ; the people rocked their bodies, listened tensely, and were deeply moved.   And suddenly, when Joseph paused after a great and moving passage, a pale and very young man said in a low convulsive voice into the silence : " That is he."

" Who am I ? " asked Joseph sternly.   And with humbly devoted, somewhat foolish eyes, the young man repeated again and again, " You are he, yes, you are he."

It appeared that the people of the little town regarded this young man as a prophet of Jehovah, and that a week before they had left the doors of their houses open all night because he had foretold that the Redeemer would appear to them.

At the young man's words Joseph was chilled to the marrow.   He became angry and shouted at the youth, and in his secret heart he furiously denied that he could be the Messiah ; it was blasphemy.   Yet he was filled more deeply than ever with the conviction that his mission was a divine one.   Only children and fools could call him the Redeemer.   But perhaps it was his mission to prepare the way for the Kingdom.

The people of Meron were not to be dissuaded that they had seen the Messiah.   They had the hoof marks of the horse Arrow cast in copper, and these hoof marks were regarded by them as holier than the tombs of the two law givers.   Joseph was angry ; he laughed at the fools and rebuked them.   But he felt a closer and closer affinity with the Messiah that was to come, and more and more longingly, almost with greed, he waited for the time when he should see him with his own eyes.

When the commission arrived from Jerusalem bringing the decree deposing him he declared smilingly that there must be some error, and that until he obtained reliable

G

information from Jerusalem he must detain the gentlemen
in case the news should leak out and lead to disturbances in
the country. The Jerusalem gentlemen asked him who
had given him authority to predict a war against Rome.
He replied that he had his authority from God. The
Jerusalem gentlemen quoted the passage from the law :
" But the prophet, which shall presume to speak a word in
my name, which I have not commanded him to speak,
even that prophet shall die." Still smiling amiably and
insolently, Joseph shrugged his shoulders, and said that
they would have to wait and see who spoke in the name of
the Lord and who didn't. He was radiant, sure of himself
and of his God. At the head of his militia and John of
Gishala's troops, he marched on Tiberias. Justus surrendered the city to him without making any resistance.
Once more they sat opposite each other, but this time,
instead of old Jannai, Joseph had the burly good-humoured
and sly John of Gishala to support him.

" You may go in safety back to your King Agrippa,"
he said to Justus. " You're a clever fellow, far too clever
to involve yourself in a war of liberty. For that one must
have faith and listen to one's inner voice. You can take
everything with you, Doctor Justus," Joseph went on in a
friendly voice, " that belongs to the King, and is of any
monetary value. Only I must ask you to leave the state
documents here with me. Go in peace."

" I have nothing against you, John of Gishala," said
Justus. " I believe you listen to your inner voice. But
your cause is lost beforehand, quite apart from everything
else, by your having this man as your leader." He did not
look at Joseph, but his voice was full of contempt.

" Our leader Doctor Joseph," said John of Gishala
with a smile, " doesn't seem to be to your liking, but

he's a brilliant organiser, a splendid speaker, and a born leader."

"Your Doctor Joseph is a scoundrel," said Justus of Tiberias. Joseph did not reply; the defeated man was embittered and unjust; it wasn't worth one's while to argue with him and confute him.

During that winter Joseph travelled happily and proudly through Galilee. Jerusalem did not dare to proceed by force against him, and when after a few weeks he wrote again to the central government, signing himself commissary, they let it pass in silence. With ease he held his frontiers against the Romans and even extended them, and he also seized part of King Agrippa's land on the western banks of the Lake of Genezareth, and manned and strengthened his towns. He organised the country for war. From the sacred air of this land new and great inspirations came to him.

Rome was silent; no tidings came from Rome. Paulinus had broken off all communications with his Jerusalem friends. Joseph's first success had been lightly won. The Romans confined themselves to Samaria and the cities on the coast, where, with the support of a population mainly Greek, they remained in assured possession of their power. King Agrippa's troops also avoided any encounter. The land was quiet.

All those who had movable property, and did not belong in their hearts to the Avengers of Israel, sought to escape with their goods into the provinces under Roman protection. During one of those attempts at flight the wife of a certain Ptolemaeus, a steward of King Agrippa's, was seized by Joseph's men; it happened in the neighbourhood of a village called Dabarita. The lady had a great deal of baggage, which included valuables evidently belonging to

the King ; it was a very good haul, and the men who had
seized it were congratulating themselves on their share of
the booty. They were to be severely disappointed. Joseph
had the lady's goods sent to the nearest Roman province
with a polite letter addressed to the safe hands of Paulinus.

It was not the first time that he had acted in this way,
and his men murmured. They complained to John of
Gishala. There was a heated interview between John,
Sapita and Joseph. Joseph pointed out that often in former
wars the Romans and Greeks had given such proofs of
chivalry. But John was furious ; his grey eyes sparkled
angrily and became bloodshot, his moustache quivered with
anger ; he was like a volcano about to erupt. He shouted :
" Are you out of your wits ? Do you think we are com-
peting at the Olympian games ? You actually dare to
come to us with your twaddle about chivalry when we are
fighting the Romans ? This is war, my dear sir, and not
an athletic contest. It isn't a matter of winning a laurel
crown, it's a matter of six million human beings who can't
breathe this air that the Romans have infected, and that's
stifling them. Do you understand ? " Joseph could do
nothing against the savage anger of this man ; he was
astonished, he felt unjustly used. He looked at Sapita,
but Sapita stood there with a gloomy look on his face ; he
said nothing, but it was clear that John had merely spoken
out what he, too, felt.

But the three men were too sensible to allow their enterprise to be endangered by a difference of opinion. They
employed the winter in organising as efficiently as they
could the defence of Galilee.

The land remained peaceful, but the peace began to
become oppressive. Joseph clung to his cheerfulness and
assurance. Yet sometimes through his airy confidence he

would hear Justus's hateful words. Although he filled his days from beginning to end with work, more and more often amid the reports of his civil subordinates and officers, amid the applause of popular assemblies, he heard those clear, calm and bitter words, "Your Doctor Joseph is a scoundrel," and he preserved them in his heart, preserved their tone, their contempt, their resignation, and their laborious Aramaic.

11

THE country of Israel was the centre of the world, Jerusalem was the centre of Israel, the Temple the centre of Jerusalem, the Holy of Holies the centre of the Temple : the navel of the earth. Until King David's time Jehovah had wandered over the face of the earth living in tents and temporary huts. King David resolved to build a house for Him. He bought the threshing floor of Aravina, and the ancient and holy mount of Sion. But he was only permitted to lay the foundations ; to build the Temple itself was denied him, because in his many battles he had shed much blood. His son Solomon, alone, was deemed worthy to carry out this sacred work. For seven years he built. No labourer died during that time, or even grew sick ; no tool was damaged ; as iron was not allowed to be employed in building the sacred edifice, God sent the King a marvellous stone drill, called Shamir, that split the stones. Often, too, the stone blocks laid themselves in the place appointed for them without the agency of human hands. The savage and holy sacrificial altar at last arose, and beside it the basins where the priests washed their hands, and the brazen chalice, resting on twelve oxen. In the outer hall two strange trees all of bronze rose towards the heavens ; their names were Jachin and Boas. The Inner Temple was inlaid with cedar wood, the floor was of cypress, and in this way all the

stone work was completely hidden. Five golden candlesticks stood against each wall, also the table with the shew-
bread.   But in the Holy of Holies, which was concealed
from all eyes by a veil, stood gigantic winged human forms,
cherubs, fashioned out of the wood of the wild olive ; and
their bird-like heads stared awfully straight before them.
With their gigantic, gold inlaid wings, they over-arched
protectively the Ark of Jehovah which had accompanied
the Jews through the wilderness.   This house stood for
more than four hundred years, until King Nebuchadnezzar
destroyed it and removed the sacred vessels to Babylon.

When they returned from their captivity in Babylon,
the Jews built a new temple.   But it was a wretched affair
compared with the first.   Until a great king arose, Herod
by name, who in the eighteen years of his reign began to
rebuild the Temple.   Employing thousands of labourers he
broadened the hill on which it stood, buttressed it with a
triple terrace, and applied so much art and labour to the
work that his Temple was regarded as beyond dispute the
most beautiful building in Asia, and by many people as the
most beautiful in the world.   The world was an eye, people
said in Jerusalem, the white was the sea, the iris the land,
Jerusalem the pupil ; but the Temple was the image that
appeared in the pupil.

It was touched neither by the brush of the painter nor
the chisel of the sculptor ; it owed its effect solely to the
harmony of its great masses and the rareness of the materials
employed.   Mighty galleries ran round it on every side ;
they provided shelter from the rain, and cool shade from
the sun ; they were greatly frequented by the people.
The most beautiful of these halls was that in which the
High Council sat.   There was also a synagogue in the
Temple, many booths, a hall where the sacrificial lambs were

sold, halls where holy and unholy perfumes were to be had, and finally the banks of the money changers.

A trellis of stone work separated these profane precincts from the holy ones. There Greek and Latin inscriptions were set in prominent positions threatening any Gentile who entered with the penalty of death. The farther one penetrated into the Temple, the smaller grew the number of those who were allowed admittance ; the sick were forbidden to enter the sacred courts, also all cripples, also any who had touched the dead. For the women was reserved one single great room ; but they were not allowed to set foot in it during the period of menstruation. The inner courts were reserved for the priests ; but, even among them, those who were not of flawless growth were forbidden to set foot in certain of the more sacred rooms.

White and golden the Temple hung on its terraces above the city ; from the distance it looked like a snow covered hill. From its roofs sharp golden spikes rose in serried ranks, so that it might not be defiled by the droppings of birds. The courts and halls were ingeniously inlaid with marble. There were terraces, gates, columns everywhere, most of them of marble, many inlaid with gold and silver, or with the noblest of metals, Corinthian bronze, that unique alloy which had resulted from the melting together of rare metals during the burning of Corinth. Above the door that led to the holy chamber Herod had affixed the emblem of Israel, a cluster of grapes. Of solid gold, it flaunted there sumptuously ; the cluster was as big as a man.

Art works of world fame ornamented the Inner Temple. There could be seen the candlestick with the seven branches, whose lights signified the seven planets : the Sun, the Moon, Mercury, Venus, Mars, Jupiter and Saturn. There was also the table with the twelve shewbreads, which symbolised the Zodiac and the months of the year. There stood the vessel with the thirteen different kinds of frankincense, all of which were wrested either from the sea, or the uninhabited wilderness, or the inhabited earth, showing that everything came from God, and existed for the glory of God.

Far within the Temple, in the most secure position, lay the Temple treasury, where the state treasures were kept ; a considerable portion of the gold and costly rarities of the earth. The vestments of the High Priests were also kept there, the sacred bands, the Temple jewels, the golden fillet that bore the name of Jehovah. There had been a long and protracted dispute between Rome and Jerusalem before these vestments were finally allowed to repose in the Temple treasury, and in that dispute much blood had flowed.

In the heart of the precinct reserved for the priests, once more shut off by a veil, was the Holy of Holies. It was dark and empty, only a rude rock rose from the bare floor, the rock Shetijah. Here, the Jews declared, Jehovah had His dwelling place. Nobody dared to enter the room. Only once in the year, on the day on which Jehovah was reconciled to His people, did the High Priest enter the Holy of Holies. All the Jews in the world fasted on that day ; the halls and courts of the Temple were packed with people. They waited for the High Priest to call on Jehovah by His name. For Jehovah's name must not be pronounced ; even to attempt it was a mortal sin. So only on this one day did the High Priest call on God by His name. There were not many who could hear the Name when it issued from the mouth of the priest ; but all thought that they heard it, and in tens of thousands they fell on their knees on the floor of the Temple.

There was much strange talk in the world about the mystery behind the veil of the Holy of Holies The Jews maintained that, as Jehovah was invisible, there was no image of Him there. But the world would not believe that the room was simply empty. These Jews sacrificed to a God, so their God must be there, visible, present in his image. Yes, certainly this Jehovah must be there, and the jealous Jews simply concealed the fact so that they might keep Him to themselves. The enemies of the Jews, above all the ironical and enlightened Greeks, maintained that it was merely the head of an ass that was worshipped in the Holy of Holies. But the mockery of the Greeks had no effect. The clever and clear-headed Romans, no less than the ignorant barbarians, became silent and reflective when the God of the Jews was spoken off; the uncanny, invisible God in the Holy of Holies remained a mystery and a source of fear to the world.

The Jews all over the world regarded the Temple as their true home, as an inexhaustible fountain of strength. Whether they lived by the Ebro or the Indus, the coast of Britain or the upper course of the Nile, always when they prayed they turned their faces towards Jerusalem and the Temple. All sent tribute to the Temple with willing hearts ; all made a pilgrimage to it, or at least planned some day to bring their lamb to the Temple at the Easter festival. When any enterprise succeeded with them they gave thanks to the invisible God in the Temple ; when they were sick and in need they prayed to Him for help. Only within the Temple precinct was the soil pure, and Jews who lived in foreign countries sent their dead to Jerusalem, so that in death at least they might be at rest. For scattered though they were, here they had a home.

G*

12

WHEN the news reached Rome that the palace in Tiberias had been sacked the Emperor was away on a cultural tour in Greece.   During his absence he had left to his private minister Claudius Helius the direction of state affairs. Helius called at once a meeting of the cabinet.   So there the thirty-seven gentlemen sat, all of them possessors of high offices in the court.   The news that rebellion had broken out in Judaea anew moved them profoundly.   Ten years before these tidings would have been an unimportant despatch from an unimportant province.   Now the unfortunate Jews had hit the Grovernment on its most sensitive spot and imperilled its most weighty project, the new Oriental campaign.

It was these thirty-seven men who had put that mighty project on a solid basis.   They had secured ports in Southern Arabia for the sea route to India, and also the financial resources for an expedition to Ethiopia and a still more daring one to the Caspian Gate.   In accordance with the military plans of the two commanders, Corbulo and Tiberius Alexander, the troops had already been set in motion.   The twenty-second legion, as well as all the troops that could be spared from Germany, England, and Dalmatia, were on their way to the East ; and the fifteenth legion had already been despatched to Egypt.   And now the whole magnificent plan was to be upset through this revolt which had burst out in the very middle of the army's route.   Oh, they had been too ready to believe the assurances of the local authorities that the province would soon return to peace of itself.   Now it was clear that that would not happen, and that to crush the revolt they would have to employ a considerable force and waste a great deal of valuable time.

The majority of the ministers were not Romans, but passionately Greek in their sympathies ; their hearts were fixed on making Greece and the Orient the real centre of the Empire. They foamed with rage, these councillors and generals of the new Alexander, when they reflected that their glorious hopes must be postponed, or perhaps ruined for ever, through the mad folly of the Jews.

But outwardly they remained grave and impassive. Many of them, indeed the majority, were sons or grandsons of slaves, and precisely for that reason were resolved to show, now that they had attained power, the icy dignity of ancient Roman senators.

Claudius Helius mentioned the bad news from Judaea, and spoke of its bearing on their great oriental project. Claudius Helius himself had been born a slave. He was flawlessly built, dark and handsome, with a face of regular and yet energetic beauty. He bore the seal of the Emperor. Anybody else in his place would have accompanied the Emperor to Greece ; it was dangerous to expose the ruler for so long to hostile influences. Claudius Helius had preferred to remain in Rome. Almost certainly any measure that he hit upon would fail to please the Emperor ; and it seemed probable that Claudius Helius would die young, by opening an artery or inhaling gold foil. That was not too dear a price for the rulership of the world.

He spoke quietly, to the point, and without extenuating anything. They had taken the disturbances in Judaea too lightly, now they must take them all the more seriously. "We have all been mistaken," he admitted bluntly, " with a single exception. I beg that gentleman to give his opinion."

Although they could not endure the withered, vulture-nosed Philip Talassos, the members of the Cabinet gazed now with respect at the Minister of the Orient. He had warned them at the beginning that they should not allow themselves to be lulled into false security by the cunning, sickly-sweet propitiatory talk in Jerusalem. He had been a little absurd with his eternal fear of the Jews, his senile hate. Now it seemed that the eye of hate had seen more clearly than the tolerantly sceptical glance of the others.

The minister Philip Talassos allowed no trace of his satisfaction to be seen. He sat in his place, small, bent and insignificant as ever. But inwardly he was uplifted with a great exultation ; it seemed to him that the very scars he had borne since the time he was a slave had vanished at last. Now, after this looting of the palace in Tiberias, surely a deed brought about by favourable gods, after this new measurelessly brazen breach of every promise, the time was ripe for the great final reckoning. Rome could not any longer content itself with a mild punishment, the execution of a few thousand rebels, a million or two in compensation, or anything like that ; the others must surely see that too. The minister Philip Talassos said : " Jerusalem must be destroyed."

He did not raise his voice, nor did it even tremble. But this was the greatest moment of his life, and whenever he should have to leave it, he could now die in peace. In his heart he shouted, " Nablion ! " Yes, in spite of all that the interpreter Zachaeus had said, it was " Nablion." He saw the soldiers falling upon this insolent city of Jerusalem, saw them seizing the inhabitants by their beards and striking them dead, saw them burning houses, tearing down walls, and rasing the vain and flaunting Temple to the ground. But nothing of this was betrayed in his voice, as he matter-of-factly, almost morosely, stated : " Jerusalem must be destroyed."

There was a silence, and somebody sighed. Claudius Helius turned his beautiful dark face towards Reginus, and asked whether the director of the Imperial Pearl Fisheries had anything to say. Claudius Reginus had nothing to say. These Galileans had really behaved too stupidly. Now there was nothing for it but to turn the army on them.

Claudius Helius summed up. He would then, with the consent of his colleagues, beg the Emperor to begin his campaign against Judaea as quickly as possible. Hitherto the couriers to Greece had been able to arrive with the fortune bringing laurel garland on their spears ; this time, so as to impress the Emperor how grave the situation was in Rome, the courier would be given the feather which foretold evil.

13

At the request of Claudius Helius the Senate ordered the Temple of Janus to be opened as a sign that the Empire was at war. The officiating senator Marullus expressed, not without irony, his regret to Claudius Helius that the ceremony had not a more brilliant excuse. For a year the world had been at peace. The city of Rome was taken by surprise now that the heavy wings of the door of the Temple of Janus groaningly opened, disclosing the image of the two-faced god, the god of doubt, for when he was seen the beginning was known, but nobody knew the end. Many had an uncomfortable feeling when they learned that the good and great Jupiter of their Capitol was beginning a war against the uncanny and formless God in the East.

In the poorer quarters people were exultant that the Emperor was at last going to deal drastically with the Jews. The Jews had insinuated themselves everywhere ; already the whole business quarter was permeated by them, and so their competitors were delighted to be allowed to give a patriotic vent to their hatred. In the taverns people told the ancient fable that the Jews worshipped the head of an ass in the Holy of Holies and at their Paschal feasts sacrificed Greek children to their sacred donkey. Obscene and threatening inscriptions were scribbled on the walls of the synagogues. In the baths of Flora the circumcised were cudgelled and flung into the street. In a cookshop in the Subura several Jews were requested to eat pork, and when they refused their mouths were prised open and crammed with the horrible and forbidden food. In the vicinity of the Gate of the Three Ways a shop which sold kosher fish sauces was looted, and the crowd broke the bottles and smeared the hair and beards of the Jews with the contents. But the police soon put an end to the distrubance.

The gentlemen of the Senate, the diplomatic service and high finance now came into their own. Countless new positions must be secured and occupied ; the scent of plunder was in the air. Old superannuated generals bestirred themselves. The Forum re-echoed with happy and excited laughter ; in the colonnades of Livia, the Campus Martius and the public baths there was a great bustle. Everybody had his own candidate to support, his particular interests to push ; the Abbess of the Vestals herself went every day in her litter to the Palatine, to see that the ministers attended to her wishes.

The price of gold, costly fabrics and slaves fell in the exchanges of Delos and Rome, for in Judaea there would be abundance of these commodities to be picked up. The price of grain soared, for the fighting troops would need considerable extra supplies. There was great activity among the shipping firms, and men worked feverishly on the wharves at Ravenna, Puteoli and Ostia. In the houses of Claudius Reginus and Junius Thrax, in the palace of the senator Marullus, couriers kept coming and going. These gentlemen regarded the war in Judaea with honest sorrow. But seeing that in any case it provided new business opportunities, why should the plums be pocketed by others?

The Jews were overwhelmed with confusion and grief. They knew quite well, from friends in Jerusalem, what had happened, knew the role that Joseph was playing. Was it credible that that man, who had lived with them and dressed like them and spoken like them, and knew Rome's power; was it credible that Doctor Joseph Ben Matthias could have set himself at the head of such a hopeless national adventure? Claudius Reginus was most bitterly annoyed of all with the members of the High Council. How could they have sent that minor essayist to Galilee? People like him should be allowed to get rid of their bile in books, but not to vent it in serious politics. Many prominent Jews in Rome hastened to the Government to express their loathing of the conduct of these fanatics and criminals in Galilee. The Government gave these stammering gentlemen comforting assurances. The five million Jews who were scattered over the Empire were loyal subjects and paid high taxes. The Government had not the slightest intention of injuring them.

The news from Galilee was a severe blow to the actor Demetrius Libanus. He felt both saddened and exalted. He invited a few intimate Jewish friends to a party, and behind carefully locked doors recited several chapters out of the history of the Maccabees. He had always known that an intense inner fire burned in young Doctor Joseph. But nobody knew better than he how foolish a war against Rome would be. Besides, at the moment he was the only one in Rome who was seriously suffering because of the disturbance in Judaea. For now the nickname Apella was once more being flung at the Jews in the streets of Rome. Already people were pressing him to give a public performance in his famous role. Should he refuse, the crowd would execrate him as boundlessly as they had acclaimed him hitherto.

The great majority of the Roman Jews were shaken, desperate, despairing. They read the books of the prophets. " O daughter of Zion, gird thee with sackcloth and wallow thyself in ashes ; make thee mourning, as for an only son, most bitter lamentation ; for the spoiler shall suddenly come upon us." They read and their hearts were filled with fear. They locked their houses, they fasted, they prayed in all the synagogues. The Romans did not disturb these services. There were a few among the Jews in Rome who saw, in the uprising of Judaea, the fulfilment of the old prophecies of a Redeemer. Among them was Irene, the wife of Doctor Licinus. She listened in silence when her husband expressed his loathing of the blasphemous madman, but in her heart she exulted. The feeling she had cherished for Joseph had not been unworthy ; she had always known that he was a great man in Israel, one of the line of the prophets, a soldier of Jehovah.

14

THE Emperor was in the capital of Greece, the gay city of Corinth, now ringing with public rejoicings, when the courier arrived with the ominous feather on his spear.

The young ruler of the world had never felt more happy in his life. Greece, the most cultivated country in the world, acclaimed him, honestly admired his literary art, his amiability, his pleasant manners. And then there was the thought that this Greek tour was only the prelude to a far greater enterprise. Like a sublime dream, and yet

not a dream, for it would presently be realised, his oriental
campaign floated before him ; he would add to his own
half of the world the other, nobler, wiser half, put the
finishing touch to the work of the greatest man that had
ever lived. He would make both halves of the world rich
and happy under the ægis of his imperial name.

To-day he had crowned his Greek tour by a great deed.
With a golden spade he had cut the first turf, thus beginning
a canal that was to divide the isthmus of Corinth. To-
morrow he would celebrate the inauguration of this canal
by a public spectacle. He had himself composed the final
verses in which the god appeared in his glory, commanding
the eagle to spread it wings for the great flight.

It was immediately after the Emperor had returned to
his palace in Corinth from the isthmus that the courier
arrived with the news of Judaea. The Emperor read the
despatch and threw it on the table on top of the manuscript
of the play which was to be performed next day. His
gaze fell on the line : " Who rules the tides of ocean, and
the sun revolves at his will." He slowly raised his beautiful,
slightly puffy face, lowered it again, raised it again, lowered
it again.

He got up with compressed lips. It was the jealousy of
the gods. They were envious of his oriental campaign.
" Who rules the tides of ocean, and the sun revolves at his
will." The whole final verse had no meaning except as a
prologue to the oriental campaign. It had no point now.

Gessius Florus, the Governor of Judaea, was dead, cut
down on the battlefield. He had escaped lightly. Of
course this Gallus fellow would have to be recalled in disgrace. A fool like that was of no use for the insolent
country of Judaea.

The Emperor considered. Whom should he send to

Judaea ? Jerusalem had the strongest fortress in all the
East ; the people there, Poppaea had told him so, were
fanatical and stubborn. The war would have to be conducted with severity. It must not last long. In no
circumstances would he allow the oriental campaign to be
postponed for more than a year. For Judaea he needed a
stern and clear-headed man. A man without imagination.
One who would use the power entrusted to him agaiust
Jerusalem alone, and not against his emperor by any chance.

Where was he to find such a man ? His advisers mentioned names. And very few at that. And when they
were considered critically they became still fewer. Finally
only one remained, Mucianus.

The Emperor closed his eyes in dejection ; even with the
senator Mucianus one had to exercise caution. The
Emperor recalled him quite clearly. A little fellow ener-
vated by excessive indulgence in pleasure, with a keen,
lined face, extremely well groomed. As he limped slightly,
he always carried a stick ; but usually he carried it behind
his back in one hand, a habit which had got on the Emperor's nerves. Nor could the Emperor endure the way
in which the man's face perpetually twitched. Certainly,
Mucianus had a clear sharp mind ; he would soon settle
the rebellious province. But so boundless was the ambition
of this man who had already fallen once and climbed to
power again, and was now on the threshold of old age, that
if one gave him more power he might easily feel tempted
to start dangerous tricks.

The Emperor sighed unhappily and sat down again before
the manuscript of the play. He glanced over it discontentedly.
" And the sun revolves." The very best lines would have
to go. He could no longer entrust the role to an actor ;
he must himself take the part of the god. No, he dared not

give this man Mucianus too much scope ; one shouldn't
put temptation in any man's way.   By now it was late in
the night.   He could not summon the concentration
necessary to rewrite the lines he had had to score out of the
final speech of the god.   He pushed the manuscript aside.
In his dressing-gown he trailed across to the room of his
mistress Calvia.   In deep dejection, his puffy face covered
with perspiration, he sat down on her bed and sighed.   He
weighed once more the pros and cons.   This and that spoke
for Mucianus.   Then send him, said Calvia.   This and
the other spoke against Mucianus.   Then don't send him.
Perhaps they would find someone else.   The Emperor
refused to brood on the matter any longer ; he had turned
over the arguments in his head quite long enough ; now he
would wait for an inspiration.   He would wait for luck,
his luck.   He would occupy his mind with the play and
nothing else.   To-morrow after the play was over he would
make his decision.

In Rome they waited in tense excitement for his decision.
It came before the performance was over.   While the
Emperor was sitting in his dressing-room in the heavy mask
and the high buskins of the god, waiting for his call, the
inspiration came to him.   Yes, he would appoint Mucianus ;
but he would not appoint him alone ; he would name a
second man to keep an eye on him.   And he already knew
who that man was to be.   All this time an old general had
been in his entourage, a man who had made a bid for the
highest offices, only to tumble headlong from them as
soon as they were attained ; a faint touch of the ludicrous
clung to him because of his perpetual failures.   His name
was Vespasian.   He looked more like a drover than a
general ; but he had shown his capacities in the British
campaign, and was regarded as an excellent soldier.   It

was true that the fellow had often irritated the Emperor. Only with the greatest pains was he able to conceal his difficulty in attending when the Emperor gave a recitation, and three days before he had simply gone to sleep ; yes, while the Emperor was declaiming the beautiful lines about Danäe and the wind-shaken leaves, he had unmistakably snored. The Emperor had at first thought of chastising him, but really he felt a certain pity for this dolt to whom the gods had denied all feeling for higher things. So far he had done nothing. He had merely refused to admit the man into his presence. To-day and yesterday he had noticed the fellow standing in the distance with a dejected and loyal look. Yes, that was his man ; Vespasian would scarcely dare to nourish overweening thoughts. He would send him to Judaea. In the first place, he would not have to see the fellow's face for a long time to come, and in the second, the sly, blunt fellow was the very man to keep an eye on the elegant Mucianus. He would divide the supreme powers, and appoint Mucianus Governor-General of Syria, Vespasian commander in Judaea. The one would have no military, the other no political, authority, and each would act as a spy on the other.

In spite of the heavy, hot mask of the god which he was wearing the Emperor smiled. Really it was an excellent solution, it was an inspiration. He stepped on to the stage and recited the sonorous verses of the god. The part was a short one ; but never, it seemed to him, had he spoken his words so perfectly as to-day. He deserved his applause.

15

TITUS FLAVIUS VESPASIAN returned from the performance to the little house in the suburbs which he had rented from the merchant Laches for his stay in Corinth. He flung

down his cloak and his gala costume, cursed the servant
because he did not fold up the precious garment with sufficient
care, drew on a clean but somewhat worn indoor garb
over his thick underclothing, for it was a cold day in
early spring, and after all he was fifty-eight and could feel
again a twinge of his rheumatism.

He stamped up and down in a thoroughly bad temper ;
there were deep puckers on his brow, his round peasant
face was gloomy, his large mouth compressed, and he sighed
loudly and despondently. The festive performance had
not been a very festive business for him. Wherever he
went an icy silence had fallen, people had hardly even
answered his greeting, and the chamberlain Gortyn, that
smooth swine, had in answer to his question if he could
pay his respects to the Emperor one of these days answered
in his impudent provincial Greek : " You can go to the
devil."

And really when he considered the situation there was
nothing else left for him to do. How on earth could he
have made that awful blunder three days ago ? Now this
whole expensive Greek tour was without any point. And
the incident during the Emperor's recitation hadn't been
half so bad as it was painted. He had fallen asleep, he
admitted it. But he hadn't snored ; it was an impudent
slander of that son of a bitch of a chamberlain. It was
only that he always breathed loudly when he slept.

The old general beat his arms to warm himself. Of
course he would never be admitted to the Emperor's presence
again after this ; even a blind man could have seen that in
the theatre that afternoon. He might count himself lucky
if he wasn't charged with lese-majesty because of his alleged
snoring exploit. The best thing for him would be to return
quietly to his Italian estate.

For himself he wasn't displeased at the thought that he could spend the rest of his days in peace. If he had been left to himself he would never have dragged his old bones after the Emperor to Greece to challenge fortune for the last time. But his dear crony, Dame Caenis, had given him no peace. Never had she allowed him to indulge his peasant sloth. Continually she had goaded him on until he had climbed to power, and then luckily fallen again.

All this had begun when he was still young, and the cursed peasant superstition of his mother was to blame for it. The fact that at his birth an ancient oak, sacred to Mars, had sent out a new and unusually beautiful shoot, had been taken by the pragmatic dame as a certain omen of good luck, foretelling that her son was destined by fate to rise higher than the tax-gatherers, provincial bankers and officers of the line who had been his forefathers. From his childhood he had loved a farmer's life ; he would have preferred to remain to the end of his days on his parents' property, disposing of its products with all the hard sagacity of a peasant. But his resolute mother had not relaxed until she had implanted in him, too, her indestructible faith in his great future, and driven him against his will into the path of political and military reputation.

The old general, when he thought of all the failures that this course had brought him, snorted aloud and compressed his lips more tightly. Three times, one after another, he had fallen from power. Finally with much labour he had succeeded in becoming Prefect of Rome. For two months everything went perfectly. His police functioned smoothly, the forces securing law and order at the athletic contests and theatrical performances were brilliantly efficient, the transport of foodstuffs to the markets was methodically regulated, and the streets of Rome were kept in admirable

condition. Yet it was the state of the streets that had let
him down. The Emperor Claudius had yielded to an
unfortunate whim; yes, just when he was showing his
capital to certain foreign ambassadors he had yielded to the
unfortunate whim of taking one of the few side streets
that were badly kept, and there the whole festive procession
had remained sticking in the mud. As an example the
Emperor had commanded that the Prefect's gala costume
should be smeared with mud and horse-dung from head to
foot.

When Vespasian thought of that affair a wry look crossed
his crafty peasant face, and he grinned. The business had
ended well enough ; he must, of course, have been a pretty
ridiculous sight with his wide sleeves filled with horse
dung ; but evidently the Emperor had imprinted this
sordidly comic spectacle on his mind as something highly
funny. In any case after that Vespasian was shown no
further sign of disfavour ; rather the contrary. He had
never had much use for dignity, and from then on, knowing
quite well what he was doing, he pestered the highest
legislative body in the Empire, the Senate, with requests of
almost clownish servility, delivered with the most innocent
air, so that even that hardened audience did not know
whether to laugh or cry. In any case they granted his
requests.

Now when, after many years, he considered what he
had done and left undone, he could not reproach himself
with inconsistency. He had married Domitilla, the dis-
carded mistress of the officer Capella, and through the
intrigues and connections of that very gifted gentleman
had come in touch with the minister Narcissus, the favourite
of the Emperor Claudius. Narcissus was a man after his
heart. With him one could talk frankly. He demanded

his commission, but he was willing to put something in the way of a capable man. Those had been great days when Narcissus sent him to crush the rebels in Britain. There his enemies were not snobbish courtiers who wove subtle intrigues against him, but very real savages whom he could shoot down and get at with his sword, and the objects that had to be won and that he did win were real objects, land, coasts, forests, islands. That was the time when he had come nearest to fulfilling the prophecy of the sacred oak. When he returned he was accorded an official triumphal entry and given for two months the highest post of honour in the state.

The general blew on his fingers to warm them and rubbed the backs of his hands. Of course after these two months in which he had risen so high, his fall had been all the greater. Well, that had been fate. A new emperor rose to the throne, new ministers were appointed ; he fell out of favour. In the meantime his mother had died, and now that her energetic faith was no longer there to spur him on, he had hoped to spend the rest of his days in quietly attending to his own affairs. He had settled down comfortably on his country estate without feeling envious of his brother Sabinus, who had risen to a high position and remained there imperturbably.

But now Caenis had entered his life. The daughter of a slave, she had attracted the attention of her betters. The Emperor's mother Antonia had had the young girl educated, and appointed her as her secretary. She knew what Vespasian wanted from life, she understood his type. Like him she did not give a farthing for dignity and display ; like him she enjoyed rough jests and the rude slyness of a soldier ; like him she thought rapidly and matter-of-factly ; like him she laughed at and was irritated by his stiff and

formal brother Sabinus. But in her heart, too, he soon
had to admit half in sorrow and half in gratification, the
faith of his mother in his high destiny had taken root, far
more deeply indeed than in himself. She goaded him on
until once more he emerged sighing and grumbling out of
his peaceful country life to take part in the dust and heat
of Rome. This time he managed to snatch the government
of the province of Africa. A position which brought him
the worst among the many bad years of his life. For the
rich province, and the people no less than the snobbish
aristocracy, wanted to have an ornamental governor and
not Vespasian, the rough peasant. His measures were
sabotaged. Wherever he showed himself there were
riots. In the city of Hadrunet he was bombarded with
rotten turnips. He did not mind the rotten turnips
any more than the horse dung he had been smeared with
in Emperor Claudius's reign ; but unfortunately they had
very practical consequences ; he was recalled. A hard
blow, for he had invested all his money in the province in
shady concerns from which the Governor might have been
able to extract a great deal of money, but a private citizen
nothing at all. So there he was left, with his talents for
finance. Returned to the estates which belonged to him
and his brother in common, he had to mortgage himself
heavily to the supercilious Sabinus to get relief from his
more crushing liabilities. During that whole year the
cheerful Vespasian found only once an occasion for laughter.
The province of Africa put up an ironical commemoration
tablet in his honour, inscribed with the words : " The
honest Governor." He still grinned when he thought of
that single positive result of his activities in Africa.

Since then everything had gone wrong with him. He
had entered the transport business, and supported by the

resolute Caenis had trafficked also in the selling of offices
and titles. But he had allowed himself to be caught in a
piece of sharp practice and had again escaped heavy punishment only through the intervention of his acidulous brother.
He was now fifty-eight ; nobody imagined for a moment
that he would once more drive in his triumphal car past the
Forum and be clothed in the robes of a consul. Wherever
he appeared people grinned and talked of rotten turnips.
Everybody called him the forwarding agent. His brother
Sabinus, now chief of the police in Rome, made a wry face
whenever his name was mentioned and said sourly : " Don't
talk of him. I can feel the smell of rotten turnips when
that man's name is mentioned."

Now, after this last miscarriage in Greece, he was finally
done for. Yet it was good in a way that he should be able
to pass the little that was left of his life as he pleased. The
very next day he would set off on the return journey. First
he would settle his affairs here in Corinth with the merchant
Laches, who had let the house to him. The man behaved
as if he was doing a favour in suffering the disgraced general
to live in his house at an extortionate rent. Vespasian
liked to dress down in the blunt old Roman fashion those
refined and affected Greeks who laughed at him to his face
and behind his back. Once that piece of business was
finished he would travel back to Italy with a happy mind,
would settle down there, spending half the year on his
estate near Cosa, the other half on his estate near Nursia ;
he would breed his mules and look after his olives, drink
wine and crack jokes with his neighbours, and spend the
afternoons with Caenis or one of his maids. And then, in
five years or ten, when he ended his days and they burned
his body, Caenis would shed many honest tears, Sabinus
would be relieved at being rid of his compromising brother,

the other mourners would grin and whisper to each other something about rotten turnips, and the beautiful young shoot of the sacred tree of Mars would have flourished in vain.

Titus Flavius Vespasian, ex-commander of a Roman legion in England, ex-consul of Rome, ex-governor of Africa, in disgrace at court, owing one million one hundred thousand sesterces of debts, and who had been requested a little while ago by the chamberlain Gortyn to go to the devil, had come to terms with himself. He was quite satisfied. He would now go down to the quay and haggle with these slippery Greeks over the price for his return journey. Then he would clap Caenis on the thigh and say : " Well, old girl, now it's settled. From now on you won't tempt me from my chimney corner no matter what you do." Yes, at bottom he was glad. With a contented sigh he flung his cloak over his shoulders.

As he was going out the merchant Laches greeted him with unusual politeness, indeed almost with confusion, and bowed repeatedly and humbly. Behind him came a grave imperial courier with a solemn official countenance, the auspicious laurel garland on his staff of office.

The courier stretched forth his spear and indicated the laurel garland. He announced, " Message from His Majesty to the consul Vespasian." For a long time Vespasian had not heard his diminished title ; in astonishment he put out his hand for the sealed letter and gazed once more at the messenger's staff. Yes, it was the laurel, not the feather ; so it could have nothing to do with that unlucky mistake of his in falling asleep in the middle of the Emperor's recitation. Very unceremoniously he broke the seal in the presence of the courier and the inquisitive Laches. His ample lips parted ; his round, broad peasant face creased into folds ; he grinned. He clapped the courier roughly on the shoulder and shouted : " Laches, you old rascal, give this fellow three drachmas to drink my health. No, stop, two will be enough." He ran upstairs to the top storey, waving the letter in his hand, clapped his old friend Caenis on the bottom, and bawled : " Caenis, old girl, we've brought it off ! "

Dame Caenis and he usually knew what each other thought and felt without needing to express it in words. But now they both talked at the same time. They seized each other by the shoulders, laughing and shouting, set each other free again, danced round the room, now together, now separately. They didn't care who heard them ; they laid bare their hearts without shame.

By Jupiter, this journey had been worth while ! The subjugation of the rebellious province of Judaea : that was a practical proposition which seemed to be almost made for a man with Vespasian's gifts. These brilliant strategists could occupy themselves with such utopian nonsense as this oriental campaign ; that was all very well for Corbulo or Tiberius Alexander. He, Vespasian, drew his cloak over his ears when people talked of such windy imperialistic dreams. But at the news of a real job like this expedition to Judaea the heart of the old general rose within him. Now the great commanders could wait ; he was the man of the hour now. These blessed Jews. Three cheers for them, and another three cheers ! They should have revolted long ago.

He was prodigiously pleased. Dame Caenis gave instructions to the merchant Laches to procure Vespasian's favourite dishes for him, no matter what they cost. Also he should secure for that afternoon a particularly appetising girl, not too thin, for Vespasian's delectation. But it

seemed that Vespasian had no gratitude for such attentions ;
he had sat down to work. He was no longer the old
peasant, but the general, the commander, who with cold
intelligence sets about the execution of his task. The
Syrian regiments were wretchedly demoralised ; he would
teach the rascals what Roman discipline was. Probably
the Government would try to fob him off with the fifteenth
legion which had just been sent to Egypt. Or the twenty-
second, seeing that it had already been despatched in any
case for this fatuous oriental campaign. But he wouldn't
allow himself to be put off in that way. He would have to
bargain with the military council for every single man.
But he wouldn't hesitate to use blunt words if it was necessary, and let these gentlemen know clearly and distinctly
what was what. Gentlemen, he would say, this time it
isn't a matter of fighting hysterical savages like the Germans ; we are confronted with a people organised for war.

He would ask for an interview at the palace that very
day. With a smirk he put on his gala uniform, which only
three hours before he had believed he would never need
again. In the imperial residence he was received by the
chamberlain Gortyn. Gortyn stretched out his arm in
greeting. A curt, stiff conversation followed. Yes, the
general could see His Majesty in about an hour. And the
prefect of the Guards ? The prefect would see him at
once. As he passed the chamberlain Gortyn to confer
with the prefect of the Guards, Vespasian said casually and
good-humouredly, "Well, my lad, who can go to the
devil now ? "

16

THE winter passed all too quickly. A good winter for
Joseph. He worked feverishly. He jeered at the technique of the Romans, but he did not disdain to imitate it.

He had accumulated experience in Rome ; he had ideas. He banished everything petty from his heart ; only one thing mattered to him : to prepare his country for the attack. His faith grew. Babylon, Egypt, the empire of the Seleukides, had they not been just as mighty as Rome ? And yet Judaea had been able to withstand them. What was the strongest army against the breath of God ? God would sweep their men from the land like empty chaff, and their engines of war into the sea like straw.

In the cities, in the halls of the synagogues, at the great places of assembly, in the circuses of Tiberias and Sepphoris, under the free sky, crowds gathered round Joseph. " Marin ! Marin ! Our Lord ! Our Lord ! " they hailed him. Lean and slender, he stood outlined against the wide landscape, uplifted his face with the burning eyes, and, his hands raised on high, spoke words of dark power, of strong confidence. Jehovah had consecrated this land ; now the Roman leprosy had spread over it. The pestilence must be rooted out, exterminated, destroyed. In what did these Romans put their trust when they marched so insolently on Judaea ? They had their armies, their ridiculous technique. Their power could be exactly calculated : their legions consisting of ten thousand men each, ten cohorts, sixty companies, and in addition sixty-five batteries. Israel had its God Jehovah. He was without shape and His power could not be calculated, but before His breath the besieging engines would fail and the legions melt away. Rome had power. But its power was already past, for it had lifted its insolent hand against Jehovah and His chosen people, who had for so long found favour in His eyes : against His first born, His heir, Israel. The time was fulfilled. Rome had been, but the kingdom of the Messiah was still to be, and it was near. He would come, to-day or to-morrow,

perhaps He had already appeared. It was unthinkable that
the people with whom Jehovah had made a covenant should
be merely tolerated in His land, and be treated as dirt by
their rulers. Let them bring on their legions through the
wastes and across the sea in ships. Judaea must believe
and fight. The Romans had their companies and their
engines of war ; the Jews had Jehovah and His hosts.

17

WINTER was over ; a beautiful spring smiled on the vineyards and olive terraces and sycamore groves of Galilee.
The banks of the Lake of Genezareth near Magdala, where
Joseph still had his headquarters, were heavy with perfumed blossoms ; the people breathed lightly and happily.
During these radiant spring days the Romans appeared.
At first their advance troops, coming from the north and
the seaports, reconnoitred the country ; they no longer
avoided the troops that Joseph sent out to skirmish. Then
the whole Roman force marched in, three entire legions
with horses and wagons and strong reinforcements from
the vassal states. In front came the light infantry. Then
the first division of the heavy infantry. Then the pioneers,
to clear the rough parts of the route, level difficult places,
cut down thickets, so that the army might not be hindered
in its march. Then the escort of the commander and his
general staff. Then the cavalry and artillery, the powerful
siege engines, the battering rams which were so greatly
feared, the ballistas and catapults ; then the standard, the
divine eagle. Then the main body of the army in ranks of
six men. Finally, the immense baggage, the commissariat,
the jurists and revenue officials. And at the very end a
crowd of civilians : diplomats, bankers, a throng of merchants consisting chiefly of jewellers and slave-dealers,

auctioneers to sell the booty, private couriers for the
diplomats and rich magnates ; and women.

When the Romans appeared the country became very
still. Many of the volunteers deserted. Slowly and
inexorably the Roman army advanced. Vespasian reduced
Galilee according to plan, both the country itself and the
coast.

It should really have been King Agrippa's business to
subjugate the west bank of the Lake of Genezareth ; for
this part, containing the cities of Tiberias and Magdala,
belonged to him. But the elegant king was an amiable,
good-natured man ; it went against his grain to undertake
himself the severe measures that would be necessary to
chastise the rebels. So Vespasian fulfilled the prayer of
this allied prince who was so devoted to Rome, and agreed
to undertake the punitive expedition himself. Tiberias
submitted to him without resistance. The strongly fortified
city of Magdala attempted to defend itself. But it could
not hold out for long against the Roman artillery, and
treachery within did the rest. Many of the rebels fled into
the great Lake of Genezareth when the Romans burst into
the city.

The rebels requisitioned the little fisher fleet, so that the
Romans were forced to pursue them on rafts. A grotesque
water fight followed, a fight that produced much laughter
on the side of the Romans, and many dead on the side of
the Jews ; for the Romans had occupied the banks of the
lake. They managed to capsize a great number of the light
boats, and on their clumsy rafts enjoyed many an exciting
chase of their drowning enemies. They gazed with interest
at the men floundering in the water ; they laid bets
whether the Jews would prefer drowning to being slain.
They debated whether they should shoot their enemies

or wait until they clung to the rafts, and then cut off their
hands.   The beautiful lake, famous for its brilliant colours,
was dyed a uniform red on that day ; its banks, renowned for
their perfumed fragrance, stank for many weeks with
unburied corpses.   Its water was poisoned, but its fish
waxed very fat in the next few months, and the Romans
were pleased with their flavour.   But the Jews, on the
other hand, including even King Agrippa himself, refused
for years afterwards to eat fish taken from the Lake of
Genezareth.   Later the Jews made a song that began :
" The lake is red with blood far and wide by Magdala,
The shore is covered with corpses far and wide by Magdala."
After exact computation it was discovered that in this lake
fight four thousand two hundred Jews had been slain.
Which brought in Captain Sulpicius four thousand two
hundred sesterces ; for he had made a bet that the number
of dead would exceed four thousand.   If it had been beneath
that number he would have had to pay four thousand
sesterces and one more sesterce for each minus in his list.

Two days later Vespasian summoned his staff to a con-
sultation.   As far as most of the inhabitants of the city
were concerned it was possible to discover with a fair degree
of certainty whether they had been on the side of peace or
war.   But what was to be done with the fugitives who had
fled from all over Galilee into the strongly fortified city ?
There were about thirty-eight thousand of them.   To
discover whether each one individually was a rebel would
take far too much time.   Simply to let them go would
not do either, for most of them were under suspicion.   To
keep them in prolonged captivity would be too burdensome.
On the other hand they had surrendered to the Romans
without resistance, believing they would be spared, and
simply to cut them down seemed to Vespasian hardly fair.

The members of his staff, however, came after some vacillation to the unanimous conclusion that where Jews were concerned everything was allowable, and if expedience could not be reconciled with decency, then the former must have the preference. After some hesitation Vespasian agreed with this opinion. In equivocal Greek, which the prisoners found it difficult to understand, he granted them their freedom, but told them that only the road to Tiberias would be left open for their departure. The prisoners wished to believe that they were granted their freedom, and so they believed it, and withdrew by the road prescribed for them. The Romans, however, had lined the road to Tiberias with troops, and would not suffer any of the prisoners to take a byeway. When the thirty-eight thousand men reached Tiberias they were escorted into the great circus. They squatted there, tensely waiting to hear what the Roman commander would have to say to them. Soon Vespasian appeared. He gave instructions that those who were over fifty-five should fall out, also those who were sick. Many of the Jews smuggled themselves in among the sick, for they imagined that the others would have to return on foot to their homes, while they would enjoy the advantage of a conveyance. But they were mistaken. When all the old and sick had been segregated Vespasian commanded them to be cut down ; they were of no use for his purposes. From among the others he had six thousand of the most powerful men picked out, and sent them to the Emperor in Greece with a courteous letter saying that they would be useful for work on the Corinth canal. The rest he put up to auction as slaves, reserving the proceeds for the upkeep of the army. He sent a few thousand also as a present to King Agrippa.

In the course of this uprising a hundred and nine thousand

Jews were put up to auction as slaves, and the price of slaves
began to fall alarmingly ; in the eastern provinces it sank
from an average of two thousand sesterces to one thousand
three hundred for each slave.

18

JOSEPH gazed out from a wall tower of the small but strong
mountain fortress of Jotapat and watched the tenth legion
advancing. Already the geometricians were measuring
out the plans for the Roman camp. Joseph knew them,
these Roman camps. He knew that through centuries
of practice the legions had learned how to set them up
at once wherever they made a halt. He knew that two
hours after the work was begun the whole would be complete. Twelve hundred tents for every legion, with streets
between them, walls, gates and towers round them ; really
a well-fortified city. Gloomily and vigilantly Joseph had
watched the Romans gradually advancing in a great circle,
had seen them occupying the mountain peaks round him
and cautiously pushing forward through the valleys and
ravines. Now they had closed him in. By this time, in
all Galilee, there were only Jotapat and two other strong
fortresses in the hands of the Jews : the mountain fortresses
of Tabor and Gishala, where John was in command. If
the Romans took these fortresses the road to Jerusalem
would lie open to them. The Jewish commanders had
decided to keep these strongholds as long as possible, but at
the last moment to fight their way through and make for
the capital ; for there a great many troops were assembled,
but they had few leaders to organise them.

When Joseph saw that in addition to the other Roman
troops the tenth legion was now encamped beneath him
he felt a sort of grim satisfaction. Vespasian was not a

nervous gentleman like Cestius Gallus ; he had at his command not one, but three legions at full strength, the fifth, the tenth, and the fifteenth. Joseph would hardly be able to capture even one of the three golden eagles that these legions bore with them. But this fortress of Jotapat had good walls and towers ; it lay high, and the advance to it was fortunately steep ; he had abundance of food, and his men, above all those under Sapita, were in good spirits. Vespasian would have to exert himself if he was to demolish the walls of this fortress, and carry away the sacred scrolls from its synagogue.

Vespasian did not attempt any attack. His army lay there as idle as a log, but also as immovable as a log. Presumably he had decided to wait for Joseph to creep out of his hole in despair, or for the garrison to die of inanition.

A message from Jerusalem was smuggled through to Joseph. The capital, wrote his father Matthias, would not send troops to raise the siege. Doctor Eleasar Ben Simon had, it was true, urgently demanded that they should be sent, but there were certain people in Jerusalem who would not be displeased if Jotapat fell, if only Joseph fell with it. So he should surrender the fortress, for without help from outside it could not hold out for a fortnight. Joseph reflected stubbornly. It was May now. If Jotapat could hold out to the beginning of July, by then it would probably be too late in the year for the Romans to advance on Jerusalem. Did they not see that, these people in the Temple ? Well, he would save the blinded city in spite of itself. He wrote back to his father that he would hold Jotapat not only for two weeks, but for seven times seven days. Seven times seven days ; the words seemed to come involuntarily to him. It was with such dream-like certainty as this that the prophets of old must have seen their visions.

But Joseph's letter never reached his father. It was intercepted by the Romans, and the general staff laughed over the boastings of the Jewish commander; it was out of the question that Jotapat could hold out for so long.

The second week came, and the Romans still refrained from attacking. The town was well provided with food, but the water in the cisterns was running short; and Joseph had to ration it strictly. It was a hot summer and the besieged suffered more grievously every day from thirst. Many stole out of the town by subterranean ways in search of water; for the mountain was threaded with a wild and confused system of underground passages. But such attempts were foolhardy in the extreme. Anyone who fell into the hands of the Romans was crucified.

The officer who attended to the executions was a Captain Lucianus. He was at bottom a good-natured man, but he suffered greatly from the heat and in consequence was often in a bad temper. When this happened to be the case he ordered the prisoner to be bound to the cross, and that meant a very lingering and painful death. When he was in a better mood he allowed his soldiers to nail the prisoner's hands to the cross, so that the inflammation caused by the wound might bring a quicker end.

Evening after evening a doleful procession climbed to the heights where the crucifixions took place; the condemned carried the crosses on their shoulders, their outstretched arms were already tied to the horizontal bars. The nights cooled their suspended bodies, but the nights were short, and as the sun rose flies and other insects came. Birds gathered, and masterless dogs waited for the meal that would be theirs. The men hanging on the crosses repeated their confession of faith as they died : Hear, Israel ! Jehovah is our God, Jehovah is the only God. They went

on saying it as long as they could speak ; they cried it to
one another as they hung on their crosses.   Soon the Hebrew
phrase became popular in the Roman camp, a welcome
theme for all sorts of witticisms.   The army doctors com-
piled statistics showing how long it took on an average for
a man to die who was nailed to the cross, and how much
longer if he was merely bound to it.   They selected particularly vigorous and particular feeble prisoners for observa-
tion, and demonstrated that the midsummer heat contributed
very greatly to hasten the lethal process.   On all the hills
round about rose the crosses, and the men hanging on them
were changed evening after evening.   The Romans could
not provide separate crosses for all the crucified ; and although the neighbourhood was richly wooded they had
to economise in timber.

They required it to raise artificial walls and galleries
round the obstinate city.   They cut down all the woods
round about and used them to build these walls.   To
protect them as they worked they employed an ingenious
construction of hide and damp leather that neutralised the
effect of the burning oil and Greek fire that the besieged
poured down upon them.   The soldiers in Jotapat envied
the Romans who could use water for such a purpose.   They
made sorties, several times they succeeded in setting fire
to their enemies' works, but these were soon repaired again,
and the walls and galleries crept nearer.

Evening after evening Joseph gazed at them from the
walls.   If the galleries reached a certain point in the north
Jotapat was lost even if Jerusalem decided after all to send
troops to raise the siege.   Slowly Joseph's eyes swept the
horizon.   Everywhere on the hill-tops stood crosses ; the
mountain paths were lined with crosses.   The heads of
the crucified lay on their shoulders, their mouths hung

open. Joseph gazed on and mechanically tried to count the crosses. His lips were dry and cracked, his gums hard, his eyes reddened ; he did not claim a greater ration of water for himself than for the others.

On the 20th of June, or the 18th of Sivan according to the Jewish calendar, the artificial walls had reached that critical point in the north. On that day Joseph commanded divine service to be held. He made his assembled men repeat the confession of sin. Wrapped in their mantles, and wearing their purple phylacteries, the men stood round, beat their breasts wildly and cried : " Oh, Adonai ! I have sinned, I have fallen short, I have blasphemed in Thy sight." Joseph stood in front as priest of the first rank, and fervently as the others he confessed : " Oh, Adonai ! I have sinned, I have fallen short, I have blasphemed in Thy sight." And he felt guilty, sinful and humbled to the ground. Then, as he began the third sentence of the confession of sin, he suddenly raised his head, for he felt the eyes of someone in the back row fixed maliciously and persistently upon him, and he saw a mouth which did not recite in chorus with the rest, " I have sinned, I have fallen short," but savagely and relentlessly formed the words, " You have sinned, you have fallen short." It was the mouth of Sapita. And when at the end of the service Joseph along with the other priests pronounced the benediction, when with raised hands and fingers extended he stood before the assembled men, who bowed their heads to the ground, when the spirit of God hovered over the priests and their blessing, then once more he saw a pair of eyes insolently raised and malignantly and persistently fixed on him, and the face of Sapita jeered at him, as though to say : " Keep your mouth shut, Joseph Ben Matthias. We prefer to die without your blessing, Joseph Ben Matthias."

Joseph was cast into the greatest bewilderment. He had turned aside from no danger ; he had accepted thirst and hardship like the humblest of his soldiers ; the measures he had taken had proved to be good and effective ; God was visibly with him ; and already he had held the city longer than anyone could have thought it possible. What did this man Sapita want ? Joseph did not feel angry with him. The man was blinded and what he had done was blasphemy.

The sortie that Joseph made next day against the wall to the north was carried out with savage fanaticism. It was better to die fighting than on the cross, and their gloomy resolve to die a soldier's death carried the Jews to their objective, in spite of the rain of arrows that met them. They cut down the defending forces and set fire to the wall and the engines of war. The Romans wavered. They wavered not only at this point, but also in the south, where they were not very urgently pressed. And soon the besieged knew the reason. Vespasian had been hit. The Roman commander was wounded. There was jubilation in the city, and Joseph commanded a double ration of water to be given out. They were now in the fifth week. If he managed to hold out to the seventh week, then the summer would be too far advanced ; then Jerusalem would be saved for that year.

It took almost a week for the Romans once more to secure their position in the north. Meantime, however, they had placed their battering rams in position on three sides of the wall. These were gigantic beams, somewhat like ships' masts, furnished at the point with a huge block of iron in the form of a ram's head. The masts were suspended by a pulley to a horizontal beam strengthened by strong supports. A squad of artillerymen pulled the beam

with the ram's head backwards and then let it rebound.
No wall, it did not matter how thick, could withstand for
long the assaults of this engine.

At last, after the battering ram had been at work for
some time, Vespasian considered the fortress ripe for a
general assault. The attack began early in the morning.
The heavens were darkened by the bombardment ; the
trumpets of the legion blared dreadfully and persistently ;
from all the catapults simultaneously flew great stone
projectiles ; the battering rams pounded dully, re-echoing
from the hills. On the artificial walls there were three
armoured towers, each seventeen yards high, occupied by
spear-men, archers, slingers, and also light catapults. The
besieged were defenceless against these armoured monsters.
Under cover of them there now crept out of the galleries
gigantic and uncanny tortoises, each composed of a hundred
picked Roman soldiers whose shields, held over their heads,
overlapped each other like the scales of a reptile, so that no
shot could pierce through them. The armoured towers
worked in strict collaboration with these tortoises, directing
their fire against the points on the wall which the soldiers
chose for attack, so that the defenders had to vacate
them. Already the attackers had reached the wall at five
points and were throwing ladders so as to gain a foothold.
But at that moment, when the Romans could not fire
without danger of hitting their own men, the defenders
poured down upon them burning oil which got under their
armour, and also scattered on the ladders a slimy decoction
of Greek fire, so that the attackers tumbled off.

Night came, but the attack did not relax. All night
through the dull pounding of the battering rams went on ;
the catapults and the armoured towers kept up their work.
Those among the defenders who were hit tumbled in

grotesque postures from the walls. Screams and groans could be heard everywhere. So full was the night of terrible sounds that the Jewish commander instructed the soldiers on the walls to stop their ears with wax. Joseph himself listened to the tumult with almost savage satisfaction. It was the forty-sixth day ; for seven times seven days he would hold the city. Then the fiftieth day would come, and there would be silence. Perhaps it would be the silence of death. In the midst of the savage hubbub he enjoyed a foretaste of the silence of that fiftieth day, and he thought of the words that had been handed down : First comes the tempest and the great whirlwind, but God appears in the stillness.

That night one of the defenders succeeded in flinging down a great rock with such violence on one of the battering rams that it knocked off the iron head. The Jew sprang down from the wall, snatched the ram's head from the midst of his enemies, bore it back amid a rain of arrows, climbed the wall, and fell, hit by five arrows, on the inside, where he collapsed. It was Sapita.

Joseph bent over the dying man. Sapita must not depart without repenting of his blasphemy. Ten men stood round him. They recited : " Hear, Israel. Thy God Jehovah is the one eternal God," so that he might die with the words in his ears. Sapita tugged painfully at a strand of his two-pointed beard. He moved his lips, but Joseph could see that it was not the words of the creed that he was reciting. Joseph bent his head closer. The little fanatical eyes of the dying man glittered malignantly, full of pain ; he tried to say something. Joseph put his ear quite close to Sapita's dry lips ; he could not make out what he was saying, but it was obviously something contemptuous. Joseph was bewildered and filled with grief

that the blinded man should die in such a state.   He thought
and then said softly and passionately :   " Listen, Sapita.
I'll prevent the Romans from advancing on Jerusalem
this summer.   I'll hold the city for three more days,
and I won't make my way through to Jerusalem as we
agreed.   I'll stay in the town to the fourth morning."
In monotonous chorus, so that the words might reach the
ear of the dying man, the ten soldiers cried, " Hear, Israel."
Joseph gazed urgently, almost imploringly, at Sapita.   The
man must acknowledge the sin he had committed and die
at peace with God.   But Sapita's bloodshot eyes had turned
up, his jaw had fallen ; Joseph had made his vow to a dead
man.

From that day Joseph allowed himself no rest.   He was
to be seen perpetually on the walls.   His skin burned, his
eyes pained him, his gums were swollen, his ears were
deafened with the din of the besieging engines, his voice
was raw and hoarse.   But he did not spare himself.   And
so he held out until the midnight of the forty-ninth day.
Then he fell into a leaden sleep.

On the morning of the 1st of July, the fiftieth day of
the siege, the Romans took the fortress of Jotapat.

19

JOSEPH had hardly been sleeping for two hours when he
was awakened by the shout : " They are here."   He reeled
up and snatched everything that he could lay his hands on,
dried mutton, bread, his priest's sash embroidered with
flowers, the decree appointing him commissary, the dice
that the actor Demetrius Libanus had once given him in
Rome.   He stumbled out into the grey light ; his men
dragged him through a subterranean passage to a deserted
cistern which widened into a fairly spacious cave.

There were about a dozen of them in the cave, one of them severely wounded ; they had food, but only one bucket of water. All day they remained full of hope, but when night came they found that there was no possibility of escape. The subterranean passage had many branches and windings, but they all returned again to the cave, which had only one exit, the one to the town where the Romans were keeping a sharp watch.

On the second day the wounded man died. On the third the water was exhausted ; on the fourth the remaining men, enfeebled by the long siege, became crazy with thirst.

On the fifth day Joseph Ben Matthias lay in a corner of the cave ; he had put the blue sash under his head and drawn his robe over his face, and he waited for the Romans to come and kill him. His stomach burned ; every now and then he tried to swallow, although he knew how painful and useless it was ; his pulse was a mere flutter ; all his limbs prickled and ached. His closed lids chafed against his inflamed eyes ; in the darkness little points and rings danced before him, swelled and shrank again, glittered and wove in and out. The thought of hastening his death, of taking his own life, was sweet and seductive ; but one hope still remained : perhaps he would manage to get a drink first. Perhaps when the Romans came they would give him something to drink before they hung him on the cross. In Jerusalem there was a benevolent association of women who gave condemned men a goblet of wine and myrrh on their way to their crucifixion. That would be a fine death. He pushed the robe off his face and smiled with his cracked lips.

Palpably he saw before him the great cistern with the rations of water, with all those rations of water. Now that the Romans were in Jotapat there was no longer any

need to spare with the water ; queer that he hadn't thought
of that until now.   He saw himself walking towards the
cistern.   A great many people were coming towards him.
But he went straight through the screaming Jews and the
Romans who stood everywhere in the streets, for he was
the commander, and so the people must make way for him ;
he kept on straight for the cistern, his thirst guiding him.
He must drink.   There is no one guarding the cistern any
longer.   But a man is standing there and will not let him
drink.   Will you not go away, Sapita ?   I'll kill you if
you won't let me drink.   Have I behaved like a coward ?
Have I turned aside when the swords flashed, when steel
and iron flew and men fell thick from the walls ?   Don't
lift up that silly ram's head with your sound arm.   I know
quite well that you're dead ; you're a common liar, Sapita,
even if you are dead a hundred times.   Go away.

The painful and hopeless need to swallow inflamed
Joseph's swollen throat and awoke him from his fantasies.
He drew the robe over his face again.   He wanted to forget
everything.   When he had been in the wilderness with Banus
the Essene, subduing his flesh, he had needed visions.   But
now he needed to bring clarity and order into his thoughts.
He had no intention of dying simply because he had drunk
nothing for a few days.   Certainly, if one drank nothing
for several days one caved in ; that was a recognised fact ;
but he wouldn't.   The others, yes, they would end by
dying of thirst.   But it was impossible that he himself
should die like that ; he had too much still to do ; there
were far too many things that he had neglected to do.
What about the women he had not enjoyed, the wine he
had not drunk, the glories of the earth he had not seen, the
books he had not written ?   Why hadn't he taken Poppaea
that time ?   Her dress had been of Coan silk, thin as a

breath, so that one could see the downy hair gleaming through. Her hair was amber yellow, right enough. There were so many women that he had not possessed. He saw their thighs, their breasts, their faces.

But no, these were not faces, but heaps of fruit such as one saw in the markets. Round juicy fruits, figs, apples, huge grapes. He longed to bite into them, to chew and swallow ; but when he tried to seize them each had the same infamous golden brown face that he knew so well. No, you cursed dog, I shall not die, I shall not give you that satisfaction ; you in particular. You silly yokel, you ape of reason, with your statues and your symmetrically worked out systems. You dare talk about Judaea ! What do you know about it ? Are you even on its side in this struggle ? Have you joined us ? You have no blood in your veins, you rascal. If Judaea did wreck your accursed palace and the idols in it, Judaea was right, ten times right, and I'm glad of it.

I'm not crazy. I'm only very thirsty, but I know quite well still that it was a dastardly thing to laugh at the Avengers of Israel in Rome. It was a paltry and shabby thing. You're a miserable fellow, Justus of Tiberias.

There was a buzzing in his head as of many voices : Marin, Marin. And a thin stubbornly devoted voice rose amid the others : That is he.

No, he had never let those words win any power over him ; he had never allowed himself to be puffed up ; he had cast off that temptation as blasphemy. It was the Tempter that was exploiting his feebleness now, that had suddenly brought back that voice again. Yes, it was nothing but an impudent trick of the Tempter, who wished to turn away Jehovah's favour from him.

With a great effort he struggled on to his knees, painfully

beat his brow against the ground, and painfully recited the confession of sin. He recited proudly : " Oh Adonai, I have not sinned, I have not fallen short, you must give me water, I have honoured your name. I desire water, let not your servant die of thirst, for I have served you well, and you must give me to drink."

Suddenly a voice sounded in the cave, the barking voice of a Roman officer, which Joseph knew so well. The others were shaking him. So it was a real voice ; that was clear. It was speaking in Greek and saying that the Galilean commander was in this cave, and that if the prisoners surrendered they would be spared. " Give me something to drink," said Joseph.

" You have an hour to think it over," replied the voice. " Then we will smoke you out."

A blissful smile distorted Joseph's face. He had won. He had overreached the dead Sapita and the insolent living Justus, who had not allowed him to eat the fruit. Now he would drink after all and live.

But among Joseph's companions there were some who would not hear of surrender. They remembered what had happened at Magdala ; they were convinced that if they gave themselves up to the Romans only Joseph at best would be spared for the triumphal procession, while the others would be crucified or sold as slaves. They decided to fight. Half mad with thirst, they planted themselves in Joseph's way. They would rather kill him than suffer him to give himself up to the Romans.

Joseph longed only for one thing : to drink. Whether the Romans would spare them or not could be considered later. In any case the Romans would give them something to drink, and these fools did not see that. Madmen and dogs, that was all they were. It would be too absurd if,

after so much suffering, he must kill himself without having
drunk first.   He summoned all his exhausted wits to argue
his case against the others, to drink and to live.

For a long time he laboured in vain to convince them.
His cracked and hoarse voice almost gave out before he was
able to make them a final proposal : that at least they
should not kill themselves, but rather fight with one another
until all were dead ; that was the lesser sin.   They agreed
to this ; they accepted the proposal, and that was his salvation ; for they let fortune decide which of them should
kill the other, and they diced with the dice which Joseph
had been given by the actor Demetrius Libanus.   They
begged each other's forgiveness and died, the words of their
faith on their lips.   When Joseph was left with the last
man he simply walked out of the cave to the Romans.
The other man stood still for a moment, then crept after
him.

20

IT was Paulinus who accepted Joseph's submission.   He
stretched out his arm in the Roman fashion, and acted
chivalrously towards his defeated enemy.   Joseph did not
even thank him.   He simply collapsed and whispered :
" Water."   They brought him water, but he kept
control over himself, and, this was the most pious deed in
all his life, pronounced the grace : " Praise be to Thee,
our Lord Jehovah, who created everything by Thy Word " ;
and only then drank.   Blissfully he let the water flow
through his lips, over his tongue, down into his throat ;
he asked for more water, and again for more, and could
hardly bear to set down the pitcher to draw breath, and
drank on.   He smiled broadly and foolishly ; his whole
face smiled.   The soldiers stood round grinning good-
naturedly and gazed at him as he drank.

They dusted Joseph's clothes perfunctorily, set food before him, and led him in fetters to the commander's quarters. He had to pass through the whole camp. Everywhere the soldiers came rushing out; they all wanted to see the enemy leader; many of them grinned good-naturedly: so that was the man who had kept them busy for seven weeks. An able fellow. Others, embittered by the death of comrades, threatened him and cursed him savagely. A few jested at his expense, for he looked very young, frail and emaciated : " Well, well, little Jew, when you hang on the cross the birds and the flies won't find much to eat on you." Ghastly as he looked, his hair matted, his cheeks unshaven, Joseph walked calmly through all the hubbub; threats and witticisms made no impression upon him, and many soldiers turned away their gaze when they caught the melancholy glance of his inflamed eyes. When one of them spat upon him Joseph did not even reply; he merely asked his escort to wipe away the spittle, for he himself was fettered and could not do so. It was unseemly that he should appear before the commander in such a state.

His way through the camp was a long one. Tents and tents and tents, and inquisitive soldiers everywhere. Then the altar of the camp. In front of it, in rough gold, hostile and menacing, the eagles of the three legions. Then tents again. It cost Joseph a great effort, in his enfeebled state, to hold himself erect; but he pulled himself together and kept his head high during that long road of shame.

When at last the commander's tent was reached, Joseph could see nobody at first but Paulinus and a young gentleman wearing the badge of the general staff; he was not tall, but broad and athletic, with a round open face and a short but jutting chin. Joseph guessed at once that this was Titus, the commander's son. The young general approached him. "I am sorry," he said frankly and kindly, "that you have been annoyed by the soldiers. You put up a splendid fight. We have underestimated you Jews; you are excellent soldiers." He saw that Joseph was exhausted, and asked him to sit down. "Your summers are hot," he said. "But it is pleasant and cool here in the tent."

Meanwhile the curtain that divided the tent in two was raised and Vespasian himself appeared in comfortable loose robes, accompanied by a stately and resolute looking lady. Joseph got up and tried to salute in the Roman fashion. But Vespasian good-humouredly gave him a sign to remain seated. "Please don't trouble. You look confoundedly young, my little Jew. How old are you?"

"Thirty," replied Joseph.

"You see, Cacnis," Vespasian grinned, "what can be done by the time one is thirty."

Dame Caenis contemplated Joseph without goodwill.

"I don't care much for this Jew," she said bluntly.

"She can't endure you," Vespasian explained to Joseph, "because she got such a fright when you wounded me on the foot. But it was a false alarm, for I'm all right again." But now that he walked up to Joseph it could be seen that he still limped a little. "Let me feel your muscles," he said, prodding Joseph as if he were a slave. "Thin, thin," he decided, breathing loudly. "Well, you insisted in holding out. You could have taken things more easy if you had liked. But you seem to have had a very variegated past, apart from that, young man. I have been told about you. The story of your three so-called innocent men who afterwards got so much on the nerves of our friend Cestius Gallus; that among other things, but that wasn't all." He was in high spirits. He was thinking that

without those grey-beards that smart fellow Cestius would
scarcely have been recalled, and in that case he himself
would not be where he was.

"What do you say, young man?" he asked jovially.
"Should I set out for Jerusalem straight away? I have a
great desire to see your great Sabbath service in the Temple.
But you've held me up so long at this Jotapat of yours.
It's quite late in the year now. And if the people in Jerusalem are as stiff-necked as you fellows here it'll be a long-
winded business."

He spoke casually and jestingly. But Joseph saw that
the eyes in the broad, hard-lined peasant face were clear
and watchful; he heard the man's loud breathing; then
suddenly, in a blinding flash, he saw that in his secret heart
this Roman did not want to march on Jerusalem; that he
had no desire for a quick victory over Judaea. Vespasian
did not look as if he would give up in a hurry whatever he
held. He wanted to keep his army, his three superb legions
which worked so well together; and once the campaign
was finished he would be deprived of them as a matter of
course, and his command would be at an end. Joseph
saw clearly that this man Vespasian did not want to march
at present on Jerusalem.

The knowledge gave him new strength. His agitations
in the cave were still working within him. He knew that
now at last he would have to fight for his life, and in that
fight the knowledge that the Roman had no desire to reach
Jerusalem gave him a tremendous advantage. Softly, but
with burning conviction, he said: "I tell you this, General
Vespasian. You will not march on Jerusalem this year.
Probably not next year either."

He saw Vespasian before him, strong and clear-eyed, a
man. Gazing intently at him, Joseph proceeded slowly, as

if he were digging the words out of himself: "You are destined for greater things."

Everybody was struck dumb by this unexpected answer; this Jewish officer who had fought so flawlessly liked, it seemed, grandiose words. Vespasian's eyes narrowed as he stared at his prisoner. "Think of that," he said chaffingly, "so it seems that the prophets have not died out in Judaea after all." But the raillery in his rough old voice was quite mild; it breathed encouragement and good nature. There were very queer things to be met in this country of Judaea. In the Lake of Genezareth there was a fish that cried in a human voice; in the fields of Sodom everything that was sown blackened and fell to ashes; the Dead Sea kept you afloat, no matter whether you could swim or not. Everything here was uncanny. Why should there not be in this young Jew some trace of the madman and the prophet, even although he was a good politician and soldier?

Meanwhile Joseph madly racked his brains. His words had hit the mark; but what could he say now to deepen the impression he had made upon this man? The Roman stood there, a burly peasant, and waited. Joseph searched every corner of his memory. Claudius Reginus, John of Gishala, "God is in Italy now." Where could he find a bone to fling to this man who held his life in his hands? Suddenly he saw distinctly before him the slow, massive, awkward men in the tavern in Capernaum, these simple, doltish olive growers and cloth weavers. "So the prophets haven't died out in Judaea after all?" the Roman had asked. Joseph knew that everything depended upon his answer; he was fighting for his life. He summoned all his strength and gave the answer: "There are not many prophets in Judaea," he said, "and their sayings are dark. They have foretold that the Messiah will go out from

Judaea. We misunderstood them and started this war.
Now that I stand before you, Consul Vespasian, in your
tent, I know the right interpretation." He bowed to the
Roman in profound reverence. "The Messiah will go
out from Judaea, but he will not be a Jew. You are he,
Consul Vespasian."

At this brazenly fantastic lie everybody in the tent became silent. They had heard of the Messiah ; the whole
Orient was full of talk about him. The Messiah : that
was the demi-god of whom this part of the earth dreamed ;
he would appear to avenge the subject East on Rome. A
dark being, mysterious, supernatural, a little ludicrous like
all the creations of eastern superstition, but still full of
seduction and of danger.

Caenis had risen with parted lips. Her Vespasian the
Messiah ? She thought of the sacred oak. The Jew could
hardly know anything about that. She stared at Joseph,
suspicious and yet fascinated. His prediction was marvellous and glorious and completely in accordance with
her hopes ; but this oriental remained uncanny to her.

A fanatical precisian, young General Titus liked to hold
people to their exact words ; and it had become an auto-
matic habit of his to take down interviews in a sort of shorthand. He had been doing this now. At this moment,
however, he looked up in surprise. It would be disappoint-
ing if this brave young soldier should turn out to be a common
mountebank. No, he really didn't look like a mountebank ;
perhaps in spite of his simple and natural bearing he was
possessed, like so many in the Orient. Perhaps long hunger
and thirst had turned his wits.

With his clear, sly peasant eyes Vespasian stared into
Joseph's, which were now filled with reverence. Joseph
supported his stare for a long time. He was sweating,

although in the tent it was not really hot ; the fetters hurt
his legs, his clothes chafed his skin.   But he supported
Vespasian's stare.   He knew that this was the decisive
moment.   Perhaps the Roman would simply turn away,
angered or even disgusted, and order him to be conducted
to the cross or to a slave ship sailing for Rome.   But it was
possible also that Vespasian might believe him.   He *must*.
In his heart, while he waited for the answer, he prayed
feverishly :   " God, make this Roman believe me.   If
you will not do it for my sake, do it for the sake of your
Temple.   For if the Roman believes, if he does not march
this year on Jerusalem, then perhaps your city and your
Temple may be saved before next year comes.   Oh, God,
you must make the Roman believe, you must, you must ! "
So he stood there praying, in fear of his life, supporting the
Roman's gaze, awaiting in tense agitation the Roman's
answer.

The Roman simply said :   " Well, well, well.   Not so
fast, young man."

Joseph heaved a sigh of relief.   The man had neither
turned away nor dismissed him.   He had won.   He went
on softly, rapidly, urgently, confidently :   " Please believe
me.   It was because I was destined to say these things to
you that I did not make my escape to Jerusalem as we had
planned, but stayed in Jotapat to the very end."

" Rubbish," growled Vespasian.   " You would never
have got through to Jerusalem."

" I received letters from Jerusalem and sent letters
there," said Joseph, " so I would have been able to get
through myself too."

From the table where he was sitting Titus said with a
smile, " We intercepted the letters, Doctor Joseph."

Paulinus modestly put in a word. :   " In one of the inter-

cepted letters it said that Jotapat would hold out for seven
times seven days. We laughed at that. But the Jews did
hold the place for seven weeks."

They all became thoughtful. Vespasian grinned across
at Caenis. "Well, Caenis," he said, "this young fellow
with his three innocent men really seems to think at the
eleventh hour that Mars didn't make a blunder with his
oak shoot after all." The General was an enlightened
man. All the same why shouldn't he believe in omens, if
it didn't conflict with his plans? Sometimes people had
erred in the interpretation of these omens, but on the other
hand there were well vouched for stories of the astonishing
reliability of certain prophets. And as for this formless
God of the Jews, who dwelt in his dark Holy of Holies
in Jerusalem; why should one throw away the hint if this
Jewish God told one things that went so well with one's
own plans? Up till now he had not himself known quite
clearly whether he really wanted to march on Jerusalem or
not. The Government was urgent; the campaign must
be finished that very summer. But it would really be a pity,
not only for him but also for the state, if this army of the
East which he had drilled so well were to be broken up again
after a rapid victory and fall into questionable hands. In
reality this fellow here with his stubborn defence of Jotapat
had done a good service, and the God who spoke out
of him was by no means a bad counsellor.

Joseph felt refreshed like a dry field after rain. God
had been gracious; it was clear that the Roman commander
believed him. And why not, after all? That man
standing there was in very truth the man of whom it had
been said that he would go out from Judaea to judge the
earth. Did it not say in the Scriptures: "Lebanon will
fall into the hands of the mighty?" Adir, the Hebrew

word for mighty, did it not mean pretty much the same as
Caesar, Imperator ?   Was there a better and more adequate
word for that massive, sly, clear-sighted man ?   He bowed
his head profoundly before the Roman and put his hand
to his brow.   The prophecy of the Messiah and the ancient
dark prediction that Jehovah would chastise Israel to save
it were one and the same, and this Roman had come to
fulfil it.   As the olive gave its oil only when it was crushed,
so Israel rendered its best when it was oppressed, and the
man who would tread it in the winepress was called Vespasian.   Yes, Joseph had found the final decisive argument.
A deep assurance descended upon him ; he felt within him
strength enough to maintain his interpretation against the
most learned doctors in the Temple.   He had wrested
good from bloodshed and fury, and even from shame great
things had come forth.   He was filled with confidence
from head to foot.

Caenis walked suspiciously round the prisoner.   " He's
afraid of the cross," she sneered.   " That's what makes him
say such things.   I would send him to Rome or Corinth.
The Emperor must judge him."

" Don't send me to Rome," begged Joseph imploringly.
" It is you who will have the power of determining my fate
and all our fates."

He felt empty with exhaustion, but it was a happy exhaustion ; he no longer had any fear.   In his heart, indeed,
he already felt superior to the Roman.   He stood there
before the Roman ; he spoke daring and flattering words,
he bowed before the Roman, but already he felt that the
other was under his influence.   This Roman was, without
knowing it, a rod in the hand of Jehovah ; he, Joseph, was
consciously and gladly an instrument of Jehovah.   His
proud feelings when he had gazed down for the first time

on Rome from the Capitol had been fulfilled in the strangest way. He had his hand on the destiny of Rome. Vespasian was the man whom God had chosen ; but he, Joseph, was the man who would move him to fulfil the will of God.

The commander said, and in his rumbling voice there was a hint of menace : " Now, my little Jew, be careful. Titus, my son, see that you take down his words. Perhaps we shall have the pleasure one day of pinning this gentleman to his statements. Can you tell me also," he turned to Joseph, " when my reign as the Messiah is due to begin ? "

" That I do not know," replied Joseph. And suddenly, with unexpected violence : " Keep me in fetters until that day comes. Have me executed if the time seems too long to you. But the time will not be long. I was a good servant to the Avengers of Israel so long as I believed that God was in Jerusalem and these men were His messengers. I will be a good servant to you, Consul Vespasian, now that I know that God is in Italy and you are His messenger."

Vespasian said : " I will take you into my private service," and when Joseph made to speak : " Do not congratulate yourself too soon, my little Jew. You can wear your priest's girdle still, but you will have to wear your fetters too until we discover how much of your prophecy comes true."

To the Emperor and the Senate Vespasian wrote that he would have to content himself for that year with consolidating what he had won.

The men who had to light the signal fires which Cestius Gallus had prepared still waited at their posts for the news that Jerusalem had fallen. Vespasian recalled them.

Book Three
CAESAREA

Book Three

CAESAREA

I

JOSEPH was kept in close attendance on Vespasian ; he was treated as an inferior, but not with cruelty. The Roman commander liked his society, although he often chaffed him and at times severely humiliated him. He listened to his advice in matters touching Jewish customs and the personal relations of individual Jews. But he showed also that he did not entirely trust the information that Joseph gave him, and often had it verified. Joseph accepted scorn and humiliation with accommodating pliancy, and made himself useful in every way he could. He improved the style of the commander's proclamations to the Jewish population, acted as an expert in disputes between the army authorities and the Jewish town councils, and soon made himself indispensable.

By the Jews in Galilee Joseph was looked upon as a coward and a traitor, though he was doing his best for them. In Jerusalem it seemed that they hated him with a deadly hatred. True, only vague tidings from the capital reached the provinces occupied by the Romans ; but one thing was certain, that the Makkabi people had become absolute masters of the city, that they had set up a reign of terror, and that they had succeeded in having Joseph publicly excommunicated. To the blare of trumpets it was announced : " Accursed, banned and outcast be Joseph Ben Matthias, formerly priest of the first rank in Jerusalem. Nobody

221

shall hold communication with him. Nobody shall rescue him from fire, tempest or flood, or any danger that may be about to destroy him. His books shall be as those of the false prophets, his children bastards. All shall think of him when in the eighteenth prayer the curse is recited, and anyone who comes in his way shall remain at a distance of seven paces from him, as from a leper."

The commune of Meron in Upper Galilee showed its loathing of Joseph in a particularly impressive manner, although it lay in the territory occupied by the Romans and its action was not without risk. In Meron a young man had once cried : " That is he," and the people of Meron had cast the hoof mark of the horse Arrow in copper, and regarded the place as holy. Now in leading sacrifices to the Temple they avoided the main street, because they had once strewn it with flowers and branches in Joseph's honour. They solemnly sowed grass on what had been their chief street, so that grass might grow where the traitor had trod, and his memory be forgotten.

Joseph's eyes narrowed, and he compressed his lips. The insult only stiffened his self-conceit. He arrived at Tiberias in Vespasian's train. There he had accomplished the decisive deed of his life ; through those streets he had rode proudly and royally on his horse Arrow, a hero, the leader of his people. He hardened his heart. He wore his fetters proudly as he walked through the streets of Tiberias, and paid no attention to the people who spat when they saw him, or those who, in their hatred and loathing, ostentatiously avoided him. He was not ashamed of the turn of fate that had transformed him, the dictator of Galilee, into the contemptuously tolerated slave of the Romans.

But before one man he could not maintain his assumed haughtiness : before Justus and Justus's inveterate disdain.

When Joseph entered the room Justus broke off in the middle
of a sentence and painfully turned away his golden-brown
face. Joseph was resolved to justify himself. This man knew
so much about the human heart ; he must understand him.
But Justus would not suffer Joseph to address a single word
to him.

King Agrippa had set about rebuilding his ruined palace.
Joseph learned that Justus was to be found almost every
day at the huge new edifice. Again and again he climbed
the hill on which the palace was being built, seeking for
an opportunity to confront Justus. Finally he found
Justus by himself. It was a clear day in early winter.
Justus was sitting on the ledge of a wall ; he looked up
when Joseph began to speak. But then he drew his cloak
over his head as if he were cold, and Joseph could not tell
whether he was listening or not. Joseph spoke eloquently
and eagerly ; he begged and implored and tried to make
the other understand. Was not a life-giving error prefer-
able to a barren truth ? Must one not have shared the
enthusiastic faith of the Avengers of Israel before one
could condemn them ?

But Justus remained silent. When Joseph had finished
he got up hastily and a little clumsily. Without saying a
word he slipped past Joseph, left him standing there where
everything smelt of mortar and newly-cut wood, and disappeared. In bitter humiliation Joseph gazed after him and
watched him climbing somewhat laboriously and wearily
over the great blocks of stone so as to get out of the new
palace by the shortest way.

2

THERE were many people in Tiberias who did not like
Justus. In these war times reason was not popular either

among the Greek and Roman population of Judaea, or among the Jews. And Justus was reasonable ; with a passionate faith in reason he had mediated between the Jews and Gentiles as long as he was in authority over the city, had striven to preserve peace, but without success. The Jews thought him too Greek, the Greeks too Jewish. The Greeks blamed him for not having proceeded more severely against Sapita, and for not having prevented the destruction of the palace. They knew that King Agrippa had a high opinion of his secretary, and when the city was restored to them they had held their silence. But now, encouraged by the presence of the Roman commander, they sent in accusations saying that the Jewish governor Justus bore the chief blame for the outbreak of the revolt in Galilee and in their city.

Doubly eager in those questionable times to show his devotion to the Romans, King Agrippa did not dare to defend his servant. On the other hand Longinus, the head judge in Vespasian's army, had made it a maxim that it was better to execute an innocent man than to let a guilty one go free. Consequently the business did not look too well for Justus. Filled with a bitter contempt for humanity, Justus defended himself without conviction. Let his king leave him in the lurch if he chose. He knew who was really to blame for all the dreadful things that had taken place in Galilee. That glittering superficial fool always managed to escape scot free from all the trouble he created. The Romans could chaff him now to their heart's content. Everything was stupid. Justus was filled from head to foot with bitter fatalism.

Out of regard for King Agrippa Longinus treated the case very seriously. He summoned Joseph as a witness. Joseph was torn this way and that, now that the fate of

Justus was given into his hands.   Justus had seen into the
dirtiest crannies of his heart ; now it was for him to decide
whether this man should vanish for ever or not.   For
everything and everybody this fellow Justus knew how to
find a sufficient explanation and excuse.   But not for
Joseph.   For him Justus had only silence and contempt.
Joseph had laid aside much of his pride ; he had learned
patience ; he went about in fetters, but contempt can pierce
through the shell even of a tortoise.   It would be a simple
matter to make the man who had insulted him vanish for
good.   Joseph did not need even to lie ; it would be sufficient
if his evidence was lukewarm.

His evidence was passionately in Justus's favour.   With
burning conviction and very good reasons he proved that
nobody had stood up more consistently for peace and for
the Romans than Doctor Justus.   And those who accused
him were either liars or fools.

Longinus laid the evidence before the general.   Vespasian snorted.   He regarded his two prisoners keenly and
guessed at once that there must have been some link between
them formerly.   But until now he had not caught his
clever Jew out in a single false assertion.   Besides, this man
Justus was a typical litterateur and philosopher, and so
quite harmless.

The General stopped the trial and sent back Doctor
Justus to his master King Agrippa.

King Agrippa greeted his severely tried secretary politely
and somewhat guiltily.   Justus saw at once how unwelcome
his presence was.   He smiled, he knew mankind.   He
offered to go on his master's service to Jerusalem to work
for peace during the winter, when military operations
would be at a standstill.   It was both a hopeless and a
dangerous task, now that the Avengers of Israel were

supreme in Jerusalem.   Nobody expected the King's
secretary to return alive.

Justus travelled with falsified passports.   As he was
setting out Joseph suddenly appeared before him.   Justus
rode past as if he were not there.

3

AT the great summer fair in Caesarea Joseph caught sight of
Alexas, the son of Nachum, the glass-blower from Jerusa-
lem.   Joseph expected that, like the majority of the Jews,
Alexas would ostentatiously avoid him.   But, behold,
Alexas came up to him and greeted him.   Neither Joseph's
fetters nor his excommunication seemed to daunt Alexas.

They went on side by side ; Alexas was stately and full-
bodied as ever, but his eyes were still more troubled and
unhappy.   He had been able to escape from Jerusalem
only at great risk ; for the Avengers of Israel prevented by
force anyone from leaving the city and putting himself under
the protection of the Romans.   Yes, madness and stupid
violence ruled in Jerusalem now.   After the Makkabi
crowd had massacred almost all of the moderate party, they
were fighting now among themselves.   Simon Bar Giora was
fighting Eleasar, and Eleasar was fighting John of Gishala,
and John again was fighting Simon, and they were united
only against one thing : against reason.   If one looked at
the matter soberly, the danger of this journey to
Caesarea was out of all proportion to what he hoped to
gain from it.   For he, Alexas, had the firm intention of
returning to Jerusalem again.   He was resolved to go on
living in that city, which was being stifled by the folly and
blind hatred of the Makkabi crowd.

It was foolish of him.   But he loved his father and

brother, he couldn't live without them, and he didn't want
to leave them in the lurch.   But in the last days he hadn't
been able to endure the madness of the city any longer.
He had felt that he must breathe a freer air for once, must
see with his own eyes that there was still some reason in
the world.

He knew that it was forbidden to stand and talk with
Joseph and if anyone heard of it in Jerusalem the Makkabi
crowd would pay him out for it.   And besides Joseph bore a
good deal of the blame for things having turned out so badly.
In Galilee he could have prevented lots of things from
developing.   But, on the other hand, he had made good
again in many ways.   He, Alexas, at least, regarded it as
a great service, a victory for reason, that Joseph had not
died with the others in Jotapat, but had surrendered with
bowed head to the Romans.   Better, he quoted, to be a
living dog than a dead lion.

In Jerusalem, he went on bitterly, people thought differently, and he told Joseph how Jerusalem had received the
news of the fall of Jotapat.   At first it had been reported
that Joseph had died with the others when the fortress
was taken.   The whole city had celebrated a wild and
splendid day of mourning for the heroes who had held
Jotapat for such an incredibly long time.   Alexas described
how at old Matthias's house the bed in which Joseph had
slept was solemnly overturned in the presence of the High
Priest and the members of the High Council.   Thereafter his
own father, Nachum Ben Nachum, clothed in sackcloth and
ashes, had, on the instructions of the chief citizens, carried
the prescribed woven basket containing the mourning meal
of lentils to old Matthias.   And all Jerusalem was present
when Joseph's father pronounced for the first time the
Kaddish, the prayer for the dead, ending with the three

words which might only be said when a great man had died in Israel.

" And then ? " asked Joseph.

Alexas smiled his quiet smile. Oh then, he said, when it was learnt that Joseph was alive and had surrendered himself to the mercy of the Romans, the revulsion of feeling was all the greater. When the priests standing on the stairs of the holy place pronounced their curse and excommunication on Joseph the halls of the Temple were as full as at a Paschal feast. Only a very few of the members of the High Council had dared to speak publicly in Joseph's favour, but among them had been the great doctor Jochanan Ben Sakkai. " Don't you worry," he said to Joseph, smiling kindly at him, showing his white sound teeth. " Whoever takes the side of reason must suffer for it."

They parted from each other. Stately, full-bodied, his ruddy face overcast, Alexas strode off between the booths. Later Joseph saw him buying powdered quartz from a dealer and stroking the fine dust tenderly with his fingers ; no doubt he had had to do without this expensive material of his beloved art for a long time.

Joseph often thought of this conversation, and with divided feelings. In Jerusalem he had already seen that Alexas had a clearer judgment than his father, but his heart had been with the foolish Nachum and against the wise Alexas. Now everybody was against him, and only the wise Alexas was for him. His fetters, which he thought he had got quite used to, irked and chafed him. Certainly the printer had been right : better to be a living dog than a dead lion. But sometimes he wished that he had perished with the others in Jotapat.

4

MARCUS LICINIUS CRASSUS MUCIANUS, Governor-General of Syria, wandered restlessly through the spacious rooms of his palace in Antioch. He had felt certain that this time Vespasian would be unable to find any further excuse for protracting the campaign. After the reign of terror begun by the Avengers of Israel had extirpated the moderates in Jerusalem, the rebels were now turning against each other. There was civil war in Jerusalem ; the reports were clear and reliable. It was madness to let this opportunity pass unexploited. Now at last Vespasian must march on the city, capture it, and finish the war. With burning impatience Mucianus had been awaiting a dispatch from military headquarters indicating the main lines of the spring campaign ; already the winter was almost over. Now the dispatch was lying before him. The overwhelming majority of the staff, including young General Titus, Vespasian's son, were in favour of marching on Jerusalem immediately. But the forwarding agent, the sly, brazen, filthy peasant, had found a new excuse. The eternal quarrels of the Jews, he said, would in a very short time make the city easy to capture, and at a far smaller sacrifice of life than at present. To march on Jerusalem now would mean squandering much good Roman blood that could quite well be spared. He was in favour of waiting, and in the meantime occupying the southern provinces, which had not been yet reduced. He was a sly fellow, this Vespasian. He might be stingy, but he was not stingy in excuses. He would not give up his command in a hurry.

His stick clasped behind his back, his lean head craning forward, Mucianus walked furiously up and down. He was no longer young ; he was already on the wrong side of fifty ; he had behind him a life of splendid dissipation which he had never regretted ; a life filled also with en-quiries into the inexhaustible abundance and diversity of nature ; a life of power and failure, of riches and sudden poverty. Now, just when he was at the height of all his faculties, and ruler over this profoundly exciting ancient province of Asia, the light-headed young Emperor had forced him to share the magnificent morsel with this dis-gusting peasant, and he boiled with rage. For almost a whole year he had had to suffer this sly forwarding agent as his equal. But now he had had enough. Of course he saw through the intentions of the general as clearly as he saw through those of the Emperor. This fellow must not be allowed to stand any longer in his way. He must be driven out of Asia ; he must finally put an end to this stupid Jewish war.

In great fury and haste Mucianus dictated a whole series of letters to the Emperor, the Minister for the Orient, and his personal friends among the senators. It was incom-prehensible why, after so many preparations, and when the enemy had been enfeebled by internal discord, the general should not consider Jerusalem ripe for capture even by early summer. He did not want to insist how gravely this languid military policy was endangering the plans for the great oriental campaign ; but one thing was certain, that if this policy of hesitation was continued the prestige of the Emperor, the Senate and the army would be jeopardised in all the Orient.

These letters reached Rome at a moment that was very unfortunate for Mucianus. For the western provinces had sent in far more important and disagreeable news. The Governor of Lyons, a certain Vindex, had risen in rebellion, and he seemed to have the sympathy of all Gaul

as well as of Spain.   The reports were extremely grave.
In these circumstances Mucianus's letters evoked real and
full sympathy only from one man, the minister Talassos.
That old gentleman regarded it as a personal insult to himself that the destruction of Jerusalem had been delayed for
so long.   He replied to Mucianus cordially, agreeing with
all his heart.   With this reply in his hands the Governor-
General decided to confront the forwarding agent in person,
and set out for Vespasian's headquarters in Caesarea.

The general received him smilingly and was visibly
pleased.   All three, Vespasian, Titus and Mucianus, dined
together in the most friendly fashion.   Gradually, after the
dishes were taken away, the conversation turned to political
matters.   Mucianus protested that it was far from his mind
to interfere in Vespasian's affairs, but Rome and the Roman
ministers were urging that the campaign should be brought
to a close.   For his part, he appreciated perfectly well the
general's motives, but the wishes of Rome, on the other
hand, seemed to him so weighty that, though it would be a
hardship to him, he was prepared to contribute troops from
his own Syrian legions if Vespasian would only agree to
march on Jerusalem.   Eager to show his martial qualities,
young General Titus agreed enthusiastically.   " Accept it,
father, accept it !   My officers and the whole army are
simply on fire to conquer Jerusalem."

Vespasian watched with inward amusement Mucianus's
keen face, ravaged with lust, greed and ambition, turned
now to Titus in gratitude which was compounded partly
of honest sympathy and partly of calculation.   The general
smiled.   Much as he loved his son, he had said nothing
to him of his real motives.   In his heart he had been convinced that Titus saw through them just as clearly as this
sly fellow Mucianus, or the Jew Joseph ;   but he was

delighted that his son should show such enthusiasm. It made it all the easier for him to conceal his personal reasons behind general ones.

Later, when he and Mucianus were alone, the latter drew out the letter he had received from Talassos. Vespasian experienced a feeling almost of respect for his persistence. The fellow was contemptible, but clever all the same ; one could talk frankly to him. Vespasian raised his hand : " Don't trouble to read that. I know you want to draw my attention to the views of some influential scoundrel in Rome, who assures you that Rome will be ruined if I don't march on Jerusalem immediately." He went over to Mucianus, he breathed loudly in Mucianus's face so that the latter had to summon all his politeness to keep himself from starting back, and said quite good-humouredly : " Even if you were to show me ten letters, my dear fellow, it would have not the slightest effect on me." He sat up straight, groaningly stroked his gouty arms, came quite close to the other man, and went on confidentially : " Listen, Mucianus. We have both braved all the winds in the compass ; we needn't pretend with each other. It turns my wine sour when I look at you, with your twitching face and your stick behind your back. And you feel sick when you hear me wheezing and smell my bad breath. Is that so ? "

Mucianus replied politely : " Please continue."

Vespasian continued : " But, unfortunately, for the time being we're both yoked to the same cart. It was a confoundedly sly thought of His Majesty. But can't we be just as sly ? A dromedary and a buffalo don't draw very well together in the same yoke ; one can play off Greeks and Jews against one another with some hope of success ; but as for two old augurs like us, what do you say ? "

Mucianus's face twitched nervously. " I have been following your line of thought attentively, Consul Vespasian," he said.

" Have you had any news from the western provinces ? " Vespasian asked brusquely, and he kept his clear eyes on the other's face.

" From Gaul, do you mean ? " asked Mucianus.

" I see that you're all there," Vespasian grinned. " You needn't think to frighten me with this letter of yours from your Roman supporter. Rome has other cares at present."

" You can't do very much with your three legions," said Mucianus uncomfortably. He had laid his stick aside, and now with the back of his small and manicured hand wiped the sweat from his upper lip.

" True," Vespasian admitted good-humouredly. " So I am going to make you a proposal. Your four Syrian legions are in a pretty miserable condition, but along with my three good ones they make up seven after all. Let us keep our seven legions together until things clear up in the west." And as Mucianus remained silent, Vespasian went on persuasively and reasonably : " Until things clear up in the west you won't get rid of me, that's certain. Be reasonable."

" Thanks for your frank and apposite statement," replied Mucianus.

Ostensibly it was scientific interests that detained Mucianus for the next few weeks in Judaea ; for he was working on a great scientific work describing the geography and ethnology of the Empire, and Judaea was full of remarkable features. Young Titus accompanied the Governor-General on his excursions and was very attentive ; often he would take down in shorthand the information provided by the natives. These, for instance, were the springs of Jericho, which for long ages had destroyed all the fruits of the soil as well as those of the womb, and brought all living things in its vicinity to death, until a certain prophet Elysseus had by his priestly arts and sacred ardour consecrated them, so that now their effects were life-giving. Mucianus also viewed the asphalt lake, the Dead Sea, in which even the heaviest things floated, the water violently casting them up if one tried to hold them down. Mucianus carefully investigated all these things ; ordered men who could not swim to be thrown into the lake with their hands tied behind their backs ; and looked on with interest while they floated about on the surface. Also he made a tour of the fields of Sodom seeking traces of the fire sent down from heaven, beheld in the lake the spectral outlines of five sunk cities, and plucked fruit which in colour and shape seemed very appetising, but crumbled to dust and ashes at a touch.

He asked questions about all sorts of things ; he was avid for knowledge, and took notes. One day he found certain notes in his own handwriting which he was certain he had not written. It turned out that young Titus was their author. Yes, that young gentleman had the capacity to immerse himself so promptly and profoundly in the handwriting of other people that they were unable to distinguish his imitation of their script from the real thing. Mucianus became reflective and begged Titus to write him a few lines in the writing of his father. Titus did so, and it really would have been impossible for anyone to take it for a forgery.

But the most noteworthy sight that Mucianus saw during those weeks in Judaea was the scholar and prisoner of war, General Joseph Ben Matthias. On his very first day in Caesarea the Governor-General had been struck by the captive Jew who walked to humbly through the streets of Caesarea, eyed by everyone on account of his fetters. When

Mucianus asked Vespasian about the man Vespasian was
curiously casual and evasive. Nevertheless he could not prevent the inquisitive Governor-General from having long and
intimate talks with the priest Joseph. Mucianus often spoke
to Joseph ; he soon discovered that Vespasian employed
his prisoner as a sort of oracle by whose utterances he was
guided in cases of doubt, without of course allowing the
oracle to perceive the importance he attached to his
words. Mucianus was deeply impressed by this Jew, for
he regarded the general as a sober-minded and sceptical
rationalist. He talked with Joseph about everything under
the sun, and was surprised again and again to find how much
deep religious eastern wisdom was mingled with the Greek
cynicism of this Jew. He had met priests of all kinds,
priests of Mithra and of Aumu, barbaric druid priests from
Britain, priests of the German Rosmerta ; but this priest
of Jehovah, little as he was distinguished externally from
the Romans, impressed Mucianus more than all the others
put together.

In spite of his conversations with Joseph, however, he
found time to clarify as far as possible his attitude to the
general. Vespasian was right ; so long as the situation
remained dubious in the West and in Rome, the two commanders in the East, the Governor-General of Syria and the
military commander of Judaea, were bound together by the
same common interests. With his crude frankness Vespasian indicated a practical policy to subserve those interests.
Neither would make any important political or military
decision without the consent of the other ; but in their
official dispatches to Rome they would as before continue
to intrigue against each other, but from now on in strict
collusion.

Stingy by nature, Vesaspian looked forward in appre-

hension to the parting gift which the extravagant and greedy
Governor-General might demand when he left.   Mucianus
asked only for one trifling thing : he asked for Joseph, the
Jewish prisoner of war.   At first surprised by such a modest
request, the general was about to say yes.   But then he
reflected.   No, he would not give up his Jew.   " As you
know, of course," he said smilingly to Mucianus, " the
forwarding agent is a miserly fellow."

But the Governor-General succeeded nevertheless in
persuading Vespasian to allow Titus to accompany him back
to Antioch for a long visit.   The general saw quite well
that Titus was intended as a sort of hostage to keep him
to the agreement he had made.   But he did not feel insulted.
He accompanied Mucianus to the ship sailing for Antiochia.
As he said good-bye Mucianus remarked in his polite way :
" Your son Titus, Consul Vespasian, has all your good
qualities without any of your bad ones."   Vespasian snorted,
then he replied :   " It's unfortunate you have no Titus,
Your Excellence."

5

IN the docks of Caesarea Vespasian was reviewing the
prisoners of war that were to be sold.   Fronto, the Roman
captain who had command over the docks, had made out a
rough list of the prisoners ; there were about three thousand.
Each wore a little tablet round his neck, on which were
marked his number, as well as his age, weight, diseases and
such particular abilities as he might possess.   The slave
dealers walked about and commanded the prisoners to
stand up, squat down, lift their legs, open their mouths,
show their muscles.   The dealers complained : these
fellows weren't much good ; to-morrow the auction would
be a pretty poor one.

Vespasian was accompanied by Caenis, a few of his

officers, and Joseph, his Jew, whom he had ordered to attend
to act as an intermediary between him and the prisoners.
He had a right to ten slaves as his share of the booty, and he
wished to select them before the others were put up for
sale. Caenis wanted a hairdresser and a good-looking
youth to wait at table. The more practical Vespasian, on
the other hand, was resolved to select a few powerful fellows
to be employed on his Italian estates as farm labourers. He
was in excellent spirits. He cracked jokes at the expense
of the Jewish slaves. "They're stiff-necked fellows with
their Sabbaths and feast-days and complicated food regulations, and all the rest of their nonsense. If you allowed
them to carry out all their so-called religious rules you would
have to look on while they passed half their lives in idleness.
And if you don't allow them they become obstinate as
bulls. Really all they're good for is being sold back to
the other Jews. I've been asking myself," he turned
suddenly to Joseph, " whether I shouldn't sell you back to
your fellow countrymen. But the prices they've been
offering are miserable ; obviously they have a superfluity of
prophets."

Joseph smiled humbly. But in his heart he did not
smile. From scraps of conversation that he had picked up
he had discovered that Dame Caenis, who could not endure
him by now, had tried to sell him to Mucianus behind
Vespasian's back. The courteous Mucianus, interested as
he was in Joseph, would certainly never have perpetrated
such coarse witticisms at his expense as Vespasian did. But
by this time Joseph felt bound to Vespasian. God had
fettered him to this man ; here was his great opportunity.
When Vespasian suggested jestingly that he should be sold
Joseph's smile was thin and somewhat wry.

They came upon a crowd of women slaves. Food had

just been set before them ; greedily and dully they devoured their lentil soup and chewed their coarse bread. It was the first very hot day, and stench filled the sultry air. The older women had been allowed to retain their clothes, seeing that they could only be employed for work now ; the younger ones were naked. Among them was a quite young girl, slender and graceful. She was not eating, but crouched with crossed legs on the ground. Her shoulders were bowed shrinkingly, her hands clasped her ankles, her body was bent forward to conceal her nakedness. Very beautiful, very afraid, she crouched there and gazed at the men with vigilant, terrified and reproachful eyes.

Vespasian was impressed by the girl. Breathing heavily on account of the heat, he walked up to her through the other women. He seized the shrinking girl by the shoulders and straightened them. Motionless with fear she gazed up at him.

" Stand up," Captain Fronto bawled at her.

" Let her sit," said Vespasian. He bent down, raised the tablet that hung at her breast, and read aloud : " Mara, daughter of Lakish, theatre attendant in Caesarea, aged fourteen, a virgin. Well, well," he added, groaningly straightening himself again.

" Won't you stand up, you whore ? " hissed the overseer. She was so terrified that she obviously did not understand.

" You must stand up, Mara," said Joseph gently.

" Let her be," said Vespasian in a low voice.

" Shall we go on ? " asked Dame Caenis. " Or do you want the girl ? I'm afraid she wouldn't be of much use as a dairymaid." Caenis had no objection to Vespasian's enjoying himself, but she preferred to select the objects of his enjoyment. The girl had now risen. Gentle and clear, her oval face was framed by raven black hair ; the full lipped mouth gave her a slightly pouting expression. She stood there, helpless, naked, young, piteous, her head swaying on her shoulders.

"Ask her if she has any special qualifications as a worker," said Vespasian, turning to Joseph.

"The great lord asks if you are good at any kind of work," said Joseph kindly and solicitously.

Mara's breath came in pants, and she looked at Joseph beseechingly with her great eyes. Suddenly she put her hand to her brow and bowed deeply, but she did not answer.

"Shouldn't we go on?" asked Dame Caenis.

"You must reply, Mara," Joseph said. "The great lord asks if you are good at any kind of work," he repeated patiently.

"I know a great many prayers by heart," said Mara. She brought this out timidly; her voice was unexpectedly deep and melodious.

"What did she say?" asked Vespasian.

"She can pray," said Joseph in reply.

The company laughed. Vespasian did not laugh. "Well, well," he said.

"Shall I send the girl to you?" asked Captain Fronto.

Vespasian hesitated. "No," he said at last. "I need workers for my estates."

In the evening Vespasian asked Joseph: "Do your women pray a great deal?"

"Our women are not required to pray," Joseph explained. "They are obliged to observe the prohibitions, but not the commandments. We have three hundred and sixty-five commandments, as many as there are days in the year, and two hundred and forty-eight prohibitions, as many as there are bones in the human body."

"That's certainly enough," said Vespasian. "Do you think that she is really a virgin ?" he asked after a pause.

"Our law punishes unchastity in women with death," said Joseph.

"Your law !" Vespasian shrugged his shoulders. "Perhaps that girl worries her head about your law, Doctor Joseph, but my soldiers certainly do not. I must confess I have found ways of getting over their scruples when they insisted on keeping the law in that particular respect. It's their great eyes, that look as though they concealed some great secret. Probably they conceal nothing at all, that's always the case in your land. A great display, and when you look more closely there's nothing behind it. How is your oracle getting on, my little prophet ?" he suddenly became spiteful. "If I had sent you to Rome, no doubt you would have been sentenced long ago and be drudging in some Sardinian mine now, instead of amusing yourself here with pretty Jewish girls."

The general's jokes did not affect Joseph much. From the first he had seen that it was not only he who was bound. "Mucianus, the Governor-General," he replied with brazen politeness, "would have paid the price of at least two dozen mine workers to get you to sell me to him. I fancy that I might have quite a good time in Antioch."

"I've allowed you to get very impudent, my little Jew," said Vespasian.

Joseph changed his tone. "My life would have been lost," he said with burning conviction, and yet humbly, "if you had sent me away. Believe me, Consul Vespasian, you are the Saviour, and Jehovah has sent me to you to tell you that, and keep on telling you that. You are the Saviour," he repeated obstinately. Vespasian glanced at him mockingly, with a faint touch of contempt. He could

not keep the fiery words of this man from stirring his old
heart again.   It annoyed him that his jokes should extract
those reiterated prophecies from the Jew.   He had become
too accustomed to the mysterious, warm and confident
voice of this man, had attached himself too firmly to this
Jew.

" If your God doesn't hurry up, my little Jew," he said
jeeringly, " the Messiah will look a bit doddering when
he finally does appear."

Joseph did not himself know from whence he drew his
assurance, but he replied quietly and inflexibly : " If before
this summer is over something does not happen that will
fundamentally change your situation, Consul Vespasian,
then I shall ask you to sell me and send me to Antiochia."

Vespasian swallowed those words greedily.   But he did
not want to show it and changed the subject.   " Your
King David was very fond of the girls, and liked them to
keep him warm in bed when he was old.   He didn't despise
pleasure.   I don't believe that you're all despisers of pleasure.
What do you say, my little Jew ; you could tell me something about that ? "

" Our people say," Joseph explained, " that when a man
has lain with a woman, God does not speak out of his mouth
for seven moons afterwards.   While I wrote my book on
the Maccabees I never touched a woman.   From the
moment when I was given supreme command in Galilee I
never touched a woman."

" It doesn't seem to have helped you much," said Vespasian.

Next day, at the auction, Vespasian secured Mara,
the daughter of Lakish, for himself.   That very evening
she was conducted to him.   She still wore the garland
which was allotted to prisoners of war who were publicly

sold, but at Captain Fronto's instructions she had been bathed, anointed, and clothed in a robe of transparent Coan silk. Vespasian looked her up and down with his clear eyes. "You dunces!" he spluttered. "You idiots! You've done her up like a Spanish whore. I wouldn't have paid a hundred sesterces for her if that was all she was." The girl did not understand the old man's words. She had endured too much, and now she was stupid with fear. Joseph spoke gently and kindly to her in her native Aramaic; she replied hesitatingly in her deep voice. Vespasian listened patiently to the strange guttural dialogue. At last Joseph explained to him: "She feels ashamed because of her nakedness. Nakedness is a great sin among us. A woman dare not show her nakedness, even though the doctors should declare that it is necessary for the saving of her life."

"Idiocy," Vespasian remarked curtly.

Joseph went on: "Mara begs you to give her a dress made of one square piece. Mara also begs you to give her a net for her hair and perfumed sandals for her feet."

"She smells quite good enough to me," said Vespasian. "But all right. She can have them."

He sent her away, telling her that she need not return that night. "I can wait," he told Joseph confidentially. "I've learned to wait. I like to save up tasty bits before I enjoy them. For my table, for my bed, all sorts of things. I had to wait for some time too before I got this job." He rubbed his gouty arm and became still more confidential. "Do you really find anything in this Jewish girl? She's shy, she's silly, and I can't talk to her, for I don't know her language. Innocence is nice, but here, damn it all, one can find much handsomer women. God alone knows what attracts one in a little animal like that." Joseph, too, was

attracted by Mara. He knew those women of Galilee ;
they were slow, shy, sometimes melancholy too, but when
they opened out they were passionate and voluptuous.
" She says," he explained with unusual frankness to the
Roman, " that she's fallen on evil days. And she's right.
This girl Mara hasn't much cause to say a prayer of
thanks for being given her new dress of one piece."

Vespasian became irritated. " Are you growing sentimental, my Jew ? You're beginning to annoy me. You're
making yourself too important. When one asks for a slip
of a girl for one's bed, you demand preparations sufficient
for a campaign. I tell you what, my prophet. Try to
teach her a little Latin. Have a talk with her to-morrow
morning. But don't try to steal a march on me, or your
prophetdom may be endangered."

Next day Mara was brought to Joseph. She wore the
traditional dress of the country, a dark brown one-piece
dress with red stripes. The general's instinct had been
sound. The purity of her oval face, the low white brow,
the long eyes, the voluptuous mouth, were set in admirable
relief by the simple dress.

Joseph cautiously questioned the girl. Her father and
all her family had been killed. That had happened, Mara
believed, because her father had spent his life in sin, and she
too, she was convinced, was being punished for his sins.
Lakish Ben Simon had been employed as an attendant in
the theatre of Caesarea. Before he accepted the post he
had asked the advice of several priests and doctors, and they
had permitted him, with some hesitation, to earn his bread
in this fashion. But others had piously denounced him
because of his occupation. Mara had believed these pious
men, had listened to the speeches of the Avengers of Israel ;
her father's daily work was sinful, and she herself was

touched with its corruption. Now she had been exposed naked to the eyes of the uncircumcised, the Romans had feasted their eyes on her shame ; why had not Jehovah permitted her to die before that day ? She lamented quietly in her deep voice ; the words came humbly from her voluptuous mouth ; she sat there before Joseph, young, sweet, and desirable. He thought, her vineyard is in blossom. Suddenly he was filled with a great desire for her, and his knees became weak ; he felt as he had done when he lay in the cave in Jotapat. He looked at the girl ; she did not turn away her long beseeching eyes under his glance ; her lips were slightly parted, and he felt her fragrant breath ; he desired her very keenly. She went on : " What should I do, my doctor and master ? It is a great comfort, a great favour, that God has let me hear your voice." And she smiled.

That smile aroused in Joseph a savage and boundless fury against the Roman. He chafed against his fetters and submitted himself again, torn this way and that. That he, a Jew, should be forced to fling this girl into the arms of that greedy Roman, that beast !

Suddenly Mara got up. Still smiling, she lightly walked up and down in her woven and perfumed sandals. " I always wear perfumed sandals on the Sabbath. It is a sign of grace to put on one's best clothes on the Sabbath, and God is pleased by it. Was I right in asking the Roman for perfumed sandals ? "

Joseph said : " Listen, Mara, my girl, daughter of Lakish." And cautiously he tried to explain to her that both of them, he and she, had been sent by God to this Roman for the same purpose. He talked to her of Esther, whom God had sent to King Ahasuerus to save her people ; and of Irene before King Ptolemy. " It is your duty,

Mara, to please the Roman." But Mara was afraid. She loathed and was terrified by the uncircumcised blasphemer, this old man who would be judged in the valley of Hinnom. With fury in his heart against himself and his master, Joseph talked to her circumspectly, in soft words, and prepared this dish for the Roman.

Next morning Vespasian described coarsely and frankly his experience with Mara. A little apprehension and shame he didn't mind; but the girl had trembled from head to foot, she had actually almost fainted, and for a long time afterwards had lain stiff and rigid. He was not a young man, he suffered from rheumatism; she was too much of a strain for him. "She seems," he said, "cram full of superstitious fancies; if I touch her she's afraid demons will eat her up, or something like that. You know better my little Jew. Listen; see what you can do with her for me. Will you? And tell me what the Aramaic is for ' Don't be stupid, my turtle dove,' or something of that kind."

When Joseph next saw her Mara was lifeless and sunk within herself. The words issued mechanically from her mouth; she was like a painted corpse. When Joseph made to approach her she started back and cried in helpless terror, as if she were a leper : " Unclean, unclean ! "

6

BEFORE summer great news arrived from Rome. The revolt in the western provinces had succeeded; the Senate had deposed the Emperor; Nero, the fifth Augustus, had taken his life, not without dignity, while providing a great spectacle to his friends. The leaders of the armies were now the rulers of the world. Vespasian smiled. He was a man who disliked display, but he put on a more dignified air ; it was a good thing that he had obeyed his inner voice and not ended the campaign too quickly. Now he had three strong legions, and counting those of Mucianus seven. He seized Caenis by the shoulders and said : "Nero is dead. My Jew is no dunce, Caenis." They gazed at each other, their stout bodies swayed a little, softly and rhythmically ; they both smiled.

When the news of Nero's death reached him Joseph rose quite slowly to his feet. He was still a young man ; he was only thirty-one, and he had experienced more ups and downs than most men of his age. Now he stood up breathing deeply, his hands on his breast, his lips slightly parted. He felt that Jehovah was with him ; he had played for very high stakes and he had not lost. Laboriously, with his fettered hands, he put on his priest's cap and recited the prayer : "Praise be to thee, Jehovah, Our Lord, Who hast permitted us to see and know this day." Then slowly and heavily he raised his right foot, then his left foot, and danced as the great lords danced before the people in the Temple at the festival of the drawing of water. He stamped about, the fetters rattled, he leapt, hopped, stamped, tried to clap his hands and smack his legs. The girl Mara appeared in his tent and stood in terrified confusion. But he did not stop ; he danced on ; he whirled about and shouted : "Laugh at me, Mara, daughter of Lakish. Laugh as his foes laughed at David. Have no fear, I am not Satan, the arch dancer, I am King David dancing before the Ark of the Covenant." Thus did Doctor Joseph Ben Matthias, priest of the first rank, celebrate God's fulfilment of his prophecies.

That evening Vespasian said to Joseph : "You can take off your fetters now, Doctor Joseph."

Joseph replied : "With your permission, Consul Ves-

pasian, I shall go on wearing my fetters.   I shall wear them
until the Emperor Vespasian sets me free from them."

Vespasian grinned.   "You're a reckless fellow, my
Jew," he said.

As he returned to his house Joseph whistled softly through
his teeth.   He very seldom did that, and only when he felt
p articularly pleased with himself.   And it was the couplet
of the slave Isidor that he whistled :   "Who is the master
here ?   Who pays for the butter ? "

7

COURIERS flew from Antiochia to Caesarea, and from
Caesarea to Antioch.   Messengers arrived post-haste from
Italy and Egypt.   The Senate and the Imperial Guard had
proclaimed as Emperor the aged General Galba, a gouty,
morose, moody old gentleman.   He would not remain
emperor for long.   The army would decide who the next
emperor would be ;   the Rhine Army, the Danube Army,
the army in the East.   The Governor-General of Egypt,
Tiberius Alexander, established closer relations with the
two commanders in Asia.   Even Vespasian's dyspeptic
brother Sabinus, the chief of police, set himself in motion,
sent messages and made mysterious overtures.

There was much to be done, and Vespasian had no time
to study Aramaic for the sake of the girl Mara.   By
Jupiter, the fool of a girl must learn to be tender to him
in Latin.   But Mara would not learn.   In fact it took him
all his time to keep her from stabbing herself.

Such lack of understanding annoyed the commander.
He felt himself in a vague way responsible to the Jewish
God ;   he did not want the girl to create any unpleasantness
between him and Jehovah.   He did not trust Joseph in
this matter, so he tried through another intermediary to

get the girl to divulge what was really troubling her.   He
was surprised when he learned it.   This slip of a girl was
full of the same naive arrogance as his Jew.   Vespasian
grinned broadly and a little maliciously.   He knew now
how he could arrange everything to the satisfaction of
himself, the girl, and Joseph.

" You Jews," he said to Joseph that day in the presence
of Dame Caenis, " are filled from head to foot with impudent barbaric superstition.   Just imagine, Doctor Joseph ;
this child Mara is firmly convinced that she is unclean
because I have taken her into my bed.   Do you understand that ? "

" Yes," said Joseph.

" Then you're wiser than I am," said Vespasian.   " Is
there any means of making her clean again ? "

" No," said Joseph definitely.

Vespasian drank the good wine of Eshkol ; then he continued comfortably :   " But she knows of a means.   If a
Jew will marry her, then, she assures me, she will be pure
again."

" That is childish nonsense," said Joseph.

" It isn't such a stupid superstition as the first one,"
Vespasian remarked conciliatingly.

" She will find it hard," said Joseph, " to find a Jew who
will marry her.   The law forbids it."

" I shall find one," responded Vespasian affably.   Joseph
looked up.   " You, my little Jew," the Roman grinned.

Joseph grew pale.   Vespasian good-humouredly reproved
him :   " You have forgotten your manners, my prophet.
You could have said thank you, at least."

" I am a priest of the first rank," said Joseph ; his voice
sounded hoarse and curiously dead.

" A confoundedly contrary lot, these Jews," Vespasian

remarked to Caenis. " Once you've touched a bit of
women's flesh they lose all appetite for it. And the Emperor
Nero and myself both married women that had slept with
other men. What do you say to it, Caenis, old girl ? "

" I am one of the Hasmonaeans," said Joseph very softly,
" my family goes back to King David. If I marry this
woman I lose for ever my privileges as a priest, and the
children born of such a union are illegitimate and without
any rights. I am a priest of the first rank," he repeated
softly and stubbornly.

" You are dirt, as far as I am concerned," said Vespasian
bluntly and finally. " If you have a child I will have a
look at it in ten year's time. Then we shall see whether
it is your son or mine."

" Will you marry her ? " Dame Caenis asked with
interest.

Joseph was silent.

" Yes or no ? " Vespasian asked with sudden violence.

" I say neither yes nor no," replied Joseph. " God
who chose that Vespasian should be emperor has given
Vespasian this desire. I bow before God." And he
bowed profoundly.

Joseph slept badly during the following nights ; his
fetters chafed him. The fulfilment of his prophecies had
uplifted him ; all the more deeply was he humiliated now
by the Roman's insolent jest. He recalled the teaching of
the Essene Banus in the wilderness. Carnal desires drive
out the spirit of God ; it had been self-evident to him that
he must renounce the society of women until his prophecies
were fulfilled. His heart had been filled with carnal desire
for the girl Mara ; now he had to pay for it. If he
had to marry this girl, who through her captivity and this
affair with the Roman had become unclean, then he would

be an outcast from God, and liable to the punishment of a public whipping. He knew the law very well on this point ; here no evasion was possible, no pretext or excuse. " The vine shall not twine its tendrils round the thorn," that was the crucial passage. And the authentic commentary on the sentence, " He who shall couple with a beast is accursed," was to the effect that the priest who fornicated with a harlot was no better than one who coupled with a beast.

Alone, Joseph swallowed down his shame to the last drop. High play demanded high stakes. His fate was bound up with this Roman ; he would take the scandal upon him.

Vespasian expended much time and energy in squeezing all the enjoyment possible out of his jest. He went exhaustively into the complicated ramifications of the Jewish marriage rites, and also studied the ceremonial of betrothal and marriage, which in Galilee was not quite the same as in Judaea. He saw to it that everything was done according to the ancient tradition.

Custom demanded that the bride's guardian, if her father were dead, should fix with the bridegroom the price for the bride. Vespasian declared himself Mara's guardian. It was usual for the bridegroom to pay two hundred sesterces if the bride was a virgin, and a hundred sesterces if she was a widow. Vespasian put down in the marriage contract a hundred and fifty sesterces as the price of Mara, daughter of Lakish, and insisted that Joseph should sign a bond acknowledging his indebtedness to him for that sum. He summoned doctors and students from the schools of Tiberias, Magdala and Sepphoris, and the chief notabilities from the occupied territories, as witnesses of the marriage. Many refused to have anything to do with such an abomination.

Vespasian imposed fines upon them and extorted contributions from their communes.

The whole population of the town was summoned by heralds to take part in the ceremony. A magnificent bridal chair had to be brought from Tiberias for the marriage procession, for this chair was always employed for the weddings of great public figures. As the representative of her dead father Vespasian said to Mara as she left his house on her myrtle-wreathed bridal chair : " May you never return here again." Then she was carried through the city ; Jews from the best families in Galilee, they too crowned with myrtle, bore the bridal chair. In front went girls bearing torches and students swinging alabaster vessels filled with incense. Libations of wine and oil were poured out where the procession passed, and nuts and burned ears of corn were strewn in its path. The crowd sang : " Thou hast no need of myrrh and frankincense, beautiful one." In all the streets the people danced ; the matron of sixty years no less than the child of six had to show her paces ; even the miserable doctors had to dance, holding myrtle sprays in their hands ; for Vespasian wished the wedding to be celebrated according to ancient tradition.

So Joseph was conducted through the city of Caesarea, a long way, and one as dreadful to him as his journey through the Roman camp that day when he was brought to Vespasian for the first time At last he stood with Mara in the bridal tent, in the Chupa. The tent was of white linen embroidered with gold ; from the roof hung clusters of grapes, figs, and olives.

Vespasian and a number of his officers, as well as the chief Jewish notabilities in Galilee, witnessed Joseph's marriage to the girl Mara. They listened while he clearly and defiantly repeated the formula, which in his mouth was a

blasphemy : " Herewith I declare that thou art entrusted
to me according to the law of Moses and of Israel."   The
earth did not open and swallow him when the priest uttered
these forbidden words.   The clusters of fruit hanging from
the ceiling of the tent swayed lightly.   The people sang :
" A garden enclosed is my sister, my spouse ; a spring shut
up, a fountain sealed," but the girl Mara gazed at Joseph
shamelessly and tenderly with her great eyes and responded
with the appropriate verse :   " Let my beloved come into
his garden, and eat his pleasant fruits."

Vespasian asked everything to be translated, and grinned
with pleasure.   " I would only give you one piece of
advice, my dear fellow," he said to Joseph.   " Stay in the
garden as long as you can."

8

PRINCESS BERENICE, daughter of the first, sister of the
second, King Agrippa, emerged from her meditations in
the wilderness and returned to Judaea.   Passionate and
sensitive, she had suffered physically with the inhabitants
of the towns in Galilee when the Romans butchered them,
and had fled to the wilderness in the south.   There she fell
into a fever, rejected food and drink with loathing, scourged
herself, let her hair grow long and matted, wore a coarse
garment that chafed her skin, and submitted her frame to
the burning midday heats and the freezing nights.   She
lived in this way for weeks and months, alone, in utter
forsakenness of spirit, seeing nobody but the hermits, the
Essene brothers and sisters.

But when rumours of the events that were happening
in Rome, of Nero's death and the chaos under Galba's rule,
penetrated by incomprehensible ways even into the wilderness, the Princess flung herself with the same fury into

politics as she had done before into renunciation and repent-
ance. She had always been subject to these sudden alternations ; now she would bury herself in the Holy Scriptures,
imperiously and wildly seeking for God ; now she would
direct the full force of her daring and ingenious mind on the
complications of government in the Empire and the provinces.

During her journey she had already begun working ;
she sent out feelers and dispatched and received countless
letters and enquiries. Long before she reached Judaea
the threads spun between the East and the West, the balance
of power in the Empire, were clearly known to her ;
she had drawn up plans and taken up her position. There
were many factors to be considered ; the Rhine Army,
the Danube Army, the troops in the East ; the Senate, the
rich magnates in Rome and the provinces ; the personal
qualities and effective power of the Roman governors in
Britain, Gaul, Spain, Africa, not forgetting the head
officials in Greece and on the Black Sea, and that greedy,
morose, very aged person, the Emperor ; finally, the countless candidates for the succession, both the silent and the
vociferous ones. The more confusion there was in the
world, the better for her purpose. That confusion had
succeeded in maintaining Jerusalem and the Temple safe
and unsullied ; perhaps it might be possible to transfer the
centre of world rule once more to the East, so that the
world would be governed not from Rome, but from Jerusalem.

The Princess weighed everything and sought some point
where she could intervene. In the East, in her East, three
men held the reins of power : Tiberius Alexander, the
Governor of Egypt, Mucianus, the Governor of Syria,
Vespasian, the military commander in Judaea. She
resolved to visit his headquarters, so as to have a look at

this general. She was filled with prejudice against him.
People called him the forwarding agent ; he was said to be
sly, a crafty peasant, rude and gross ; in any case he had
dealt with her land brutally and bloodily. Her strong,
voluptuous lips twisted wryly when she thought of him.
And unfortunately she could not help thinking of him a
great deal ; he had become very pre-eminent ; he seemed
to have fortune on his side. The whole Orient was full of
rumours of divine omens and prophecies which pointed
to him.

Vespasian hesitated far longer than politeness permitted
before he gave an audience to the Princess. He, too, was
filled with prejudice against her, He had heard a great
deal about this precious dame, about her whims and
moods, her hectic love affairs, and her relations to her
brother, which were by no means sisterly. The snobbish
and affected bearing of this eastern woman was repellent
to him, but it would be madness to turn her gratuitously
into an enemy. She had countless connections in Rome,
she was considered very beautiful, she was enormously
rich ; even her wild mania for building—she and her brother
had scattered palaces over the whole Orient—had not
noticeably made any breach in her wealth.

For her audience with Vespasian Berenice attired
herself soberly and ceremoniously. Her noble face, still
tanned with the sun, rose regally from the complicated
folds of her robe ; her short, rebellious hair was without
ornament, her stiff brocade sleeves almost hid her beautiful,
tapering hands, still roughened by her life in the wilderness.
After a few introductory words she came at once to the
point : " I thank you, Consul Vespasian, for having spared
the city of Jerusalem so long." Her voice was deep, full
and rich, but there was a tiny, nervous tremor in it, and it

also sounded slightly broken, thickened by a faint, agitating
huskiness. With his hard, clear eyes Vespasian coolly
looked the lady up and down, then he said somewhat coldly :
" To be quite frank, I have not really spared your Jerusalem,
I have merely spared my soldiers. If your countrymen go
on as they are doing, then I fancy I shall be able to take the
city without any sacrifice of life."

Berenice replied courteously : " Please go on, Consul
Vespasian. It's a pleasure to listen to your Sabine dialect."
She herself spoke an easy and flawless Latin.

" It's true," Vespasian admitted good-humouredly, " I'm
an old peasant. That has its advantages, but its disad-
vantages too. For you, I mean."

Princess Berenice got to her feet ; she walked up quite
close to Vespasian, a little jauntily, in her celebrated walk :
" Why, really, are you so irritable with me ? Perhaps
people have been telling you stupid things about me. You
mustn't believe them. I am a Jewess, a granddaughter of
Herod and the Rasmonaean. My position is a somewhat
difficult one while your legions are in the country."

" I can quite understand, Princess Berenice," replied
Vespasian, " your indulging in all sorts of ingenious dreams
while there is a very old emperor in Rome who refuses to
name his successor. I should be sorry if I were compelled
to regard you as an enemy."

" My brother Agrippa is in Rome paying his homage to
Emperor Galba."

" My son Titus has left for Rome for the same purpose."

" I know that," said Berenice coolly. " Your son has
gone to lay his homage before Galba, although you have
reliable information from intercepted letters that the
Emperor wants to have you assassinated."

" When a very old gentleman," replied Vespasian, still

more coolly, " finds himself sitting on a very shaky throne,
he lays about him a little so as to keep his balance. That is
natural enough. If we two were as old as that we would
probably do just the same. What really is your game,
Princess Berenice ? "

" What is your game, Consul Vespasian ? "

" You orientals always like to get the other fellow to
lay his cards on the table first." The Princess's animated
and changing face was suddenly transformed with a great
and daring assurance. " I want," she said in her deep and
agitating voice, " the ancient and holy East to take it's due
share in the government of the world."

" That is a little too general for my Sabine peasant mind.
But I'm afraid our wishes are pretty divergent. For I
want all this melodramatic rubbish that has flowed into the
Empire from the East to stop. The oriental plans of Nero
and his eastern sympathies have plunged the Empire in
debt to the tune of several millions. I think that is a little
too much to pay for the holy wisdom of the ancient East."

" If Galba dies," Berenice asked bluntly, " won't the
eastern army want to have some say in the appointment of
the new emperor ? "

" I am for law and justice," said Vespasian.

" So are we all," replied Berenice, " but people's opinions
of what law and justice are sometimes differ."

" I would really be grateful to you, my dear lady, if you
would tell me clearly what you want."

Berenice gathered herself together ; her face became
quite calm. With quiet and savage intensity she said :
" I want you not to destroy the Temple of Jehovah."

Vespasian had been sent to the East with a mandate to
subjugate Judaea by every means that he considered justified.
For one moment he was tempted to answer : " The mainten-

ance of the Roman Empire unfortunately doesn't always
allow of a tender consideration for architecture." But he
saw her motionless and tensely composed face, and he only
grunted : "We aren't barbarians."

She did not reply. Full of melancholy uncertainty
she fixed her great tear-filled eyes on his, and he became
uncomfortable. Wasn't it a matter of complete indifference
to him whether this Jewess considered him a barbarian or
not ? Curiously enough, it was not a matter of complete
indifference. With her he felt the same slight embarrassment that he felt occasionally in the presence of Joseph.
He tried to pass it off by saying : "You mustn't try to
appeal to my vanity. I am no longer young enough for
that."

Berenice came to the conclusion that the forwarding
agent was a hard and tough fellow, confoundedly sly in
spite of all his frankness. She tried another tack. "Show
me a picture of your son Titus," she begged. He sent a
messenger to fetch the picture. She contemplated it with
interest and said a great many flattering things that should
have warmed the heart of a father. But Vespasian was old
and knew the world, and he saw quite clearly that she did
not in the least like the picture. They parted outwardly
on friendly terms, but both the Roman and the Jewess
knew that they were enemies.

9

WHEN at her command Joseph Ben Matthias called on
Berenice, she stretched out her hand with a gesture of
repulsion and cried : "Don't come nearer. Remain
where you are. You must not come within seven steps
of me."

Joseph turned pale, for she shrank from him as from a leper.

Berenice began : " I have read your book ; twice."

Joseph replied : " It would inspire any writer to write about ancestors such as ours."

Berenice violently tossed back her short, rebellious hair. It was true ; the man was related to her. " I regret bitterly, Cousin Joseph," she said, " that we are related to each other." She spoke quite quietly, and the vibrating huskiness was only a soft overtone to her voice. " I can't understand how you could remain alive when Jotapat fell. Now there is no one in Judaea who doesn't loathe the name of Joseph Ben Matthias."

Joseph thought of the words of Justus of Tiberias : " Your Doctor Joseph is a scoundrel." But women's chatter did not bother him. " Certainly a great many hard things are being said about me," he replied, " but I fancy that no one has said that I am a coward. I ask you to reflect that sometimes it isn't very hard to die. It would have been easy for me to die ; it was a great temptation. It needed resolution to live. It needed courage. I re-mained alive because I knew that I was an instrument of Jehovah."

Berenice's lip curled ; her whole face expressed scorn and contempt. " There's a rumour flying through the Orient," she said, " that a Jewish prophet has declared this Roman to be the Messiah. Are you the prophet ? "

" I know," said Joseph quietly, " that Vespasian is the man of whom the Scripture speaks." Berenice leaned forward over the space which she had insisted on setting between them. It comprised the whole breadth of the room ; braziers were standing there, for it was a cold winter day. She contemplated this man ; he still wore his fetters, but he looked well groomed. "I must have a good look at this prophet," she sneered, "who willingly swallowed what the Roman threw up, when he was told to do so. It made me sick with shame when I heard that the doctors of Sepphoris had to look on at your wedding."

"Yes," said Joseph quietly, "I swallowed that too."

All at once he looked small and wretched. Something else tormented and humiliated him more than his marrying that girl. In the bridal tent he had made a vow that he would not touch Mara. But then Mara had come to him ; she had sat down on his bed, young, fresh, ardent, full of expectation. He had taken her, had been as incapable of refusing her as he had been incapable of refusing the water that was offered him when he came out of the cave. Ever since Mara had clung to him. Her great eyes remained fixed on him with the same devotion when he took her, and when, after it was all over, he roughly and contemptuously sent her away.

Berenice was more than justified. He had not only swallowed what the Roman rejected ; he had found pleasure in it. When Berenice turned to another subject Joseph heaved a sigh of relief. She began to speak of politics and raged against Vespasian : "I won't have this peasant planting himself on the neck of the world. I won't have it !" Her voice was hoarse with passion. Joseph stood quietly regarding her. But he was filled with ironical amusement when he thought of her impotence. She saw that quite clearly. "Go and tell him, Cousin Joseph," she said scornfully. "Betray me to him. Perhaps he will give you a still richer reward than the slave girl Mara."

Separated by the breadth of the room they stood there, these two people of Jewish blood, both young, both beautiful, both driven on by a burning desire towards the goal they

had set in front of them.   Eye to eye they stood, filled with
scorn against each other, and yet at heart very alike.

"If I told the general," said Joseph mockingly, "that
you are his enemy, Cousin Berenice, he would laugh."

"Then make him laugh, this Roman master of yours,"
said Berenice.   "Perhaps it's for that he keeps you beside
him.   But I shall wash my hands, Cousin Joseph, I shall
take a good bath when you are gone."

Joseph smiled to himself on the way back.   He preferred
to be reviled rather than treated with indifference by a
woman like Berenice.

10

At Vespasian's headquarters in Caesarea appeared an aged
Jewish gentleman, who was received with great respect ; he
was very small and very dignified ; it was Doctor Jochanan
Ben Sakkai, Rector of the Temple University and Chief
Justice of Judaea.   In the Jewish circles of Caesarea he
had told in his frail voice of the abominations that filled the
capital.   How the leaders of the moderate parties
had been butchered, including the High Priest Anan, most
of the aristocrats, and also many of the Scriptural Believers ;
and how at present the leaders of the Avengers of Israel
were savagely warring among themselves.   They had even
set up engines of war in the outer halls of the Temple, and
people bearing their offering to the altar had been hit.
Occasionally employing the ancient phrase, he would
emphasise what he said by adding : "Mine eyes have seen
it."   He, too, had been able to steal out of Jerusalem only
at great peril to himself.   He had given out a report
that he was dead ; then his scholars had borne him in a
coffin outside the walls of Jerusalem to be buried.

He begged for an interview with the Roman general,

and Vespasian sent for him immediately. The great
Jewish doctor appeared before the Roman ; his skin was
yellow with age, but his blue eyes looked remarkably alive
in his wrinkled face fringed with the little white beard.   He
said : " I have come, Consul Vespasian, to discuss peace
and submission.   I have no power at my back.   The
Avengers of Isreal hold the power in Jerusalem ; but the
authority of the law is not yet dead, and I have brought
with me my seal as Chief Justice.   That is not much.
But nobody knows better than Rome that a great empire
cannot hold together for long except with the help of justice,
the law and its seal ; and so it is perhaps not such a very
little thing after all."

Vespasian replied : " I am delighted to talk with the
man who bears the most honourable name in Judaea.   But
I was sent here solely to wield the sword.   Only the
Emperor in Rome and his Senate can negotiate a peace."

Jochanan Ben Sakkai shook his little old head.   Slyly
and softly, in the singsong of the Orient, he continued :
" There are many who call themselves emperor.   But
there is only one with whom I would exchange my seal
and pledge.   Was it because of Galba that Lebanon fell ?
He who wrought the fall of Lebanon is the mighty man, the
Adir.   It was not Galba that wrought the fall of Lebanon."

Vespasian gazed suspiciously at the old man.   Then he
asked : " Have you spoken to my prisoner, Joseph Ben
Matthias ? "

Jochanan Ben Sakkai said no, and looked somewhat
surprised.   Vespasian added awkwardly, almost apologetically : " Forgive me.   I know you haven't spoken to him."

Then he seated himself, so that he might not have to
look down at the old man, and said : " Please tell me what
you have to offer, and what you want in exchange."

Jochanan stretched out his withered hand and said : " I
offer you in writing and under my seal the submission of
the High Council and doctors of Jerusalem to the Senate
and people of Rome.   In return I ask only one thing :
Give me a little town where I can found a university, and
allow me to teach in freedom there."

" You're hatching a fine quarrel between me and Rome,"
Vespasian grinned.

Jochanan Ben Sakkai became still smaller and humbler.
" What more do you wish ?   I only want to plant a tiny
shoot from the mighty tree of Jerusalem.   Give me, let
us say, the little town of Jabne.   Jabne, it would be such a
very little university ! "   He eagerly assailed the Roman,
gesticulating, insisting on the smallness of his university.
Oh, it would be such a little thing, his university at Jabne,
and he opened his little hand and closed it again.

Vespasian replied :   " Very well, I shall convey your
suggestion to Rome."

" Don't do that," Jochanan implored.   " I would much
rather deal with you, Consul Vespasian."   And he reiterated
stubbornly :   " You are the Adir."

Vespasian got up ;   broad and stalwart, a peasant, he
stood in front of the seated doctor.   " To be quite frank,"
he said, " I don't quite understand what sort of fool you
take me for.   You are an old man, wise, and from all
appearances relatively honest.   Won't you explain ?   Don't
you find it a little hard, for instance, that I should be the
Adir in the land that your God Jehovah allotted to you ?
I have always been told that you Jews are far more bitter
against foreigners than any other people."

Jochanan had closed his eyes.   " When the angels of
God," he said, " wanted to raise a hymn of joy after the
Egyptians were drowned in the Red Sea, Jehovah said :

My creatures are drowning and you want to raise a hymn of joy ! "

The general went up quite close to the little scholar, tapped him lightly and confidentially on the shoulder, and asked slyly : " But you must admit this much. You don't regard us as quite genuine and authentic human creatures ? "

With his eyes still shut Jochanan replied quietly, almost absently : " At the feast of the wine grape we sacrifice seventy oxen to God as an atonement for the Gentiles."

Vespasian said with unaccustomed courtesy : " If you are not too tired, Doctor Jochanan, I should like you to tell me a few more things."

" I'll be glad to answer your questions, Consul Vespasian," said the venerable doctor.

Vespasian leant his hands on the table. Bending across he asked eagerly : " Has a Gentile an immortal soul ? "

Jochanan replied : " There are six hundred and thirteen commandments which we Jews are bound to keep. The Gentile is bound to keep only seven commandments. If he keeps them, then the Holy Ghost will descend upon him too."

" What are these seven commandments ? " enquired the Roman.

Jochanan raised his wrinkled brows ; his blue eyes, suddenly very clear and young, gazed into the grey eyes of Vespasian. " There is one beginning ' thou shalt ' and six beginning ' thou shalt not,' " he said. " The Gentile must live justly, he must not deny his God, nor worship idols, nor murder, nor steal, nor commit adultery, nor treat animals with cruelty."

Vespasian reflected for a little, and at last said regretfully : " Then there is unfortunately little hope that the Holy Ghost will descend upon me."

The doctor went on coaxingly : " Surely you don't think there's any danger to Rome in my teaching such things in my little university in Jabne ? "

Vespasian replied stubbornly : " It may be dangerous or not, and your university big or little ; what real inducement have I to grant you such a favour ? "

The old man put on a sly expression, raised his little hand and brought it down again, and replied once more in his oriental sing-song : " Until you are Adir you can have no reason to conquer Jerusalem ; for you will probably need your troops so as to become Adir. And once you are appointed, probably you won't have any time to conquer Jerusalem. But in that case it might be to your advantage to take back with you to Rome, if not the news that Jerusalem is captured, at least the submission of Judaea. Perhaps that is worth the small concession I have asked you for."

He stopped ; he seemed exhausted. Vespasian had listened with the keenest attention. " If the other Jews were as sly as you," he said with a smile, concluding the interview, " then possibly I should never have been in a position to be greeted by you as Adir."

11

THERE were sins for which the venerable doctor, in spite of his mild clemency, could show no indulgence, and Joseph's heart beat apprehensively when he was commanded to appear before the old man. But Jochanan did not insist that Joseph should remain at a distance of seven paces. Joseph bowed his head, his hand to his brow, and the old man blessed his favourite scholar.

Joseph said : " I have used the words of the prophets equivocally. I am guilty of falsehood. Much misfortune has been caused by this."

The old man replied : " Jerusalem and the Temple were
ripe for destruction before you did what you did ; the gates
of the Temple fly open now if one but breathes on them.
You are presumptuous even in your accusation of yourself.
I want to talk to you, Doctor Joseph, my scholar," he went
on.   " In Jerusalem people thought that your heart failed
you once, and so they excommunicated you ; but I believe
in you, and I want to say a few words to you." These
words refreshed Joseph like dew at the turn of the year,
and his heart opened.

" Our kingdom is lost," said Jochanan.   " But it is not
the kingdom that holds us together.   Other peoples, too,
have founded kingdoms ; they have fallen ; and new kingdoms will arise, and they too will fall.   The kingdom is
not the greatest thing."

" What is the greatest thing, my father ? "

" It is not the people that create a community, nor the
state.   Our fellowship is not in the kingdom, but in the
law.   So long as the doctrine and the law endure, we have a
bond firmer than any state.   The law endures as long as
there is a voice to proclaim it.   As long as the voice of
Jacob is heard the arms of Esau are powerless."

Joseph asked hesitatingly : " Have I the voice, my
father ? "

" The others believe," replied Jochanan, " that you have
renounced your Jewish heritage, Joseph Ben Matthias.
But when the salt is dissolved in water it is still there, and
when the water evaporates the salt still remains."

These words of the old man both exalted and humbled
Joseph, so that for a long time he could not speak.   Then
softly and shyly he said to his teacher : " Will you not tell
me, my father, what your thoughts are ? "

" Yes," replied Jochanan, " I shall tell you.   We shall

surrender the Temple. In place of the visible house of God we shall build an invisible one ; we shall shield the breath of God within walls of words instead of stone. What is the breath of God ? The doctrine and the law. No one can divide us as long as we have tongues to speak or paper on which to inscribe the law. That is why I have begged the Roman for the town of Jabne, so that I might found a university there. I believe that he will give it to me."

" Your thought, my father, will need the labour of many generations to realise it."

" We have time enough," replied the old man.

" But will not the Romans prevent it ? " asked Joseph.

" They will certainly try to hinder it ; power is always suspicious of the spirit. But the. spirit is resilient. No door can be closed tightly enough to keep it out. They will destroy our state and our Temple ; we shall build instead our doctrine and our law. They will forbid us the word ; we shall communicate with one another by signs. They will forbid us the Scripture ; we shall invent secret codes. They will bar the straight road against us ; God's greatness will not be diminished if those who know Him have to seek Him by tortuous ways."

The old man closed his eyes, opened them again and said : " It is not given to us to consummate the work, but it is laid upon us never to cease from striving. It is for that that we are chosen."

" And the Messiah ? " asked Joseph with a final despairing hope. The conversation had begun to exhaust the doctor, but he summoned up all his strength ; it was essential that he should pass on his knowledge to his favourite scholar Joseph. He made a sign to Joseph to bend down, then whispered in a feeble voice into his ear. " It is a question," he whispered, " whether the Messiah will ever come. But

one must believe in Him. We must never count upon the
advent of the Messiah, but we must always believe that He
will come."

On his way back Joseph felt dejected. The faith of
this great old man was not a resplendent faith that inspired
one, but something laboured and tortuous, perpetually
involving itself with heresy, always guarding itself agains
heresy, a burden to the spirit. In spite of the difference
in their ages there was not much real difference between
Jochanan Ben Sakkai and Justus of Tiberias. Joseph felt
despondent.

12

THE venerable doctor had heard a great deal of scandal
about Joseph's marriage. He commanded Mara, the
daughter of Lakish, to come to him, and spoke to her. He
sniffed the scent that rose from her sandals. She said :
" When I pray I always put on these sandals, for I like to
kneel before God clean and fragrant." She knew many
prayers by heart ; it was not permissible merely to patter
them off ; they must come from the heart, and one must
carry them in the heart. She addressed him trustfully.
" I have heard that it takes five hundred years to pass from
the earth to heaven, and five hundred years again to pass
from one heaven to another, and another five hundred years
to traverse each of the heavens. And yet when I stand
behind one of the pillars in the synagogue, and merely
whisper, it is as if I were whispering into Jehovah's ear.
Is it a presumptuous sin, learned doctor, for me to believe
that Jehovah is as near to me as the ear to the mouth that
whispers into it ? "

Jochanan Ben Sakkai listened with interest to the thoughts
that took shape behind the girl's white brow, and discussed
them as gravely with her as he would have with any of the

doctors of the Temple. When she took her leave he laid his soft withered hand on her head and pronounced the old blessing : " May God make thee as Rachel and Leah."

He heard that Joseph was resolved to divorce Mara as soon as Vespasian removed his opposition ; it was not difficult to get a divorce. In the Scripture it said clearly and simply : " When a man hath taken a wife, and married her, and it come to pass that she find no favour in his eyes, because he hath found some uncleanness in her ; then let him write her a bill of divorcement, and give it in her hand, and send her out of his house." Jochanan said : " There are two things which, though they cannot be heard by the physical ear a mile away, cry from end to end of the earth. The one is the crash of a tree that has been felled while it is still bearing fruit ; the other is the sigh of a woman whom her husband sends away while she still loves him."

Joseph said defiantly : " Have I not found uncleanness in her ? "

Jochanan replied : " You have not found uncleanness in her ; her uncleanness was before you married her. Examine yourself, Doctor Joseph. I shall not be a party to your divorcing this woman."

13

VESPASIAN'S relations to the Emperor Galba were not quite so simple as he had represented to Princess Berenice, Titus had gone to Rome not to pay his homage, but principally to ask for the high state post that he still lacked. But he had also a higher aim. Vespasian's brother, the stiff and sullen Sabinus, had hinted that it was not impossible that the old and childless Emperor might adopt Vespasian's son in order to bind the army in the East to him. This news had put an end for the moment to the uneasy negotiating between Vespasian and Mucianus. Again and again each had generously assured the other that he had no intention of seizing supreme power ; if either should be in a position to do so, then the other would share in the glory. In reality each of them knew that he was not strong enough to fight the other, and so the letter from Sabinus had provided a welcome way out.

But in mid-winter news arrived which put an end to all these plans. Supported by the Imperial Guard and the Senate, a man who did not take the East into his calculations at all had seized power ; Otho, Poppaea's first husband. The old emperor was murdered ; the young emperor had courage, ability, and the sympathies and respect of the people. No one knew whether Titus would continue his journey and lay his homage before the new ruler or simply return again. Here in the Orient, at any rate, one did not feel that there was much hope of opposing the young emperor with success, and then whom was the East to choose ? Old Galba's end had come too soon, with the East still undecided ; Vespasian and Mucianus made their troops swear allegiance to the Emperor Otho.

Meanwhile nobody believed that the new emperor's rule would be lasting. Otho could depend on the Italian troops, but he was out of touch with the armies in the provinces. The young emperor did not sit any more firmly on his throne than the old one had done.

Every day Princess Berenice received detailed reports from Rome. After her life of renunciation in the wilderness she flung herself with redoubled ardour into politics. She intrigued with the Imperial ministers, the senators, the governors and generals in the East. The East would not be confronted a second time with a *fait accompli*. This very spring it must make itself ready to conquer the capital.

It dared no longer be disunited ; it must have one head, and that head must be Mucianus. First of all she must secure the explicit consent of Mucianus, if she was to set him up as Vespasian's rival.

With a great and magnificent train Berenice proceeded to Antioch. She cautiously sounded Mucianus. That experienced gentleman was very capable of appreciating the talents of the Jewish princess, her beauty, intelligence, taste, wealth, and passionate devotion to politics. They soon understood each other. But Berenice was unable to bring Mucianus to the point. With the greatest frankness he confessed all his inner desires. Yes, he was ambitious, and he was not a coward, but he was exhausted. To conquer Rome with an army from the East would be a confoundedly ticklish business. He wasn't the man for the job. He could deal with diplomats, with senators, governors, and business men. But the army held the whip hand at the moment, and to haggle with these promoted sergeants went against his grain. He kept his keen, melancholy, insatiable gaze fixed on the princess. " One gets tired of burning out the eyes of these Polyphemuses. There is no relation between the risk and the profit. As things stand to-day, Vespasian is really the only man. He has the necessary coarseness and vulgarity to be popular in our age. At bottom he's such a pure incarnation of the age that sometimes I feel I almost like him. Make him emperor, Princess Berenice, and let me finish in peace my book on the natural history of the Empire."

Berenice did not relax her efforts ; she did not employ words only ; she squandered money with a free hand to obtain support for her candidate. Her arguments became more and more urgent ; she flattered and goaded Mucianus by turns. A man with so much inner vitality must not hold back, must not shrink from the fray. He replied smilingly : " If I only had a lady like you, Princess, sincerely on my side, then I might be tempted to dare this stupid hazard in spite of all my scruples. But you aren't really for me, you're only against Vespasian."

Berenice flushed and denied that it was so ; she spoke at length and eloquently, and tried to shake his decision. He listened courteously and pretended that he was impressed by her words. But while she went on pouring out her heart she saw that he was scribbling some words in the sand, Greek words certainly not intended for her eyes, yet she could decipher them. " To some the gods give talent, to others good fortune." As she read all the conviction died out of her voice.

When Joseph Ben Matthias himself appeared in Antioch Berenice realised at last that her journey to Mucianus was hopeless. She guessed at once and rightly that Joseph had been sent by Vespasian to undermine her plans.

Joseph did not go bluntly about his task. He waited until the governor came to him. Mucianus was delighted to hear again the strange, ardent and moving voice of the Jewish prophet. He spent hours in questioning Joseph about the customs, traditions and antiquities of his people. By this route they reached the Jewish kings and Joseph told Mucianus the story of Saul and David.

" Saul was the first king in Israel," said Joseph. " But among us very few people are called Saul and a great many are called Samuel. We hold Samuel to be a greater man than Saul."

" Why is that ? " asked Mucianus.

" The man who confers power," replied Joseph, " is greater than the man who holds it. The king-maker is greater than the king."

Mucianus smiled. " You are a proud people."

" Perhaps we are proud," Joseph admitted frankly.
" But doesn't it seem to you, too, that the power that guides
events from the background is finer, more spiritual and
more fascinating than the power that displays itself before
the eyes of the whole world ? "   Mucianus neither agreed
nor disagreed.   Joseph went on, and his words were words
of knowledge purchased by much painful experience.
" Power makes one stupid.   I was never more stupid than
during the short time that I possessed power.   Samuel was
greater than Saul."

" The figure I like best in your history," said Mucianus
with a smile, " is the young David.   A pity," he sighed,
" that young Titus's plans have been wrecked."

Soon after Joseph's appearance in Antioch Berenice
said farewell to Mucianus.   She renounced her hopes.
She went to meet her brother, who was expected in Galilee
in a few days.   He had been in Rome, but in his heart he
expected Otho's reign to last only for a few weeks longer,
and had quietly left the city while there was still time, so
as not to be obliged to swear allegiance to yet another
Roman Emperor.   Berenice took heart, now that she was
to see her longed-for brother ; the bitterness of failure would
be alleviated by that joy.   " Sweet Princess," said Mucianus
in farewell, " now that I shall be missing your company, I
can't understand why, to please you, I didn't set myself up
as a candidate after all."

" I, too, find that difficult to understand," replied Berenice.

15

SHE found her brother in Tiberias.   The new palace was
completed.   More beautiful than ever, white and golden,
it shone over city and lake.   Certain windowless halls were

built of a Cappadocian stone so transparent that even when
the doors were closed a subdued light filled them.
The whole palace was airy, not overladen with ornamentation, as was the fashion at that time in Rome.   The
architect's masterpiece was the dining-hall.   It's domed
roof was so high that one's struggling gaze could scarcely
reach the expanse of ivory ceiling ; and in the ceiling was a
sliding door from which flowers and scented water could
be showered down upon the guests.

Brother and sister walked through the palace ; they
held each other's hands, filled with a deep joy in one another.
Spring had come, already the days were longer, and with
expanded breasts the beautiful pair wandered through the
airy galleries ; with the eyes of connoisseurs they took in
the symmetrical proportions of the building and the rareness
of the material. Agrippa spoke sarcastically of the new palaces
he had seen in Rome, of their gigantic and meaningless
dimensions, their tastelessly redundant ornamentation.
Otho had given fifty millions towards the completion of
the Golden House begun by Nero ; but Otho himself would
hardly see the work finished.   Berenice curled her lip.
" They are only collectors, these Roman barbarians.   They
think that if they inlay some very rare marble with another
equally rare and embellish it with as much gold as possible,
it's the last perfection of architecture.   They have no talent
except for power."

" A very profitable talent, all the same," said Agrippa.

Berenice paused.   " Must I really put up with this
Vespasian," she lamented.   " Can you ask that of me, my
brother ?   He is so coarse and vulgar ; he pants when he
breathes like a dog that has been running."

Agrippa said gloomily : " When I visited him recently
in Caesarea he set fish before me and drew my attention

repeatedly to the fact that they were caught in the Lake of Genezareth. When I refused to eat that loathsome dish he chaffed me cruelly. I had lots of good answers I could have given him, but I swallowed them down."

"He drives me almost crazy with exasperation," Berenice burst out. "When I hear his doltish witticisms it's as if I were in a swarm of stinging midges. And we're to help this man to become Emperor!"

Agrippa said gravely: "Any Emperor that the West sets up will be pitiless to the East. The general is clever and moderate. He will take what he needs. And the rest he will leave us." He shrugged his shoulders. "It's the army that makes emperors, and the army swears by Vespasian. Be my clever sister," he implored her.

16

TITUS was in Corinth on his way to Rome when the news of Galba's murder reached him. There was no point in proceeding farther. He had felt certain that Galba would adopt him; and the Emperor's premature death was a hard blow. He had no desire to pay homage to this Otho, in whose place he had himself dreamt he would sit. He remained in Corinth, spent fourteen wild days in the light city, days crowded with women and boys and vice of every kind. Then he tore himself away, and though it was a bad time of the year returned to Caesarea.

On the ship his grandmother's ambitious dream flamed up wildly in him. General Titus, young as he was, had a chequered life behind him. His father's ups and downs, the alternations from consul to forwarding agent, from pompous ostentation to crushing poverty, had affected him too. He had been brought up with Prince Britannicus, had sat at the same table as that brilliant young candidate for the throne, had eaten of the food with which Nero had poisoned his companion, and had himself been very ill. He knew the magnificence of the Palatine and the squalor of his father's needy town residence, the quiet life of the country and the perils of campaigns on the German and British frontiers.   He loved his father ; his sober wisdom, his capacity, his sound commonsense.   But often, too, he hated him for his boorish ways, his caution, his lack of dignity.   Titus would endure for weeks and months poverty and hardship ; then suddenly a savage desire for luxury and dissipation would overcome him.   He admired the unaffected dignity of the old and noble Roman families, and his heart was exalted by the hieratic and sumptuous pomp of the ancient royal lines of the Orient.   Urged on by his uncle, Sabinus, he had married while very young an austere and dried-up lady of noble family, Marcia Furnilla ; she had presented him with a daughter, but that had not increased his affection for her ; she sat forlorn and wretched in Rome ; he never saw her or wrote to her.

When the ship neared Cyprus he felt he could not pass the mysterious island without having a look at it.   He visited the dark shrine of the Paphian Venus, contemplated the altars which no rain could wet although they stood under the open sky, and the strange image of the goddess, which was without human form, an equivocal figure, broad at the base and narrowing to a point.   He was not content with the general empty predictions provided by the priest ; he desired to be told more particular things, personal things regarding himself, and finally the priest was able to see his future distinctly :   great spaces and throngs of people. This prophecy made Titus happy for the rest of his tempestuous voyage.

Old Vespasian received his son with a grin, half regretful

and half pleased. " Evidently our fate has only a single line, my son, the line leading up and then down again. We must see to it that the next time we get up earlier in the morning and set about things more wisely. The Saviour is to go out from Judaea. You are young, my son, you mustn't blame my Jews."

17

AGRIPPA and his sister sent out invitations for a feast to celebrate the rebuilding of their palace in Tiberias. Vespasian could not endure the Princess, so he sent his son instead.

Titus was not displeased with his mission. He loved Judaea. Its people were old and wise, and though they started brainless enterprises they had an instinct for the beyond, for the eternal. The strange and invisible God Jehovah allured and teased the young Roman. King Agrippa with his elegance, his melancholy grace, impressed him. Titus departed for Tiberias in good spirits.

Agrippa greeted him with great cordiality and showed him round the palace. Titus admired the symmetrical beauty of the building and also, with a slight feeling of envy, the unostentatious firmness with which Agrippa controlled his servants. He noted that the King's sandals were of bast, but that each was embellished with a great precious stone ; he himself would never had hit upon such a practical and yet elegant solution of the problem of how to devise a shoe that could be worn comfortably during a long repast.

Greatly as Agrippa and his palace charmed him, Titus was deeply disappointed by the Princess. He was presented to her just before dinner. He was accustomed to become intimate with women quickly, but to his first sentences she merely listened with polite and indifferent attention. He thought her cold and haughty ; her deep and slightly husky voice repelled him. He paid little attention to her during dinner, and so had all the more to devote to the rest of the company. He was a merry talker, an amusing story-teller, and he was listened to with attention and appreciation. With a certain Captain Jachim he got on specially well ; he forgot the Princess, and during the long meal they only exchanged a few words. The meal came to an end. Berenice rose ; she was dressed according to the Judaean fashion in a robe consisting of one piece, a precious, stiffly falling brocade. She nodded to Titus with polite indifference and began to ascend the stairs, her hand lightly resting on her brother's shoulder. Titus mechanically stared after her. He had involved himself in a sham fierce debate on military technique with Captain Jachim. Suddenly he broke off in the middle of a sentence, his restless inquisitive eyes became vigilant, and he gazed intently at the pair going up the stairs. His somewhat too short lips were slightly parted. His knees trembled. Without ceremony he left the captain standing and hastened after Berenice and her brother.

How beautifully that woman walked ! No, she did not walk, there was only one word to describe her, she floated. It was ridiculous, no doubt, to employ such a poetical term, but for the walk of this woman nothing else would serve. " You seem to be in a hurry," she said in her deep voice. Until now its slight huskiness had made him uncomfortable, had almost repelled him. Now it agitated him and was full of mysterious allurement. He said something to the effect that the army must always hurry ; it was rather feeble, he usually found better repartees. He was filled with the awkward adoration of a boy. Berenice was quite aware of the impression she had made upon him, and she thought him quite likeable, of a certain angular charm.

They talked about the sciences of physiognomy and graphology. These were a great rage at that time both in the East and the West. Berenice asked to see Titus's handwriting. Titus pulled out his gilt-edged writing tablet, smiled maliciously and wrote. Berenice was astonished ; for to the most minute flourish it was the writing of his father. Titus admitted that he had played a joke upon her ; really he had no handwriting of his own left, he had so often trespassed on that of others. But now she must show him her writing. She read what he had written. It was a sentence from a modern epic : " The eagles of the legions spread their wings for flight, upbearing with them the soldiers' hearts." She became grave, hesitated for a moment, then she erased his sentence and wrote : " The flight of the eagles cannot hide the Invisible One in the Holy of Holies." The young general contemplated the script ; it was somewhat childish and conventionally correct. He thought for a moment, then without rubbing out the sentence he wrote underneath : " Titus would like to see the Invisible One in the Holy of Holies." He handed the tablet and the pencil back to her. She wrote : " The Temple of Jerusalem must not be destroyed." Now there was only a little space left on the tablet. Titus wrote : " The Temple of Jerusalem shall not be destroyed."

He made to put away the tablet. She begged him to let her keep it. She laid her hand on his shoulder and asked when this horrible war was going to end. The worst thing of all was the heart-breaking, hopeless waiting. A quick end was a merciful end. Wouldn't he take Jerusalem and be done with it ? Titus hesitated ; he felt flattered. " That doesn't depend upon me." Berenice—how could he ever have thought her cold and haughty—went on persuasively and confidently : " But it does depend upon you."

After Titus had gone Agrippa asked his sister what her impression was. " He has a weak, ugly mouth, don't you think ? "

Berenice smiled. " There are lots of things that I dislike in this youth. He has many points of resemblance with his father. But Jewish women have been able to manage barbarians before this. For example, Esther and Ahasuerus, and Irene and the seventh Ptolemy."

Agrippa said, and Berenice was quite well aware of the gentle warning in his words : " On the other hand our great grandmother, Mariamne, lost her head playing at that game."

Berenice rose and walked up and down. " Be easy in your mind, dear brother," she said, and her voice remained gentle, but she was very sure of herself and very triumphant. " This boy Titus will not have my head cut off."

18

IMMEDIATELY on his return to Caesarea Titus assailed his father with prayers to begin the siege of Jerusalem. He became quite violent. He couldn't endure this state of affairs any longer. He felt ashamed before his officers. Such prolonged hesitation couldn't be interpreted except as weakness. Roman prestige in the East was in peril ; Vespasian's prudence bordered on cowardice. Stately Dame Caenis listened disapprovingly. " What are you thinking of, Titus ? Are you stupid, or only pretending to be stupid ? "

Titus replied angrily that Caenis could not understand such things ; she could not be expected to understand a soldier's sense of honour. Vespasian strode up massively to his son. " But I expect you, my lad, to apologise to Caenis at once."

Caenis remained quite calm. " He's right, I really haven't much sense of dignity. Dignity is always more popular with young people than commonsense. But he must see for himself that only an idiot would give up his army at such a time."

Vespasian asked : " Have they been getting at you in Tiberias, my boy ? Or has the Paphian oracle that prophesied great spaces and crowds of people gone to your head ? Nothing but prophecies nowadays. First comes my Jew and next your Paphian priest. I'm only sixty yet. You'll have to wait in patience for another ten years."

When Titus was gone Caenis burst out against the filthy pack in Tiberias. Of course it was these Jews that were behind Titus. That soft-stepping king, that peacock Berenice, and that unctuous, uncanny fellow Joseph. Vespasian would do better to leave the oriental rabble out of account altogether and treat with Mucianus, and in the Roman way. The general listened attentively. Then he said : " You're a clever and resolute woman. But you don't understand the East. In the East I shan't be able to get on without the money and cunning of my Jews. In this country the most crooked roads are the shortest."

News came that the northern army had proclaimed their commander Vitellius as emperor. Otho had fallen, and the Senate and people of Rome had acknowledged Vitellius as their new master. The world gazed tensely towards the East, and the new ruler, who was a thick-witted glutton, started apprehensively whenever the eastern commander was named. But Vespasian behaved as though he saw nothing. Calmly, without hesitation, he commanded his legions to swear allegiance to the new emperor, and reluctantly and sullenly Tiberias Alexander followed his example in Egypt, as Mucianus did in Syria. From every side pressure was exerted on Vespasian. But he pretended not to understand and remained stubbornly loyal.

To secure his position in the West the Emperor was forced to send huge divisions to the capital, four legions from the Lower Rhine, the two Mainz legions, and forty-six auxiliary regiments. Vespasian watched with narrowed eyes. He was a skilful soldier, and he knew that things could not be very pleasant in a city like Rome with a hundred thousand demoralised mercenaries quartered there. The soldiers who had proclaimed Vitellius emperor were waiting for their pay. There was little money to pay them with, nor, if Vespasian knew the army, would they content themselves merely with their pay. They had behind them a very arduous period of service in Germany. Now they were in Rome and would look forward to enjoying the advantage of the shorter period of service and the higher pay of the Imperial Guard. Twenty thousand men, if it came to the pinch, could be garrisoned in Rome ; but what could Vitellius do with the others ? In the eastern armies a rumour grew more and more persistent that Vitellius intended to send these soldiers to the beautiful and warm East as a reward for their services. When they took their oath of allegiance the eastern troops had managed to raise only a thin cheer for their new ruler ; now they publicly showed their discontent. They held meetings, and swore that there would be trouble if anyone tried to send them to the rigours of Germany, or the mists of Britain. The commanders in the East noted with pleasure these signs of insubordination. Pressed by their officers to divulge how much truth there was in the rumoured redistribution of the army, the generals remained silent and shrugged their shoulders expressively and regretfully. Wilder and wilder news arrived from Rome. The Imperial finances were in hopeless disorder, trade was at a standstill, over all Italy, including the capital itself, there had been looting, the new and disorganised court was lazy, gluttonous and shameless, the Empire was going to the dogs. In the East the general indignation grew. Tiberius Alexander and King Agrippa fed it with bribes and rumours. Over all the great territory from the Nile to the Euphrates the prophecies of Vespasian's future greatness grew ; again the marvellous prediction made by the captive Jewish General, Joseph Ben Matthias, in the presence of witnesses, was in every mouth. The Saviour would go out from Judaea. When Joseph, still wearing his fetters, went through the streets of Caesarea, he was greeted everywhere with reverence and awed whispering.

19

THE air of that early summer was magically light and exhilarating on the coasts of Judaea. With his hard, clear eyes Vespasian gazed out over the shining sea, waited and watched. He became more and more taciturn, his stern face became sterner and more imperious, his stiff body tauter, the man visibly grew. He studied the dispatches from Rome. Chaos everywhere in the Empire, the finances ruined, the army demoralised, and law and order at an end. The Saviour would go out from Judaea. But Vespasian compressed his lips and curbed his impatience. Things would have to ripen ; he must let them come to him.

Caenis gazed at the broad impassive man and did not know what to make of him. Until now he had never kept any secrets from her ; but now he was secret and incomprehensible. The man had grown greater ; he was too great for her. She loved him more than ever.

She wrote an awkward, housewifely-anxious letter to Mucianus. All Italy was waiting for the eastern army to

arise and save the fatherland. Vespasian did nothing, said
nothing, made no move. She felt helpless. In Italy she
would have been able to do something against Vespasian's
strange passivity ; but in this accursed, uncanny Judaea
nobody knew where one was. She urgently begged
Mucianus, as Roman to Roman, to try to shake Vespasian
out of his lethargy.

This letter was sent off at the end of May. In the
beginning of June Mucianus arrived in Caesarea. He, too,
noticed at once the change in the general. With envy and
embarrassed respect he saw this man growing greater, the
nearer great things approached him ; and it was not without
admiration that he chaffed him about his stolidity, his
slowness and his bulk. " You are taking this philosophically,
my friend," he said. " But I would urgently beg you not
to philosophise too long." He stabbed an invisible enemy
with his stick.

A burning desire filled him to goad the general out of
his complacent calm. The old jealousy gnawed at him.
But now it was too late. The army swore by Vespasian ;
from now on Mucianus must be prepared to play second
string. He recognised this, submitted himself to fate, and
spurred on his rival. He saw that the rumours that the
Syrian and Judaean troops were to be sent to the West were
growing more definite. Already actual dates were being
mentioned. The legions were to set out at the beginning
of July.

In the beginning of June Agrippa appeared before Vespasian. He had been in Alexandria staying with his friend
and relative Tiberius Alexander. The whole Orient, he
told the general, was against Vitellius ; bewildered by the
wild reports from Rome, Egypt and Asia were waiting in
agitated and longing expectation for the divinely chosen

Saviour to set about his task. Vespasian said nothing ;
he gazed at Agrippa and remained obstinately silent.   Then
Agrippa went on with unaccustomed vigour ; there were
men, he said, who were firmly resolved to further this
divine project.   He knew for a fact that the Governor-
General of Egypt had resolved to make his troops take the
oath of allegiance to Vespasian on the first of July.

Vespasian controlled himself, but he could not keep his
breathing from becoming loud and quick.   He walked up
and down a few times ; at last he said, but it sounded more
like an acknowledgment than a threat :   " Listen, King
Agrippa.   If such a thing should happen, I shall have to
regard your relative Tiberius Alexander as a high traitor."
He went up quite close to the King, laid both hands on his
shoulders, and breathing hard into his face said with unusual
cordiality :   " I am very sorry, King Agrippa, that I chaffed
you because you wouldn't eat the fish from the Lake of
Genezareth."

Agrippa replied :   " I beg you to count on us, Emperor
Vespasian, on our blood and our wealth."

July was approaching.   Everywhere in the East there
were rumours that just before his death the Emperor Otho
had sent a letter to Vespasian imploring him to be his successor and to save the Empire.   And one day Vespasian
actually found this letter on his desk.   The dead Otho
conjured the commander in the East in urgent and awful
terms to avenge him on the glutton Vitellius, to establish
order, and save Rome from ruin.   Vespasian read the letter
very carefully.   He told his son Titus that he was really a
great artist ; his art almost made one apprehensive.   He
was afraid, he said, that one morning he might waken up to
find a document in front of him in which Titus was proclaimed Emperor.

The fourth week of June arrived. The tension became unendurable. Caenis, Titus, Mucianus, Agrippa, Berenice, lost their nerves, and kept desperately imploring Vespasian finally to declare himself. But the stolid man was not be be moved. He gave evasive answers, grinned, made jokes, and waited.

20

ON the night of the 27th of June Vespasian summoned Jochanan Ben Sakkai to him in strict secrecy. " You are a very learned man," he said. " I beg you to instruct me still further on the nature and faith of your people. Have you a fundamental law, a golden rule, which sums up all those strange and countless commandments of yours ? "

The venerable doctor nodded his head, closed his eyes and said : " A hundred years ago there lived among us two celebrated doctors, Shammai and Hillel. A Gentile came to Shammai and told him that he would embrace our religion if Shammai could instruct him in its nature during the time that he could remain standing on one leg. Doctor Shammai was angry and sent him away. Then the Gentile went to Hillel. Doctor Hillel complied with his request. He said : ' Do not unto others what you would not that others should do unto you.' That is all."

Vespasian reflected deeply. Then he said : " Such maxims are good ; but it is hardly possible by their help to keep a great empire in order. Seeing that you possess these maxims, you should confine yourselves to writing good books and leave politics to us."

" The opinion you have just expressed, Consul Vespasian," the Jew admitted, " is one that your servant Jochanan Ben Sakkai has always upheld."

" In my opinion, learned doctor," the Roman continued, " you are the best man in this country. I am anxious that you should understand my motives. Believe me, it is only relatively seldom that I am a scoundrel, and only when I have absolutely no choice. Let me assure you that I have nothing at all against your country. But a good farmer puts up a fence round his property. We must have a fence round the Empire. Judaea is our fence against the Arabs and the Parthians. Unfortunately, when you are left to your own devices you are a bad fence. So we must ourselves stay on the spot. That is all. How you choose to act in other respects is not our concern. Leave us in peace, and we shall leave you in peace."

Jochanan's eyes looked very bright and young in his faded, wrinkled face. " It is rather unpleasant," he said, " that your fence should happen to run across our country. It is a very thick fence, and it leaves very little of our land to us. Still, so be it, make your fence. But, we too, need a fence. Another kind, a fence round our law. The thing I asked you for recently, Consul Vespasian, was that fence. It is a humble and insignificant one compared with yours ; a few scholars and a little university. We shall not resist your soldiers, if you will only give us the university of Jabne. Such a tiny university," he added coaxingly, and he indicated its smallness with a wave of his hand.

" Your proposal isn't a bad one, it seems to me," said Vespasian slowly. He got to his feet, suddenly a different man. With his sure instinct Jochanan caught the change at once. Until now an old Sabine peasant had been talking in a friendly manner with an old Jerusalem scholar ; now it was Rome speaking to Judaea. " Be prepared," said the general, " to receive papers from me the day after to-morrow granting your request. You shall then, my learned doctor, be pleased in return to hand over to me a declaration of Judaea's submission sealed by the High Council."

For the great occasion Vespasian solemnly summoned an
assembly in the Forum of Caesarea. The authorities of
all the provinces occupied by the Romans were commanded
to attend, also deputations from all the regiments. It was
universally expected that now at last the event so long
yearned for by the troops would come to pass and Vespasian
be acclaimed emperor. Instead, the general appeared on
the tribune of the Forum with Jochanan Ben Sakkai. A
high legal official made a speech, and a herald announced
in a ringing voice that the rebellious province had seen the
error of its ways and had returned repentantly under the
protection of the Senate and people of Rome. In sign of
this the venerable doctor, Jochanan Ben Sakkai, would
hand over to the Roman commander the attestation and
seal of the highest authorities in Jerusalem. The Jewish
war, to wage which the Emperor had sent Titus Flavius
Vespasian to Judaea, was therewith ended. The only
thing that still remained to be done, the chastisement of
the city of Jerusalem, was a police rather than a military
measure. The soldiers gaped at one another, dumb-
founded and disappointed. They had hoped to hail their
commander as emperor, to receive assurance of their future
security and perhaps also a huge donation. Instead they
were now the witnesses of a legal proceeding. As Romans
they knew that documents and all the paraphernalia of law
were important ; nevertheless they could not understand
what Vespasian meant by this proclamation. Only a
very few, such as Mucianus, Caenis, and Agrippa, were
able rightly to interpret the ceremony. They saw that
Vespasian, being a methodical man, was resolved, before he
returned to Rome as emperor, to receive from his opponents
letter and seal to the effect that he had successfully fulfilled
his task.

The soldiers made wry faces, and some of them openly expressed their dissatisfaction. But Vespasian had thoroughly disciplined his troops, and when they were commanded to evince their joy at the conclusion of peace they actually managed to assume the gratified expression which the military regulations prescribed for such occasions. The army defiled before the little doctor from Jerusalem. The ensign and standards were borne past him. The Roman legions greeted him with uplifted arms in the Roman fashion.

Had not Joseph once seen something that reminded him of this? Yes, he had seen an eastern king thus honoured in the city of Rome while the Emperor Nero looked on; but the king's sword had been nailed fast to its sheath. Now the Roman army were paying homage to the Jewish divinity, but only after they had broken the sword of Judaea. Joseph watched this drama from a corner of the great square; he stood quite at the back among the humble people and slaves; he was jostled and pushed and shouted at. He stared straight ahead and paid no attention to the people round him. The little old doctor still stood on the tribune; but presently, as he was visibly exhausted, a chair was brought for him. Again and again he raised his hand to his brow in salute, while his old head kept nodding and his mouth faintly smiled.

21

THE ceremony finished, the disappointed fury of the army burst out. Mucianus and Agrippa were convinced that the general had deliberately provoked the anger of the troops. They assailed him with entreaties, telling him that the fruit was more than ripe, and he must now proclaim himself emperor. But when, this time too, he insisted on sticking to his naive and cautious pose, they sent Joseph Ben Matthias to him.

It was a pleasant, cool night, with a fresh wind blowing from the sea, but Joseph felt hot and worried. His goal was almost reached ; his Roman would be emperor ; and he himself was largely responsible. He did not doubt that he would succeed in goading the vacillating Roman to a decision. Of course the hesitation was nothing but a politic pose. Just as runners put on shoes weighted with lead ten days before the race so as to harden their feet, so the expectant candidate for the throne would at first wish to retard his course with excuses and affected scruples, so that at last he might reach his goal all the more swiftly. Joseph resolved that he would be so ardent in his expressions of devotion, confidence, and knowledge of fate, that Vespasian would have no choice but to bow to God and his destiny and consent.

But Vespasian refused to be driven. The man was as arrogant and obstinate as a mountain goat. He refused to take the smallest single step of his own volition ; till the very end he would insist on being shoved and pushed to his goal.

" You're a fool, my little Jew," he said. " Your petty eastern kings can cement their crowns with blood and mud if they like ; that's nothing to me. I am a Roman peasant, and I have no intention of doing such a thing. With us it is not arbitrary violence that raises an emperor to power, but the army, the Senate and the people. The Emperor Vitellius was raised to power by legal means. I am not a rebel. I am for law and order."

Joseph ground his teeth. He had spoken with all his eloquence and his words had simply rebounded off this obstinate man. Vespasian wanted the impossible, he wanted to be appointed lawfully and unlawfully at the same time. It was senseless to talk at him any longer; there was nothing left but to give up the whole thing.

Yet Joseph could not find it in his heart to leave, and Vespasian did not send him away. For five long minutes the two men sat in silence, Joseph resigned and empty, Vespasian calm and sure of himself.

Suddenly the commander once more took up the theme, and said softly, yet as if weighing every word: "You can tell your friend Mucianus that I will not be led, that I will yield to nothing but absolute coercion."

Joseph looked up, gaped at Vespasian, and heaved a great sigh of relief. To make doubly sure he asked: "But you *will* yield to coercion?"

Vespasian shrugged his shoulders. "Of course I should be very unwilling to be killed by my soldiers. Sixty is no great age for a hardy peasant like me."

Joseph took his leave as soon after that as he decently could. Vespasian knew that he would go at once to Mucianus, and that to-morrow he himself would be forced to become emperor, against and yet not against his will. He was a matter-of-fact fellow; he had refrained from building on this eventuality, and had forbidden Caenis also to build on it until it was achieved; but now he savoured all its sweetness. He blew a great breath through his nostrils. He had never yet enjoyed a life of luxury and ease; he stamped in his heavy military boots on the cool stone floor of the room. "Flavius Titus Vespasian, Emperor, Imperator, God," he muttered, grinning broadly, then his face became serious again. "Well, well," he said. He went over the Latin and eastern words, confusing them all together: Caesar, Adir, Imperator, Messiah. It was really funny that his Jew had been the first to acclaim him.

It annoyed him a little ; he felt more closely bound to this man than he desired.

He had a great desire to waken Caenis, the woman who had for so long now shared his ups and downs with him, and say to her : " Well, we've arrived at last." But that lasted only for a moment. No, he must be alone now ; he must not see anyone.

Yes, there was one he could see. A complete stranger who knew nothing of him and of whom he knew nothing. Again his great face grinned, broadly, maliciously, contentedly. In the middle of the night he sent to Joseph's house and summoned Joseph's wife, Mara, daughter of Lakish of Caesarea. Joseph had just returned after his interview with Mucianus, exulting in the consciousness that to-morrow his Roman would be emperor, and that he himself would be so largely responsible for that consummation. Now he was plunged into dejection. He was overwhelmed with disappointment and shame that this Roman should humiliate in such a way the man who had given him his great idea. The insolent barbarian would never allow him to emerge from the scandal of this marriage. In silence he went over the jeering names which Vespasian had earned : forwarding agent, lousy peasant. And he supplemented them with the filthiest terms that he could think of, in Aramaic and Greek ; everything that came into his mind.

The girl Mara, no less overwhelmed than himself, asked quietly : " Joseph, my master, shall I take my life now ? "

" Fool," said Joseph. White and wretched, she crouched before him in her shirt. She said : " The blood that should have come three weeks ago has not come. Joseph, my husband, given to me by the Lord, the Lord has blessed my womb." And when he remained silent she added

humbly, expectantly, quite softly : " Do you not want to
keep me with you ? "

" Go ! " he said.   She fell to the ground.   After a while
she raised herself and crept to the door.   But when she was
about to go as she was he added roughly and imperiously :
" Put on your best clothes."   She obeyed timidly and
hesitatingly.   He examined her and saw that she was
wearing ordinary shoes.   " Put on the perfumed sandals
too ! " he shouted at her.

During the time she was with him Vespasian had no
cause for complaint, and enjoyed her with all his senses.
He knew that to-morrow would be the day, to-morrow they
would acclaim him emperor, and then he would leave this
East for ever and go where he belonged, to his city of Rome,
where he would establish order and discipline.   In his
heart he despised the East with a sort of indulgent affection.
This country of Judaea at any rate had been to his liking ;
the strange, fortune-bringing, violated land had been a
good footstool for his feet ; it had shown an admirable
willingness for submission, and this girl Mara, too, was very
much to his taste, simply because she was so docile and full
of contemptuous submissiveness.   He subdued his harsh
voice, laid her white moonlike head on his hairy chest,
paddled with his gouty hands in her black hair, and spoke
kindly to her in the few Aramaic words that he knew :
" Be loving, my girl !   Don't be stupid, my turtle dove ! "
He repeated this several times as mildly as he could, yet a
little absently and contemptuously.   He snorted ; he felt
pleasantly tired.   He ordered her to wash and clothe herself,
summoned his chamberlain, commanded him to let her out,
and a moment afterwards had forgotten her and fallen
asleep in secure expectation of the morrow.

The night was a short one and morning had not yet

come when Mara returned to Joseph.   She walked heavily,
as if she were weighed down by the separate weight of all
her limbs ; her face was stupid and expressionless, and as
if it were made of some damp and heavy stuff.   She took
off her dress.   Slowly and painfully she tugged at it, tugged
at it until the cloth parted, tore it into little pieces, laboriously
and ceremoniously.   Then she seized the beloved perfumed
sandals, tore at them with her nails and her teeth, slowly
and soundlessly as before.   Joseph hated her for not complaining, for not reviling him.   There was only one thought
in his mind : " I must get away from her, far away from
her.   I shall never rise from my shame as long as I breathe
the same air as her."

When Vespasian left his room the soldiers and guards
gave him the salute of honour which was accorded only to
the Emperor.   Vespasian grinned.   " Lost your wits,
my lads ? "   But now appeared the officer on duty and other
officers, and they also gave him the salute reserved for the
Emperor.   Vespasian showed signs of annoyance.   But
presently arrived a crowd of captains and generals, Mucianus
at their head.   The whole building was suddenly filled
with soldiers ; the spacious square outside was also packed,
and again and again, more and more tempestuously, they
hailed him as emperor, while the whole city went mad with
enthusiasm.   Meanwhile Mucianus assailed the commander with urgent and eloquent appeals not to allow the
fatherland to go to ruin.   The others punctuated his
speech with wild applause ; they pressed forward more and
more audaciously, and finally they actually drew their
swords and threatened, seeing that they were rebels now in
any case, to kill Vespasian if he did not consent.   Vespasian
replied in his favourite phrase : " Well, well. Not so fast, lads.
If you absolutely insist upon it, then I won't say no."

To the eleven soldiers on guard he assigned a punishment of thirty blows and a donation of seven hundred sesterces for their audacious salute. If they wished they could buy exemption from the thirty blows for three hundred sesterces. The five soldiers who accepted both the blows and the sesterces he promoted as sergeants.

To Joseph he said : " I think, my little Jew, that you can take off your fetters now." Joseph raised his hand to his brow without much sign of gratitude ; his pale, brown face was sullen and filled with aversion.

" Did you expect anything more ? " Vespasian chaffed him. And as Joseph remained silent he added brutally : " Open your mouth when *I* speak to you. *I* am *not* a prophet." He must have known quite well what Joseph wanted, but it amused him to force the Jew to ask for it. But now the good-humoured Titus intervened. " I expect that Doctor Joseph wants his fetters to be struck off." That was the manner in which it was usual to deliver men who had been unjustly imprisoned. "Well, so be it," said Vespasian, shrugging his shoulders. And he commanded the striking off of Joseph's fetters to be conducted with great ceremony.

A free man now, Joseph bowed deeply to Vespasian and asked : " May I from now on bear the family name of the Emperor ? "

" If you think it will do you any good," replied Vespasian. " I have no objection."

And Joseph Ben Matthias, priest of the first rank in Jerusalem, called himself from that moment Flavius Josephus.

Book Four
ALEXANDRIA

Book Four

ALEXANDRIA

A LONG narrow rectangle, Alexandria, the capital of the
East, stretched along the coast. After Rome it was the
greatest city of the known world and certainly the most
modern. It was sixteen miles in circumference. Seven
great avenues ran from end to end of it, twelve across from
side to side ; the houses were high and spacious, and all
were furnished with running water.

Standing at the intersecting point of three continents,
at the meeting place of the Orient and the Occident, and on
the main route to India, Alexandria had raised itself to the
position of the greatest trading centre in the world. In
the long stretch of sea coast lying between Joppa in Asia and
Paraetonium in Africa, the harbour of Alexandria was the
only one that was safe in all weathers. Here were piled up
gold dust, ivory, tortoiseshell, Arabian spices, pearls from
the Persian Gulf, precious stones from India, Chinese silks.
Factories employing the most modern technique sent world-
famous linens as far as Britain, wove precious carpets and
tapestries, and produced national costumes for the Arabian
and Indian peoples. They manufactured beautiful glass
and famous perfumes. They supplied the whole world
with paper, from the thinnest letter paper for ladies to the
roughest packing paper.

Alexandria was an industrious city. There even the
blind found something to do, nor were the aged idle. Work

was profitable, and the city did not conceal its wealth. While in the narrow streets of Rome and the hilly streets of Jerusalem all heavy traffic was forbidden during the day, in Alexandria the spacious avenues resounded with ten thousand vehicles, and a never-ceasing procession of pleasure chariots was to be seen in the two Corsos. In the spacious park rose the gigantic palace of the ancient kings, the museum, the great library, the mausoleum with the crystal coffin containing the dead body of Alexander the Great. It took strangers weeks to see all the countless sights. For there was also the shrine of Serapis, the theatre, the circus, the Isle of Pharos crowned with its famous white lighthouse, the huge industrial and harbour buildings, the basilica, the stock exchange which fixed prices for the whole world, and not least the great pleasure resort which extended as far as the luxurious bathing place of Canopus.

Life in Alexandria was comfortable and gay. The cook-shops and taverns, in which the celebrated barley beer was sold, were countless. On all the statutory holidays per-formances were given in the theatres, the circus, and the arena. In their city palaces and their villas in Eleusis and Canopus, or on their yachts, the rich magnates gave sophisti-cated and skilfully planned entertainments. The banks of the long canal, twelve miles from end to end, which con-nected Alexandria with Canopus, were lined with restaurants. Yachts plied up and down the canal ; the cabins were so constructed that they could be curtained off when the sun was hot ; everywhere along the banks, in the shadow of the trees, these boats were to be seen anchored It was here in Canopus that people located the Elysian fields of Homer ; in the provinces the middle-classes dreamt of a few weeks of splendid debauchery in Canopus, and saved up for a visit to Alexandria.

But the city offered also more noble pleasures. The museum contained more objects of art than those of Rome and Athens, the splendid library employed continuously the services of nine hundred clerks. The academies of Alexandria were superior to the schools of Rome. In the science of war, perhaps also in jurisprudence and political economy, the capital of the Empire was, it may be, superior ; but in other intellectual disciplines the academies of Alexandria undoubtedly took the lead. The Roman families of the ruling caste preferred to consult doctors who had studied anatomy in the Alexandrian schools. Also, on the advice of its physicians, the city practised a more humane type of execution for its criminals, employing the bite of a poisonous adder bred for this purpose and whose effects were very rapid.

In spite of all their modernity, the Alexandrians clung to their traditions. They maintained their temples and shrines with peculiar piety and austerity, were not to be turned aside from the primitive Egyptian magic handed down to them by their fathers, and stuck to their ancient customs. As in the earliest days they worshipped their sacred animals, the ox, the sparrow hawk, and the cat. If a Roman soldier, even without intending it, happened to kill a cat, no power could save him from execution.

In this way lived these twelve hundred thousand human beings, impetuously flinging themselves into pleasure when their work was done and into work when their pleasure was exhausted, always greedy for novelty and yet stubbornly and piously clinging to their ancient customs, very changeable, swinging round from the most cordial friendship into the bitterest enmity in a moment, greedy for wealth, clever, of a quick and malicious wit, boundlessly impudent and temperamental, and politicians to the very marrow. From all the ends of the earth they had thronged to this city ; but soon they forgot their native countries, and from that moment felt they were Alexandrians. Alexandria ; that spelt for them the city of the East and the West, the city of mystical philosophy, of gay art, of keen business, of unceasing labour, of overflowing pleasure, of ancient tradition, and of the most modern fashions. The Alexandrians were boundlessly proud of their city, and it did not bother them in the least that their overweening and insolent local patriotism produced exasperation everywhere.

In the midst of this community lived a group of human beings still older, still richer, still more cultivated, still more arrogant than the others : the Jews. They had behind them a turbulent history. Ever since, seven hundred years before, gallant Jewish soldiers had gained his greatest victory for King Psammetich, the Jews had remained in the country. Later, Alexander of Macedon and the Ptolemies had settled them in colonies, until there were a hundred thousand of them. Now in the city of Alexandria alone they amounted to almost half a million. Their religious isolation, their riches and their insolence had again and again led to savage pogroms. Only three years before, when the revolt broke out in the province of Judaea, fifty thousand Jews had lost their lives in a savage butchery in Alexandria. Even now there were whole districts in the Delta quarter, where most of them lived, that still lay in ruins. They deliberately left these ruins standing, nor did they wash from the walls of their synagogues the blood which had defiled them. They were proud even of these attacks, which were an acknowledgment of their power. For it was they in reality who ruled Egypt, as once Joseph, the son of Jacob, had ruled the land under Pharaoh. Tiberius Alexander, the Governor-General of Egypt, was of Jewish descent, and the leading

men in the province, the administrators, textile manufacturers,
customs officers, armourers, bankers, corn dealers, shippers,
paper manufacturers, doctors, and teachers in the schools
were Jews.

The chief synagogue in Alexandria was one of the wonders
of the world. It could hold more than a hundred thousand
people ; and after the Temple of Jerusalem it was the
greatest Jewish building in the world. Seventy-one chairs
of pure gold stood in it ; these were for the great masters
and presidents of the High Council. No voice, however
powerful, could fill the vast hall ; and flags had to be waved
to tell the congregation when to respond with their Amen
to the leader of prayer.

The Alexandrian Jews looked down haughtily on their
Roman compatriots, on those Jews of the West, most of
whom lived needily and were not able to raise themselves
out of their proletarian existence. They, the Alexandrians,
skilfully and harmoniously adapted their Jewish qualities
to the forms of life and the general ideas of the Grecian
Orient. A hundred and fifty years before they had translated the Bible into Greek, and they found that this Bible of
theirs went very well with the Greek world.

Yet in spite of all this, and although they had their own
temple in Leontopolis, they regarded Mount Zion as the
centre of their life. They loved Judaea ; they looked on
with deep pity when they saw the Jewish nation threatening
to fall as a result of the political incapacity of Jerusalem.
They were filled with a great hope that at least the Temple
might remain untouched. Like all other Jews they sent
their dues to the Temple, they pilgrimaged to Jerusalem,
they had there their own hotels, synagogues and burial
places. Many of the monuments in the Temple, gates,
columns and halls, had been erected by them. Any life

without the Temple in Jerusalem was unthinkable even to the Alexandrian Jews.

They maintained their outward arrogance, they did not let anybody see how much they were distressed by the events in Judaea. Business flourished, the new emperor was gracious to them. In their luxurious conveyances they drove on the Corso, sat like princes in their high chairs in their private boxes at the Basilica, gave their great entertainments in Canopus and on the Pharos. But when they were together their proud faces were often overcast. Their breathing became uneasy, and their haughty shoulders were bowed.

2

THE Jews of Alexandria received Joseph cordially and respectfully when he stepped off the ship among the train of the new emperor. The part he had taken in the election of Vespasian seemed to be quite well known, indeed to be overestimated. Joseph's youth, his restrained intensity, the grave beauty of his lean and ardent face, touched everybody's heart. As once in Galilee, so now in Alexandria people cried when he appeared in the streets : " Marin, Marin, Our Lord, Our Lord."

After the gloomy fanaticism of Judaea and the severities of a Roman military life, Joseph now drank in with joy the unrestrained gaiety of the great city. He had left behind him in Galilee all his dull and savage earlier life, and his wife Mara. His sphere did not include the intrigues of actual politics, nor the harsh tasks of military organisation ; his sphere was that of the intellect. He wore with pride at his belt the golden writing apparatus which young General Titus had given him as a mark of esteem when he left Judaea.

Sitting by the side of the Great Master Theodore Bar

Daniel, he drove on the Corso. He showed himself in the library, in the baths, in the splendid restaurants of Canopus. The Jew with the golden writing tablets was soon known everywhere. In many of the classrooms the teachers and students rose at his entrance. The manufacturers and merchants were proud when he came to view their factories and warehouses, and the literary men felt honoured when he was present at their readings. He led the life of a great gentleman. The men listened to him, the women pursued him.

Yes, he had been right in his prophecies : Vespasian was really the Messiah. It was true that this Messiah was redeeming the world in a different fashion from what he had expected, gradually, soberly, matter-of-factly. The redemption consisted in the fact that the Emperor was breaking the shell of Jewish culture to enable that culture to spread over the world and smelt Greece and Judaea into one. Into Joseph's view of the world more and more of the clear and sceptical spirit of these Eastern Greeks was insinuating itself. He no longer understood how he could once have felt disgust for all that was not Jewish. The heroes of Greek myth and the prophets of the Bible did not exclude each other ; and there was no incompatibility between the Heaven of Jehovah and the Olympus of Homer. Joseph began to hate the limitations which once had meant for him election and privilege. What mattered was to let the goodness in him flow out to others and draw into himself the goodness of others.

He was the first man to live deliberately in accordance with this conception. He was a new kind of man, no longer a Jew, nor a Greek, nor a Roman, but a citizen of the whole civilised world.

Alexandria had always been a centre of the Antisemites.

Here Apion, Apollonius Molo, Lysimachos and the Egyptian High Priest Manetho, had taught that the Jews were descended from lepers, that they worshipped in the Holy of Holies the head of an ass, that they ate in their Temple the bodies of young Greeks, slaughtering them at their Easter Festival and every year swearing a secret Jewish oath against all other peoples while they drank the blood of their victims.   Thirty years earlier two directors of the Gymnasium, Dionysus and Lamponius, had very efficiently organised the Antisemite movement.   The white shoes worn by the pupils of the Gymnasium had gradually grown into a symbol, and now the Antisemites over all Egypt called themselves " The White Shoes."

With the arrival of Joseph a new plague had descended upon Alexandria according to the White Shoes.   When he haughtily drove about the streets accepting public homage he became in their eyes the very incarnation of Jewish insolence.   In their clubs, or wherever they met, they sang verses, some of them really witty, about the Jewish hero of freedom who had deserted to the Romans, about the pushing Maccabee who had insinuated himself everywhere and wore his cloak to catch the wind of favour.

One day as Joseph was about to enter the Agrippa Baths he found he had to pass a group of young men in white shoes in the entrance hall.   Scarcely did the White Shoes catch sight of him before they began a snuffling, guttural chorus : " Marin, Marin," obviously trying to parody the enthusiastic cries with which the Jews greeted Joseph.

Joseph's pale brown face grew paler than ever.   But he went straight on, turning his head neither to the right nor to the left.   When they saw that he took no notice of them the White Shoes redoubled their chorus.   Some of them cried : " Don't go too near him in case you catch the disease." Others cried : " How do you like our pork, little Maccabee ? " then from every side they bawled and shouted at him : " Joseph the Maccabee ! The circumcised Livy ! " and Joseph saw in front of him a wall of jeering faces filled with hatred. " Do you want anything ? " he asked the face nearest to him, which was an olive brown one, and his voice was very quiet. The youth replied with exaggerated and impudent humility : " I only wanted a piece of information, little Maccabee. Was your father a leper too ? " Joseph stared him in the eyes and said nothing. A second White Shoe, pointing to Joseph's golden stylus and tablets, chimed in : " Did some one give these to your father when he was hunted out of Egypt ? " Joseph still said nothing. Suddenly, with terrifying quickness, he drew the heavy tablets from his belt and struck the questioner over the head. The man sank down. They all became quite silent. Without turning to look at his fallen enemy Joseph passed into the baths. The White Shoes made to follow him, but the attendants and visitors repulsed them.

The wounded man, his name was Chaereas and he belonged to a prominent family, was gravely injured. Action was taken against Joseph, but presently quashed. The Emperor said to Joseph : " Well, well, my lad, it was bravely done. But we didn't give you the writing gear to do that with it."

3

EVERY year the Alexandrian Jews celebrated a great festival on the Pharos in memory of the completion of the Greek Bible. The second Ptolemy and the curator of his library, Demetrius of Phaleron, had three centuries before ordained the translation of the Holy Scripture into Greek. Seventy-two Jewish doctors who were equally conversant with

Hebrew and Greek had accomplished this heavy task, which threw open the Word of God to the Jews of Egypt who could no longer understand the original. The seventy-two doctors had worked in seclusion, each strictly isolated ; nevertheless the translation of each of them agreed word for word with the translations of the others. This miracle by which Jehovah showed that he approved the friendly spirit of the Jews and their peaceful relations with the Greek population, the Alexandrians celebrated by this annual festival.

All the leading men and women of the city, including even the Gentiles, appeared that day on the Pharos ; only the White Shoes absented themselves. The Emperor himself took part, along with his son Titus, and all the leading figures from Rome and the various provinces whom the presence of the imperial court in Alexandria had drawn there.

To Joseph fell the task of making the speech of welcome to the strangers who had been invited to the festival. He spoke in a light vein, yet with an undercurrent of seriousness, praised in glowing words the art of literature which bound peoples together, and the great city of Alexandria which performed the same office. To speak well he always needed to read the effect of his words from the faces of his listeners, and he was in the habit of fixing upon a face at a venture, so as to discover from it the impression he was making. This time his eye happened to fall on a fleshy and yet severe and very Roman face. But the face was closed against him and remained impassive during his whole speech. Sour and strangely blank, the Roman face stared through him and past him with a curious dull arrogance that almost discomposed him.

His speech finished, Joseph enquired who the gentleman was to whom the face belonged. He turned out to be Caius

Fabullus, Nero's court painter, who had executed the frescoes in the Golden House. Joseph took a good look at this man who had listened to his speech with such boorish indifference. The body on which that strong and severe head was planted was thickset, fat, almost shapeless. Yet Caius Fabullus was very carefully dressed and held himself stiffly and with dignity, which considering his fatness gave him a slightly ludicrous appearance.

In Rome Joseph had heard a great deal of the queer whims of this man. The painter, a convinced Hellenist whose art was light, easy and sensuous, was exaggeratedly grave in his bearing ; he insisted on painting in gala dress, he was extremely arrogant, and he never spoke to his slaves, communicating with them only by signs. Famous and sought after as his art was—there was none among even the small provincial towns which did not display frescoes and paintings in imitation of his—he had not succeeded in being received by the great Roman families. Finally he had married a Hellenised Egyptian woman and by that step had ruined for ever all hope of entering the highest society.

Joseph was surprised that Fabullus should be there at all ; he had been told that he was among the most zealous supporters of the White Shoes. Joseph disliked all painting ; it conveyed nothing to him. The commandment of the Scripture, Thou shalt not make any graven image, had sunk deep into him. In Rome, too, writers were much looked up to, while painters were regarded as members of a lower caste ; so that Joseph regarded this conceited artist with a double portion of contemptuous dislike. The Emperor sent for Joseph. In a very beautiful copy of the Greek Bible which had been presented to him he had found by pure instinct certain erotic passages, and now in his

wheezy voice he bade Joseph explain them.   "Why, you've
been putting on fat, my little Jew," he said suddenly in a
surprised voice.   He turned to Fabullus who was standing
near : "You should have seen my Jew in Galilee, Master.
At that time he was splendid.   Unshaven, lean as a rake,
and dirty.   A prophet that any artist would have died to
paint."   Fabullus stood stiffly at attention with a sour look
on his face ; Joseph smiled politely.   "Since coming
here," Vespasian went on, "I've put myself under the
physician Hecateus.   He makes me fast one day a week.
That agrees with me splendidly.   What do you say, Fabullus ?   If we make this fellow fast for a week, will you paint
him for me after that ? "   Fabullus stood stiff as a stock ;
his face was wry.   Joseph said smoothly : "It's a great
pleasure to me, your Majesty, to know that you are in a
position to-day to joke so pleasantly about Jotapat."   The
Emperor laughed.   "When the weather changes," he
said, "I can still feel a twinge in my foot where your people
hit it that time."   He pointed to a lady who stood beside
the painter.   "Your daughter, Fabullus ? "   "Yes," said
the painter dryly and reluctantly, "my daughter Dorion."
They all gazed at the girl.   Dorion was moderately tall,
slender and fragile, her complexion a golden brown ; her
face was long and thin, with a high and slanting forehead,
and eyes the colour of the sea.   She had high cheek bones, a
blunt nose with wide nostrils, and a pure, delicate profile ;
her mouth, large and challenging, was startling in such a
fine, proud face.   "A pretty girl," said the Emperor ;
then, turning away : "Well, think it over, Fabullus, this
matter of painting my Jew."   With that he left them.

For a little while the others stood together in embarrassed
silence.   Fabullus had attended the festival merely out of
fear of offending the new regime.   With difficulty he had

induced Dorion to go with him. Now he was sorry that he had come. He had no intention of painting a portrait of this lazy, conceited Jewish scribbler. For his part Joseph had no intention of allowing his portrait to be painted by this insolent and dull-witted dauber. All the same it could not be denied that the girl Dorion was a striking creature ; a pretty girl, the Emperor had said. That was to put it very tamely, and erroneously besides. As she stood there, delicate to the verge of fragility, graceful and yet proud in her bearing, a quite tiny triumphant smile on her mouth, Joseph could not help being attracted against his will by her somewhat savage charm.

"Well, well," the girl Dorion repeated somewhat mockingly the favourite expression of the Emperor, "shouldn't we be going too, father ?" She had a high, thin, malicious voice. Joseph opened his mouth to speak to her, but though usually so ready, he could think of nothing to say. At that moment he felt something rubbing against his legs. He looked down ; it was a great, reddish-brown cat. Cats, as sacred animals, were much petted in Egypt ; but the Romans and Jews could not stand them. Joseph tried to shoo it away. But it remained and annoyed him. He bent down and seized the animal. Suddenly the voice of the girl leapt at him : "Put down that cat !" It was a shrill, unpleasant voice. Strange how gentle it became when the girl now turned to the cat. "Come, my pet, my love, my little goddess ! That man doesn't understand you. Did he frighten you ?" And she stroked the cat. The ugly beast purred.

"Pardon me," said Joseph, "I didn't mean to offend your cat. They're useful animals when there's mice about." Dorion caught quite well the sneer in his words. She had had an Egyptian mother and an Egyptian nurse. The cat

was divine ; in it there still lingered something of the
lion-goddess, Bastet, something of the strength and violence
of primeval times. The Jew was trying to humiliate her
god, but the Jew was too small for her to answer. She
shouldn't have come to this festival. Her father's art was
unique ; no government, no emperor could do without
him ; he had no need to make this concession to the new
regime. She said nothing, but stood quietly with the
cat in her arms, presenting quite a pretty picture which
might have been entitled, " Girl with Cat on the Pharos."
As she stood there with a pleasantly excited feeling of being
the target of many eyes she thought over what had happened.
A pretty girl, the Emperor had said. Her father had to
paint this Jew. A rude and pointless joke. But the Emperor was coarse, a true Roman. A pity that her father
hadn't sufficient presence of mind to protect himself against
jokes of that kind. The only defence he could bring up
was a somewhat sour gravity. The Jew with his servile
irony had come better out of the business. She saw quite
well that in spite of his rude remarks about the cat, Joseph
was attracted by her. If she were to say something now,
no doubt he would respond with many flattering and repentant
words. But she decided to say nothing. If he spoke again,
then she might reply if she felt inclined. If he didn't
speak she would leave, and this would be her last encounter
with the Jew.

On his side Joseph was thinking ; this girl Dorion is a
proud and sarcastic piece. If he were to become intimate
with her there would soon be differences and unpleasantness.
The best thing would be simply to leave her standing with
that hideous cat of hers. How extraordinary the brown of
her hands was against the ugly brown of the cat. Unusually
long and frail hands she had. She was like a figure in one

of those old, harsh and angular pictures that one saw everywhere here.

" Don't you think it is expecting a little too much of me
to make a skeleton of myself so that your father may paint
me ? " he said, and while he spoke he was already regretting
not having gone away.

" It seems to me that a little fasting isn't too high a price
for being immortalised for ever," replied Dorion in her
high childish voice.

" I fancy," retorted Joseph, " that if my name is to live
it will live because of my books."

This reply irritated Dorion. There it was again, the
arrogance for which these Jews were notorious. She
sought for a reply that would crush the man ; but before
she could find it Fabullus said dryly and in Latin : " Let
us go, my daughter. It doesn't depend on us or on him
whether I shall paint him. If the Emperor commanded
it, I would paint even the rotting body of a dead pig."

Joseph gazed after them as they disappeared in the pillared
hall which led from the mole to the town. He had not
come out of it very well, but he didn't regret having spoken.

4

IT was during these days that Joseph wrote the psalm which
was later to be known as the Psalm of the Citizen of the
World.

O Jehovah, give me a truer ear and a truer eye
That I may see and hear the greatness of Thy world.
O Jehovah, give me a greater heart
That I may comprehend the diversity of Thy world.
O Jehovah, give me a greater voice
That I may proclaim the glory of Thy world.

Attend, ye peoples, and take heed, ye nations.
Do not be niggardly, saith Jehovah, with the spirit that I
    pour out upon you.
Squander it lavishly, saith the voice of the Lord.
For I spew out of my mouth the niggard and the miser.
And he who guards his heart and his possessions,
From him I turn away my countenance.

Cast thyself free from thine anchor, saith Jehovah.
I love not them that dally in the harbour.
And an abomination to me are they that rot in sloth.
I have given feet to men to bear them over the earth,
And legs that they might run.
That they might not remain for ever where they are, like
    a tree rooted to its place.

For a tree has only one food.
But man nourishes himself on all things
That I have created beneath the heavens.
And a tree knows only what is round it,
But man has eyes, so that he might drink in all things
    that are strange,
And hands that he might touch and feel what he sees.

Praise God and be ye dispersed among the nations.
Praise God and scatter yourselves over the seas.
Praise God and lose yourselves in infinite spaces.
A slave is he who binds himself to a single country.
The Kingdom that I promise you, its name is not Zion,
Its name is the earth.

So Joseph transformed himself from a citizen of Judaea
into a citizen of the world, and from the priest Joseph Ben
Matthias into the writer Flavius Josephus.

5

IN Alexandria too there were supporters of the Avengers
of Israel. In spite of the palpable risk, men were to be
seen in the streets with the forbidden arm band bearing the
initials Makkabi which signifies : Who is like Thee, O Lord ?
Ever since Joseph's arrival the Makkabi adherents had
shown in every possible way how much they despised him,
a traitor to the cause. After his encounter with Chaereas,
the White Shoe, they had become a little quieter. But now,
after the Citizen of the World's Psalm, they raised a redoubled outcry against this suspect and much vilified
man.

At first Joseph laughed. But soon he could not help
seeing that the agitation of the Avengers of Israel had
spread also to the more moderate elements, and that even
the members of the High Council were beginning to cold
shoulder him. Doubtless the Jewish leaders in Alexandria
were of the same opinion as himself in their hearts ; but
for the majority of the Jewish community Joseph's psalm
was wild heresy, and less than a fortnight after its publication
there was a violent scene in the chief synagogue.

If an Alexandrian Jew considered that the Great Master
and his officers had given an unjust decision in some important matter, there was an ancient usage which allowed
him to appeal to the whole community. The appeal had
to be made on the Sabbath, standing before the open Scripture. The sacred ceremonial of the Sabbath, the reading
of the Scripture, must be postponed until the whole community had come to an immediate decision on these appeals.
It was dangerous, however, to ask for such a decision ;
for if the community did not find for the complainant he
was sentenced to excommunication for three years. As a

result, people very seldom made use of this right ; in the last twenty years it had been invoked only three times.

Now that for the first time since the publication of his poem Joseph appeared in the great synagogue it was invoked a fourth time. On that particular Sabbath a passage beginning with the words : " And Jehovah appeared to him among the Terebinthians," was to be read out. Scarcely had the Scripture roll been deposited on the pulpit where the reading was to take place, scarcely was it unwrapped from its splendid coverings and opened, when the leader of the Avengers of Israel with several of his supporters rushed to the pulpit and forbade the reading. They accused Joseph Ben Matthias. It was true that the jurists in the community had declared, quoting all manner of complicated clauses, that the excommunication of Jerusalem did not apply to Alexandria. But the overwhelming majority of the Jews in Alexandria thought otherwise. This man, Joseph Ben Matthias, was responsible for the disasters in Galilee and Jerusalem ; he was a double traitor. His accursed and ignominious marriage with Vespasian's concubine was enough in itself to exclude him from the fellowship of the synagogue. Amid tempestuous assent the speaker demanded that Joseph should be driven out of the sacred place.

Joseph stood very still, with compressed lips. The congregation in the synagogue consisted of the same people who a few weeks before had greeted him with the shout : " Marin, Marin." How was it that there were so few to lift a finger for him now ? He glanced at the Great Master, Theodore Bar Daniel, and the seventy members of the High Council on their golden chairs. They sat there whiter than their praying mantles and never opened their mouths. No, these men could not protect him and would not protect him. Nor did even the fact that he was the

friend of the Emperor help him now.   He was driven with
ignominy out of the synagogue.

Some, when they saw him going out so sadly, said to
themselves : " There is a great wheel.   It is a water
wheel, it turns round and round, and it fills the empty
vessel, and it empties the full.   And that is what it has done
to this man, for yesterday he was proud, and to-day he is
covered with shame."

6

JOSEPH himself did not seem to take the matter very seriously.
He continued to live the same gay life as formerly, associating
with women, literary men, actors and actresses ; and he
was a much welcomed guest in the most luxurious circles
of Canopus.   Titus showed him favour still more ostentatiously than before, and was to be seen almost perpetually
in his company.

But when Joseph was alone, lying in his bed at night, he
felt sick with rage and shame.   His thoughts turned against
himself.   He was defiled, he was full of leprosy within and
without, and not even Titus could cleanse him.   His
shame was public, everyone could see it.   It had a name,
the name of Mara.   He must get rid of this source of
misfortune, and for ever.

After waiting for a few weeks he went, without having
consulted anyone, to the Supreme Judge of the Jewish
community, Doctor Basilides.   Since his ejection from the
synagogue Joseph had not visited any of the great men among
the Jews.   His visit made the Supreme Judge uncomfortable ;
he sought painfully for some phrase of excuse, twisted in
his chair, and made a few lame remarks.   But Joseph pulled
out his tattered priest's hat as the ritual prescribed in such
cases, laid it down before the Supreme Judge, tore his garments and said : " My Doctor and Master, I am your

servant, Joseph Ben Matthias, formerly priest of the first rank in Jerusalem. I have committed the sin of lustful inclination. I have married a woman whom it was forbidden in the law that I should marry, a war prisoner who had traffic with the Romans. I am deserving of the punishment of excommunication."

When Joseph spoke these words Doctor Basilides grew pale ; he knew quite well what they signified. Some time elapsed before he answered in the prescribed formula : " The punishment of excommunication, transgressor, is not in the hands of men, but in the hands of God." Joseph went on, asking once more in the prescribed words : "Is there any means, my Doctor and Master, through which the transgressor can turn aside the punishment of excommunication from himself and his family ? " The Supreme Judge replied : " If the transgressor take upon himself the punishment of forty lashes, then Jehovah will have pity upon him. But the transgressor himself must request to be granted this punishment." Joseph said : " I request you, my Doctor and Master, to grant me the punishment of forty lashes."

When it became known that Joseph had decided to take upon himself the punishment of a public scourging, there was immense excitement in Alexandria ; for a public scourging rarely took place, and usually it was only slaves who were subjected to it. The Avengers of Israel raised their eyebrows and fell silent, and many who in the synagogue had shouted loudly for the ejection of Joseph now regretted it in their hearts. But the White Shoes smeared all the house walls with caricatures of Joseph being whipped, and satirical verses were sung in the taverns.

The Jewish authorities did not make public the date of the scourging. Nevertheless on the appointed day the

courtyard of the Augustan Synagogue was packed with
people, and the adjacent streets were crowded with curious
spectators. Brown and lean, his burning eyes fixed straight
ahead, Joseph advanced towards the Supreme Judge. He
raised his hand to his brow, and very loudly, so that it could
be heard in the farthest corner of the courtyard, he said :
" My Doctor and Master, I have committed the sin of
lustful inclination. I request to be granted the punishment
of forty lashes." The Supreme Judge replied : " Then I
hand you over, transgressor, to the servants of the court."

The executioner, Ananias Bar Akashia, made a sign to
his two assistants and they tore Joseph's clothes from his
back. The doctor went over and examined him to see
whether he was capable of enduring the punishment without
unseemly physical consequences ; for that would be humiliating and the law declared : " Thy brother shall not
be humiliated in thy sight." It was Julian, the head doctor
of the community, who examined Joseph. He tapped his
chest and back and tested in particular his heart and lungs.
Many among the spectators were convinced that the doctor
would declare Joseph unfit to endure the whole punishment,
or capable at least only of a smaller one. In his heart Joseph
himself hoped for some such decision. But the doctor
washed his hands and declared : " The transgressor is
capable of enduring forty lashes."

The executioner told Joseph to kneel down. The
assistants bound his hands to a stake, so that his body was
drawn tautly forward from the knees and everybody could
see the smooth pale skin of his back stretching under the
strain. Then they bound a heavy stone to his chest to
pull his body downwards. The executioner Ananias Bar
Akashia seized the whip. The crowd could see Joseph's
heart beating against his ribs, while the executioner very

carefully fastened the broad strap of ox hide to the handle, tested it, loosened it, tightened it, then loosened it again. The tip of the whip lash had to reach the chest of the offender. That was the law.

The Supreme Judge began to read out the two Scriptural verses concerning the punishment of scourging. " And it shall be done as follows : if the offender is deserving of lashes, the Judge shall order him to kneel down, and he shall be whipped in the sight of the Judge according to the measure of his offences. Forty lashes he shall have, but no more. So that thy brother should not be humiliated in thy sight." The executioner gave Joseph thirteen lashes on the back. The second judge counted ; then the assistants bathed the offender's back. Then the third judge said : " Strike," and the executioner gave Joseph thirteen lashes on the chest. Then the assistants bathed his chest. Finally the executioner gave Joseph another thirteen lashes on the back. The crowd became very still while he struck. One could hear the sharp smack of the whip, could hear Joseph's breath whistling painfully, and see his heart fluttering.

Joseph lay bound and panted for breath under the whip. The blows were sharp and short, but the pain was like an endless whirling sea ; it came in huge waves, bearing Joseph away with it, then sank again leaving him naked, then returned again and broke over his head. Joseph panted, his breath whistled ; he smelt the odour of blood. All this was happening because of Mara, the daughter of Lakish ; he had desired her, he had hated her, now he was having her whipped out of his blood. He prayed : " From the depths I cry to Thee, O Lord." He counted the lashes, but the numbers confused him ; he had already counted many hundreds, and yet the executioner still went on. The law prescribed that there should not be forty, but only thirty-nine lashes ; for in the Scriptures the words were " but no more," and so there should be only thirty-nine lashes. Oh, how mild was the interpretation of the doctors ! Oh, how harsh was the Scripture ! If they did not stop now he would die. It seemed to him that Jochanan Ben Sakkai would presently announce that they must stop. The great doctor was in Judaea, in Jerusalem or Jabne ; but all the same he must be here, and he would speak. All that mattered was to hold out until then. The ground and stake swam from beneath him, but Joseph collected himself. A command was laid upon him to see everything clearly, to watch the ground and the stake very carefully until Jochanan Ben Sakkai came. But Jochanan Ben Sakkai did not come, and finally Joseph lost consciousness and could see no longer. Yes, at the twenty-fourth lash he fainted and lay unconscious in his bonds. But after he had been bathed he came to himself again, and the doctor said, " He can endure it," and the judge said, " Strike on."

Princess Berenice was among the spectators. There was no public platform and no reserved space. But the night before she had sent her most powerful Cappadocian slave to keep a place for her. Now she stood in the second row, jostled by the crowd, her lips half-parted, her breath coming in gasps, her dark eyes persistently fixed on the offender. In the courtyard everything was absolutely still. Only the voice of the Supreme Judge, who was reading out the verses of the Scripture very slowly, three times in all, could be heard, and from the distance the shouts of the crowds in the streets. Berenice watched very attentively while her proud relative Joseph endured the lashes that were to rid him of that woman to whom he had to give his name. Yes, he was a true cousin of hers after all. Petty sins were not for him, nor petty duties. To humiliate oneself so as afterwards to rise all the more proudly ; she could understand that. In the wilderness she had herself tasted the keenness of such humiliations. She was very pale ; it was not an easy matter to look, but she looked. Her lips moved soundlessly, mechanically counting the lashes. She was glad when the last lash fell ; but she could have stood and watched longer. Her gums felt dry.

Joseph was carried, bloody and unconscious, into the building. Under the superintendence of the doctor he was washed, anointed with oil, and given a drink composed of wine and myrrh. When he came to himself he said : " Give the executioner two hundred sesterces."

7

MEANWHILE Mara the daughter of Lakish went about happily, rejoicing in the thought of the child that she was to bear, and taking a thousand precautions to protect it. She was very busy ; but now she did not turn the handmill, lest the child might be a drunkard. She refrained from eating unripe dates, so that its eyes might not water ; she drank no beer, so that its complexion might be clear ; ate no mustard, so as to preserve it from gluttony. On the other hand she ate eggs, that the child's eyes might be large, red mullet, that it might find favour in the eyes of men, and citron, that its skin might be fragrant. She anxiously avoided everything ugly, lest she might have a miscarriage, and sought out the company of handsome people. With much difficulty she procured a precious stone with magical powers, a stone with a hollow in the centre containing a smaller stone, an image of the pregnant mother.

When her hour came Mara was set on the bearing-chair, a construction of lattice work in which she could

recline in a half-recumbent position, and her attendants
bound a hen to the chair, so that its fluttering might hasten
the birth.   It was a painful birth, and for days afterwards
Mara's body still felt bitterly cold.   The midwife spoke
encouragingly to her, told stories, called on her by her name,
and told more stories.

But then the child was there, and behold it was a boy.
He was covered with a filthy blackish caul of blood, but he
screamed, he screamed until the walls re-echoed.   That
was a good omen, and it was a good omen, too, that the child
had seen the light on a Sabbath.   Warm water was prepared
for the bath, despite the Sabbath, and wine was poured among
the water, precious wine of Eshkol.   Cautiously they
stretched the babe's limbs and laved its tender head with a
brew made of the juice of ripe grapes to scare vermin away
Then they anointed it with warm oil, strewed it with
powdered myrrh, and wrapped it in its swaddling bands ;
Mara had denied herself new clothes so as to buy the best
linen for it.

Janik, Janiki, Jildi, my child, my babe, my baby, Mara
crooned, and next day she proudly planted a cedar, for she
had been granted a son.

During all the time she had been carrying the child she
had been trying to think of a name to give him.   But now
that the week of circumcision had come and she had to
decide, she hesitated for a long time.   At last she decided.
She summoned a scribe and dictated a letter to Joseph :

" Mara, daughter of Lakish, greets her master Joseph,
the son of Matthias, priest of the first rank, the Emperor's
friend.

" O Joseph, my master, Jehovah has seen that your
handmaid was displeasing in your sight, and He has blest
me and granted me the great joy of bearing you a son.

He was born on a Sabbath, and he weighed seven litra and sixty-five zus, and he screamed until the walls rang. I have called him Simeon, which means the son of prayer, for Jehovah listened to me when I was without favour in your sight. Joseph, my master, accept my greeting and become great in the sun of the Emperor, and may the Lord let his countenance shine upon you.

" And do not eat of the cabbage palm, because it will give you a pain in the chest."

8

ABOUT the same time, and before Mara's letter had reached him, Joseph appeared in the hall of the Jewish community in Alexandria. He was still pale and sore from the scourging, but he held himself erect. Beside him stood as witnesses the Great Master, Theodore Ben Daniel, and Nicodemus, the President of the Augustan Ward. The Supreme Judge Basilides himself presided, and three doctors acted as counsel. The secretary of the Augustan Ward wrote at the dictation of the Supreme Judge ; he wrote, for such was the law, on parchment made of calf's hide ; he wrote with a goose quill and with very black ink, and saw to it that the document comprised just twelve lines, according to the secret cipher of the word Get, the Hebrew word for divorce.

While the goose quill was scraping over the parchment Joseph heard in his heart a louder sound. It was the sharp tearing sound with which Mara the daughter of Lakish had rent her clothes and her sandals, slowly, ceremoniously, on that grey morning when she had returned from the Roman Vespasian. Joseph had thought that he had forgotten that sound ; but now he heard it again and it was very loud, louder than the scraping of the quill. But he made his ears deaf and his heart impassive.

The secretary wrote as follows : " On the 17th day of the month Kislev in the year 3830 after the creation of the world, in the city of Alexandria on the Egyptian Sea.

" I, Joseph Ben Matthias, also called Flavius Josephus, finding myself now in the city of Alexandria on the Egyptian Sea, consent of my own freewill and without compulsion to set you free and to part from you, my wife Mara, daughter of Lakish, residing now in the city of Caesarea on the Jewish sea coast.   You have been my wife until now, but now be free and depart from me, and dispose of yourself as you desire, and marry whom you please.

" Herewith you receive from me the announcement of your deliverance, and the letter of divorce according to the law of Moses and Israel."

The document was handed to a special messenger with written instructions to give it to Mara the daughter of Lakish in the presence of the president of the Jewish community of Caesarea, as well as of nine other Jewish men of mature age.

On the day after the courier reached Caesarea Mara was summoned.   She could not make out what it was all about. In the presence of the president of the community Joseph's deputy handed her the document.   She could not read, so she begged that it might be read out to her.   It was read, but she did not understand ; it was read again, and explained to her, and she fell to the ground.   The secretary tore the document in two, in token that it had been lawfully handed over and read, put it among his other documents, and gave the courier a receipt.

Mara managed to reach her home.   She saw that she had not found favour in Joseph's eyes.   When a woman did not find favour in her husband's eyes the husband had

the right to send her away.   She harboured no evil thoughts
against Joseph.

From now on she devoted all her time and love and care
to little Simeon, Joseph's first-born.   She strictly renounced
everything that might injure her health, and avoided salt
fish, onions, and certain other vegetables.   She did not
persevere in calling her child Simeon, but called him presently
Bar Meir, which means the son of the radiant one, then Bar
Adir, which means the son of the mighty one, then Bar
Niphli, which means the son of the clouds.   But the president of the Jewish community summoned her a second time
and forbade her to give her child such names, for cloud and
mighty one and radiant one were titles given to the Messiah.
She put her hand to her brow, bowed her head, and obediently
promised.   But when she was alone in the night and
nobody could hear she still went on calling little Simeon
by these names.

She faithfully guarded all the things that Joseph had
ever touched, the towels with which he had dried himself,
the plates out of which he had eaten.   She wanted her
child to be worthy of its father.   She foresaw that this
would involve great labour.   For the son of a marriage
between a priest and a woman prisoner was not recognised
as legitimate, and her child was an outcast from the community.   But in spite of that she would find a way.   On
the Sabbath and on feast days she showed little Simeon all
that remained of his father's things, the towels and the
plates, and she told him of the greatness of his father, and
exhorted him also to become a doctor and master.

After Joseph had handed over the receipt for the letter
of divorce to the competent official in Alexandria he was
solemnly called to give a reading out of the Scripture in the
chief synagogue.   For the first time after a long period he

wore once more his priest's hat and the blue, flower-em-
broidered sash of a priest of the first rank. He ascended
the great pulpit from which a few weeks before he had
been driven. Amid a breathless silence he recited over
the heads of the crowded congregation the prayer of thanks :
" Praise be to Thy name, Jehovah, Our God, who hast given
us Thy word and planted in us the seeds of eternal life."
Then in a loud voice he read the passage from the Scripture
that was prescribed for that Sabbath.

9

BY the middle of winter, just when the new year was
beginning, Vespasian knew that the Empire was firmly in
his hands. The work of the soldier was finished ; now
began the more difficult work of the ruler. The things
that had been done in his name in Rome up till now had
been badly and unwisely done. With cold greed Mucianus
was draining Italy of whatever wealth it had, and the
Emperor's younger son, Domitian, whom he had never
liked, a waster and a ne'er-do-well, was dealing out favour
and punishment haphazardly at Regent. Vespasian wrote
to Mucianus saying that he did not wish the land to be so
severely purged, for people had died of that remedy before.
To the ne'er-do-well he wrote asking him to be so kind as
to leave his father in office for another year. Then he
summoned three men from Rome to Alexandria, the aged
finance minister Etruscus, the court jeweller and director
of the Imperial Pearl Fisheries Claudius Reginus, and the
steward of his Sabine estates.

The three experts went over each other's figures and
checked them. The imperialistic oriental policy of the
Emperor Nero and the chaos after his death had used up a
great deal of money ; the total of the Empire's debts,

according to the three men's calculations, was a high one. Reginus undertook the somewhat thankless task of informing the Emperor of the total.

Vespasian and the financier had never met before. Now they sat opposite each other on comfortable chairs. Reginus blinked ; he looked sleepy ; he crossed one fat leg over the other ; his untied shoe laces dangled from his foot. He had had hopes of this Vespasian once before, at a time when one could expect to make only small profits out of him. He had established relations with Dame Caenis, and when the question of large deliveries for Vespasian's armies in Judaea and in Europe came up he had paid out considerable sums in the way of commission to her. Vespasian knew that the financier had shown himself to be an open-handed fellow in his dealings, not in the least niggardly. With his clear hard eyes he scrutinised the fleshy and melancholy countenance of Reginus. The two men considered each other ; they rather liked each other.

Reginus mentioned his figure ; forty milliards. Vespasian did not wince. He breathed a little more loudly, it may be, but his voice was calm as he replied : "Forty milliards. You're a brave fellow, but haven't you estimated a few items too highly ? " With composure Claudius Reginus persisted in his unctuous voice : " Forty milliards. That figure must be looked in the eye." " I'm looking it in the eye," said the Emperor, breathing hard.

They discussed the necessary financial measures. Immense sums could be got hold of if one confiscated the property of those who had still adhered to the former emperor after the proclamation of Vespasian. It was the day that the Emperor fasted at the command of his doctor Hecateus, and so his mind was more than usually keen. " Are you a Jew ? " he asked suddenly. " Half a Jew,"

replied Reginus, "but every year I look more Jewish."
"I know a way," Vespasian's eyes narrowed, "of ridding
myself at one stroke of half the forty milliards."   "I am
full of curiosity," said Claudius Reginus.   "If I were to
decree," Vespasian said thoughtfully, "that in the chief
synagogues an image of myself must be set up——"   "Then
the Jews would revolt," Claudius Reginus completed the
sentence.   "Right," said the Emperor.   "And then I
could take their money off them."   "Right," said Claudius
Reginus, "by my reckoning that would produce twenty
milliards."   "You're a quick reckoner," the Emperor
said appreciatively.   "You would cover the first half of
your debts by doing that," Claudius Reginus went on.
"But you would never be able to cover the second half,
for industry and credit, and not only in the Orient, would
be destroyed for ever."   "I'm afraid you're right," sighed
Vespasian, "but you must admit that the idea is tempting."
"I admit it," Claudius Reginus smiled.   "It's a pity that
we're both too clever to do such a thing."

Reginus could not endure the Alexandrian Jews.   They
were too insolent, too fashionable.   It annoyed him, too,
that they should look down on the Roman Jews as if they
were unpresentable poor relations.   Nevertheless the
Emperor's proposal seemed to him too radical.   He would
think out later some other way of tapping the wealth of
the Alexandrian Jews ; he did not want to bleed them to
death, but merely to give them something to remember him
by.

For the time being he recommended a tax which would
affect everybody and which until now nobody had dared to
impose in the East ; a tax on salted fish.   He did not
conceal the danger of such a tax.   The Alexandrians'
tongues were as sharp as daggers, and the Emperor would

soon hear from them. But Vespasian had no fear of satirical couplets.

The popularity of the Emperor in Alexandria suddenly came to an end when the text of the salt fish tax was published. The population swore savagely at the increase in the price of their favourite food, and once, when Vespasian was driving out, they pelted him with rotten fish. The Emperor laughed uproariously. Mud, turnips, and now rotten fish ; it amused him that even when he was Emperor he could not escape such attentions. He commanded that the affair should be enquired into, and the ringleader was sentenced to deliver as many goldfish to the Emperor's steward as there had been rotten fish in his cart.

Vespasian saw very little of Joseph during these days. He had grown with his office, he had withdrawn from his Jew, had become strange, western, a Roman. Once he said to Joseph : " I hear that on account of some superstition or other you've had yourself given forty lashes. I wish," he sighed, " I could get rid of my forty milliards of debts in that way."

10

JOSEPH and Titus were lying in the great open dining-hall of the villa in Canopus where the young Roman was accustomed to pass a great part of his time. They were alone. It was a mild winter day, and though evening was coming on they felt no need to go inside. The sea was quite still ; the cypresses were motionless. Titus's favourite peacock strutted through the hall picking up crumbs.

From his couch Joseph could see through an opening in the wall the terrace below him and the garden. " Are you having your box-hedge made in the form of a letter ? " he asked, and nodded his head in the direction of the gardeners at their work below. Titus was munching a sweet ; he was in a generous openhanded mood ; there was a smile on the broad boyish face surmounting his somewhat too short body. " Yes, my Jew," he said, " I'm having the box-hedge made in the form of a letter. I'm having the box-hedge in my villa in Alexandria, too, made in the form of a letter, and the cypresses as well." " The letter B ? " Joseph asked smilingly. " You're a sly fellow, my prophet," said Titus. He moved nearer ; Joseph was sitting ; Titus lay with his arms under his head and gazed up at him. " You've said," he went on confidentially, " that I resemble my father. You don't like my father. I can understand that, but I find that I'm getting less and less like him. I hadn't an easy time of it with my father," he complained. " He's a great man, he knows what human beings are, and if one knows that can one help laughing at them ? But he does it a bit too whole-heartedly. The other day at dinner, when one of his generals was defending himself against the charge of being too fat, he asked him without more ado to strip and show his bottom. It was great to see the Princess ignoring the incident. She sat still, saw nothing, heard nothing. We can't do things like that," he sighed. " We would become embarrassed or nasty. How can one do such a thing without its seeming nasty ? " " It isn't so very difficult," said Joseph, still gazing at the gardeners, who were busy with the box-hedge. " You have only to rule an Empire for three hundred years, and then it comes quite naturally." Titus said : " You're very proud of your cousin, but you have reason to be. By now I know women from all parts of the world. At bottom they're all the same, and with a little experience one can soon get them to the point where one wants them to be. But I can make nothing of her. Has it ever occurred to you that a man of my years and in my position can be shy ?

Only a few days ago I said to her : ' By rights we should declare you a prisoner of war, for in your heart you're with the Avengers of Israel.' She simply said, ' Yes.' I had intended to go further, I had intended to say : ' Seeing you're a prisoner of war, I claim you as my private property.' I would have said that to any other woman, and I would have taken her too." His pampered boyish face was actually worried.

Joseph looked down at the Emperor's son. Joseph's face had become harder, sometimes it expressed unconsciously a gloomy and repellant arrogance. He knew now a good deal better what power was, what humiliation was, and what was meant by pleasure, pain, death, success, failure, freedom and bondage. His knowledge had been well earned, a hard-won prize. He liked the young Roman ; he found in him a ready sympathy, and he had much to be thankful to him for. But now, in spite of all his goodwill, he looked down upon him from his dearly purchased knowledge. He, Joseph, was finished with women ; for him Berenice had never been a problem, and in Titus's place he would long ago have come to the end of that affair. But it was good that things were as they were, and now that Titus begged him boyishly, confidentially and a little awkwardly to advise him how he should act to win Berenice's favour, asking whether Joseph could do anything with the Princess for him, after a little reflection Joseph said thoughtfully and not too eagerly that he would, and pretended that it was a difficult task.

It was no difficult task. Since his public whipping Berenice had changed towards him. Instead of the old alternation between hatred and attraction they now felt a quiet friendship for each other, the fruit of the similarity of their natures and their aims.

Berenice did not stand on ceremony before Joseph ; she
let him see into her life without let or hindrance.   Oh,
she had never held back for long when she found a man to
her liking ; she had slept with many men, she had had
experiences.   But none of these connections had lasted for
long ; there were only two men without whom life would
be· unthinkable for her.   One was Tiberius Alexander, to
whom she was related.   He was no longer a young man,
he was the same age as the Emperor.   But how immensely
tactful, how courteous and understanding he was in spite
of all his sternness and resolution.   Just as firm of will as
the Emperor, and yet never coarse and boorish, he was a
great soldier.   He kept his legions under the strictest
discipline, and yet never departed from the most ceremonious
politeness and most exact taste.   Then there was her
brother.   The Egyptians had been wise when they had
ordained that brother should marry sister to perpetuate
their line of kings.   Wasn't Agrippa the cleverest and nicest
man in the world, mellow and strong like wine of a late
vintage ?   One became wise and good by merely thinking
of him, and love for him enriched one.   Joseph noticed,
not for the first time, how her daring face softened and her
eyes grew dark when she spoke of her brother.   He smiled ;
he felt no envy.   There were women, too, whose faces
changed like that when they spoke of him.

He cautiously steered the conversation in the direction
of Titus.   She asked at once : " Have you been sent here
to sound me, Doctor Joseph ?   Titus can be infernally
clever ; but when I'm in question he becomes clumsy, and
his clumsiness has infected even a clever man like you.
He's awkward, my Titus, a great big baby.   Really the
only thing I can call him is a baby, Janik.   He's thought
out a special shorthand symbol for that word ; I call him

by it so often. For he takes down almost everything I say. He hopes to find some sentence he can pin me down to. He's a Roman, a good lawyer. Tell me, is he really good-natured? Most of the time he's good-natured; then, suddenly, out of pure curiosity, he makes some experiment that costs thousands of lives and destroys whole towns. His eyes become queer and cold when he's like that, and I never dare to open my mouth then." " I like him very much; he's a great friend of mine," said Joseph seriously.

" I'm often afraid for the Temple," said Berenice. " If God has inclined Titus's heart towards me, tell me yourself, Joseph, can it be for any purpose but to save His city? I've become very humble. I've no longer any hope that the world will be ruled from Jerusalem. But the city must remain. They daren't destroy the House of Jehovah." And quietly and fearfully, with a simple and sublime gesture, she asked: " Is that asking too much? "

Joseph's face grew dark. He thought of Demetrius Libanus; he thought of Justus. He thought also of Titus, who had reclined beside him and gazed up at him with frank and friendly eyes. No, it was unthinkable that that amiable young fellow with his reverence for ancient and holy things should lift his hand against the Temple. " Titus will not make any of his cruel experiments with Jerusalem," he said with a great certainty.

" You're very confident," said Berenice. " I'm not. I half suspect that he would have got out of hand as it is if I had dared to say a word against his experiments. He stares after me wherever I go; he finds that my face is better modelled than those of other women; well, who doesn't? " She walked up quite close to Joseph, laid her hand, a white, manicured hand, on his shoulder, and no trace was to be seen on it of the roughness of the wilderness. " We know the world, my dear Joseph. We know that the passions of mankind are always to be counted on, that they are strong, and that a clever man can achieve a great deal if he knows how to exploit those passions. I thank God that He has implanted in this Roman that desire for me. But believe me, if I were to accede to his wishes to-day he would pay no further heed to my words the next time he wanted to start his experiments again." She sat down ; she smiled, and Joseph became aware that she saw her road for a long distance ahead. " I'll keep him on the curb," she decided coolly and cynically. " I won't let him become too familiar." " You're a wise woman," said Joseph. " I don't want the Temple to be destroyed," replied Berenice.

" What am I to say to my friend Titus ? " Joseph wondered aloud. " Listen to me, my dear Joseph," said Berenice. " I'm waiting for a sign. You know the village of Thekoa, near Bethlehem ? When I was born my father planted a pine grove there. Although during the civil war there was severe fighting round Thekoa, the grove didn't suffer. Now listen to me. If the grove is still standing when the Romans enter Jerusalem, then Titus can make me a bridal bed out of the wood of my pines."

Joseph thought hard. Did this proposal arise from her fear of Titus or her concern for the fate of her country ? Did she want her acceptance of Titus to be conditional on his sparing her land, or did she merely want to secure herself against the man's cruel experiments ? And should he communicate her message to Titus ? What really did she want ? He was on the point of asking her, but the Princess's long, keen face was haughtily impassive ; the hour for frankness was gone, and Joseph knew that it would be stupid to ask any further.

I I

ONE morning when Joseph attended the usual reception in the Imperial Palace he found set out in Vespasian's bed-chamber a portrait of Dame Caenis, which the painter Fabullus had executed in all secrecy at the Emperor's instructions. The picture was intended to adorn the head office of the Imperial Treasury. Originally Vespasian had asked that the god Mercury should be shown in the picture standing beside Dame Caenis in a protective attitude, also the goddess of good fortune with the horn of plenty, and perhaps also the three Parcae spinning golden threads. But Fabullus had declared that he could not manage all that, and had presented Dame Caenis in the most realistic fashion, sitting at her desk and checking accounts. Her brown eyes, hard and clear, stared out of her broad, strong face. She was quite still, yet seemed uncannily alive ; the Emperor said jokingly that they would have to bind the picture at nights so that she mightn't walk out of it. So she was to sit above the desk of his head treasurer, with her sharp eyes perpetually on the pounce, to see that there should be no cheating or tampering with the accounts. The Emperor regretted that his favourite god Mercury was not in the picture, but it delighted him nevertheless. Dame Caenis too was content ; only one thing irritated her, that the painter had refused to give her a splendid coiffure.

Anyone who examined the portrait closely could easily see that it was painted by a master, but not by a friend of Caenis. She was a great business woman, capable if necessary of understanding and looking after the finances of the whole Empire, and filled with a genuine devotion to Vespasian and to the people of Rome. In the picture she had become a calculating and niggardly housewife. And was not her resolute, dignified bearing exaggerated in the picture until it bordered on the gross ?   It was as if the painter Fabullus, the devout admirer of ancient Roman senators, had expressed in his picture without knowing it all his hatred of this self-made woman.

From the spacious reception hall a great open door led into the Emperor's bed-chamber. Here, in accordance with ancient custom, Vespasian was robed by his servant before the eyes of all his visitors, and here the living Caenis sat beside the painted one.   Her friend, the man in whom she had believed when he was still in very humble circumstances, was Emperor now, and she was by his side. All that was essential in her was in the picture, and she was prepared to stand up for it. Laboriously the waiting courtiers pushed their way out of the reception hall into the bed-chamber, crowded round the picture, and passed on slowly, an endless line ; each brought out a few words of insincere admiration and flattery.   Dame Caenis listened intently and Vespasian smiled.

The picture made Joseph uncomfortable.   He was afraid of Dame Caenis, and he saw clearly enough that there were things in this picture to nourish and justify his dislike of her.   Nevertheless he felt again that such pictures were blasphemous, for they had the hardihood to recreate what the invisible God had already created.   Jehovah it was who had implanted in this woman her coarseness and her cold and calculating temper ;   the painter Fabullus showed presumption when he now endowed her, on his own initiative, with these qualities.   Filled with repulsion Joseph stared at the painter.   Fabullus was standing near the Emperor.   His severe, fleshy, very Roman face gazed through the visitors ;   sour, haughty and indifferent, he stood there listening to the words of flattery.

The girl Dorion, too, was there.   Her too full but
finely cut lips smiled, a happy radiance lay on her fragile
and haughty face.   Her father had his whims, no one knew
better than she ; but the picture was a masterpiece, full of
skill and knowledge, and this woman Caenis would live
for ever now in the semblance her father had chosen to
give her ; all her coarseness and her sharp greed were brought
to light and made visible to men's eyes for ever.   Dorion
had a passionate love for pictures and could follow the
technique of painting to the most subtle detail.   Her
father had perhaps painted more effective pictures, but this
was his best portrait ; here he had touched the limits of his
genius, and that was saying a great deal.

The reception hall was packed.   Tall, slender, fragile,
her golden brown frail face thrown back, Dorion was leaning
against a pillar.   She breathed softly, her lips were slightly
parted, she enjoyed the effect the picture was producing,
enjoyed the somewhat embarrassed discomfort of the spectators no less than their admiration.   She was elated when
she caught sight of Joseph ; he was a good distance away,
but with a quick side glance she saw that he had noticed
her, and she knew that presently he would come across
to her.

She had not seen the young Jew since the festival on the
Pharos.   When she was told of his whipping she had made
a few spiteful and witty jests at his expense, but had felt as
if she were in a swing high in the air, just before it comes
down again ; for she was firmly convinced that this impudent, handsome and brilliant man had taken the whipping
upon himself simply that the way to her might be left free
to him.

Filled with pleasant anticipation she noticed that he was
slowly making his way towards her.   But when he greeted

her she pretended at first not to know who he was. Then
she remembered. Oh, of course, the young Jewish gentleman whom the Emperor had wanted her father to paint.
Now the Emperor's conditions were more near to being
fulfilled ; she had heard that since she saw him last Joseph
had submitted of his own free will to all sorts of severe
punishments. His face, at any rate, had become much
thinner, and she could see quite well that with a little more
effort he would produce the prophetic impression that the
Emperor had found lacking. With slow, provoking
curiosity she looked him up and down, and in a clear, thin
voice asked whether the scars of the lashes were healed
yet.

Joseph gazed at her frail brown hands, then at the picture
of Dame Caenis, then again at Dorion, obviously comparing
the two women, and said : ' You and Dame Caenis are
the only women here in Alexandria who can't endure me."
As he had intended, Dorion was annoyed at being classed
with Dame Caenis. " I fancy," he continued, " that my
portrait will never be painted. Your worthy father has as
little love for me as for a dead pig, and you, Dorion, find
that I need fasting and whipping to become a good model.
It seems to me that future generations will have no choice
but to know me from my books instead of the paintings of
Fabullus." But he lowered his voice while he was uttering
these sarcastic words so that they sounded almost like a
flattery, and their inflection was of more importance to
Dorion than their meaning. " Yes, you're right," she
replied, " my father can't stand you, but you should try
to remove his dislike. Believe me, it would be worth your
while. A man like you, Doctor Joseph, who submit to
forty lashes of your own free will, shouldn't bear a grudge
so long against the great painter Fabullus for a hasty

phrase." Her voice was no longer shrill, but as gentle as when she had spoken to her cat that afternoon.

Because of the crush Joseph was standing so close to her that they were almost touching. He went on talking softly and familiarly, as if he did not want the others to hear He became serious. " Your father may be a great man, Dorion," he said, " but we Jews hate his art. That isn't a prejudice ; we have good reasons for it." She gazed at him mockingly out of her sea-green eyes, and replied in the same soft and confidential tone : " You shouldn't be so fainthearted, Doctor Joseph. For it's simply that you're fainthearted. You know very well that there's no better means for getting at the reality of things than art. You don't dare to create art. That's all." Joseph smiled pityingly from the height of his superior knowledge. " We have pierced to the invisible that lies behind the visible. That's the only reason why we no longer believe in the visible ; it's too cheap." But the girl Dorion now spoke from her heart, and her voice became quite shrill with eagerness. " Art reveals the visible and the invisible in one stroke. Reality hobbles in the wake of art ; it's only an unfinished, imperfect imitation of art. Believe me, the great artists lay down life's laws for it. My father has done that too, whether he knows it or not." Her childish head was quite close to his ; she almost whispered into his ear as if she were telling him a secret. " Do you remember how Drusilla died ? By a dagger blow on her left side, straight into her heart. Nobody knows who struck the blow. A year before it happened my father painted her portrait. He put a mark on her bare bosom, a mark that looked like a scar ; he did it on technical grounds, the mark had to be there. And it was at that point on her breast that the dagger went in." They stood together in the bright high room ; round about them well-dressed ladies and gentlemen were chatting together ; it was an ordinary Tuesday, but about the two of them lay secrecy and mystery. With a smile Dorion emerged out of this twilight atmosphere. " Really," she said in a polite conventional voice, " such things as these should help to draw together the prophet Joseph and the painter Fabullus."

Simply because the girl's arguments had made an impression upon him, Joseph stubbornly maintained the superiority of the word to the picture. The superiority, above all, of the divinely inspired Jewish word. The girl Dorion puckered her, lips, smiled, then burst into laughter, her high, shrill, malicious laughter. From all that she had heard of Hebrew books, she said, she had little use for them ; they were full of stupid superstitions. She had asked someone to read a passage from his book on the Maccabees to her. She was sorry, but it seemed to her empty, sounding phrases. If Joseph himself was as empty as the book, then she didn't care whether his portrait was painted or not. Joseph himself had a few days before disclaimed his book on the Maccabees quite violently. But now he found her criticism impertinent and silly, and it annoyed him. He hit back, asking politely after her gods, certain animal gods, and enquiring if they liked to lick plates and steal milk. She replied angrily, almost rudely, and they seemed to be the most discourteous couple in the great hall.

12

As Titus had commissioned Fabullus to paint a portrait of Berenice, the girl Dorion now became a temporary member of the gay circle in the villa at Canopus. She met Joseph almost daily. He noted how the others behaved towards her ; very politely, very gallantly, but at bottom

contemptuously, as the gentlemen in Alexandria were
accustomed to behave to pretty women. Towards other
women he, too, behaved in this way, but he could not
in her case. That exasperated him. He violently gave
way to his vexation. When she was present he sneered
bitterly at her, only to praise her boundlessly when she was
gone. With the clear-sightedness of a clever child she
saw through him, saw his desire to shine, his vanity, his lack
of dignity. She had learned what dignity meant. She
saw how filled with envy her father was because the aristocracy refused to admit him to their society ; she saw how
the Romans looked down upon the Egyptians. Her
Egyptian mother and nurse had impressed upon her the age
and holiness of her ancestry ; her forefathers slept beneath
high, pointed, triangular masses of stone. And weren't
the Jews the most contemptible of all peoples, ridiculous as
apes, not much better than unclean animals ? Now she
couldn't tear herself free from this Jew, and it was precisely
his lack of dignity that attracted her, his boundless devotion
to whatever absorbed him at the moment, the sudden alteration from one enthusiasm to another, the shamelessness
with which he spoke out whatever he felt. She stroked
her cat Immutfru. " He's stupid to you. He has no
heart, he doesn't know what you are really, or what pictures
really are, or what the land of Kemet means to us. Immutfru, my little god, scratch me until the blood flows, for my
blood must be evil seeing that I love him ; I must be a
ridiculous girl for loving him." The cat sat on her lap
and gazed at her with round, glittering eyes.

Once during a violent quarrel with Joseph in the presence
of others, she said, her voice filled with hate and triumph :
" Why, if you think I'm so silly, did you have yourself
whipped so that you might be free for me ? " The words

startled him. He was about to laugh, but immediately
controlled the impulse and remained silent.

When he was alone he was torn by doubt. Was it a
warning, an omen, that this Egyptian girl interpreted his
punishment as she had done ? He had been quite right to
let her words pass ; a silent lie like that was permissible
when one wanted to win a woman. But was it a lie ?
He had always wanted to win this woman, and could he
ever have imagined that she would yield to him without
his making some sacrifice ? It was a great temptation, the
thought of marrying her. But it was forbidden to him as a
priest, even if she were to embrace the Jewish religion.
Why had he taken the punishment upon him if the next
moment he was to transgress the law anew ? The Makkabi
crowd would raise an outcry ; worse, they would laugh.
Well, let them. It would be a pleasure, it would be a joy,
to make sacrifices for this Egyptian girl. His offence
when he had married the Roman's cast-off concubine had
been loathsome and disgusting. This sin glittered in
brilliant hues. It was a very great sin. Thou shalt not
lie with the daughter of strange peoples, said the Scripture,
and when Pinchas saw that one of the Israelites was whoring
with a Midianite woman he took a spear and followed the
man to the house and transfixed both the man and the woman
with one blow. Yes, it was a very great sin.

On the other hand his namesake Joseph had married the
daughter of an Egyptian priest, Moses had married a Midianite, Solomon an Egyptian woman. Humbler folk must
put up with a lesser allowance of freedom, for they ran the
danger of losing their customs among the daughters of strange
people, and of worshipping strange gods. But he, Joseph,
was one of those who were strong enough to accept strange
customs without being swallowed up by them. Cast thy-

self free from thine anchor, saith Jehovah. Suddenly he understood the dark saying that man should love God with all his powers, the evil as well as the good.

On his next meeting with Dorion he talked of their betrothal and marriage as of an old and often discussed plan. She only laughed her thin piping laugh. But he pretended not to have heard ; he was possessed by his plan and by the thought of his sin. He began to discuss the details of the ceremony, the date, the formalities necessary for her joining the Jewish religion. Had not women of the highest rank in Rome as in Alexandria gone over to the Jewish religion ? The whole business was somewhat complicated, but the ceremony did not last so very long. Dorion did not even laugh ; she simply stared at him as if he were mad.

Perhaps it was the very madness of his proposal that attracted her. She thought of her father's face, her father whom she loved and reverenced. She thought of her mother's father whose embalmed body slept under the stone pyramid. But this Jew swept every pretext away with the fanaticism of a madman. For him there were no difficulties, and all the reasons she brought up were so much air to him. His ardent eyes beaming with happiness, he told Titus and the guests at the villa at Canopus of his engagement to Dorion.

The girl Dorion laughed and said : " He's mad." But that did not worry Joseph. Wasn't every great and import-ant idea looked upon as mad at first ? Gradually before his ardour, before his unbending obstinacy, she gave way. When others told her that this marriage project was insane, she brought out Joseph's arguments. Soon the idea seemed no longer ridiculous. Already she listened attentively when Joseph spoke of the details of the marriage, and began to quarrel with him over these very details.

To go over to the Jewish religion was not a matter of

great difficulty. Women were not obliged to keep the countless commandments imposed upon believers; they were only bound to observe the prohibitions. Joseph was willing to make wider concessions. He was prepared to be content with the assurance that she would not transgress the seven commandments imposed upon Gentiles. She laughed and rebelled. What, she must renounce her gods, Immutfru, her little cat god? Joseph tried to persuade her. He told himself that before he could soften her heart he must first let it grow harder. He remained silent and summoned all his patience. He did not grow weary of going over the old arguments again and again.

But when he was with Titus he did not restrain himself, and complained bitterly of the girl's obstinacy. Titus was very sympathetic. Nor had he any dislike to the Jewish creed and customs; a community that produced women like Berenice was deserving of all respect. But that anyone bound to another religion from birth should renounce the visible gods of her fathers and go over to the invisible Jewish God, was not that asking a little too much? Titus rummaged among his shorthand notes; he had set down a few particularly abstruse articles of faith and theological clauses from the Jewish doctors. No, to embrace such superstitions; he wouldn't have thought the girl Dorion capable of such a thing. They reclined at the banqueting-table, the three of them, Joseph, Titus and the girl Dorion, and discussed eagerly and gravely what might be demanded of a proselyte, and what might not. The little god Immutfru sat on Dorion's shoulder, opened it's brilliant eyes, shut them again and yawned. To renounce Immutfru, no, never; Titus, too, was of the opinion that that was going too far. After much hesitation Joseph agreed at last that Dorion's conversion to the Jewish religion should be reduced to a formal declaration before the competent official of the community that she had taken that step.

But now came the girl's counter-demand. Tall, languid and fragile, she lay outstretched on the couch. She smiled ; she did not put herself about ; her voice remained thin and polite, but she would not be turned aside from her demand. She thought of her father, of his life-long battle to be accepted by society, and she persisted with childish obstinacy that Joseph must obtain the rights of a Roman citizen.

Supported by Titus, Joseph tried to make her understand what a difficult and wearisome business that would be. She shrugged her shoulders. " It's impossible," he shouted at last in a furious voice. She shrugged her shoulders ; her face grew paler and paler, with that slow ebb of the blood which characterised her. But she persisted : " I must be the wife of a Roman citizen." She saw that Joseph's eyes had grown dark, and in a high piping voice she announced : " I ask you, Doctor Joseph, to make yourself a Roman citizen within ten days. Then I shall be ready to declare my conversion to your God before the officials of your community. But if you can't be a Roman citizen within ten days, then I think it would be better for us not to see each other any more." Joseph gazed at her thin brown hands, which were caressing the long reddish-brown fur of Immut-fru, he saw her slanting childish forehead, her light and pure profile ; he felt bitter against her and filled with love for her. He knew with absolute certainty that she would stick to what she said. If in ten days he did not obtain his rights as a Roman citizen, then that golden girl lying there so languidly would never be seen by him again.

Titus intervened. He thought Dorion's demand high, but was Joseph's so very modest ? He weighed Joseph's chances coolly ; he contemplated the whole business in a

purely sporting spirit, as a battle of wills. It wasn't altogether out of the question that the Emperor, seeing that he
liked Joseph, might grant him the rights of Roman citizen-
ship. Certainly the affair couldn't be done on the cheap,
probably Dame Caenis, as everyone knew, didn't give
anything for nothing. Ten days was a short time. " You
must put all your strength into it, my Jew," he said, and
then : " Tighten your belt ! Get off the mark ! " he
shouted laughingly, as if he were encouraging a runner at
the public games.

The girl Dorion listened to the other two while they
were discussing the whole matter. Her eyes flew from the
one to the other. " Things will be made easier for him
than for me," said she. " Please, Titus, remain impartial,
and don't do anything either for him or against him."

13

JOSEPH went to see Claudius Reginus. If anybody could
get him his citizen's rights in ten days, then it was the
great financier.

In Alexandria Claudius Reginus had become still more
taciturn, still more inconspicuous, still more unkempt than
usual. Few knew the role that he was playing. But
Joseph knew it. He knew that this Reginus was responsible
for the fact, for instance, that the members of the Jewish
community here now regarded the Western Jews with far
different eyes than formerly. He knew that when nobody
else could help you this man Reginus always had an extra
trick up his sleeve. How simply had he succeeded in making
Vespasian the darling of the people again, after the tax on
salt fish had made him unpopular with all Alexandria !
He had merely got the Emperor to perform a miracle. In
the East miracles were always calculated to make the miracle

worker popular, but this man from the West had had to come before anyone thought of employing such a hackneyed trick. Joseph himself was present when the Emperor had cured a cripple known to the whole city and had given back his sight to a blind man by the laying on of hands. Since that day Joseph had been more uncomfortably convinced than ever of Reginus's capacities.

Fat and slovenly as ever, the publisher listened, shooting side glances from his sleepy eyes, as Joseph somewhat stiffly and haltingly explained that he must obtain the civic rights of a Roman. He remained silent for a little while when Joseph was finished. Then, somewhat contemptuously, he remarked that Joseph had always had expensive tastes. The proceeds from the granting of civic rights was one of the most important of the province's sources of revenue. So as not to depreciate the value of those rights, one had to grant them sparingly and keep the fees high. Joseph replied stubbornly : " I must have my rights quickly." " How quickly," asked Reginus.

" In nine days," said Joseph.

Reginus lolled in his chair, his hands hanging languidly over the side. " I require my civic rights, because I want to get married," said Joseph obstinately. " To whom ? " asked Reginus.

" To Dorion Fabulla, the daughter of the painter," said Joseph. Reginus shook his head. " An Egyptian. And you're marrying her ! And you must have civic rights, too ! " Joseph sat on with a haughty and impassive face. " First you wrote the Citizen of the World Psalm," Reginus reflected aloud, " and that was good. Then by very drastic means you won back your priest's sash, and that was better. Now you want to fling it away again. You're a wild young fellow," he concluded. " I must have this woman," said

Joseph. "You always want to have everything you set your eyes on," Reginus said reprovingly in his unctuous voice. "You want everything at the same time, Judaea *and* the world, books *and* fortresses, the law *and* your pleasure. I beg to point out that one has to be very rich to be able to pay for all that." "I must have this woman," Joseph persisted savagely and fatuously. He became urgent. "Help me, Claudius Reginus! Get me my civic rights. Besides, you owe me a little thanks. Isn't it a blessing for us all and you in particular that Vespasian is emperor? And don't I have some credit for it? Was I a false prophet when I called him Adir?"

Reginus regarded the palms of his hands, closed his fingers, and then regarded his palms again. "A blessing for us all," said he. "True. Another emperor might have listened more to Talassos than to old Etruscus and me. But do you fancy," and he suddenly transfixed Joseph with a surprisingly keen glance, "that Jerusalem will be left standing because he is emperor?" "Yes, I do believe it," said Joseph. "I don't believe it," said Claudius in a tired voice. "If I believed it I wouldn't lift a finger to help you to marry this woman and throw away your priest's sash." A cold shiver ran over Joseph. "The Emperor isn't a barbarian," he objected. "The Emperor is a politician," replied Claudius Reginus. "Probably you're right," he went on, "probably it is really a blessing for us all that he is emperor. Probably he really has a desire to save Jerusalem. But," he gave a sign to Joseph to draw nearer and his unctuous voice became soft, cunning and mysterious, "I'll tell you something in confidence. At bottom it's quite unimportant who is emperor. Of ten political decisions that a man may make, no matter what position he's in, nine are imposed upon him by external circumstances. And the higher a man stands, the more his freedom of decision is circumscribed. Society is a pyramid, the Emperor is the pyramid's tip, and the whole pyramid keeps on revolving, but it isn't the man at the tip that revolves it, but those at the bottom. From all appearances the Emperor acts of his own free will. But his fifty million subjects prescribe his actions. Any other emperor would have to act just like Vespasian in nine cases out of ten."

Joseph did not want to admit this. He asked rudely : " Will you help me to get my rights ? " Reginus stopped, a little disappointed. " It's a pity that you have no taste for serious conversation," he said. Then he agreed to sound Vespasian on Joseph's business.

14

Now that his power seemed secure and the time for his return to Italy grew nearer, Vespasian became more and more insensible to the claims of the East. He was a great Roman peasant who had been sent out to establish Roman order in the world. His country was Italy, and Caenis was his conscience. He was elated at the thought of returning. He felt strong and firm on his legs. It was no great distance from Rome to his Sabine estates. Soon he would be smelling the good Sabine soil and having a look at his fields, his vines and herds.

Now more than ever he insisted on method even in his private affairs. He kept pedantically to the programme drawn up for each day. Every Monday he fasted, according to the prescription of his doctor. Three times in the week, on Sunday, Tuesday and Friday, he summoned, immediately after dinner, a girl to come to him, always a different one. After these visits he was usually in a good

humour.   Dame Caenis extorted a considerable commission
for these audiences.

It was after one of these visits and on a Friday that
Reginus managed to secure an audience for Joseph with
Vespasian. The Emperor was always pleased to see his
Jew ; he also liked novel experiments of all kinds.   For
instance, he intended to try to rear African pheasants and
flamingoes and Asiatic citrons and plums on his Sabine
estates. Why shouldn't he grant his Jew the rights of a
Roman citizen ?   But he would make the fellow sweat
for it. " This is presumption, Flavius Josephus," he said
reprovingly.   " You Jews are confoundedly exclusive as
it is.   If I wanted, for instance, to sacrifice in your Temple,
or even if I only wanted to be allowed to read out of your
Holy Scriptures here in Alexandria, you would put all the
difficulties you could in the way.   I would have at least to
acknowledge your religion and God knows what else.   But
you simply come to me and ask me to give you the rights of
a Roman citizen, just like that.   Do you fancy that your
services to the state are really so very great ? "   " I think,"
replied Joseph modestly, " that it was a service to have been
the first to declare that you are the man who will save the
Empire."   " Aren't you inclined to make too much of a
splash, my Jew," the Emperor grinned, " where women
are concerned ?   And how is the little Jewess getting on ?
I've forgotten her name."   He tried to remember the
Aramaic phrases : Be loving, my dove, be gentle, my girl.
" You know the one.   Has she a child ? "

" Yes," said Joseph.

" Is it a boy ? "

" Yes," said Joseph.

" Forty lashes," the Emperor grinned.   " You Jews are
really exclusive, you don't give yourselves away."

He sat comfortably in his chair and gazed at the Jew, who stood respectfully before him. "You've no right really," said he, "to appeal to your former services. People tell me that you're whoring all over the place. Consequently, according to your own theory, you must have lost what gifts you had." Joseph remained silent. "We'll just see," Vespasian went on with a look of sly satisfaction, "whether you have any of your prophetic gifts left still. Come, prophesy whether I'm going to give you your civic rights or not." Joseph hesitated only for a moment, then he made a deep bow. "I only use my reason, and not any prophetic powers, in thinking that a wise and good ruler can have no occasion to refuse me the rights of a citizen." "You haven't answered, you eel of a Jew," the Emperor insisted. Joseph saw that what he had said was inadequate. He must find something better. He sought desperately and found it. "Now," he began, "that everybody recognises who the Saviour is, my first task is fulfilled. I have a new task." The Emperor looked up. Gazing at him with his eager, ardent eyes, Joseph went on daringly, with sudden decision : "The task laid upon me is to perpetuate the past, and not to foretell the future." He concluded resolutely : "I wish to write a book about the deeds of Vespasian in Judaea."

With astonishment Vespasian turned his hard, steely glance on his petitioner. Then he moved closer to him, breathing in his face. "H'm. That is'nt at all a bad notion, my lad. All the same, I had a different idea of my Homer." Joseph said humbly and yet confidently, with his hand to his brow, "The book will not be unworthy of you." He saw that the project attracted the Emperor ; so he went on recklessly, raising his voice : "Give me my civic rights. It would be a great and noble mark of favour, and I would thank your Majesty for it on my knees till the end of my days." And opening his heart he added with humble yet savage frankness : " I must have this woman. Everything will go to ruin with me if I don't have her. I can't work, I can't live without her."

The Emperor laughed. He replied not unkindly : " You're fairly going it, my Jew. You carry out your affairs with spirit. I've noticed that already. Rebel, soldier, author, agitator, priest, penitent, rake, prophet ; whatever you do, you do it with all your heart. But tell me, how about the other woman ? Do you send that little thing in Galilee a good supply of cash, at least ? Don't you neglect your duty there, my Jew. I won't have my son going hungry."

Joseph lost his humility. Challengingly and foolishly he replied : " I'm not a miser."

Vespasian's eyes narrowed.

Joseph was afraid that he was about to break out, but stood his ground. The Emperor, however, had already regained his composure. " You aren't a miser, my dear chap ? It was a mistake to say that," he went on in a fatherly and reproving voice. " A mistake, for which you'll have to pay. For I'm a miser. I had intended to ask a hundred thousand sesterces for your civic rights. Now you'll pay me that hundred thousand, and over and above you'll send fifty thousand to that poor thing in Caesarea."

" I can never get together so much money," said Joseph hopelessly.

Vespasian approached him. " But you're writing a book. A book that'll bring you in a lot. Mortgage the book to me," he said.

Joseph was desperate. Vespasian gave him a clap on

the shoulder and grinned. " Keep your heart up, my Jew. In six or seven years we'll have the boy sent to Rome and have a look at him. If he's like me then you'll get your fifty thousand back."

15

JOSEPH had never bothered very much about money. His properties in the new town in Jerusalem had been confiscated, it was true, by the Makkabi party, but when the Romans reduced things to order again they would be returned to him. For the time being he was living on the salary that he drew from the Imperial Treasury as an interpreter and court official. A portion of his salary was set aside for Mara. As he was almost always a guest of Titus, he could live in Alexandria well and comfortably without incurring much expense. But to raise from his own means the 150,000 sesterces that the Emperor demanded was out of the question.

He would have been able perhaps to borrow the money from rich men in the Jewish community, but he dreaded all the outcry, the savage and melodramatic execrations of the Makkabi crowd, the keen scurrilous witticisms of the White Shoes. His quick fancy already saw the walls of the houses decorated with inscriptions in which his name and Dorion's were lewdly associated. No, he must find some other way.

After a night filled with bitter thoughts he plucked up courage and went to see Claudius Reginus. The publisher shook his head. " I simply can't believe," he persisted stubbornly, " that your heart is still in the Temple. Otherwise you wouldn't fling away your priest's sash."

Joseph replied : " My heart is still in the Temple, but my heart longs for this Egyptian girl, too."

" I've been six times in Judaea," said Reginus. " I've

been six times in the Temple, of course only in the outer
court reserved for the Gentiles, and I've stood before the
door that the uncircumcised aren't allowed to enter. I'm
not a Jew, but I would give a lot to stand for a seventh
time before that door."

" You'll stand there yet," said Joseph.

" Perhaps I shall," Reginus smiled coldly. " That is
if the door is still in existence."

" Will you give me the hundred and fifty thousand sesterces ? " asked Joseph. Reginus gazed at him with his
disagreeably cold eyes. " Come for a drive with me into
the country," he suggested. " I'll think the matter over
there."

The two men drove out. Reginus dismissed the carriage,
and they went on on foot. At first Joseph did not know
where they were. Then he saw a building rising, not a
very big building, white, with a three-cornered gable. He
had never been here before, but he recognised from pictures
he had seen that this was the tomb of the prophet Jeremiah.
Bare, harsh, and forlorn, it stood in the desolate sand in
the bright sunlight. During the morning crowds of pilgrims were accustomed to visit the tomb of the great prophet
who had foretold the destruction of the first Temple and
had lamented it so heart-breakingly ; but it was afternoon
now, and the place was deserted. Reginus made straight
for the tomb and Joseph followed awkwardly over the
sand. Twenty paces from the tomb Joseph stopped ; as a
priest he was not allowed to approach any nearer to the
dead. But Reginus went on and when he reached the
tomb crouched on the ground in the posture of a mourner.
Joseph stood where he was and waited to see what his companion would do or say. But Reginus said nothing, he
crouched there in an uncomfortable posture in the sand

N

and dust, rocking his fat body almost imperceptibly. At last Joseph realised that the man was sorrowing for Jerusalem and the Temple. As more than six hundred years before, when the old Temple still rose in splendour and Judaea was still in its pride, the prophet who lay buried here had preached submission and recited that roll of the Scripture which was full of such wild grief over the destruction of a city that was still intact, so the great financier crouched now in the sand, a wretched heap of misery and despair filled with wordless sorrow over the new city and its Temple. The sun sank, the air became piercingly cold, but Reginus still remained crouching where he was. Joseph stood and waited. He set his teeth, he stamped his feet, he shivered with cold, he stood and waited. It was brazen impudence of this man to compel him to look on and witness his sorrow. It was probably intended as a reproach. Joseph refused to acknowledge the reproach. But he was standing here to get his money and he dared not make any objection. Gradually his thoughts turned away from the man and the money, and irresistibly there rose in his mind the lamentations, exhortations and curses of the prophet who lay buried here, those famous and constantly quoted lamentations, the most wild and poignant ever uttered by a human tongue. The cold became keener, his thoughts grew bitterer, the frost and his bitter thoughts seared and consumed him. When at last Reginus got up Joseph felt that he could scarcely move his limbs.

Reginus still said nothing. Joseph crept after him like a dog ; he felt small and contemptible in the eyes of his companion and in his own eyes ; meaner than he had ever felt before in his life. And when they reached the carriage and Reginus in his usual unctuous voice asked him to get in, Joseph refused and walked by himself the long dusty way back to the town, his heart filled with acrid and painful thoughts.

Next day Reginus asked him to call. As usual the publisher was brusquely genial. "You've written nothing for a long time," he said. "I hear from the Emperor that you're thinking of a book on the war in Judaea. I've a proposal to make to you, Flavius Josephus. Dedicate the book to me."

Joseph looked up. Reginus's words were in effect the first offer for the book, and much as he disliked the man he valued his judgment and was proud of receiving his offer. Luck was on his side. God was on his side. He had been a source of trouble to everybody, to Jochanan Ben Sakkai, to the Emperor, to Claudius Reginus. But when it came to the point they believed in him and stood by him. "I intend to write the book," he said. "Thanks for what you say."

"You can have the money," said Claudius Reginus somewhat gruffly.

16

Now that Joseph had faithfully fulfilled her conditions, the girl Dorion also stood by her decision, absurd and unimaginable as this marriage was. With unshakable energy she went about the necessary preparations for the wedding. First of all, and hardest of all, she told her father of her decision. She brought the news out in a casual, somewhat amused tone, as if she were joking at her own expense. For the fraction of a second Fabullus seemed not to understand. Then he understood. His eyes bulged with apprehension; but he remained sitting where he was and compressed his lips until they became a thin line. Dorion knew him; she had not expected him to stamp and swear, but she had thought he would make some cutting and sarcastic remark. Now that he sat there silent, his lips closed in a thin line, it was far worse than she had imagined it would be. She left the house in great haste, almost as if she were in flight from something, and waiting only long enough to take her cat Immutfru with her, went to Joseph.

Calmly and haughtily she submitted to the formalities of her betrothal and her conversion to the Jewish religion. She contented herself with responding yes and no in her thin childish voice at the necessary moments. The Emperor would have been very willing to celebrate the marriage of his Jew with the Egyptian girl as pompously as he had celebrated Mara's nuptials. Titus, too, would have been glad to arrange a splendid wedding for Joseph. But Joseph declined. Quietly and without ostentation they retired to the pretty little house in Canopus that Titus had let them have for the period of their stay in Alexandria. They climbed to the top storey, which was arranged to look like a tent, and it was in this tent that they lay the first time they lay together. Reclining beside this woman Joseph knew that he was committing a great sin. Thou shalt not lie with the daughters of strange peoples. But the sin was a pleasant one and good to the taste. This woman's skin was fragrant as sandalwood and her breath smelt like the perfumed air of Galilee in spring. Yet strangely enough Joseph could not think what her name was. He lay with closed eyes but could not remember it. With an effort he opened his eyes. She lay there, long, slender, golden brown ; her sea-green eyes glittered through her almost shut lids. He loved her eyes, her breasts, the breath that came from her half-parted lips, all of her, but he could not hit upon her name. There was only a light coverlet on the bed, the night was cool, her skin, too, was smooth and cool to the touch. He stroked her very softly, his hands had grown soft and smooth in Alexandria, and as he did not know her name he whispered little terms of endearment into her ear, Hebrew words, Greek, Aramaic : " My love, my shepherdess, my bride, Janiki."

From below came the soft throaty sing-song of her Egyptian servants, a few notes endlessly recurring. For these people did not need much sleep, and often they sat up all night and never grew weary of singing their little store of songs. They sang : " Oh, my lover, it is sweet to bathe before thee in the pool. Let me show thee my beauty and my shift of the finest royal linen which clings to my body now that it is wet."

Joseph lay motionlessly, the woman lay beside him, and he thought : " The Egyptians forced us to build their cities, the cities of Piton and Rameses. The Egyptians forced us to immure our first born alive in the walls of their houses. But then the daughter of Pharaoh found Moses on the banks of the Nile, and when we marched out of Egypt the children leapt out of the house walls and came to life again." And he stroked the body of the Egyptian woman.

Dorion kissed the scars on his back and chest. He was a man and full of vigour, but his skin was as smooth as a girl's. Perhaps the scars could be charmed away, so that they became invisible ; many people had had their scars removed in that way. But she did not want him to have the scars removed. He must never allow it, never. He had got these scars for her sake, sweet scars received in her honour ; he must guard them.

All that day they admitted no one, not even any of the servants, no one. They did not wash, so that they might lose nothing of each other's fragrance ; they did not eat, so that they might lose nothing of each other's savour.

They loved each other ; there was nothing in the world that existed save themselves. All that was beyond the confines of their bodies did not exist.

On the second night, towards morning, they both lay awake. And everything was strangely altered. Joseph lay thinking. Dorion with her plate-licking, milk-stealing cat had become like a figure in one of her father's hateful pictures, and she was quite foreign to him. Mara had been an outcast, the rejected concubine of Vespasian, but she had never been strange to him, never. She had borne him a son, a bastard, it was true. Yet when one clasped Mara one felt there was a heart beating in her body. But what did one clasp when one embraced this Egyptian woman ?

Dorion lay, her full sensual lips half-parted ; between her regular teeth her breath came lightly and easily. From below rose the throaty monotonous sing-song of the Egyptian servants. Now they were singing : " When I kiss my beloved and she parts her lips my heart is filled with gladness though I have no wine." Sometimes Dorion mechanically hummed a snatch of the song. How much she had sacrificed to this man who was a Jew, and, the gods be thanked, it was good. She had allowed herself to be bought like a chattel according to the absurd and contemptible laws of the Jews, and, thanks to the gods, it was very good. She had renounced her father, the greatest artist of the age, for this man who was dull and blind and could not distinguish a picture from a table, and, the gods be thanked, it was very good. She had sworn allegiance to the silly Jewish demon in whose Holy of Holies people adored an ass's head, or perhaps, which was worse still, nothing at all, and if she were to ask this man to sacrifice to her lovely little god Immutfru, he would simply laugh at her, and yet the gods be thanked, it was very good.

Joseph saw her lying there naked in the posture of a little girl, and her golden brown face was weary with the fatigue of love. She was pale, her skin was cold, her eyes were sea-green, and she was very strange to him.

The brilliant day rose. They had slept for a few hours ; they felt refreshed ; they gazed at each other and were pleased ; they were very hungry. They breakfasted on strongly seasoned dishes that the cook had to prepare to their instructions ; lentil soup, a pasty of nondescript flesh, and beer. They were happy, satisfied with each other and with fate.

In the afternoon they went through the whole house. Among Joseph's things Dorion found a few queer-looking dice with Hebrew letters on them. Joseph became thoughtful when she showed them to him. He said they were amulets for bringing luck, but now that he had her he did not need an amulet. In his heart he resolved never to play with false dice again. Even for Dorion he had played with false dice, for had he not let her believe that he had taken on his public scourging for her sake ? With a laugh he flung the dice into the sea while she looked on.

17

VESPASIAN followed vigilantly all the actions of his son, and Dame Caenis also kept a sharp eye on him. Many tongues and hands were plotting to plant Titus on the throne of his father. The youth had courage and prudence, and his troops were devoted to him. Besides, that hysterical Jewish princess was always spurring him on, and in her fanatical faith she expected far greater things for Judaea from this young man who was so madly in love with her than from the cold-blooded Vespasian. The Emperor saw all this very clearly. He found it best always to call

things by their names. Often he pulled up his son and
sarcastically computed how long he would still have to wait
for the paternal throne. Often, too, there were violent
scenes. Pointing to the wide powers his brother, that
waster Domitian, enjoyed in Rome, Titus insisted that he
himself should be given more authority in the East. The
tone in which father and son addressed each other was frankly
rude. Vespasian warned his son against the Jewess in a
vein of jocular paternal rebuke. Mark Antony had at
least conquered Rome before he began to whore and go
the pace with the Egyptian woman ; he, Titus, had only
conquered a few mountain forts in Galilee and so had not
yet acquired the right to carry on amours with these orientals.
Titus struck back. He retorted that his taste for oriental
women was not a new phenomenon ; he had it by birth.
He reminded his father of Mara. Vespasian roared with
laughter. Right, Mara had been the wench's name. Now
at last he had her name fixed in his mind. He had completely forgotten it, and the Jew Joseph, dog that he was,
had refused to divulge it when she had been mentioned
recently.

For the rest he relied on his son's good sense. Titus
would never be so stupid as to make a doubtful and risky
bid for power, when in a few years the ripe fruit must fall
in his lap in any case. Vespasian loved his son, he wanted
to secure the dynasty ; he decided to give Titus a chance of
winning fame. He himself had accomplished the most
difficult part of their task in Judaea. He would leave to
Titus the glory of concluding it.

Again, however, he kept his entourage painfully waiting
before he came out with his decision. The Alexandrian
winter was passing. With its end he would have to resume
operations in Judaea in case the Jews should risk an in-

convenient countermove. Would the Emperor himself wind up the campaign, or to whom would he entrust the task ? Why was he hesitating ?

At this stage Joseph was summoned by the Emperor. Vespasian chaffed him at first in his accustomed style. " Your marriage must be a happy one, my Jew," he began. " You look properly pumped dry, and I fancy that isn't caused merely by inward contemplation and ecstasy." He maintained his chaffing tone, but Joseph perceived the seriousness behind it. " All the same," Vespasian went on, " you must give your inner voice another chance. That's to say, if you've still any intention of describing the Jewish campaign. For it will be finished off within the next few months. But I'm going to leave the final settlement of your revolt to my son Titus. You're free to chose whether you're to go to Rome with me in a few weeks, or with Titus to Jerusalem at once."

Joseph's breast filled with elation. The decision for which everybody had been waiting with such painful anxiety had been divulged to him first by this old man. But at the same time, he felt keenly how hard was the choice that the Emperor imposed upon him. Was he to go to Judaea and look on while the thing of which he had had that foreboding by the tomb of Jeremiah was actually happening under his eyes ? Was he to drink all the bitterness of seeing his city brought to destruction ? The eyes of this man sitting before him were again narrowed, and they had a damnably hard look in them. That man knew how bitter the choice was ; he was trying him and waiting.

An inner bond had attached him to this Roman from the first moment he had seen him. If he went to Rome that bond would become closer ; Vespasian would give ear to him and he would rise in the world and achieve many

N*

things.   A bond also attached him to the Egyptian girl.
Her arms were brown and smooth, her hands were brown
and fragile, and with all his being he yearned for her.   He
felt jealous when with her fragile brown hands she stroked
the cat Immutfru.   Some day he would no longer be able
to restrain himself and would kill her god Immutfru, not
out of hatred of idolatry, but out of pure jealousy.   He must
flee from this Egyptian woman ; he would be ruined if he
stayed longer with her.   His inner eye was already almost
blind, and his heart was dead and no longer had any feeling
for spiritual things.   He must flee from this man, too, for
if he stayed any longer with him his longing for power
would grow more and more.   And power made one stupid.
And stifled the inner voice.

Power was sweet ; one walked on air when one enjoyed
power.   The world became an easy place to live in, and one
breathed deeply and easily.   Dorion's arms were brown and
smooth.   Her limbs were long and supple and yet like those
of a little girl, and to love her was pleasant and delightful.
If he went to Rome his life would be a happy one, for he
would have the Emperor, and Dorion would be there with
him too.   But if he went to Rome he would see nothing of
the destruction of his city, and his country and the House
of God would go down unsung ; the Temple would be
rased to the ground and nobody in later ages would know
anything of its destruction.

Suddenly an immense longing for Judaea filled him.   He
had a mad yearning to be there, to gorge completely his
eyes and his heart when the white and golden marvel of the
Temple was being destroyed, when the priests were being
dragged along by their hair and their sacred blue robes were
torn from their backs, and the golden cluster of grapes over
the door of the inner Temple melted and dropped into a

mire of blood and mud and filth. Yes, and together with the Temple his whole race would be exterminated in a reek of savage butchery, a burnt offering to the Lord.

Into the midst of his feverish imaginations broke the harsh voice of the Emperor. " I am waiting for your decision, Flavius Josephus."

Joseph put his hand to his brow and bowed deeply in the Jewish fashion. He replied : " If the Emperor will permit me, I should like to see with my own eyes the consummation of the campaign which the Emperor began."

Vespasian smiled faintly ; his expression was resigned and morose ; all at once he looked very old. He was fond of his Jew, he had given much to his Jew. Now the Jew had decided in favour of his son. Well, his son Titus was young ; but he himself had still ten years of life in him, or at least five, or at most fifteen.

18

DORION still lived by herself in the little villa in Canopus which Titus had lent to her. It was a lovely winter, and she drank in with all her senses the fresh coolness of the air. Her god Immutfru lived on excellent terms with the sparrow hawk, and the peacock strutted majestically through the tiny rooms. Dorion was happy. Formerly she had always needed to have crowds of people about her ; her father's ambition had infected her too, she had had to shine, to chatter, to be admired. Now even the occasional presence of Titus became a burden, and all her ambition was wrapped up in Joseph.

How handsome he was. How ardent and lively his eyes were, how strong and gentle his hands, how wild and sweet his passion ; and besides he was the cleverest man in the world. She told her animals about him. In her thin voice, which was hardly more melodious than that of her peacock, she sang to them the old love songs she had learned from her nurse. " Oh, stroke my breasts, my beloved. Do not leave me when you are hungry. Drink from my breasts, for their milk overflows for love of you. My love for you penetrates every inch of my body as the oil penetrates the pores of the skin." She begged Joseph again and again to recite the verses of the *Song of Songs* to her, and after she knew them by heart nothing would do but that he must repeat them in the Hebrew original, and she pattered them after him joyfully, mispronouncing the words. The days, short as they were, were too long for her, and the nights, long as they were, too short.

It would be difficult, Joseph reflected, to convince her that he must go to Jerusalem and leave her here. It would be a very painful break for him too, but he was resolved to make it at once and without dilly-dallying.

When he told her she did not understand at first. When she did understand she grew pale, quite slowly as was usual with her ; the pallor started at her lips and spread until it covered her cheeks and her brow. Then she fell forward on the ground, very slowly and lightly, and without making a sound.

When she came to herself he sat down beside her and began cautiously to reason with her. She stared at him ; her sea-green eyes were confused and wild. Then with a frightful grimace she bared her teeth and vented on him all the abuse she knew, cursing him in the most scurrilous terms in Egyptian, Greek, Latin, and Aramaic. She called him the son of a stinking slave and a leprous whore. He was lower than dirt ; the eight winds had swept together all the offal in the world to create him. Joseph looked at her. She was hideous as she crouched there and screamed

at him in her breaking voice. But he could understand ;
he was filled with pity for her and himself, and with intense
love for her. Then suddenly her mood changed ; she
clung to him and her face became hopeless and woebegone.
She whispered to him all the little terms of endearment
that he had taught her, whispered them imploringly, beseechingly, filled with despairing love.

Joseph was silent. Very softly he stroked her as she lay
limp against him. Then gently and cautiously he tried
to make things clear to her. No, he didn't want to lose her.
It was hard, what he asked from her : that she, who was so
full of life, should sit there and wait ; but he loved her and
did not want to lose her, and asked this from her. No,
he wasn't cowardly and inconstant, nor was he wooden and
feelingless, as she had accused him of being. He was only
too capable of appreciating and loving and devoting himself
completely to a being so dear to him. He wouldn't stay
away for long, a year at most.

" That is for ever," she interrupted him.

And his going away, he went on seriously and urgently,
ignoring her interruption, was for her sake no less than
his own. Hope and expectation dawned in her eyes, and
a touch of suspicion. Still cautiously caressing her, he
explained his plan, modifying it to suit her wishes. He
believed in the power of the word, of his word. His words
would achieve something that she, too, desired in her heart.
Yes, his book would gain her the place and rank among
the ruling classes for which her father had all his life striven
in vain. She denied it violently, but already she was somewhat shaken. Softly and fanatically he whispered into her
ear, into her heart. The Empire would go out from the
East ; the East was destined for sovereignty. But the
East had set about things too clumsily until now, too coarsely

and materialistically. The sovereignty and the power, these were not the same. The East would determine the destiny of the world, but not from without, but from within. Through the word, through the spirit. And his book would be an important milestone on that road. " Dorion, my girl, my sweetheart, my shepherdess, don't you see that this is a second and deeper bond between us ? Your father eats his heart out because the Romans look upon him as a curious animal, a king pheasant, or a white elephant. I, your husband, will achieve the golden ring of the second aristocracy. You, an Egyptian despised by the Romans, I, a Jew regarded by Rome with mistrust and unwilling respect : we together will conquer Rome."

Dorion listened, she listened to his words with her ear and her heart and drank them in. She listened like a child ; she had wiped away her tears, she still sniffed a little now and again, but she believed him ; he was so clever, and his words were so sweet to her. Her father had painted all his life, and that in itself was certainly a great vocation ; but this man had roused his people to rebellion, had fought battles, and then had won over the victor himself, so that now Vespasian was devoted to him. Her husband, her beautiful, strong, clever husband ; his empire stretched from Jerusalem to Rome ; the world was as wine to him which he poured into his beaker ; and all that he did was right.

Joseph stroked her and kissed her. She felt his breatn, his hands, the smell of his skin, and after they had melted together in the final embrace she was completely convinced. She sighed happily and clung to him ; then she curled up with her knees to her chin and went to sleep.

Joseph lay awake. He had persuaded her more easily than he had anticipated. It would not be so easy for him.

Cautiously he detached himself from her arms. She muttered a little, but she went on sleeping.

He lay awake thinking of his book. He saw his book before him, vast, threatening, a heavy burden, a hard task, and yet it filled him with joy. Vespasian's remark about Homer had struck him. He would not be Vespasian's Homer, nor Titus's. He would sing his people, the great war of his people.

If utter destruction were really to come, then he would be the tongue of that utter destruction ; but he no longer saw destruction, but peace and joy. He himself would negotiate a peace between Rome and Judaea, a reasonable peace assuring honour and prosperity. The word would conquer. The word demanded that he should go to Judaea. He looked down at Dorion sleeping. He smiled and lightly touched her hair. He loved her, but his thoughts were far away from her.

The interview in which Vespasian told Titus of his decision to entrust him with the conclusion of the campaign in Judaea was brusque and cordial. Vespasian seized his son by the shoulder, walked him up and down, and spoke faithfully to him like a good father. The powers that he gave him were comprehensive and embraced the whole Orient. Moreover, he would let him have four legions for his task in Judaea instead of the three that his predecessor had had to be content with. Full of joyful gratitude, Titus frankly laid bare his mind. He was not working to oust his father from the throne. He was without his brother, the waster's, lust for power ; he had a Roman heart. Perhaps later, after Vespasian had ruled in peace and prosperity for a time, he would be prepared to take over an empire all in ship-shape order, and he pinned his hopes firmly on that, and wasn't such a fool as to exchange it for a mere gamble

Vespasian listened to him with approval and believed him. He looked into his son's face. That face, burnt a brick-red by the summer in Judaea, had become paler in Alexandria ; but it was still a face formed to please the army and the multitude. The brow was not bad, the chin was short, firm and military ; only the cheeks were somewhat flabby. And sometimes there came into the young man's eyes a somewhat mad and reckless look that the father did not like at all. The boy's mother Domitilla had also had that look occasionally ; and at such times she acted in an idiotic and hysterical manner, and probably it had been for that reason that Capella, her former husband, had wanted to get rid of her. However that might be, the boy wasn't stupid and he would easily manage what was left to be done in Judaea, especially as Vespasian had given him a particularly clever chief of staff, Tiberius Alexander. By Hercules, everything would be splendid if the boy would only take more interest in the oriental men and less in the oriental women.

In the same familiar tone Vespasian cautiously touched the old sore theme of Berenice. " I can understand," he began with a friendly smile, speaking as man to man, " that this Jewish lady may possess charms as a mistress that Greek or Roman women may not have." Titus's brows shot up ; he looked now really like a child ; he tried to avoid the theme, which acutely embarrassed him ; but he could not bring himself to tell his father that the Jewess was not actually his mistress ; for Vespasian would overwhelm him with a cataract of chaff. So Titus compressed his thin lips and remained silent. " I admit," the old man continued, " that these Eastern people have been given certain gifts by their gods that we don't possess. But believe me, these gifts are of no great importance." He put his hand on his son's shoulder and went on in a paternal tone. " For, you

see, the gods of the East are old and feeble. This invisible
god of the Jews, for instance, has given his worshippers
excellent books, but he can only fight on the water, as I have
been informed on dependable authority. All that he could
do against Pharaoh was to make the water close over him
and drown him, and at the very beginning of his reign the
only way he could get even with mankind was to send a
great flood against them. On land he's feeble. Our
gods, my son, are young. They don't insist on your having
so many scruples of conscience as the Eastern ones ; they
aren't too refined ; they content themselves with a few
oxen and swine and a man's oath. I advise you not to
become too intimate with the Jews. It's a good thing to
know that there are other ways of looking at the world
than those of the Forum and the Palatine. There's no
harm in your letting yourself be carried away at moments
by Jewish prophets and Jewish women ; but, believe me,
my son, the Roman military discipline and the political
hand-book of Augustus are things that will serve you better
in life than all the sacred scriptures of the East."

Titus listened attentively and in silence. Much that
the old man said was true. But in his mind he saw Princess
Berenice ascending the steps of the terrace, and at that vision
all the political wisdom of Rome vanished to the four winds.
When she said : " Give me, dear Titus, until we're in
Judaea and I feel my feet on my native soil. Then I shall
know what I am to do and not to do "—when she said
those words in her deep, agitating, slightly husky voice, he
could not withstand her. One might want to win the
rulership of the world and to see one's legions stretching
from end to end of it ; but the sovereignty of this woman
was more ancient, more legitimate and royal than any such
solid and matter-of-fact empire. His father was an old

man.   At bottom it was fear that made itself heard in the
words of this old man.   The fear that a Roman might not
be equal to the subtle temptations of the East, its fine logic,
its profound morality.   But Rome had digested the wisdom
and sentiment of Greece.   It was cultured enough now to
swallow without danger the sentiment and the wisdom of
Judaea.   At any rate, he, Titus, felt himself strong enough
to unite both things, the Eastern darkness and profundity,
and the direct and clear ruling spirit of Rome.

19

The news that Titus was to conclude the Judaean campaign and afterwards follow the Emperor to Rome roused
great excitement in Alexandria.   The White Shoes breathed
a sigh of relief.   They were elated at the thought of getting
rid of the Emperor and their austere Governor Tiberius
Alexander, and it filled them with satisfaction that now
at last four legions were to be sent to deal with those insolent
Jews.   The old catchword of the Jew Apella was revived
again.   Wherever the Jews showed themselves the word,
" Apella, Apella," was bawled at them.   But presently it
was superseded by another catchword, a shorter and more
pungent one that soon spread over the city, over the East,
over the whole world.   It had been invented by Chaereas,
the young man whom Joseph had once struck down with
his writing apparatus.   It consisted of the initials of the
sentence : Hierosolyma est perdita, Jerusalem is lost.   So
now the word, " Hep, Hep," was shouted everywhere that
the Jews showed themselves.   The children in particular
were always screaming, " Hep, Hep," and presently they
coupled the two words, and all through the town the shout
was to be heard : " Hep Apella, Hep Apella, Apella Hep."
Joseph did not allow himself to be annoyed by these shouts.

He, Berenice, Agrippa and Tiberius Alexander, who was
a Jew by birth, were the sole hope of the Jews, and wherever
he appeared he was once more saluted with the cry : " Marin,
Marin." He radiated confidence. He knew Titus. It
was inconceivable that Tiberius Alexander, whose father
had embellished the Temple with its most splendid monuments, would allow the Temple to be destroyed. The
campaign would be a short and severe one. Then Jerusalem
would surrender, and the country, rid of the Avengers of
Israel, would blossom again. Already he saw himself one
of the chief men in Judaea, either as a member of the Roman
administration or of the Jerusalem government.

True, the immediate ask that lay before him was a hard
one. He wished to be an honest mediator between the
Jews and the Romans. Both parties would distrust him.
When the Romans suffered a rebuff they would put the blame
on him ; when things went badly with the Jews it would
be his fault. But, however that might be, he would not
allow himself to become embittered, he would keep an open
eye and an open heart. " O Jehovah, give me a greater
heart, that I may understand the diversity of thy world
O Jehovah, give me a greater voice, that I may declare the
splendour of thy world." He would keep his eyes and his
senses open ; and this war in all its madness, its horror and
its greatness, would live again for later generations in his
words.

20

THE Egyptian winter was over ; the Nile floods had
subsided. The torrential rain, which made the swampy
country near Pelusium almost impassable, had now ceased,
and the army could be transported up the Nile from Nicopolis,
so that it might have a clear line of march to Judaea along
the old desert road.

The leaders of the Alexandrian Jews marched proudly with the others, their faces composed and their bearing calm ; but in their hearts they were deeply troubled. They had themselves assisted in the mobilisation of the troops, and they had made high profits on the equipment and the victualing. Also they were filled with indignation against the agitators in Judaea and were glad with all their heart that Rome had lifted its foot at last to trample those agitators into the dust. But how easy it would be for the Roman boot to trample down not only the agitators, but the city too, or even the Temple. Jerusalem was the strongest fortress in the world ; the rebels were so blinded by hatred that they were rending each other ; and when a city is taken by violence, where is the violence to cease, and who can command it to cease ?

Rome's attitude towards the Alexandrian Jews was one of polite benevolence. This war was being waged merely against the rebels in the province of Judaea, not against the Jews in the Empire. But if the Imperial Government made this distinction, the masses did not. Alexandria had to give up most of the soldiers in its garrison, for the campaign. The Jews showed no sign, but they were filled with apprehension lest there might be a pogrom similar to the one four years before.

They strove all the more eagerly to show their loyalty to the Emperor and his son. In spite of the black looks of many members of the Jewish community the great master Theodore Bar Daniel gave Titus a farewell banquet. The Emperor was there, Agrippa, Berenice, and Titus's chief of staff, Tiberius Alexander. Joseph and Dorion had also been invited.

Dorion's face was serious and calm and startlingly pale, and everybody looked at her.

So there they lay on their banqueting couches, a hundred human beings, Jews and Romans, and drank in honour of the campaign that was to begin next morning, when four legions, the fifth, the tenth, the twelfth and the fifteenth, would set out from various points in Syria and Egypt to besiege the insolent Jewish capital and humble it for ever. " Thy destiny, Roman, is to rule the world, shielding the humble and crushing the insolent." So had the poet sung when the founder of the Empire had seized supreme power, and to make his words true they were now all resolved, Romans and Jews alike, to employ every resource of the sword and the law.

The banquet did not last for very long. Titus replied to a short address by the great master. He wore the parade uniform of a general ; he no longer looked like a youth ; his eyes were hard, cold and clear, and everybody saw how much he resembled his father. He spoke of the Roman soldier, of his discipline, his mercy, his pitilessness, his traditions. " Others have thought more deeply," he said, " and others have felt more beautifully ; to us the gods have granted the ability to do the right thing at the right moment. The Greek has his sculpture, the Jew has his book ; we have our camp. It is strong and yet easy to shift, it rises every day anew, a little city. It is the shield of the humble who obey the law, and the terror of the insolent who defy the law. I promise you, my father, I promise Rome and the world, that Rome will be in my camp, the old Rome, stern where it must be stern, and mild where it can be mild. It will not be an easy campaign, but it will be a good one, conducted in the Roman fashion." It was not mere words that the young general uttered ; it was the meaning and essence of his race, the masculine nature in its purity, the masculine virtue that had made of the first dwellers in the little settlements on the hills of Tiber the rulers of Latium, Italy, and the whole globe.

The Emperor listened to his son with pleasure and approval ; softly and mechanically he stroked his gouty leg. No, the Jewess would not get round this son of his. And he glanced at Berenice with a faint, secret smile. She was listening, her dark, keen face supported motionlessly on her hand. She looked very sad. This man had completely forgotten her now, had driven her out of the last corner of his heart. He was a soldier and nothing more, a man who had learned to stab, to kill, to destroy. It would be difficult to stay his hand once it was raised.

The brilliant hall was very still while Titus spoke. The painter Fabullus was there. His portrait of Princess Berenice was finished. But Titus did not want to take it with him on the march, and the painter felt greatly flattered ; for the picture, Titus had said, was so living that it would be disturbing to have it near him, and as he had to conduct a campaign now, he could not afford to be disturbed. Fabullus looked older, his face was still more stern and severe, and he had lost fat. He stared in front of him blankly, as was his custom ; but the blankness of his gaze was deceptive. This man who had grown so old in the last few weeks could see very well. He saw all the hundred faces, the Romans, those masters of the world who were setting out to chastise a race of lepers and slaves, and the Jews, the chastised, who licked their masters' hands. The painter Fabullus was a man of few words, for words came with difficulty to him ; but he was a great painter, and without needing words he understood what was happening behind those faces, no matter how impassive they looked. He saw Tiberius Alexander, cold and elegant, who had achieved with ease what he, Fabullus, had striven for painfully all his life ; and he saw

that that stern, gifted and powerful gentleman was not
happy. No, not a single one of those Jews was happy,
neither King Agrippa, nor Claudius Reginus, nor the great
master. Only the Romans were happy and satisfied with
themselves and their destiny. They weren't profound ;
wisdom and beauty weren't problems to them. Their road
was simple and direct. It was a hard road and very long,
but they had strong legs and courageous hearts. They
would walk their road to the end. The Jews and Egyptians
and Greeks in the hall were quite right to look up to them
as their masters.

He saw also the face of the man for whom his daughter
had deserted him, that scoundrel, that dog, that waster on
whom she had thrown herself away. But, behold, his face
was not that of a scoundrel ; it was the face of a fighter who
had long resisted superior power and had gained knowledge
in the process, and now bowed to power and recognised it,
but with a thousand crafty reserves : the face of a fighter
who acknowledged power but had not surrendered to it.
Fabullus knew nothing about literature ; he did not want
to know about it ; he hated it and was filled with bitter
rage because Rome recognised its writers, but not its artists.
Nevertheless Fabullus knew something about faces. He
gazed at Joseph listening to Titus's speech, and he knew
that this man, the husband of his daughter, the scoundrel,
the dog, would presently follow Titus and look on while
his city was being destroyed, and afterwards describe it.
He saw all this in the man's face. And a little while after
Titus had finished he went over to Joseph somewhat
hesitatingly, and not quite so firm and grave in his bearing
as usual. Dorion gazed at him apprehensively, fearing
what might happen. But nothing happened. Fabullus
said to Joseph, and his voice was not quite as assured as

usual : " I wish you luck, Flavius Josephus, with the book
on the war that you're going to write."

Next day at Nicopolis Joseph embarked on the long ship
that was to take him up the Nile. The quay was crowded
with soldiers, packing cases and baggage. Very few civilians
had been admitted, for a military order had gone out that
soldiers were to say farewell to their friends in Alexandria.
Only one man had insisted on accompanying Joseph to
Nicopolis : Claudius Reginus. "Keep your heart and
your eyes open, young man," he said as Joseph stepped on
to the ship, "so that your book may be worth something.
One hundred and fifty thousand sesterces is a pretty considerable advance to make."

Immediately before his embarkation Titus gave instructions that the sentries whom Vespasian had recalled were
to return to their posts at the signal bonfires that should
announce to Rome the fall of Jerusalem.

Book Five
JERUSALEM

Book Five

JERUSALEM

I

FROM the first of Nissen there began to appear on the roads of Judaea pilgrims making for Jerusalem to sacrifice their Easter lambs on the Altar of Jehovah and hold the ritual supper in the holy city. The civil war was still going on, the roads were filled with robbers and soldiers ; but these incomprehensible Jews refused to forego their Paschal pilgrimage. Singly and in great bands they appeared, all of them males over thirteen years. Most of them came on foot, carrying their pilgrim's staffs and their water-skins, and with their horns containing food for the journey slung over their shoulders. Others came riding on asses, horses, or camels ; the rich people journeyed in carriages or litters. The very rich brought their wives and children with them.

They came from Babylon by the great wide Road of the Kings. They arrived from the south by many wretched field paths ; they crowded the three fine army roads constructed by the Romans. They cursed when they passed the columns in honour of the god Mercury which had been set up along those roads ; they cursed when they paid the high road and bridge tolls. But then they at once became cheerful and put on again the joyful face commanded by the law. In the evenings they washed their feet, anointed their heads, recited the blessing, and looked forward with gladness to seeing the Temple and the holy city, and to

379

enjoying the flesh of the Easter lamb, the male yearling lamb
without a blemish.

But behind the pilgrims came the Romans. Four whole
legions at full fighting strength, swollen by the reinforcements from the vassal states : in all about a hundred thousand
men.   On the 23rd of April, the 10th of Nissen according
to the Jewish calendar, they had set out from Caesarea ;
on the 25th they struck their camp in Gabath Saul, a big
village not far from Jerusalem.

Marching in rows of six men, the soldiers took up the
whole breadth of the road and crowded the pilgrims into the
field paths.   Otherwise the pilgrims were not molested.
Only those who wore the provocative arm-band with the
word Makkabi were seized by the soldiers.   A cold shiver
ran down the spines of the pilgrims when they saw that
gigantic serpent creeping onward towards the city, and
perhaps one here and there hesitated for a moment ; but
they did not turn back ; instead these incomprehensible
people hastened faster.   They hurried on with averted
faces, and finally their haste turned to flight.   And when
on the 14th of Nissen, the day before the Paschal Feast, the
day of the ritual supper, the last pilgrim reached the city,
the gates were immediately closed, for behind on the surrounding heights the vanguard of the Romans had already
appeared.

From immemorial time it had been counted a great
wonder, a great miracle by which Jehovah showed his love for
his people, that at the Paschal Feast Jerusalem should be
able to hold all the pilgrims.   But this year, as they were
crowded inside its walls and cut off from the villages around,
which usually could offer hospitality to some, the city was
bursting with people.   But the pilgrims did not worry
about that.   They thronged the gigantic halls and courts

of the Temple and gazed at the splendid sights of Jerusalem. They had brought money with them and so they went the round of the bazaars. They rubbed shoulders with one another in the most friendly spirit, courteously made place for one another, good-humouredly haggled with the vendors, and bought presents for their friends. In this month of Nissen Jehovah had rescued the Jews out of the hands of the Egyptians. They gazed at the approaching Romans with astonishment and curiosity, but without fear. They felt they were standing on sacred ground. They felt secure and happy.

2

TITUS and the gentlemen of his suite were making a survey from one of the hilltops. At their feet in the sun lay the city, cloven by its deep ravines.

Now that for the first time he saw this celebrated and rebellious city of Jerusalem, Titus savoured its beauty to the full. It looked up at him from where it lay, white and splendid, on its precipitous hills. Behind it the country stretched waste and empty, with many bare peaks, slopes girdled with cedar and pine-woods, valleys cut into fields, olive terraces, vineyards, and far away the distant gleam of the Dead Sea ; but the city itself was bursting with crowds who hardly left a passage way for pedestrians in the deep ravine-like streets, and filled every inch of space with their tents. As the silent landscape ended in the swarming city, so the city again conducted one's eye to the white and golden Temple, the Temple buildings, which, huge as they were, seemed to float in the atmosphere with an infinitely tender and pure fragility. Yes, the highest points in Jerusalem, Fort Antonia and the roof of the Temple, lay far lower than the point at which Titus was standing, and yet it seemed to him as though he and his horse were firmly clamped to the ground, while the city and the Temple floated, light and unattainable, in the air.

Titus saw the beauty of the city. Simultaneously, with the eye of the soldier, he saw its impregnability. Ravines on three sides. A huge wall encircling the whole. And when that was taken the lower town had a second wall, the upper town a third ; and the Temple on its high steep hill and the upper town on its mount were two fortresses in themselves. It was only from the north, where he was standing, that the land descended more gently to the city and the Temple. But the walls and forts on this side were the strongest of all. Arrogant and invincible, the city gazed up at him. More and more intense within him grew the longing to tear down those spacious and defiant palaces and force his way with fire and sword through the thick walls into the heart of the disdainful city.

Titus gave his head a little uncomfortable toss. He felt Tiberius Alexander's eyes fixed on him. Titus knew that the general was the first soldier of his age and the chief support of the Flavian house. He admired the man ; his bold features and his airy walk reminded one of Berenice. But he felt like a raw schoolboy in the man's presence ; the general's polite superiority oppressed him.

In spite of his years Tiberius Alexander sat well on his Arab horse. His long sharp-nosed face quite impassive, he gazed down at the city. How complicated everything was. It was insane, the way these people crowded into the city for their religious festival, packed themselves there as close as salted fish. He had been Governor of Jerusalem for several years, and he knew. How was the town to provide for all those multitudes of people for any length of time ? Did the leaders, this Simon Bar Giora and this John of Gishala, think that they were going to get rid of the

Romans ? Did they imagine they could drive off a hundred thousand men with their twenty-four thousand ? He thought of his artillery, of the battering rams of the tenth legion, of Big Julius in particular, that marvellous modern engine. The old and experienced soldier gazed down almost pityingly on the city.

They were still fighting each other, these incorrigible people, within their own walls. They hated one another more intensely than they hated the Romans. In their mad intestinal struggle they had burnt down their huge supply of grain ; and John had set up artillery in the outer halls of the Temple itself to fire against Simon. Quietly and a little wearily the general's eyes took in the familiar sight of the Temple buildings and lingered there. His own father had endowed the Temple with the nine inner gates ; of gold, silver and Corinthian bronze, their value amounted to the revenue of a whole province for two years. Nevertheless his father, though he was great master in Alexandria, had allowed him, Tiberius Alexander, while he was still a lad, to forsake the Jewish community. The general was still thankful to his wise father for that. It was criminal folly for a people to cut themselves off from an incomparably rich province of culture.

With a faint and mocking smile he glanced at the commander's secretary and interpreter, who was also looking down at the city with an embarrassed air. That fellow Josephus wanted to have both things at the same time, the Jewish culture and the Greek. That can't be done, my dear fellow, Jerusalem *and* Rome, Isaiah *and* Epicurus ; you can't unite such incompatibles. You just have to decide for the one or the other.

King Agrippa's handsome but somewhat too full face wore its usual courteous smile. He would have preferred to come here as a pilgrim, rather than at the head of five thousand horsemen. For four years he had not seen the city, never indeed since the day when these foolish people had driven him out after his great appeal for peace. A passionate lover of architecture, he now gazed down with deep love and pity on Jerusalem lying white on its hills and with all those people inside its walls. He himself had done a great deal for it. When the eighteen thousand labourers who had built the Temple were thrown out of work at the conclusion of their task, he had set them to pave the whole city anew. Now the Makkabi crowd had forced those labourers to become soldiers. One of them, a man called Phanias, they had actually chosen as High Priest to show their scorn for the aristocrats. And what horrible damage they had done to his houses, to the Palace of Herod, the ancient Palace of the Maccabees. It was hard to keep one's heart and face composed at such a spectacle.

All round the soldiers were at work. Into the silent contemplation of their commanders, who stood motionless on the hill in the light breeze, broke the sound of spades and axes. The soldiers were setting up their camp and evening the ground for that purpose, filling it up here and levelling it down there. The country round Jerusalem was like a great garden. Now they were cutting down the olive trees, the fruit trees, the vines. They were tearing down the villas on the Mount of Olives, and the shop of the Brothers Chanan. They were levelling the ground to the same undistinguished flatness. Solo adaequare was the technical expression for it. One had to adopt this measure at the beginning of any siege ; it was an elementary rule which every student of military art was taught at the very beginning. The Jewish King sat lazily and elegantly on his horse ; his face looked a little tired, but calm as ever.

He was just forty-two ; he had always been pleased with
the world, although it was full of stupidity and barbarism.
To-day he found a little difficulty in being pleased with it.

Joseph was the only one who could not quite conceal his
emotions. Once he had looked out with the same eyes
from Jotapat at the legions closing their narrowing ring.
He knew that resistance was hopeless. His brain was at
the service of those who were standing round him. But
his heart was with the others, and it cost him a great deal
to endure the sound of the axes, hammers and spades with
which the soldiers were laying waste the beautiful surroundings of the city. A startling bellowing sound arose from
the Temple quarter. The horses became uneasy. " What
is that ? " asked Titus. " It is the Magrepha, the great
shawm," Joseph explained. " It can be heard as far as
Jericho." " Your God Jehovah has a powerful voice,"
Titus admitted.

Then at last he broke the long, embarrassed silence.

" What do you say, gentlemen ? " and his voice had a
violent, almost a menacing ring ; it was more like a
command than a question. " How long shall we need ?
I estimate that if things go well it may take three weeks,
and if they go badly two months. In any case I would
like to be back in Rome for the October equestrian games."

3

Up to now three leaders, claiming to be dictators, had been
fighting each other in Jerusalem. Simon Bar Giora held
the upper town, John of Gishala the lower town and the
southern corner of the Temple quarter, and Doctor Eleasar
Ben Simon the rest of that quarter, the Temple itself, and
Fort Antonia. Now that on the day before the Paschal
Feast the pilgrims thronged to the Temple in great crowds

to sacrifice their lambs to Jehovah, Eleasar did not dare to forbid them entrance to the inner courts. But John of Gishala ordered a great number of his soldiers to mingle with the pilgrims, and no sooner were these within the Temple than they threw off their pilgrims' garments in front of the huge altar where the burnt offerings were sacrificed, and drew their swords. They cut down Eleasar's officers, and took Eleasar himself prisoner. Having in this way gained possession of the whole Temple quarter, John of Gishala proposed to Simon Bar Giora that thenceforth they should unite in repelling the enemy from the walls, and invited him to partake of the Paschal lamb at his headquarters, the palace belonging to Princess Grapte. Simon accepted.

In the evening John was waiting, sly and exultant, within the open door of Princess Grapte's house, for his former enemy and future comrade to appear. Passing John's sentries, who accorded him a salute of honour, Simon ascended the steps before the house. He and his escort were armed. For a moment this vexed John; he himself was unarmed; but he immediately regained his composure. As custom demanded he obsequiously took three steps back, bowed deeply and said: " I thank you heartily, Simon, for coming."

They went inside. The palace of Princess Grapte, who was a Transjordanian noblewoman, had been once furnished with great splendour, but was now in a forlorn state, a mere barrack. With his small brown eyes Simon Bar Giora scrutinised his companion as they walked side by side through the bare rooms. This man John had done him all sorts of injury; he had abducted his wife to extort concessions from him; they had fought against each other like wild beasts, and he hated the man. Nevertheless he had a feeling of respect for the other's cunning. Perhaps Jehovah would never forgive this fellow for commanding his men to conceal swords under their pilgrim's garments and draw those swords before His altar, which was made of unhewn stone, for steel had never been suffered to touch it ; but all the same it was a daring thing to have done, crafty and brave. Somewhat sulkily, though with respect, he walked on by John's side.

The lamb was roasted over the fire in accordance with the law ; that is, the whole animal except for the four legs and the entrails. They said grace and recited the prescribed passage regarding the exodus from Egypt ; they ate with relish the unleavened bread and bitter herbs in memory of their bitter servitude in the land of Egypt which the ritual obliged them to partake of on such occasions. Actually all the plagues with which Jehovah had afflicted Egypt sounded a little ludicrous compared with the plagues that had descended upon them now, and the Roman army was certainly more dreadful than the army of the Egyptians had been. But that did not matter. They were sitting together in the same room, tolerably reconciled. The wine too was good, it was wine of Eshkol, and it warmed their bitter hearts. Simon Bar Giora, it was true, still looked grave, but his companion seemed quite in good spirits.

After their meal they sat closer and drank fraternally the last of the four beakers of wine which were obligatory. Then the two commanders sent their women and followers away and were left alone.

" Will you let me and my men have some of your artillery ? " Simon Bar Giora began after a pause, gravely and distrustfully, and it sounded more like a demand than a request. John gazed at him. They were both lean and tattered, embittered with pain and disappointment and many labours. How could one be so young and yet so morose, thought John. Only three years before there had been a radiance round this man like that round the Temple itself.

"You can have all my artillery," he said frankly, almost gently. "I don't want to fight Simon Bar Giora; I want to fight the Romans."

"Thank you," said Simon, and now there was something of the old savage confidence in his small brown eyes. "This is a happy Paschal Eve, seeing that Jehovah has opened your heart towards me. We shall hold Jerusalem, and the Romans will be scattered." Slender and erect, he sat facing his broad-shouldered companion, and one saw that he was very young.

John of Gishala's clumsy peasant hand was fiddling with the great wine beaker. It was empty and one was not allowed to drink more than the prescribed four beakers. "We shan't hold Jerusalem, Simon, my brother," he said. "It isn't the Romans, but we, who will be scattered. But it is good that there are still men with such faith as yours," and he gave Simon a frank and cordial look.

"I know," said Simon passionately, "that Jehovah will give us the victory. And you believe it too, John. If you don't, why did you embark on this war?" John gazed reflectively at his arm-band with the initials Makkabi. "I won't try to explain to you, brother Simon," he said complacently, "why my faith here in Jerusalem is not so firm as it was in Galilee."

Simon controlled himself. "Don't speak about the blood and injustice," he said, "that have been between us. You weren't to blame."

"Well," John threw in casually. "You taught them a lesson anyway. They hopped about like Syrian rope-dancers, the grave doctors in their long robes. Anan, the old High Priest who put on airs in the High Council as if he were Jehovah Himself in His wrath ; he lay dead and naked and filthy in the streets, and he wasn't very splendid to look at then. He never ordered you a second time out of the Quadern Hall."

"Well," said Simon, and now a faint smile appeared even on his harassed face. "You, John, weren't so very correct either. The way you settled with the surviving sons of the High Priest, and chose the building labourer as High Priest instead, and then made the yokel go through the whole ceremony of investiture and all the rest of the tomfoolery ; you can hardly set that up as an example for pious people to follow."

John grinned. "Don't you say anything against my High Priest Phanias, brother Simon," he said. "He's a bit slow, I admit it, but he's a good man and he's a worker, not an aristocrat. He's one of us. And, after all, the whole business was decided by lot." "But didn't you help a little ? " asked Simon. "We come from the same district," said John, laughing. "Your Gerasa and my Gishala are not so far from each other. Come, brother Simon, my countryman, kiss me."

Simon hesitated for a moment. Then he opened his arms and they kissed each other.

Then, towards midnight, they made a tour of inspection to see that the sentries were at their posts on the walls. Sometimes they stumbled over a sleeping pilgrim, for the houses had not enough room for everybody, and in all the doorways, in all the streets, lay pilgrims, sometimes sheltered in primitive tents, often simply wrapped in their cloaks. The night air was fresh, but it was filled with a dense odour of human beings, smoke, wood, and roasted flesh. Signs of the civil war were to be seen everywhere ; outside the walls stood the enemy ; the streets of Jerusalem did not provide a very comfortable resting place. But the pilgrims slept well. This was the night on which Jehovah watched over them, and He would fling the Romans, man, horse, and chariot, into the sea, as He had once done with the Egyptians. Simon and John tried to step as gently as possible, and when they came to a sleeping man they walked round him. Each was filled with professional curiosity regarding the other's defensive measures. Everywhere the discipline was excellent, and the sentries challenged them promptly and alertly.

Morning was approaching. Outside the walls the signals of the Romans could be heard. Then from the Temple came a loud groaning noise, showing that the gate to the holy place was being opened, then was heard the powerful blast of the shawm, the Magrepha, which announced the beginning of the Temple service, and it drowned the shouts of the Romans. The legions began to throw up trenches ; they were shot at from the walls and replied in turn. When the heavy projectiles came whistling across the monotonous shout of the sentries could be heard : " Look out," and the soldiers with a laugh took cover.

From the tower of Psephinous Simon and John watched the struggle beginning. " It will be a good day, brother Simon," said John.

The white projectiles of the Romans came across, whistling as they flew through the air, and visible from a great distance. The shout came : " Look out," and the soldiers threw themselves down. But then came projectiles which were not visible, for the Romans had painted them. They swept a group of defenders from the walls, and after that nobody laughed.

4

On the 11th of May the glass-blower Alexas left his house and workshop in the Street of the Salve Makers and went to see his father Nachum in the new town. On the previous night the Romans had managed in spite of all hindrances to bring their battering rams within reach of the walls, and through the whole new town could be felt the dull blows of Big Julius, their greatest battering engine. Now at last Alexas would surely be able to persuade his father to seek safety for himself, his people and his property in the upper town, where Alexas himself lived.

Nachum Ben Nachum was squatting inside the door of his workshop beneath the great glass cluster of grapes, squatting on cushions with his legs crossed. Buyers were in the shop haggling over gilded toys made of glass, a golden Jerusalem, or some ornament for a woman's hair. Somewhat apart, quite undisturbed by the bargaining, Doctor Nittai rocked his body and muttered to himself passages out of the law in a monotonous sing-song.

Nachum Ben Nachum did not make the slightest attempt to influence his buyers. They went at last, still undecided. Nachum turned to his son. "They'll come back again, they'll buy all right. In a week at most the sealed letter of purchase will be lying in the archives." Nachum's square beard was well tended, and his cheeks were ruddy as ever, and his words confident. But Alexas guessed at his father's concealed anxiety. If with the sound of the battering ram in his ears Nachum still behaved as if his day's work would go on as usual, it must be because he recognised that the whole new town, including his house and his workshop, was in danger. In a few weeks, perhaps even in a few days, the Roman army would be where they were sitting at present quietly talking. His father must be forced to admit that and move to the upper town. One had only to walk a few steps to reach the walls and see the engines of the Romans at work.

Meanwhile Nachum Ben Nachum comfortably continued his optimistic chatter. Wouldn't it have been criminal folly if he had given way to Alexas's persistence and fled from the city before the Paschal Feast ? Never before had he done such good business. Wasn't it a blessing that the pilgrims wouldn't be able to leave the town for a while ? As it was there was nothing they could do but wander about all day from one shop or bazaar to another. It was a great blessing that he hadn't allowed himself to be led away by his son's talk. To what could one compare a man who accepted advice from someone younger than himself ? To one who ate grapes before they were ripe.

Alexas let his father go on talking. Then, quietly and stubbornly, he began : " The soldiers in Fort Phasael themselves admit now that they can't hold the outer wall. Most of the shops in the Street of the Smiths and the Street of the Clothiers have closed down already. They've all moved up to the upper town. Be reasonable ; put out the furnace and come up to my house."

His young brother Ephraim appeared. He burst out furiously : " We'll hold the new town. You should be reported to Fort Phasael. You're worse than Yellow Face himself." Yellow Face was a prophet who jeered at the Makkabi prople and counselled the Jews to negotiate with the Romans for surrender. Alexas smiled his quiet smile. " I wish," he said, " that I had Yellow Face's command of language."

Nachum Ben Nachum nodded his head and stroked the thick raven hair of his youngest son. But at the same time he weighed in his heart the advice of his first-born, the wily Alexas. The blows of the battering ram really came with terrifying regularity. It was true, also, that many people living in the new town had fled to the upper town, which was safer. Nachum had seen it happening with his own eyes, and the fact that the Avengers of Israel were permitting it meant a good deal. For the Avengers of Israel, the present masters of the city, were very strict in such matters. Too strict, thought the glass-blower Nachum Ben Nachum. But he did not say it aloud. For the Makkabi people had keen ears and Nachum Ben Nachum had often been forced to see acquaintances of his, respected citizens, led as prisoners to Fort Phasael or even to the walls, to be executed because of some unconsidered utterance.

Nachum turned to Doctor Nittai : " My son Alexas advises us to move into the upper town. What should we do, my Doctor and Master ? " Withered old Doctor Nittai turned his savage little eyes on Nachum. " The whole world is a gin and a snare," he said. " Only in the Temple is safety."

The glass-blower Nachum did not come to any decision that day. But next day he put on his old working garb, fashioned out of a single square piece of cloth. He had not worn it for many years, for he had confined himself to looking after his customers. Now, however, he got out his old working garment, put it on and crouched down before the furnace. His sons and workmen stood round him. Employing the old-fashioned method which his son Alexas had long before abolished, he lifted out of the oven with a shovel the thin mass of melted glass, snipped off with a pair of pincers the piece he wanted to shape, and by hand moulded a beautiful round beaker. Then he gave instructions to put out the great oval furnace, which had burned continually for so many decades.   He looked on while it was being quenched and repeated the prayer which is spoken at the news of someone's death : " Praise be to Thy name, Jehovah, righteous Judge."   Then he betook himself with his wife, his sons, assistants, slaves, horses, asses, and all his belongings to the house of his son Alexas in the upper town.   " A man who rushes into danger," he said, " is courting destruction.   Jehovah removes the protection of His hand from the man who delays too long.   If you will give us shelter we shall live in your house until the Romans have gone."   Alexas's eyes lost their gloomy and worried expression.   For the first time for years he looked happy and very like his father.   Reverently putting his hand to his brow he took three steps back and said with a deep bow : " My father's decisions are my decisions.   My humble house will be privileged if my father will set his foot in it."

Three days later the Romans took the outer wall.   They looted the new town and sacked the shops and workshops of the clothiers, the smiths, the iron workers, the potters, and also the workshop of the glass-blower Nachum.   They rased the whole quarter to the ground, so as to make room for the engines with which they now intended to attack the second wall.

The glass-blower Nachum Ben Nachum stroked his thick, black, square beard, in which a few grey hairs now showed, nodded his head, and said : " When the Romans are gone we'll build a bigger furnace."   But when he was alone a look of dejection came into his fine eyes, and the whole man looked worried and very like his son Alexas. " The pity of it," he thought.   " Nachum's glass factory was the best in Israel for a hundred years.   The doctors allowed me to shorten my beard, that Jehovah made so long and fine, so that it might not be singed by the hot glass ; and Doctor Nittai lived on what he got from Nachum's glass factory. And where is Nachum's glass factory now ? No doubt the Makkabi people are brave and they fear God. But the blessing of Jehovah cannot rest on an enterprise that ends in the destruction of Nachum's glass factory. They should have negotiated with the Romans ; my son Alexas always said that. They should still negotiate even now. But unfortunately one mustn't say such things, for they might land one in Fort Phasael."

By this time the price of food in Jerusalem had already risen very high. Alexas bought whatever he could get his hands on ; his father Nachum shook his head. His brother Ephraim was always wildly inveighing against him because of his pessimism. But Alexas went on buying whatever he could hunt out in the way of food. He buried a part of his store in a secret place.

5

ON the 30th of May the Romans stormed the second wall. They had to pay for their victory with great loss of life and material ; for Simon Bar Giora had defended the wall with obstinacy and skill. For a whole week the Romans had had to remain under fire day and night. Titus granted his exhausted men a breathing space. During it they were given their pay, and the commander announced that he would review his troops on a certain day, when decorations would be publicly given out to officers and men who had distinguished themselves.

Since setting out from Caesarea Titus had renounced completely the society of Berenice. He had not even set up in his tent Fabullus's beautiful portrait, because he feared that her presence, even in a picture, might distract him from his duty as a soldier. Now he felt that he could afford to allow himself some relaxation and amusement, and sent a courier post haste to her asking her to come.

But even as he rode out to meet her he knew that he had made a mistake. It was only when he was away from this woman that he felt clear-headed and sure of himself, a good soldier. As soon as she appeared his mind was cast into confusion. Her face, her perfume, her walk, the slight huskiness of her deep voice, robbed him of his calm assurance.

On the morning of the 3rd of June, with Princess Berenice by his side, he watched his troops marching past. Within sight of the besieged, but too far away for Jewish artillery to reach them, the Roman troops displayed their strength. The legions filed past in rows of six men, fully armed and with drawn swords. The horsemen led their caparisoned steeds by the bridles. Decorations sparkled in the sun, and everywhere there was a glitter of silver and gold. On the walls of Jerusalem the besieged stood and regarded the spectacle. The whole northern city wall, the roofs of the Temple colonnades and of the Temple itself, were crowded with people who crouched in the glaring sunlight and contemplated the power, the numbers, and the splendour of their enemies.

After the march past Titus distributed the honours. These decorations, consisting of little banners, spears, and gold and silver chains, were doled out very sparingly. Among the hundred thousand men composing the Roman army scarcely a hundred were distinguished in this way. One man was singled out for special recognition, Pedanus, a subaltern officer, centurion of the first cohort of the fifth legion, a square built man of some fifty years with a great red face and fair hair turning grey. Above his impudent nose with the wide nostrils appeared two eyes whose expression was very disconcerting, for one was blue and lively and the other quite dead : it was artificial. Pedanus already possessed the highest decoration that a soldier could win, the garland of grass which was given not by the commander but by the troops themselves, and only to such men as had rescued the whole army from danger by their prudence and gallantry. The garland that Pedanus wore was woven of grasses plucked in a high plateau in Armenia, the neighbourhood in which, under the command of General Corbulo, he had cunningly and coolly hacked a way for his legion through superior Parthian forces who were trying to encircle it. With his impudence, his mad daring, his ready and coarse tongue, Pedanus was the darling of the army.

The chain of honour that Titus handed him now was no great matter. The first centurion of the fifth legion repeated formally the prescribed words of thanks. Then in his hoarse voice, which could be heard everywhere, he added : " One question, General. Do you suffer from lice, too ? If we don't make an end of things here soon you'll get some, that's certain. If you want to do Pedanus a favour, General, then take your chain back and give him leave to be the first to set fire to the accursed hole where these filthy Jews hide their god." Titus saw Berenice's face growing tense as she waited for his answer. He said somewhat constrainedly : " What we're to do with the Temple is for my father, the Emperor, to decide. And no one will be more delighted than myself if I have to give you a second decoration." He was annoyed that no better answer than this wretched one had come into his mind.

Joseph, too, received a decoration, a little medal to be worn on his breast-plate. " I beg you to accept, Flavius Josephus," said Titus, " the thanks of the commander and

the army." Joseph stared with divided feelings at the silver
medal that the commander held out to him : it represented
the head of the Medusa. Doubtless Titus thought he was
doing him a favour in including him, the Jew, among the
few that were singled out for honour. Yet so little pains
had Titus taken to understand him that he had chosen the
head of the Medusa, which was not merely an image of
the human face, forbidden by the Jewish law in any case,
but an idolatrous symbol. There was no understanding
possible between Jews and Romans. Doubtless the thought
had never even entered Titus's head, much as he liked Joseph,
that such a badge would be an insult rather than a mark
of distinction in a Jew's eyes. Joseph was overcome with
disappointment and dejection. But he controlled himself.
" It is I," he replied formally and respectfully, " who
should thank the commander and the army. I shall try
to be worthy of this mark of favour." And he put out his
hand for the medal. Berenice stood and looked on, her
keen face impassive. On the walls the Jews sat silently
in the glaring sun.

Meanwhile Titus was oppressed with a deeper and deeper
vexation. What was the sense of this parade ? Berenice
knew the strength of the Roman army as well as he did.
To display it before her so blatantly was tactless and barbarous. Over there those Jews were squatting on their
walls and roofs, packed there in thousands, all silently looking
on. If only they had shouted or jeered. Their silence
was a deeper reproach. Nor had Berenice spoken a single
word during the whole march past. This Jewish silence
tortured him.

In the midst of his arrogance and vexation an inspiration
came to him. He would institute a new and more serious
attempt at negotiation. As the prelude to such a step this

military parade would take on some meaning, some point. The commander of such an army could afford to invite his enemy to treat without running any danger of its being interpreted as a sign of weakness. But it was not easy to come to this decision. His father still maintained the fiction that this was not a military campaign, but only a punitive measure. That was not Titus's opinion. He and his army saw before them as the reward and crown of their labours a triumphal procession in Rome. A splendid and glittering spectacle. But if the business ended with a composition he would have to forego his triumphal procession. All the same he was not here for his own ends. Rome's policy had to be far-sighted. He would propose that negotiations should be started.

This resolution once taken, Titus became cheerful. Now his review had a meaning, and also the presence of this woman had a meaning. Titus's eyes and voice became youthful and confident. The sight of his soldiers filled him with elation, and he was glad that Berenice was there too.

6

THE meeting of the Roman and Jewish representatives took place not far from the Tower of Psephinus, within range of the Jewish artillery.

The Romans watched from the walls of their camp, the Jews from their city walls, to see how their ambassadors comported themselves. Joseph was the mouthpiece of the Romans, while the speaker for the Jews was Doctor Amram, Joseph's friend as a youth. The Jews maintained punctiliously a distance of seven paces from Joseph, and when he spoke their faces remained stonily impassive. They did not direct a single word to him, and addressed only his two Roman escorts.

They met on a little square of naked sun-warmed soil.
Joseph was unarmed.   He had put all his heart into this
speech that was to convert the Jews in the city to reason.
Every day they had made him feel their hatred.   Often
leaden bullets and other projectiles shot from the walls had
been brought to him with the words scribbled on them in
Aramaic script : " This is for Joseph."   His father and
brother were lying in the dungeons of Fort Phasael, where
they had been tortured in the most cruel way.   He refused
to let his mind dwell on that.   He had torn all bitterness
from his heart.   He had fasted and prayed that Jehovah
might give power to his words.

When he began to speak he could not remain seated, and
sprang to his feet.   He stood there, looking very lean in
the sunshine, a new fire in his eyes from his fasting and his
resolve to win over his hearers.   Before him he saw the
savage, closed face of Doctor Amram.   Since the fall of
Jotapat Joseph had heard nothing about Amram, except
that it was he who had demanded his old friend's excommunication.   It was not a good sign that the Jews had
sent as a negotiator this old schoolmate of his, who had loved
and now hated him with such passion.   But, however that
might be, the proposals that Joseph had to offer were extremely generous.   Reason demanded that they should be
weighed.   Imploringly, yet using the keenest logic, Joseph
pleaded with the Jewish delegates.   The Romans, he
announced, pledged themselves to restore the status quo
throughout the whole country.   They guaranteed the lives
of all the civilians in the besieged town, also the autonomy
of the Temple.   Their sole demand was that the garrison
should surrender to the discretion of their conquerors.
Joseph turned to Doctor Amram persuasively, adopting
the sing-song voice which learned doctors assumed in

theological or legal disputes and had been familiar to them both from the time when they had been students together. He went on : " What have you to lose if you surrender the city ? What have you to gain if you do not surrender it ? Surrender the city, for then the civil population, the Temple, and the service of Jehovah will be saved. But if the city has to be taken by violence, then all will be lost, army, people, Temple, everything. You may, perhaps, say that the army is no more culpable than yourselves, and that it has only carried out your will. That may be so. But do you not send the scapegoat out into the wilderness and make him bear your sins ? Send the army to the Romans ; let a few suffer rather than all." In the passionate earnestness of his pleading he walked up to Doctor Amram. But the other retreated before him and kept the distance of seven paces.

When Joseph had finished Doctor Amram coldly communicated to the Romans the counter-demands of the Jews. He would certainly have preferred to speak in Aramaic, but he did not want to have speech with Joseph, so he expressed himself in Latin. He demanded a safe retreat for the garrison, marks of honours for the Jewish leaders, Simon Bar Giora and John of Gishala, and a guarantee that a Roman army would never march against Jerusalem again. These demands were of an unheard of insolence and were obviously intended simply to ruin the negotiations.

Slowly, in laborious Latin, this impudent rubbish masked as commonsense flowed from the lips of the wild-eyed Amram. Joseph listened, wearily sunk on the ground, in despair at his own impotence. From the walls a throng of faces looked down. One face, a stubborn fanatical face with stupid eyes, tormented Joseph especially ; it paralysed him ; it was like part of the wall ; one might as well speak to the wall as to it.   At the same time he fancied that he had seen that face before.   It was like the faces that had gazed up at him in dumb worship in Galilee.   Perhaps the young man was one of those who had greeted him at that time with the shout : " Marin !   Marin ! "

Paulinus tried to help matters with a few friendly and sensible words.   " Don't let us part like this, gentlemen," he said.   " Make some other proposal, one that we can consider."

For a while Doctor Amram took whispering counsel with his two companions.   Then, again in his laborious Latin, he said politely, but very loudly : " Good.   We have another proposal.   Surrender to us those whom we hold to be guilty, and we shall accept your conditions."

" Whom do you mean ? " asked Paulinus suspiciously.

" We mean," replied Doctor Amram, " the man Agrippa, formerly King of the Jews, the woman Berenice, once a princess in Judaea, and the man Flavius Josephus, formerly priest of the first rank."

" It's a pity," said Paulinus, and the Roman delegates turned to go.

At that moment a shrill cry came from the city wall : " For Joseph," and with the cry came the arrow.   Joseph had seen the bow being bent.   Then he fell to the ground. It was the young man with the dull, fanatical face who had shot.   The arrow had merely grazed Joseph's arm.   It was probably the shock more than the wound that had made him fall.

7

TITUS was very angry at the ludicrous outcome of the negotiations.   It was that woman who was to blame for his taking such a stupid step.   She robbed him of his clearness of vision and made the straight way crooked.   He must make an end of this affair with Berenice.

What was the condition she had insisted on ? If when the Romans entered Jerusalem the pine grove of Thekoa was still standing, she gave him leave to make a bridal bed for her out of its wood. Her condition was fulfilled. That he would take Jerusalem there could be no doubt now. He had given orders to Valens, the commandant of Thekoa, to fell three of the pines. The bed could be ready by that evening. He would have supper with Berenice, alone. He would not wait any longer. He sent some of his men to fetch the bed.

It turned out that there was no bed. The pine grove of Thekoa was no longer standing ; the commander's instructions could not be fulfilled. Titus raged. Had he not given explicit orders to spare the grove ? Yes, Valens had received those orders, but afterwards, when the wood for the trenches and the encircling walls ran short, General Tiberius Alexander had sent counter-orders. Valens had hesitated and sent back a query. He could now point to the written instructions of the general, commanding him to fell the grove in spite of the commander's original order.

When he was told this a terrifying change came over Titus's face. The composed harsh features of the soldier turned into those of an insanely furious boy. He summoned Tiberius Alexander and spluttered at him, panting with rage. The more angry Titus grew, the colder became the general. He explained politely that there was an order, which was moreover signed by Titus himself, commanding, on danger of the severest penalties, all available timber to be requisitioned. The needs of the army came before the personal needs of the individual. In all the campaigns that he had conducted hitherto he had always insisted upon that and allowed no exception to the rule. Titus did not know what to reply. The man was right, and Titus was disgusted both with him and with himself. He acquired a violent headache which, beginning at his temples, bound his skull in a ring of pain. Everything grew grey around him. He loved Berenice. He must make an end of the business. He would.

Beautiful and serene as ever, Berenice wandered about the camp outside Jerusalem. But under her serenity she was in revolt. She had counted the days which she had spent in Caesarea without Titus. She refused to admit it, but she had missed him. Since he had taken over the command of the army he was no longer the good-natured youth with the boyish face ; he was a man, a soldier absorbed in his task. She told herself that it was for Jerusalem's sake that she was there beside him, but she knew it was a lie.

She had set out with elation when Titus summoned her to the camp. But when she saw the countryside round Jerusalem, round her Jerusalem, her joy vanished. The beautiful surroundings of the city were as bare as if they had been laid waste by locusts ; the orchards, the olive terraces, the vineyards, the country houses, the fine shops on the Mount of Olives : all were trampled to the same horrible bleak flatness. When she stood on the tribune beside the Roman commander and saw the troops marching past, it had seemed to her as if all those multitudes on the city walls and the roofs of the Temple were gazing accusingly at her, and at her alone.

Her life had been a wild one ; she was not sentimental, and she was used to the smells of camps and the atmosphere of a military life. But her stay here in front of Jerusalem was more painful than she had ever thought it would be. The plenty and order of the camp, and the hunger in the stifling city packed with human beings ; Titus's business-

like military air, the cold politeness of Tiberius Alexander,
the naked and violated surroundings of the city : everything
tortured her.   Like Titus, she too wanted to make an end
of the affair.   Several times already she had been on the
point of asking :   " What about the grove of Thekoa ?   Is
the grove of Thekoa still standing ? "   But she did not
know whether she wanted to hear a ' Yes ' or a ' No ' to
her question.

She was tired and overstrung when she came to Titus
that evening.   He was gloomy, passionate and persistent.
She felt empty, all her strength of will seemed to have left
her ; she made only a feeble resistance.   He took her
brutally ; his eyes, his hands, all of him seemed filled with
a savage brutality.

Afterwards Berenice lay as if broken, her mouth dry,
her eyes dull and fixed, her dress torn.   She felt old and
forlorn.

Titus stared at her with compressed lips ; his face was
that of an angry, helpless child.   So now he had got his will.
Had it been worth it ?   It had not.   It had not been much
of a pleasure, indeed anything but a pleasure.   He wished
he had not done it.   He was exasperated at himself, and
he hated her.   " And I may tell you," he said spitefully,
" that if you really imagine that the grove of Thekoa is
still standing, or that this bed is made of its wood, you're
very much mistaken.   We had other uses for the timber.
Your own uncle gave the order to cut down the grove."

Berenice slowly got up without looking at him, nor did
she address any reproach to him.   He was a man, a soldier,
a nice youth at bottom.   It was this camp, this war, that
was to blame.   This war was ruining everybody, turning
all these men into beasts or savages.   Every kind of abomination had been committed within and without the walls ;

human beings had been violated, the country violated,
Jehovah, the Temple. It was like the combats with lions
in the arena on the Roman holidays ; one could hardly tell
the human beings from animals. Now this man Titus
had taken her against her will ; he had betrayed her and
afterwards jeered at her, although she loved him. It was
this camp, this war. It was this foul stinking hole, and it
served her right for coming here.

She got to her feet painfully and laboriously ; she pulled
herself together, she tugged and tore at her dress to shake
off the filth of the camp. Then she went. She had no
reproaches for Titus, but neither had she any parting greeting
for him. Her walk even at that moment of extreme weariness and humiliation was still the walk of Berenice.

Titus stared after her in dull dejection. His plan had
been to get this woman out of his blood. He had not
wanted his campaign to be ruined and his thoughts distracted
from his aim through this woman. He had wanted to put
her behind him, and then to capture Jerusalem, and then,
with his foot on the neck of the conquered city, to decide
whether he should resume his relations with her or not.
It had been a beautiful plan, but unfortunately it had miscarried. Unluckily it seemed that nothing could be effected
with this woman by violence. She was by no means out
of his blood. His forcing of her had done nothing ; he
might as well have had some other woman. She was more
strange to him than ever. He racked his mind ; he knew
nothing about her. He did not know the fragrance of her
flesh, her sweetness, her passion, her surrender. She had
remained locked to him with six locks and hidden from
him with seven veils. These Jews were infernally clever.
They had a deeply ironical phrase for the act. They did
not say " Lie with a woman," or " Pass the night with a

woman." They said : "Know a woman." No, he did
not know this accursed woman Berenice. And he would
never know her until she gave herself to him.

Meanwhile Berenice was running through the streets of
the camp. She could not find her litter, so she ran on until
she reached her tent. There she gave hasty and panic-
stricken instructions, left the camp and fled to Caesarea.
And from there she fled to her brother in Transjordania.

8

ON the 18th of June Titus summoned a council of war. The
attacks on the third wall had miscarried. With immense
labour his troops had set up four mounds opposite the walls
and Fort Antonia, so as to provide an emplacement for
their armoured towers, artillery, and battering rams. But
the Jews had dug tunnels beneath these mounds, had filled
the tunnels with pitch and bitumen, and then had set this
mixture on fire and brought down the mounds and the
artillery with them. So these artificial works erected with
so much labour and peril had been destroyed.

At the council of war everyone was nervous and exasperated. The younger officers demanded a general attack
with all available resources. That was the straight but
stiff road to the victory that hovered before all their eyes.
The older officers were against the proposal. To storm a
fortress defended with cunning and guile without the assistance of armoured towers and battering rams, a fortress
moreover manned by twenty-five thousand desperate soldiers,
was no joke, and even if it should succeed would involve
terrible losses. No, wearisome as it might be, the only
thing that remained was to build new mounds and walls.

A dejected silence set in. Titus had listened despondently
and attentively and without opening his mouth. He asked

Tiberius Alexander for his opinion. " If we must wait a
long time for the general attack," began the general, " why
shouldn't we lengthen the wait still further for the benefit
of our enemies ? "

The other officers stared in expectant perplexity at his
thin lips.

" We have information to the effect," he went on in
his gentle, courteous voice, " and we can also see with our
own eyes what a valuable ally we have in the increasing
hunger in Jerusalem.   I propose, gentlemen, that we should
put more dependence on that ally than in the past.   I
propose that the blockade should be tightened.   I propose,
moreover, that to that end a blockade wall should be erected
round the city, so that not even a mouse will be able to get
in or out.

" That is one point.   The second is this.   Until now
we have proudly published a list of those who, in spite of
all the measures taken by the besieged, have deserted to
us.   We have treated these gentlemen with great kindness.
I fancy that that does more honour to our hearts than our
heads.   I see no reason why we should rid these gentlemen
in Jerusalem of the anxiety of providing food for such a
considerable number of their people.   Can we really be
expected to know whether those who desert to us are
civilians or men who have borne arms against us ?   I
suggest, gentlemen, that in future these deserters should be
treated without exception as rebel prisoners of war, and that
all the wood we can spare should be set aside for crucifying
these rebels.   That, I fancy, will make the people in Jerusalem remain inside their walls in future.   Already a great
number of them have to sit down to empty tables.   I hope
that presently all of them, including the troops, will have to
sit down to empty tables."   The general's voice was gentle

and extremely courteous. " The more ruthless we are
in the coming weeks, the more humane can we be afterwards. I propose that we should instruct Lucianus, the
officer who attends to the executions, not to exercise too
great mercy in crucifying the rebels."

The general had spoken without raising his voice, as if
he were carrying on an ordinary conversation. But the
room had become quite still while he was speaking. Titus
was a soldier. Nevertheless he gazed somewhat strangely
at this Jew who in such a casual voice proposed such harsh
measures against the Jews. Nobody had any objection to
advance against Tiberius Alexander's proposal. It was
resolved to build the blockade wall and in future to crucify
deserters.

9

FROM Fort Phasael the Jewish leaders Simon Bar Giora
and John of Gishala watched the blockade wall rising.
John estimated its length at four and a half miles, and with
practised eyes indicated to Simon thirteen points where
towers obviously were to be set up. " A rather shabby
trick, brother Simon, don't you think ? " he asked, smiling
quietly. " I would have believed it of the old fox himself,
but the young one with his boast of manliness and military
virtue should really have thought of some more decent
stratagem. Well, well. Now we'll have to eat locusts
soon, or perhaps we're at that point already."

The wall was finished, and the roads and hills round
Jerusalem were lined with crosses. The executioners
became inventive in thinking out new postures for the
crucified. They nailed their victims to the cross upside
down, or bound them diagonally across it, twisting their
limbs into the most ingenious patterns. At first the new
measures of the Romans had the effect of reducing the

numbers of the deserters. But presently the hunger and terror in the city grew more intense. The people felt that they were lost. Which was the wiser course ? To stay in the town and die of hunger with the crimes of the Makkabi people against God and man always before one's eyes ? Or to desert to the Romans and be hung upon a cross ? One was lost if one remained within the walls, and lost if one went outside them. When a stone falls on a pitcher, woe to the pitcher. When a pitcher falls on a stone, woe to the pitcher. Always, always, woe to the pitcher.

The number increased of those who preferred death on the cross to death in Jerusalem. A day hardly passed without several hundred deserters being brought in. Soon there was no more room left for the crosses and no more crosses for the deserters.

10

THE glass-blower Nachum Ben Nachum lay for most of the time on the roof of the house in the Street of the Salve Makers. Alexas's wife and the two children lay there too, for one felt one's hunger less under the open sky. When one drew one's robe or one's belt tighter, that too lessened one's hunger a little ; but only for a short time.

Nachum Ben Nachum had lost a great deal of his plumpness ; his thick beard was no longer well tended or square, and it was shot with many grey hairs. Sometimes the quietness of the house troubled him, for exhausted people have not much desire to talk. Then Nachum would go to the narrow bridge that led to the Temple from the upper town and pay a visit to his relative Doctor Nittai. The priests of the eighth rank, the Abija rank, had been chosen for service, and Doctor Nittai lived and slept now in the Temple. His savage eyes were dulled and the complacent sing-song of his voice came somewhat laboriously from his feeble lips. It was a marvel that the famished man could hold himself erect at all, but he held himself erect. Indeed he was less taciturn than usual ; he had no anxiety now about his Babylonian accent ; he was happy. The whole world was a gin and a snare and only in the Temple was security. Nachum's heart too was uplifted when he saw that in spite of all the misery the Temple service was being carried on as usual with all its thousand splendid and cere-monious usages, its morning and evening sacrifice. The whole city was going to destruction, but Jehovah's house and table remained abundantly provided for, as it had done for hundreds of years.

From the Temple the glass-blower Nachum often took his way to the market, the Kippa. In spite of the famine a great number of citizens still met there from old habit. It was true, the things one haggled over now were not caravans of spices, or fleets loaded with timber, but scraps of food. A pound or two of mouldy flour, a handful of dried nuts, a little bottle of fish sauce. At the beginning of June bread had been worth its own weight in glass, then its own weight in copper, then its own weight in silver. On the 23rd of June one had to pay for a bushel of wheat forty mane, but before the beginning of July it had risen to a whole talent.

Of course such transactions had to be carried out secretly ; for long before the military authorities had requisitioned all the available means of life for the troops. The soldiers ransacked the houses to the last corner. With their daggers and swords they jokingly tickled the sides of the house-holders until they extracted the last ounce of food.

Nachum was filled with gratitude towards his son Alexas. Where would they have been without him ? He fed the whole house, and his father was given the biggest portion. Nachum did not know where Alexas kept his stores hidden, nor did he want to know. One day Alexas came home in great agitation, bleeding from a severe wound. Probably he had been caught by soldiers in their rounds when he was visiting one of his hidden stores.

Filled with fear and grief the glass-blower Nachum sat beside the bed where his first-born lay grey-faced and feeble and unconscious. Oh, why hadn't he taken his son's advice sooner ? Alexas was the wisest of men, and he, the father, had not dared to take his side, simply because the spies of those in authority were everywhere. But now he would not keep his mouth shut any longer. When Alexas rose from his bed again he would go with him to this man whom people called Yellow Face. For in spite of the reign of terror a host of new prophets were emerging from the confused system of subterranean passages and caves beneath Jerusalem, and preaching peace and submission, and vanishing again into the underworld before the Makkabi people could seize them. Nachum was convinced that his son was intimate with the leader of these prophets, with that dark and mysterious figure who was called by everybody Yellow Face.

His anger against the Makkabi people grew until he no longer felt his hunger ; the violence of his indignation drove his hunger out. He felt furious against his son Ephraim above all. Ephraim gave a portion of his abundant soldier's ration to his father and his family ; but deep in his heart Nachum suspected that it was Ephraim who had set the soldiers on Alexas's track. Nachum was almost out of his mind with suspicion, impotence and rage.

Alexas got better. But the scarcity grew worse and worse ; the little food that was left was always the same ;

the summer was hot. Alexas's youngest son died. He
was only two. A few days later he was followed by the
other son, who was four. Alexas had enough strength
left to bury his youngest son. But when his eldest died
the task of burying the little body was too heavy for him,
and he had to content himself with letting it be consigned to
the ravine outside the city walls. Nachum, his sons and
his daughter-in-law carried the little corpse to the south-
east gate, so that the officer Mannaeus Bar Lazarus, who
attended to the burials, should have it cast into the
ravine. Nachum wanted the prayer for the dead to be
said, but being lightheaded with weakness he forgot little
Jannai Bar Alexas and told Mannaeus that as he had now
dealt with 47,203 corpses, thus earning 47,203 sesterces,
he would be able to buy with that sum almost two bushels
of wheat at the market.

Alexas crouched on the floor and observed the seven
days of mourning. He wagged his head and stroked his
filthy beard. He had paid dearly for his love to his father
and his brother.

When after that interval he went out into the street
again he was appalled. He had thought that the misery
could not grow worse ; but it had grown worse. Formerly
Jerusalem had been celebrated for its cleanliness ; now a
horrible stench hung over the whole city. In certain
quarters the dead had been gathered into great public buildings, and when these were full they had been locked up.
But still more disquieting than the stench was the great
silence that lay over the once so noisy city ; for now even
the most garrulous had lost all desire to talk. Silent and
noisome, and filled with thick swarms of flies, the white
city lay in the summer sunshine.

On the roofs, in the streets, the exhausted people gazed

about them with dry eyes and gaping mouths. The bodies of some were swollen, of others shrivelled to skeletons. The kicks of the soldiers no longer could move them from the places where they sat. Starving, they lay about, stared at the Temple, which up on its hill hung white and golden in the radiant light, and waited for death to come. Alexas saw an old woman scratching among refuse and fighting a pack of dogs for some crumb to eat. He knew the woman. It was old Chanana, the widow of the High Priest Anan. Once carpets had been spread before her when she stepped into the street ; for her foot was too delicate to be defiled by the dust.

And then came a day when Alexas, the wisest of them all, sat down dully and could think of nothing more to do. His wife was at the point of death, and in spite of the great risk he visited his hiding place in the underworld but found it empty ; someone had discovered the remainder of his store.

After Nachum had laboriously extorted this unfortunate news from his son he sat for a long time in reflection. It was a meritorious act to bury the dead ; and it was a highly meritorious act in the eyes of Jehovah, the greatest that any-one could achieve, to see to one's own burial if there was no one else to do it. Nachum Ben Nachum resolved to accom-plish this final deed of merit. Anyone who looked as if he would live no more than one or two days was allowed by the soldiers on guard to pass out through the city gate. They would let him pass. He laid his hand in blessing on the head of his son Alexas, who was dully staring at his dying wife. Then he took a spade, his ledger, the key of the old workshop, also a little frankincense and myrrh, and dragged himself to the southern gate.

In front of the southern gate lay a huge cave filled with

human skeletons. For during a quiet interval about a year before, when the corpses of the slain had been picked almost to the bone, these bones had been assembled in little limestone coffins, and the coffins ranged in rows against the walls of the cave. True, the besieging forces had trampled down the cave containing the coffins and reduced it to ruins, so that now it had lost all its seemliness and was merely a heap of splintered limestone and broken bones. But all the same it still remained a Jewish cemetery Nachum sat down on the yellowish white sun-warmed soil of this burial ground. Round him lay other starving men, all staring at the Temple. Sometimes they would say : " Hear, Israel, one and eternal is our God Jehovah." Sometimes they would think of the Jewish soldiers and the priests in the Temple who had bread and dried fish to eat, or of the soldiers in the Roman camp who actually had beef ; and then their rage would drive out their hunger for a short, a very short time.

Nachum was very weary, but it was not an unpleasant weariness. The heat of the sun was soothing. At the beginning, when he was an apprentice, the pain had been terrible when he burned his hands with the molten glass. Now his skin had got hardened to it. It had been wrong of his son Alexas to replace all the handwork with blow pipes. Besides, Alexas was too ambitious altogether. It was because Alexas was so haughty that his children had died and his wife was dying and his store of food had been stolen from him. What did it say in the book of Job ? " He hath swallowed down riches, and he shall vomit them up again. The increase of his house shall depart, and his goods shall flow away in the day of his wrath." But which of them was really Job, he or his son Alexas ? That was very difficult to tell. True, he had a spade with him, but was it to scratch his sores with ?   It was not ; consequently his son Alexas was Job.

If one showed honour to the dead one gained merit in God's sight, especially if it was oneself one was burying. But first he must have a look into his ledger, to see whether the last entries were correct ; for he wanted his accounts to be balanced before he took the ledger into his grave with him.   He had once heard the story of a certain Maria Beth Ezob.   Tempted by the smell of cooking meat, the soldiers of the Avengers of Israel had forced their way into the house of this Maria and had discovered some roasted flesh.   It was the flesh of Maria's own baby and she had proposed a bargain with the soldiers ; as she had borne the child she was to have half of it, and the soldiers could have the other half.   That had been a methodical woman.   Of course the agreement should really have been made in writing and sworn to before the magistrates.   But that was difficult just now.   The officials were never there.   They said they were hungry, but still it wasn't right that people should simply stay away from their work because they were hungry.   True, some had died of hunger.   The day of death was happier than the day of birth, and these people had an excuse in a way.

His son Alexas was sitting there in his house.   He was the cleverest man in the world, and yet in spite of all his cleverness he had nothing to eat.   Suddenly Nachum felt an overwhelming pity for Alexas.   Yes, Alexas was the real Job.   Alexas's beard was greyer than his own, although Alexas was far younger.   Yet his own beard was no longer square now, and if a pregnant woman were to look at it, it might not be good for her unborn child.

All the same, it was annoying that there was nobody to show the last respects to him, Nachum Ben Nachum, the glass-blower, the great merchant. It was a hard punishment from Jehovah that he himself should be his sole mourner, and he could understand Job ; and now it became quite clear to him that he himself, and not Alexas, was Job. " I have said to corruption, thou art my father ; to the worm, thou art my mother, and my sister." And now come, my spade, dig, my spade.

With great labour he raised himself to his feet, groaning faintly. It was a hard business ; for to dig one must be able to see. It was these disgusting flies that clung to one's face and made everything dark round one. Very slowly he let his eyes wander over the greyish yellow soil, the bones and the splinters of the stone coffins. There, quite near to him, he saw something glittering, something opal-hued, it was strange that he had not seen it before ; it was a piece of myrrhine glass. Was it genuine ? If it was not genuine, then it must have been by a very skilful processs that such a clever imitation was manufactured. Who could know of such a process ? Where was such glass made ? In Tyre ? In Carmania ? He simply must know where this artificial glass was made, and how it was made. His son Alexas would know. What was all his cleverness worth if he did not know that ? He would ask his son Alexas.

He crept over and lifted the piece of glass and carefully put it away in his belt. It might be part of a perfume flask that had been laid in one of the little stone coffins with its former owner. He had the piece of glass anyway. It wasn't genuine, but a marvellous imitation ; only an expert could recognise the difference. He had no longer any thought of lying down in his grave ; only one desire filled him, the desire to ask his son Alexas about this marvellous piece of glass. He stood up, yes, he was able to support himself, he advanced his right foot, then his left, he shuffled forward, stumbling now and then over bones and rocks, but he made progress. He would return to the gate, a matter of about eight minutes' journey ; and behold, it took him quite a short time, it did not take him even an hour, and there he was at the gate. The Jewish sentries chanced to be in a good humour ; they opened the little postern gate and asked : " Have you found anything to eat, dead man ? Then you must share it with us." He proudly showed them his piece of glass. They laughed and let him pass, and he went back to the house of his son Alexas.

11

THE Romans raised four new mounds against the city. The soldiers who were not engaged on the work went through their prescribed camp duty, drilled, idled about, gazed at the quiet city, and waited.

The officers made up hunting expeditions to drive away the demoralising tedium and kill off the herds of animals that, attracted by the stench of death, had flocked round the city. For many animals that had not been seen in this neighbourhood for generations now showed themselves. From Lebanon came wolves, from the Jordan district lions, from Gilead and Bashan panthers. The foxes grew fat, and without having to exert their cunning ; the hyenas and the howling droves of jackals had a good time. On the crosses that lined all the roads the ravens sat in thick rows, and on the hill-tops the vultures watched and waited.

For a joke the archers occasionally employed as targets the famished Jews who sat about in the burial places outside the walls. Other Roman soldiers sometimes appeared singly or in bands before the walls, keeping out of range of the Jewish artillery, but approaching near enough to be seen clearly, and displayed to the defenders on the walls the abundance of their rations ; then ate, chewed and swallowed, shouting the while : " Hep, Hep, Hierosolyma est perdita."

12

SEVEN weeks had now passed since the beginning of the siege. The Jews celebrated their Whitsun feast, a wretched Whitsun feast ; but there was no change. The whole month of July passed ; no change. The Jews made sorties against the new Roman walls, without success. Nevertheless this campaign was getting on the nerves of the Roman legionaries far more than many a sterner one had done. Gradually the besiegers were overcome with impotent fury before the silent and noisome city. If the Jews succeeded in destroying the four new mounds there was no possibility of building new ones ; the timber was at an end. So nothing remained but to wait until the people within the city starved to death. The soldiers stared grimly at the Temple, which stood there on its hill, white and golden as ever, and untouched. They did not think of it any longer as the Temple ; in their rage and disgust and fear they called it " That thing over there," or " That thing." Were they to remain for ever before this white uncanny fortress ? The Roman camp was filled with tense gloom, with actual desperation. No other city had ever stood out for so long against civil dissension, hunger and war. Would they never be able to bring these rascally famished madmen to reason ? As for returning to Rome for the October equestrian games, that was out of the question. From the generals of the legions to the humblest foot-soldier sent by the vassal states, everyone was filled with rage at this God Jehovah who kept the military art of the Romans from triumphing over the fanaticism of Jewish barbarians.

13

ONE day towards the end of July Titus commanded Joseph to accompany him on a tour of inspection. The two men walked without speaking through the great silence. Titus had not put on any badge of his rank, and Joseph was unarmed. The challenge of the sentries came mechanically, and mechanically they gave the password : " Rome, advance." The whole country round Jerusalem for a radius of twelve miles lay waste and bare, and the words of the Scripture seemed to be fulfilled : " Therefore thus sayeth the Lord God : Behold, mine anger and my fury shall be poured out upon this place, upon man, and upon beast, and upon the trees of the field, and upon the fruit of the ground."

They came to the ravine into which the people in Jerusalem now flung their dead. A terrible, choking stench rose from it ; the bodies lay piled up in a loathsome heap of corruption. Titus paused. Joseph halted obediently. Titus cast a side glance at his escort, to see how he was enduring the foul vapour. Only that day Titus had once more received a confidential report saying that Joseph was acting as a spy and holding secret communications with the besieged. Titus did not believe a word of it. He knew quite well how difficult Joseph's position was, and that he was looked upon as a traitor both by the Jews and the Roman soldiers. He liked the man and looked upon him as a friend. But there were moments when Joseph was just as strange and uncanny to him, Titus, as to his soldiers. Here, looking down at the ravine filled with corpses, he tried to find some sign of repugnance or of grief on Joseph's face. But Joseph's face was impassive, and Titus was overcome with a cold and strange sensation : How could the Jew endure such a sight ?

It was as though a torturing impulse drove Joseph to the place where the horrors of the siege were to be seen at their worst. He had been sent here to be the eye that should witness all those horrors. It was easy to be shocked by them. To stand still and contemplate them because one must was far harder. Often he was seized with a keen, gnawing pain at being outside the walls, and a mad longing would rise in him to be among the others in the city. They were well off. To be allowed to fight and suffer along with the others ; that was worth while.

By mysterious ways an unsigned letter from the city had reached him. " You are making things worse. You should disappear." He knew that Justus had written that letter. Once more that fellow was right and he was wrong. His attempts at negotiation had been hopeless ; his presence ruined all hope of agreement.

It was a bitter summer for Josephus, that summer outside the walls of Jerusalem. The wound in his right arm was not serious, but it pained him and made writing impossible. Once or twice Titus asked him jestingly whether he wouldn't like to dictate his history ; he himself was the best stenographer in the camp. But perhaps it was a good thing that Joseph could not write for the time being. He was not concerned with art, eloquence, sentiment. He wanted his whole body to be an eye, and nothing but an eye.

So he stood beside Titus gazing at the bare landscape that had once been one of the most beautiful in the world and his home. Now it was as waste and empty as before the creation. His ragged countrymen were standing with savage faces on the only remaining wall of the city ; it was already shaken, and they knew in their hearts that they would be defeated, and they hated him more than any other man in the world. They had set a price on his

head, a gigantic price, the highest they knew of ; a whole
bushel of wheat. He stood silently staring into space.
Behind him, before him and all round him were crosses
on which men of his blood were hanging ; at his foot was
the ravine in which men of his blood were rotting ; the
air, the whole waste land was full of loathsome birds and
animals waiting for their food.

Titus opened his lips. He spoke softly, but in the
desolation his words sounded quite loud. " Do you think
it was cruel of me, Joseph, to force you to come here ? "
Joseph replied still more softly than Titus, slowly, as if
weighing his words : " It is my wish."

Titus laid his hand on his companion's shoulder. " You
are bearing up well, Joseph. Is there any request that I
can grant you ? "   Still without looking at him, Joseph
answered in the same subdued voice : " Let the Temple
remain standing,"   " That's my wish no less than yours,"
said Titus. " I would like you to ask something for
yourself."

At last Joseph turned to the Roman commander. He
saw that Titus's face was eager and curious, but not unfriendly. " Give me," said he slowly and hesitatingly,
" give me out of the plunder when the city falls——" he
stopped. " What shall I give you, my Jew ? " asked Titus.
" Give me," Joseph said, " seven rolls of the Scripture and
seven prisoners."

Standing there they seemed very tall in the bare landscape. Titus smiled. " You shall have seventy rolls,
my Joseph, and seventy prisoners."

14

THE priests of the officiating rank assembled daily in the
Quadern Hall to decide by lot who were to perform the

various rites of the sacrifice. On the morning of the 5th of August, the 17th of Tanus, according to the Jewish calendar, there appeared among the assembled priests the leaders of the army, Simon Bar Giora and John of Gishala, both of them armed, and accompanied by their secretary Amram, and a troop of armed soldiers. The Head Priest of the Temple service, who officiated at the casting of lots, asked, with difficulty maintaining his composure :

" What do you want ? "

" You needn't cast lots to-day, my Doctor and Master," said John of Gishala. " And you needn't cast lots in future either. You can all go to your homes, gentlemen, all of you, priests, Levites, and attendants. The service of the Temple has ceased."

The priests stood in silent horror. Hunger had lined their faces, now white as their robes ; and their strength was gone. Some of them, such as Doctor Nittai, were still held erect simply by their devotion to their office. They were too feeble to shout ; and it was only a curiously thin wailing sigh that broke out after John had spoken.

" How many sacrificial lambs have you still left ? " Simon Bar Giora demanded roughly. " Six," replied the Head Priest with a painful attempt to appear firm.

" You are mistaken, my Doctor and Master," Amram softly corrected the priest, and he bared his teeth in a polite and malicious smile ; his teeth looked huge, yellow and dry in the midst of his tangled beard. " There are nine."

" Come, out with your nine lambs," said John of Gishala almost genially. " Jehovah has been for too long the only one to eat flesh in this city. The lambs shan't be wasted. Jehovah has had enough of the sweet smell of His burnt offerings. Those who fight for the Temple must also live from the Temple. Hand over the nine lambs, my Doctors and Masters."

The Head Priest of the Temple service swallowed painfully and sought for an answer. But before he could speak Doctor Nittai stepped forward. He fixed his inflamed, savage eyes on John of Gishala. " There are gins and snares everywhere," he spluttered in his harsh Babylonian accent. " Only in the Temple is security. Do you want to set your snares in the Temple next ? You will come to a shameful end." " Time will tell, my Doctor and Master," John of Gishala coolly replied. " Perhaps it has come to your notice that Fort Antonia has fallen. The Romans have advanced to the walls of the Temple itself. The Temple is no longer Jehovah's dwelling place ; it is Jehovah's fortress." But Doctor Nittai went on in his hoarse complaining voice : " Do you want to rob the altar of Jehovah ? If you steal Jehovah's bread and meat you rob Israel of its sole support." " Be silent," Simon broke in harshly. " The Temple service has ceased."

But Amran went up to Doctor Nittai, laid a hand on his shoulder, and said in a conciliatory voice, smiling with his yellow teeth : " Be content, brother. What does it say in Jeremiah ? ' Thus saith the Lord of Hosts, the God of Israel : Put your burnt offerings unto your sacrifices, and eat flesh. For I spake not unto your fathers, nor commanded them on the day that I brought them out of the land of Egypt, concerning burnt offerings or sacrifices.' "

John of Gishala ran his grey eyes over the horrified ranks of the priests. He regarded the harsh, insane looking skull of Doctor Nittai. In a polite and conciliatory voice he said : " If you want to continue your service, gentlemen, then sing, play your musical instruments, and recite your prayers ; you have full liberty to do so. But whatever bread, wine, oil and flesh there is here is requisitioned."

The High Priest Phanias appeared ; he had been told the news. When the power of John of Gishala had placed him in the highest office in the city and Temple, the burly dull-witted fellow had submitted to the decree of God with heavy sorrow. He was aware of his ignorance ; he knew nothing ; he had neither the secret knowledge of the Doctors, nor any acquaintance with the simplest interpretation of the Holy Scripture ; all that he had learned was to mix mortar and lift stones and set them on top of one another. Now Jehovah had invested him with the sacred robe, whose eight pieces absolved him from the eight deadliest sins. But poor as he was in understanding and learning, he was a pious man. Yet his piety was a hard burden to him. These soldiers had given orders that the Temple service should cease. That would never do. But how should he act ? Everybody looked at him and waited for him to say something. Oh, if he had only donned his vestments, Jehovah would certainly have put the right words into his mouth. Now he stood there as it were naked, quite helpless and at a loss. Finally he opened his mouth. " With the nine lambs," he said, turning eagerly to John of Gishala, " you can't feed your army. But we could carry on the sacred service for four more days with them." To the priests Phanias's words seemed to come out of the pious and sturdy wisdom of the people, and the Head Priest of the Temple service immediately sprang to his support. " If these men are still alive," he said, pointing to the priests standing round him, " it is only because of their determination to carry on the service of Jehovah according to the Scripture."

But Simon Bar Giora said darkly : " The walls of the

Temple have seen you long enough filling your bellies with
the sacrifices due to Jehovah." And his soldiers forced
their way into the hall where the lambs were kept. They
seized the lambs. They pushed their way into the wine
cellars and seized the wine and the oil. They thronged
into the holy place itself. Never during the existence of
the Temple had anyone but priests set foot there. Now
the soldiers advanced clumsily, grinning with embarrassment,
into the cool, severe, shadowy hall. The seven branched
candlestick stood there, the censer, the table with the
twelve golden loaves and the loaves of flour. Nobody
bothered about the golden loaves, but Simon pointed to the
fragrant wheaten ones and commanded : " Seize them ! "
He spoke roughly to conceal his uneasiness. The soldiers
went up cautiously, on tiptoe, to the table where the shew
bread stood. Then, with a sudden movement, they snatched
the loaves. They carried their booty awkwardly, as if
the loaves were young infants with whom one had to be
very careful.

The High Priest Phanias had followed the doings of
the soldiers with a rather dazed look ; he was very unhappy,
ill with speculating on what he should do next. He kept
his eyes fixed fearfully on the veil of the Holy of Holies,
the dwelling place of Jehovah which only he was permitted
to enter on the day of reconciliation. But Simon and John
did not touch the veil, but turned back. An immense
burden fell from the High Priest Phanias.

The soldiers breathed freely again once they were out of
the forbidden chamber. They had escaped unhurt ; no
fire had fallen on them from Heaven. They carried away
the loaves. The loaves were of fine white bread, yet they
were only bread after all ; nothing dreadful happened to
one for touching them.

15

THAT evening Simon and John invited the members of their staff to supper, also their secretary Amram. For weeks none of them had eaten flesh, and now they sniffed greedily the smell of roast lamb. Also there was abundance of noble wine, wine of Eshkol ; and there was bread on the table, enough bread not only to eat, but also, the men laughed heartily, to wipe their plates clean. They had bathed and anointed themselves with the oil of the Temple, and shorn and combed their hair and beards. They gazed at each other in astonishment ; how dignified and elegant everybody looked now, after all those weeks of neglect.

" Make yourselves comfortable and eat your fill," John of Gishala encouraged them. " It's probably the last time that we'll be able to do it, and we deserve it." The soldiers bore in basins of water for them to wash their hands ; Simon Bar Giora said grace and broke the bread ; it was an abundant meal, and they gave the soldiers of what was left over.

The two leaders were in a mild and softened mood. They thought of Galilee, their home. " I remember the locust trees in your town Gerasa, my brother Simon," said John. " It is a lovely place." " I remember the fig and olive trees of Gishala, my brother John," said Simon. " You came to Jerusalem from the north and I from the south. We should have joined forces then." " Yes," John smiled. " We were fools. We were like fighting cocks. The servant carries them by the feet into the yard to kill them, and they peck at each other with their beaks while they are dangling head downwards in the air."

" Give me the brisket that you have on your plate, brother John " said Simon, " and let me give you this

piece of shoulder. It's fatter and juicier. I love you
and admire you, brother John." "I thank you, brother
Simon," said John. "I never knew before what a handsome
and fine man you were. I only see it now that we're going
to die." They exchanged plates and drank to each other.
John began to sing the song celebrating the deeds of Simon,
how he had burnt the Romans' artillery and engines of
war ; and Simon struck up the song in praise of John,
recounting how behind the first wall of Fort Antonia he
had built a second. "If we had as much luck as we have
courage," John said with a smile, "the Romans would
have been gone long before this." They sang drinking
songs and scurrilous songs and songs praising the beauty of
Galilee. They thought of the cities of Sepphoris and Tiberias, and Magdala with its eighty weaving factories, which
the Romans had destroyed. "The lake is red with blood
far and wide round Magdala," they sang. "The shore is
strewn with corpses far and wide round Magdala." They
wrote their names on their arm-bands marked with the
initials Makkabi, and then exchanged them.

From outside came at regular intervals the dull blows of
the battering ram against the wall. That was Big Julius,
the celebrated battering ram of the tenth legion. "Let
him pound away," the officers laughed, "we'll burn him
to-morrow." They lay on their couches, ate, joked and
drank. It was a good banquet, and it was their last.

The night was advancing. They became more thoughtful ; a dark and gruesome gaiety filled the great room.
They thought of the dead. "We have neither lentils
nor eggs," said John of Gishala, "but we'll drink the ten
mourning beakers, and we'll turn the cushions on the
other side." "A great many are dead," said Simon Bar
Giora, "and we should have had a better banquet in

their honour. I drink to the dead officers "—there had been eighty-seven officers, all of whom were versed in the Roman military art ; of these seventy-two had fallen— " their memory be blessed." And they drank. " I drink to the High Priest Anan," said John of Gishala. " He came in very handy for the wall." " He was a villain," said Simon Bar Giora violently, " we had no choice but to kill him." " We had to kill him," John agreed, " but he was a good man. His memory be blessed." And they drank again.

" I drink to another of the dead," said Amram in a savage voice. " He was the friend of my youth, and he is a dog. We learned the mysteries of the law in the same room. His name is Joseph Ben Matthias. May his memory never be forgotten." Then he was struck by an idea from which he promised himself a great deal of amuse-ment. He winked at Simon and John, and they ordered the Doctor and Master Matthias, Joseph's father, to be brought from his dungeon in Fort Phasael.

The withered old man had lain for a long time in the loathsome stench of the foul dungeon ; he was terribly feeble, but he pulled himself together. He was terrified at these rough soldiers. They had slain so many people that it was a wonder they had left him alive ; he would have to do everything they said. He put his trembling hand to his brow and greeted the company. " What do you want, gentlemen," he stammered, " of a defenceless old man ? " His eyes blinked in the light, and in spite of him-self he greedily sniffed the odour of the food. " Things aren't going well, my Doctor and Master Matthias," said John. " The Romans will soon be where we are now. As for what we're to do with you, old man, we haven't been able to decide yet. Whether we are to leave you to

the Romans or kill you ourselves." The old man stood
with bowed shoulders, silent and trembling. "Listen,"
said the secretary Amram, "food is scarce in the city, as
you perhaps know. We haven't any meat left; we're on
short commons. What you see there on the table are the
bones of the nine last lambs intended for the altar of Jehovah. We've eaten them. Don't look so horrified.
They tasted all right to us. Do you see the writing of
doom on the wall? I don't. At the beginning of our
struggle your son stood shoulder to shoulder with us. Since
then he has changed his mind. It's only right that now, at
the end, you should be with us. We belong to the same
race. We invite you to take part in our last meal. There
are still quite a number of bones there, as you see. Also
you can have the bread that we wiped our plates with."

"Your fine son is a scoundrel," said John of Gishala,
and his sly, grey eyes were angry, "a blackguard. You
brought a cur into the world, my Doctor and Master
Matthias, priest of the first rank. Our soldiers deserve the
bones and bread more than you do. But we'll keep the
promise of our friend Doctor Amram; we invite you to
sit down." Simon Bar Giora was not so polite. He
threatened the old man with his gloomy little eyes and
shouted at him: "Eat."

The old man trembled violently. He had been boundlessly proud of his son's rise to power. He himself had
never dared to hazard the risks of fortune. He knew, oh,
he knew very well that Joseph had later gone over to the
Romans. But these men did not understand; they hated
his son and would like to see him dead. So now he was to
eat. Perhaps it was only a test, and if he ate they would
jeer at him and strike him dead because he had tried to save
what was left of his life by such a blasphemous act. After

the bad air of the dark dungeon he was almost mad with
hunger and exhaustion. He looked at the bones ; they
were juicy bones, full of marrow, the bones of young lambs,
and so soft that one could easily crunch them up and swallow
them. And there was the bread, lovely and fragrant,
and steeped besides in the gravy of the meat. The old man
told himself to stay where he was, but his feet would not
obey him. Something dragged him forward, and he went
with reluctant steps. He snatched at the bones greedily
with his filthy hands. He gnawed at them so eagerly that
the gravy ran down his matted white beard. He did not
even say grace ; for that would have been a double blasphemy. He knew that the flesh was from Jehovah's altar
and the bread from Jehovah's table, and that what he was
doing was sufficient to damn his soul ten times over, exclud-
ing him and his descendants from salvation for ever. But
he squatted down on the floor with a bone in each hand ;
and with his feeble teeth he gnawed at the bones and bit
through them, and while he chewed and swallowed he was
happy.

The others sat and looked at him. " Look," said Doctor
Amram, " see him eating at the cost of his salvation."
" These are the people, brother John, who have brought
us to this pass," said Simon. " These are the people,
brother Simon, that we're dying for," said John. Then
they were silent. In silence they looked on while the
Doctor and Master Matthias crouched on the floor of the
room gnawing his bones in the light of the torches.

16

NEXT morning, the 6th of August, Doctor Nittai wakened
the priests who were to officiate that day. The Head Priest
of the Temple service had collapsed, but Doctor Nittai

had without further ado taken over his functions, and the priests obeyed him. They followed him into the hall, and Doctor Nittai said : " Come and cast lots to see who is to kill the lamb, who is to sprinkle the blood, who is to carry the sacrifice to the altar, and who the flour and the wine." They cast lots. Then said Doctor Nittai : " Go out, you who are chosen for the task, and see whether the time has come to slay the sacrifice." When the time had come the priest on watch cried : " The day is dawning. The sky is bright in the East." " Is it bright on Hebron ? " asked Doctor Nittai, and the priest who was watching replied : " Yes." Thereupon Doctor Nittai commanded : " Go and fetch a lamb from the hall where the lambs are kept," and the priests allotted for that task went as they were told. They did not see that no lamb was there ; they fetched the lamb that was not there and in accordance with the law gave it to drink out of the golden chalice.

Those to whom the lot had fallen meanwhile betook themselves with two great golden keys to the holy place, and opened the massive door. At the moment when the mighty sound of the door opening on its hinges reached his ear, the allotted priest in the other room slew the sacrifice that was not there. Then they bore the lamb that was not there to the marble table and flayed and divided it according to the law, and carried each of the nine pieces, a priest bearing each piece, to the table before the altar. Then they cast lots who should lift the sacrifice from the table and lay it on the altar. The Temple attendants appeared and put new robes on the priest allotted for this task. Then they kindled the sacrificial fire and with golden spoons poured frankincense into the golden vessels. And they took the great shawm, the shawm with the hundred notes, and made all the hundred notes ring out together. When

that mighty blast was heard, drowning every other sound
in Jerusalem, everyone knew that the sacrifice was being
brought to the altar, and the people threw themselves down
on their faces.

The wine was handed to the priest. Doctor Nittai
ascended one horn of the altar and stood waiting with a
cloth in his hand. The priests threw the nine parts of the
offering into the fire. As soon as the priest bent to pour
out the wine, Doctor Nittai gave the signal and waved the
cloth. The column of smoke arose. The Levites standing on the steps of the Holy Place struck up the psalm. The
priests beside the altar pronounced the blessing on the
kneeling people.

Thus did the allotted priests of the eighth rank, the
Abija rank, celebrate on that 6th of August the burnt offering
with great ostentation and strictly holding to the many
hundred conditions imposed by the law. These feeble
men, prepared to die that day or the next, did not see that
the hall where the lambs were kept and the altar of their
God were empty. The faith of Doctor Nittai was within
them ; and that faith was so strong that they saw the lamb.
They brought it to the altar, and that sacrifice was the
meaning and crown of their lives. Only for the sake of
celebrating it did they draw the air into their lungs with so
much labour and breathe it out again ; only that task still
stood between them and death.

17

WHEN it was reported to Titus that the Jews had stolen
and eaten the last nine lambs reserved for their god, he was
deeply impressed. These people were uncanny, indeed
insane ; the gods had blinded them. Why did these in-

comprehensible people, who had no defence left except Jehovah, rob Jehovah's altar ?

However that might be, the besieged were now at the end of their resources. He was strongly tempted to order an assault at once on the enfeebled city. After the long, demoralising siege the army was eager for it. It was also the shortest and surest path to victory. His father had no reason now to keep up the fiction that this was merely a punitive expedition. Vespasian was established firmly enough in Rome, although he had not himself finished the campaign. If Titus stormed the city now Rome could not very well refuse him a triumphal procession.

Titus passed a restless night filled with doubts. A triumphal procession would be very welcome. But had he not made a vow both to Berenice and himself that he would not wreak on the Temple his fury against the rebels ? He had not gained much by employing violence against Berenice. If he spared her in this matter, if he waited until she came to him of her own will, would not that blot out the offence he had been guilty of against her ?

He entrusted Joseph with the task of again and for the last time initiating negotiations. He authorised him to offer terms far more favourable than any offered before.

Joseph's hopes soared extravagantly. He bowed profoundly to Titus and put his hand to his brow. The Roman's terms were a magnanimous gift granted by a strong hand which in reality had no need to give where it could take. He must succeed in making the people in the city see that. Now, in spite of everything, some meaning was given to his being here with the Romans outside Jerusalem instead of being inside the walls like that fellow Justus.

At the appointed hour, clad in simple robes, alone, unarmed, and without any badge of his priestly rank, he

appeared before the walls. He stood there between the
besiegers and the besieged, a tiny human being planted on
the bare soil ; and before him the city wall was thick with
Jews, and behind him the blockade wall was as densely
thronged with Romans. The heat and stench oppressed
him, and the silence was so tense that he could hear the
throbbing of his blood in his ears. On his back he felt the
cold, satirical gaze of Tiberius Alexander ; before him he
saw Simon Bar Giora's eyes filled with hatred, his old
friend Amram looking at him savagely, and John's contemptuous stare. He shivered from head to foot in spite
of the hot sun.

He began to speak. At first his words sounded empty
and strange, but then something rose within him, and he
spoke more simply and directly and eloquently than ever
before in his life. If the city surrendered, he said, the
Romans would treat those who bore arms as prisoners, but
the lives of all would be spared. The Romans, he went
on, would that very day admit sacrificial lambs into the
çity for the Temple service on the condition that the High
Priest would accept as formerly an offering from the Emperor, people, and Senate of Rome.

The Jews on the wall had gloomily and dejectedly watched
Joseph approaching. Now many even among the Makkabi
people gazed eagerly at Simon and John. This was indeed
a mild and magnanimous offer, and in their hearts they
hoped that the leaders would close with it.

But the leaders had no intention of doing so. If they
surrendered what would their lives be afterwards ? First
they would be led as prisoners in a triumphal procession,
and then they would be sent as slaves to some mine. And
even if the Romans set them free, could they go on living
among the Jews after all that had happened ? The other

Jews would never leave them in peace all their lives. But these were not the only considerations that influenced them ; there were deeper reasons. They had gone too far, they had persisted until the countryside was rased flat and the Temple turned into a burial place and a bloodstained fortress ; they had eaten of the lambs destined for Jehovah, and now they were resolved to go their road to the very end.

So that without even knowing what the Roman offer was to be they had already prepared their answer. They did not spit when Joseph reached the end of his speech ; they did not shake the dust from their shoes, nor did they take the trouble of returning a long answer expressing all their anger and contempt. No, they simply opened the little postern gate ; and out came a pig squealing and grunting. Yes, they had managed to capture a few pigs from the Romans, and now they set one on Joseph.

Joseph's face grew white. The pig went up to him grunting and snuffling, and the crowd on the wall laughed. And then they intoned in chorus and in Latin, and that could not have been an easy matter for these exhausted men, they must have practised it for a long time : " Have you grown a new foreskin now, Flavius Josephus ? " They laughed, and the Romans could not help laughing too. These damned Jews had managed to let off a really good joke for once. But Joseph stood alone between the two camps with his pig, within sight of the violated Temple bristling with artillery, and the Jews and the Romans roared with laughter at him.

During those moments, which were like years to him, Joseph expiated all the insolent pride of his life. " Your Doctor Joseph is a scoundrel," that yellow-faced fellow had said once ; the people of Meron had sowed grass on the road that he had arrived by ; others had kept at a distance of seven paces from him as if he were a leper ; to the sound of trumpets the decree of excommunication had been pronounced against him in Alexandria ; he had been tied to the stake, had been scourged. But what were all these things compared to this moment ? He had come with a clean heart ; he had wished to save the city, man, woman, child, and the house of Jehovah. And they had sent him a pig in reply. He knew that he must go now, but he still hesitated. The walls seemed to hold him there. He had to summon all his will to move. He put one foot behind the other, he went backwards, his gaze still fixed on the walls. An icy chill ran over him, he seemed stripped of everything, pride as well as pain. He belonged neither to the Romans nor to the Jews ; the earth was waste and empty as before the creation ; he was alone, and round him was scorn and laughter.

When the Jews let the pig out through the postern gate Titus did not laugh. Really, he was thinking, I should feel pleased. I have done my best. I wanted to make good what these madmen did against their god ; now I stand better with this Jehovah than my enemies. But this comforting thought soon faded. He gazed across at the white and golden Temple. Suddenly, with terrifying force, he was overcome by a longing to trample that disturbing and troubling thing beneath his feet. The Jews themselves had violated it ; he would reduce it to the dust once and for all, that lovely and mocking thing with its accursed purity. Through his mind ran the word which he had so often heard his soldiers shouting, rhythmically, savagely, " Hep, Hep," and with every " Hep " skulls smashed and houses fell in.

He came to himself in dismay. He was sorry for having thought such things. No, he hadn't the least intention of picking a quarrel with this Jehovah. He left that to these gentlemen within the walls.

A dark fit of melancholy seized him, a passionate longing for the Jewess. He thought with helpless fury of the fanaticism of the Jews, of their blindness. Berenice was one of them, incomprehensible as they, and never would she really belong to him.

He went to see Joseph. Joseph was lying on his bed in deathly exhaustion, covered with cold sweat in spite of the heat of the summer day. He made to raise himself. " Lie where you are," Titus begged him, " but talk to me. Perhaps my anger at these men blinds me. Explain to me, my Jew, what they want. They can't gain their ends now ; so why do they prefer to die rather than live ? They could keep the Temple that they're fighting for ; why do they do their best to have it burnt to the ground ? Do you understand it, my Jew ? " " I understand it," said Joseph, in a voice of infinite weariness, and his face had the same mournful expression as the faces on the wall. " Are you an enemy of ours, my Jew ? " asked Titus very softly. " No, my general," said Joseph. " In your heart are you with those people within the walls ? " asked Titus. Joseph painfully pulled himself together and remained silent. " Are you with those people within the walls ? " Titus repeated more urgently. " Yes, my general," said Joseph. Titus looked at him without hostility, but never had the two of them been stranger to each other. Titus went out, sadly and reflectively, his eyes still fixed on the Jew.

18

IN the beautiful secluded house in Tiberias on the hill above the lake Berenice tried to tell her brother Agrippa what had happened in the camp. When she arrived dis-

hevelled and wild-eyed he had not put any questions to her.
Now she was the more frank in relating her story. Did
she hate Titus because of his violence ? No. That was
the worst of all, that she could no longer summon up any
anger against his barbarity. Behind the spiteful and stubborn
boy's face that he had finally shown her she saw that of the
strong and unshakeable soldier, and though she made fun
to her brother and herself of Titus's crude pedantry and silly
shorthand, it did not alter matters. In his stinking camp
on the trampled waste round Jerusalem Titus was a man,
the man for her.

Agrippa understood quite well his sister's laborious
explanations. Hadn't this terrible war got on his nerves
just as badly ? He had led his own contingent to join the
Roman army, but then had immediately returned to his
Transjordanian principality, and desired to hear as little
as possible of what was happening in the Roman camp. His
beautiful palace in Tiberias, his pictures, books, statues,
were spoilt for him. " Things are easier for you, sister,"
he said in his gentle, courteous voice, a faint, melancholy
smile on his handsome, somewhat too full face. " You can
love Judaea, the country and its spirit, in your heart, and love
your Roman too ; and the problem is solved as far as you're
concerned. Love your Titus. I envy him, but I daren't
warn you against him. But what is left for me, Berenice ?
I understand both peoples, the Jews and the Romans. But
how am I to keep faith with both ? If I could only be
like those people in Jerusalem, or like the Romans ! I can
see the fanaticism of the one and the barbarism of the other,
but I can't find any solution, I can't come to any
decision."

In the quiet house in Tiberias Berenice waited tensely for
news from the camp outside Jerusalem. For a time her

eyes still saw the empty waste into which the beautiful surroundings of the city had been transformed; in her nostrils was the stench of the camp, in her ears the howling of the beasts waiting for their food. But gradually these memories lost something of their horror, and she began to be infected with the mad seduction of war. War : she saw a great spectacle of blood and fire ; war : she saw savage and pious faces, the faces of men longing for a quick and glorious death. Amid the quiet beauty of Tiberias she was overcome by a more and more violent longing for the sublime and grandiose tumult of the camp. Why did Titus remain silent ? Why did he not write to her ? Had she not pleased him ? She turned all her rage and shame against herself, not against the Roman.

When news came that the fate of the Temple was to be immediately decided, and that an Imperial Council was at that moment considering it, she held back no longer. Now she had reason enough to return to the camp.

An intense feeling of elation filled Titus when her arrival was announced to him. Since this woman had fled from him he had spent two almost unendurable months waiting with painfully strained nerves in the hot noisome camp for the fall of the city. He had tried to drown his restlessness in work ; he had made progress too ; he had carried war to the very walls of the Temple, and where Fort Antonia had once stood rose now his tent with its hree divisions, a workroom, a bedroom and a dining-room. He no longer denied himself the presence of Berenice's portrait. Disturbingly alive, like everything that Fabullus painted, it stood in his workroom ; often he stared into the great, brownish golden eyes in the portrait. How could he have ever been so stupid as to treat her as he had done ? That was the face of a strange woman, very remote and

very foreign. He longed for her as he had done the first
day they had met.

He looked up his notes, searching for words of hers that
he had taken down ; he collated and pondered them. Then,
full of doubt, he stood for a long time before the portrait.
He restrained himself, did nothing, and waited.

So now she had come of her own free will. He rode out
to a great distance from the camp to meet her. Berenice
was gentle and maidenly and had no reproaches for him.
The waste landscape round Jerusalem, the multitudes of
the dead on their crosses, the carrion birds, the savage and
threatening bearing of the soldiers ; this vale of Hinnom,
this landscape of the dead did not terrify her. For Titus
walked with a firm step through this Hades, and at his
side she felt a great peace.

They had supper together. He told her about his men,
his soldiers. These Jews were making things very difficult.
They were fanatical, mad as wild boars pierced with an
arrow. They risked their lives for a sackful of wheat, and
were always thinking out new and gruesome tricks. For
instance, they had stuffed the roofs of the halls connecting
Fort Antonia and the Temple with bitumen, dried wood and
pitch, enticed the Romans on to these roofs, and fried them
there like fish. But his fellows were not to be joked with.
Titus told all this as if he were not speaking of vitally serious
things, but of a good piece of sport. He did not spare himself
when it came to the scratch ; he flung himself into the
midst of the battle ; he had been twice wounded, his horse
had been struck down under him, his officers were always
trying to persuade him that he, the commander, should leave
the ordinary business of fighting to his army.

Titus went on garrulously, in the best of spirits, scarcely
noticing whether she was listening. Suddenly he caught

her glance fixed upon him. These were not the eyes in
the portrait. The veiled, adoring look that was in them
now he had seen in other women's eyes. Softly, with one
movement, both firm and gentle, he locked Berenice in his
arms, still continuing what he was saying. She fell against
him, he did not finish the sentence he had begun; his
words broke off, they sank down and melted together.

Afterwards she lay silently smiling with closed eyes.
Titus pressed his broad peasant face, that now looked fresh
and young, against her breast. " I know," he said, subduing
his harsh military voice, " I know that you didn't come for
my sake. But let me believe that you did. My sweetheart, my empress, my beloved. I expect that it was for
the sake of your Temple that you came. My blessing on
your Temple, seeing that you've come. It was my firm
purpose that it should be left standing. And if I have to
sacrifice ten thousand men, it shall remain standing, sweetheart. It is your Temple. It is a frame for your image,
and ten thousand men's lives are not too high a price for
that. And I'll rebuild your mother's palace too. You'll
walk up the steps, Berenice, with that walk of yours that
delights me, and behind you will be the Temple."

Berenice lay smiling with closed eyes. She drank in his
words. Quite softly she said : " My man, my child,
Janik, Janiki. I came for your sake, Janiki."

19

ON the 21st of August, the 1st of Ab, according to the Jewish
calendar, Big Julius, the great battering ram, was set to work
against the outer wall surrounding the Temple quarter.
It kept going for six days without a break, other engines
were brought up, and on the 27th of August all the engines
were working together. Without effect. Then a direct

attack was attempted, ladders were set up, and two cohorts in tortoise formation tried to scale the walls. The Jews flung down the ladders thronged with armed men. A few legionaries, the bearer of the colours among them, managed to reach the walls, but they were cut down and the Jews took possession of the colours.

Titus next tried to set fire to the gate. The outer colonnades, he said to reassure Berenice and himself, were really not a part of the Temple itself. So the gate was set on fire ; and the silver, dropping off, opened a way for the flames to the wooden beams. All day and the following night the fire raged. By that time the northern and western pillared halls of the Temple precinct were burned down, and now the Romans stood before the lofty Temple itself.

On the 28th of August, the 8th of Ab, by the Jewish calendar, while the Roman fire brigade were labouring to cut a way through debris, ashes, fire and falling beams to the Temple walls, Titus summoned a council of war. He wished to decide what method of attack should be adopted against the Temple.

At the council of war were present Tiberius Alexander, also the generals commanding the four legions, Cerealis of the fifth legion, Lepidus of the tenth, Liternius of the twelfth, Phrygias of the fifteenth, and Mark Antony Julianus, the Governor of Judaea. Titus asked Joseph to attend as secretary.

First Titus ordered a letter from the Emperor to be read. Berenice had been rightly informed ; the Emperor had summoned an Imperial Council so as to take the opinion of his advisers on the question whether the Temple should be allowed to remain standing. Several of his ministers thought that this bulwark of revolt, this centre and symbol of rebellious Jewish national pride, should be rased to the

ground. Only in that way could the Jews be deprived once
and for all of their rallying point. Others were of the
opinion that as they were waging war against human beings
and not lifeless things, Rome's cultural prestige demanded
that such a celebrated piece of architecture should be spared.
The Emperor himself, the letter concluded, had come to
the decision that his commanders should if possible spare
the Temple.

The generals listened gravely, with intent faces, while
the letter was being read. They knew that their triumphal
procession was at stake. If they stormed the Temple that
would be the glorious conclusion of the campaign, and nobody
could talk any longer of a mere punitive expedition ; then
the Senate must grant them their triumphal procession.
Seductively before them hovered the splendour and glory
of that day, the greatest of their lives to all who marched as
victors through the streets. But they dared not speak of
that here ; they dared not make any more mention here of
the interests of the army than if they were sitting at the
Emperor's council table.

They could quite well picture to themselves what had
happened at the Imperial Council. Stout old Junius
Thrax would have put in a few soft words for the Temple ;
also fat Claudius Reginus would have uttered a few vague
and conciliating phrases. But the minister Talassos would
certainly have advocated all the more sharply the destruction
of the Temple. Finally this compromise had emerged,
this letter that pushed the responsibility for all that might
or might not happen on to the army. Well, the army
could quite well bear the responsibility. The army wanted
its triumphal procession ; and the temper of the troops,
who savagely longed to trample under foot that thing up
there, that temper had also infected many of the leaders.

The cry " Hep, Hep," also ran through their heads. " To spare the Temple if possible," it was easy enough to say that in Rome. " If possible," what did that mean, and how much did it cover ?

Tiberius Alexander was the first to speak. He knew that the others wanted their Roman triumphal procession ; he himself desired the submission of the country on reasonable terms. He spoke briefly and courteously as ever. If they spared the building, it would involve sacrifices. But ten thousand soldiers could be replaced ; the Temple was unique and could not be replaced. With their hundred thousand men against the some fifteen thousand now left within the walls, they could not but win. It was quite possible to spare the building.

General Phrygias of the fifteenth legion took up the other side, encouraged by shouts of approval from General Liternius. Certainly it was possible to spare the Temple for the Empire and the world at the sacrifice of some ten thousand Roman legionaries. But he did not believe that the Emperor, the soldiers' friend, had wanted to stretch his idea of what was possible to that extent. Already many thousands had been slain, mangled and roasted because of the unfair fighting of the Jews. They dared not add another ten thousand to that sum. The soldiers were thirsting to burn down the thing and get hold of its golden ornaments. If they were denied that cheap revenge, then it would cause justified discontent among the troops.

While General Liternius noisily agreed, Tiberius Alexander smiled politely as ever. This fellow Phrygias was the very type of officer that he hated. Obstinate and vain of his authority, he simply wanted his triumphal procession, and that was all. A man like him could never appreciate a building that had been created by the spirit of centuries. He would simply walk over it in his military boots to his triumphal procession, and be turned neither to the right nor to the left.

But now Mark Antony Julianus, the Governor of Judaea, raised his voice. He was a state official, and he was worried over his own job : the future administration of the province. He did not want, he said, to shoulder any further responsibility. He did not doubt, he went on, that the army could crush the rebellion and also spare the Temple. But that was a solution that would serve only for a little while, not permanently. Nobody could admire the value of the building as a work of art more sincerely than he did. But the Jews had now turned the Temple into a fortress, and a fortress it would remain after the uprising was crushed. And when had Rome ever left rebel fortresses standing in conquered provinces ? The Temple would have to be destroyed, if they did not want the Jews to hatch a new rising as soon as the Roman troops began to withdraw. If they spared the building these restless and insolent people would most certainly take it as a sign, not of clemency, but of weakness. He, who as Governor of Judaea was responsible both to Judaea and Rome for law and order in this unruly province, felt himself bound to urge that the Temple should be rased to the ground. They simply could not leave it standing.

Titus listened to all that was said ; sometimes he took down, somewhat mechanically, a sentence in shorthand. He understood quite well the feelings of his soldiers and generals ; did not he himself long for the triumphal procession ?

But this Jehovah was a dangerous enemy. The very obstinacy with which these people fought for him proved that in spite of all his absurdities he was neither a powerless

nor a contemptible god. "If possible." He sighed
inwardly. He wished that Vespasian's letter had been
clearer.

Meanwhile all the officers had expressed their opinion.
It appeared that three were in favour of letting the Temple
stand, and three for destroying it. In tense excitement
they waited for the commander's decision. Even the
composed Tiberius Alexander could not restrain a slight
nervous twitching of the face.

Joseph scribbled nervously with his stylus on the writing
block. He listened keenly to every word that was spoken ;
he took it down perfunctorily, but his memory could be
relied upon. The reasons brought forward by these soldiers
were quite good reasons. And a still better one was at the
back of their minds : the wish for a Roman triumph. Titus
had promised him and Berenice that he would spare the
Temple. But Titus was a soldier. A soldier's highest
aim was a triumph in Rome. Would Titus stick to his
word ? Would he endanger his triumph in Rome to
preserve Jehovah's house ?

Titus was reflecting. But not on the reasons and counter-
reasons advanced by his officers. This Jehovah, he was
thinking, is a very cunning god. Probably it was he who
implanted in me this disturbing passion for the Jewess. She
has given her heart to me ; I know her ; perhaps it is this
Jehovah that prevents my thirst for her from ceasing. How
my father would grin if he heard that I had burnt the
Temple ! "Well, Caenis, old girl," he would say, "he
simply couldn't resist it. Let's give him his triumphal
procession."

There had been silence for a little while. "I agree,"
said Titus, "with those who think that it is possible to
spare the Temple. I fancy that our Roman legions will

stick to their discipline even if they don't like their orders.
I thank you, gentlemen."

20

THAT evening, as was the ancient custom, the music corps
assembled before Titus's tent to sound the salute, the army's
symbolical homage to the commander's power. Titus
stood at the door of his tent ; it always gave him a particular
pleasure to listen to the salute. The players, there were
about two hundred of them, took up their position. The
signal was given, and then the sound was released, discordant
but powerful ; a thud of drums, a piping and shrieking of
horns and flutes, a blare of trumpets, a snarling peal of
cornets ; and Titus's heart filled with elation at the sight
of the gay, parti-coloured ranks of the musicians and the
sound of their obsequious greeting.

Then they withdrew, and now came a more important
task, the giving out of the pass-word and the order of the
day. This was always gone through with ceremonious
solemnity. Each day in turn the four legions sent their
first centurion to receive from the commander the pass-word
and the order of the day, afterwards with equal solemnity
and ceremony to pass them on.

Titus was unpleasantly surprised when on this evening,
it was the 28th of August, Pedanus, the first centurion of
the fifth legion, appeared to receive instructions. The
command Titus had to give was very important, and he had
three times modified it. He handed the little tablet to the
centurion. Pedanus took it in his broad, stubby, dirty hand.
He read : " Pass-word ; Down with Judaea. Order of
the day : In the course of the 29th of August the fire
extinction and path clearing duties on the north and west
sides of the Temple must be finally completed, so that by

the early morning of the 30th the ground may be clear for
the attack.   If the soldiers engaged on these duties are
molested the enemy must be repulsed with energy, but with
every care to avoid injuring the buildings belonging to the
actual Temple."

In accordance with the regulations, Pedanus read out the
order in a loud voice.   The first centurion of the fifth
legion was a quick-witted fellow, and with his crafty eye
and brain he had grasped the meaning of the order long
before his raucous voice repeated it.   So he read out the
order very slowly.   With his bare, red face, powerful
shoulders and bull-neck, he stood there before his commander.   The words of the order came very slowly from
his gross mouth.   The words " the enemy must be repulsed
with energy " were uttered very distinctly and emphatically ;
and although Pedanus did not slurr over the concluding
phrase :   " but with every care to avoid injuring the buildings," it sounded somehow casual, an afterthought.   While
he read he kept his eyes fixed, the living as well as the dead
one, on his commander more than on the tablet, with an
enquiring and doubtful expression, as though he could not
have read rightly.   Once more under this glance Titus
was filled with the same repulsion that he had often felt
already for this rude and blatant fellow, along with the same
strong temptation, the same mad desire, that had seized him
while the generals were speaking, to carry fire and destruction further still, to carry it into the heart of that building
over there.   There was a short silence.   Pedanus still
gazed at him, incredulous, waiting.   Yes, no doubt about
it, he was waiting for something.   You're quite right,
Pedanus, but the others are right too.   Do as you please.
Responsibility for things is always pushed on to somebody
else.   Everybody wants to do it, but nobody wants it to

be done. You're a man, Pedanus ; you do it. Such was roughly what Titus felt while Pedanus was standing there waiting. It was hardly a thought, and far less was it a thought that could be formulated ; Titus was careful not to risk that. The only indication he gave was a faint, almost imperceptible smile. But the first centurion of the fifth legion saw that smile. Had Pedanus said something ? It had sounded like, " Hep, Hep." But that was impossible, of course. Pedanus took the tablet, saluted formally, outstretching his arm with the hand open. Titus said : " That is all, thanks." Pedanus disappeared and nothing had happened.

Titus passed that night with Berenice. He was restless, and once Berenice heard him saying : " Give me back the tablet."

21

MEANWHILE Pedanus returned to his tent. The words of the order were clearly fixed in his head ; nevertheless he drew out the tablet again and read it yet once more. His wide mouth stretched still wider in a happy grin. True, the heat of this country, the disgusting flies that seemed to favour particularly his fair rosy skin, the exasperating boredom of the siege—he was weary of all these, and the bearer of the grass garland, the darling of the army, could have avoided them too if he had liked. During the year before, when military operations were at a standstill in Judaea, he had gone with a detachment of Mucianus's troops to Italy to take part there in the campaign against Vitellius. He should have stayed there, should have joined the Imperial Guards and demanded to be made a general. But now, with this tablet in his hand, he was not sorry that he had returned as first centurion to his legion, to this measly place Jerusalem and this accursed siege.

Pedanus was a born soldier. He had risen from the ranks. He liked plain and abundant fare, he liked to booze and bawl out scurrilous songs. He had learned to slash and bludgeon and trample enemies underfoot, and in spite of his girth he was uncannily agile and powerful. He was quite satisfied with himself. He loved to gaze at his reflection, not only in the costly gold mirror that he always carried with him in all his campaigns, but in any pool that he passed, or in his shield. His face pleased him. When he lost his eye he ordered a new one from the best-known of the artificers who turned out eyes for statues. His face pleased him still better after that, and he did not regret the loss of his eye. He loved danger. He loved plunder as well. From his share of plunder and the donations granted him for daring achievements, as well as from private deals in the camp, he had gathered together a tidy property which was lying safe with a banker in Verona and piling up high interest. Some time, when he was old and toothless, he would return to Verona, and there the bearer of the grass garland, the darling of the army, would be a big man and make the town dance to his tune.

For the time being, however, he had something better to do. For instance there was this curious order. An extremely satisfactory order, which only he himself really understood, and which he knew how to use. This curious order in itself repaid him for returning from a life of luxury in Italy to his legion. For the first centurion of the fifth legion, who was usually indifferent to other people, sportively hewing down his opponents without taking any further interest in them, this Pedanus had one great hatred : his hatred of the Jews.

Everything about these people, their speech, their customs, their religion, their appearance, their smell, exasperated him.

The other eastern peoples too were filthy barbarians with obsolete customs.   But, it was past belief, these Jews were so fond of idleness that nothing, not even the threat of death, could bring them to the point of lifting a finger on their seventh day.   They had actually a river in their country, the Sabbath River, that stopped running on that day.   And at the beginning of the war, he had seen it with his own eyes, they had let themselves be slain on their seventh day without making any defence, simply on principle, out of lawfully ratified laziness.   The dunces believed that the souls of those who kept their filthy commandments would be preserved alive for eternity by this god of theirs.   That was what made these swine so impervious to things that attracted or terrified others.   They considered themselves better than other people, just as if they were Roman legionaries.   They hated and despised other people.   They had themselves circumcised just to be different from other people.   They were exasperatingly different from other people and stubborn as wild goats.   When they died, when they were crucified, they shouted, " Jeh, Jeh ; Jeh is our God."   When he heard this " Jeh, Jeh," he had thought at first that their god was a donkey, and some people actually said that they worshipped a donkey in their Holy of Holies. But that wasn't the case ; these madmen and criminals believed in a god that one could neither see nor taste, a god as criminal as themselves, who was only present in their minds.   For his private amusement he had often tickled up some of the Jews hanging on the crosses, to see whether he couldn't, by threats and promises, drive some sense into them.   But no.   They really believed in their invisible god ; they screamed " Jeh, Jeh," and died.

Pedanus was a savage and inveterate opponent of such nonsense.   He longed to exterminate it.   Life wouldn't be worth living if there was any truth in the stuff they believed in, even the faintest trace of truth. But what they said wasn't true, mustn't be true.

In his rolling walk Pedanus went to his tent, his wide mouth twisted in a sarcastic grin. If there was any truth in the existence of this god Jehovah, then he must be able to protect his house. But he couldn't, the first centurion of the fifth legion would see to that. That was the only point in his remaining during this hot, sweltering summer outside this measly place Jerusalem. He would show this god Jehovah what was what. He would prove to him that he didn't exist, and that that thing over there, his house, was nothing but an empty snail's house.

While he again read the notes on the tablet Pedanus saw Titus's face before him. " But with every care to avoid injuring the buildings that belong to the actual Temple." What did " to avoid injuring " mean ; what did " the actual Temple " mean ? " The enemy must be repulsed with energy." That was clearer. That was something one could understand.

Hep, Hep, thought Pedanus to himself. He was in a particularly good mood all that evening. He drank, told smutty stories, and his wit was so pungent that even the older soldiers, who looked upon him as a rival, had to admit that he had every right to be called the darling of the army.

22

NEXT morning Pedanus and his men set out to clear away the smoking ruins. They shovelled the glowing debris to the side ; they bowed their backs and kept on shovelling ; a broad and straight path must be made to the very gate. The gate itself, which was inlaid with gold, was not very big ; somewhat to the left of it, at a height of some twelve feet, was a small window with a golden frame. The rest of the wall stared out white, gigantic, impregnable, its surface broken only by a few small windows at a very great height.

The soldiers' work among the debris was dirty, hot and exhausting. The Jews gave no sign ; no face was to be seen at any of the windows in the wall ; the gate remained barred. Pedanus became exasperated. Here he and his men had to clear away the Jews' muck for them. They worked on, sweating and cross. Pedanus ordered them to sing. He himself struck up the song of the fifth legion in his hoarse voice :

> Who can beat the good old Fifth ?
> A soldier's never at a loss.
> He can fight and he can wash,
> Fling down thrones or cook the soup,
> Cart the dung or guard the Emperor,
> Suckle infants, if he's asked to.
> A soldier's never at a loss,
> The good old Fifth can beat the lot.

While they were singing this song for the third time the enemy appeared. The gate was not so small as it had looked ; at any rate it was big enough to vomit out in an incredibly short time an incredible number of Jews. The soldiers exchanged their shovels for shields and swords. They had very little space to fight in, and any man who was driven in among the smoking ruins was past help. " Makkabi ! " shouted the Jews. " Down with Judaea ! " answered the Romans. It was a real set to. Many of the Jews were also driven in among the glowing debris, but they did not care. A dense crowd of them pressed round the Roman standard. The standard bearer fell, a second soldier

seized the standard and was cut down. " Makkabi ! "
cried the Jews ; they had the standard. In triumph they
bore it into the city.

Reinforcements were sent to the Romans. In their
next sortie the Jews were not so successful, but the little
gate kept on vomiting out one band after another. Pedanus
cursed and drove on his men with a cudgel. They flung
the Jews back, a few of the Romans surged in through the
gate, the gate closed. Those who had got inside were lost.
But the enemy had been repulsed with energy.

Pedanus grinned. The enemy had not been repulsed with
sufficient energy ; Pedanus drew up his men into tortoise
formation. They gaped at him in astonishment. The
gigantic walls rose before them ; the battering engines had
not even been in action ; there was no artillery to support
them. What was the first centurion after ? Were they
supposed to tear down the wall with their bare hands ?
But they interlocked their shields above their heads, obeyed
the command, and went forward. Strangely enough,
however, Pedanus did not tell them to attack the gate, but
a part of the wall somewhat to the left, where the window
with the golden frame was.

They kept on advancing ; now they were at the wall and
the men in front were already standing pressed against it.
And now a thing happened such as the first cohort of the
fifth legion had never seen before, accustomed as it was
to strange and wild occurrences. In his heavy armour
Pedanus swung himself up on to the shoulders of the men in
the last rank, and in his hob-nailed boots crept cautiously
forward over the groaning shields. He did not fall ; he
was keeping his balance, by Hercules ; in one hand he held
a burning brand, and now he flung it, he flung it through
the opening with the golden frame and then shouted :

"Give me another," and the men handed him another piece of burning wood from the debris, and yet another. The soldiers under the shields, sweating and panting, painfully holding themselves upright, did not know what was happening above their heads ; they only heard the centurion shouting : "Hand me another," and "Hep ! Hep !" But, like those who were fetching the burning wood, they were filled with tense expectation of what was to happen next. Their first centurion Pedanus, the darling of the army, certainly knew what he was doing ; certainly something was going to happen.

And Pedanus did know what he was doing. He had seen a ground plan of the Temple, and he knew that at this point, in the room with the golden window, was kept the store of wood which the Jews bore to the altar at the feast of the wood-bearing ; the citizens of Jerusalem no less than the pilgrims, every man his little bundle. The enemy had been repulsed with energy. He ordered more firebrands to be handed up to him, he threw, he shouted : "Hep ! Hep !" and "Hand me another," and they heard his hob-nailed boots clattering on the shields, they obstinately held out with bowed shoulders, and groaned under the strain.

And now at last there came shouts from within and smoke, more and more smoke, thicker and thicker smoke, and then Pedanus ordered : "Bring the ladder." The ladder was too short ; so he planted it on the shields, he clambered up, the ladder rocked wildly, but the soldiers under their shields stood their ground, and through the smoke Pedanus clambered in through the window and disappeared. He leapt into the midst of the smoke and tore at the bar of the gate ; in the opening appeared his blackened and grinning face. And as a little before the gate had vomited out an incredible number of men in an incredibly short time, so now it swallowed in an instant Pedanus's soldiers, fifty at first, and in the next breath a hundred.

The inside walls of the Temple were inlaid with cedar beams ; the summer was hot, the wood dry. Already the smoke had turned to flames. And before the soldiers knew what had happened a great shout came from the Roman camp. " Hep ! Hep ! " the soldiers shouted, and " Set fire to the place," and " Advance your shields." They waited for no command and kept no order. The little gate swallowed them up in hundreds, and presently they had torn open the other gates as well. The Jews who were trying to put out the fire were slain, the legions pressed on in double file, shoulder to shoulder, with shields locked, cutting their enemies down right and left.

23

THE greater part of the Jewish forces was posted in the forts and towers of the upper town ; in the Temple itself there were only a thousand men. When the Romans set fire to the Temple the Jewish soldiers raised a wild cry and tried to put out the flames. At first it was only a feeble fire, but it was stubborn and went on burning. Soon the Jews saw that it was impossible to fight the advancing Romans and extinguish the fire at the same time. John and Simon Bar Giora, summoned urgently from the upper town, recognised that the Temple could not be held against the flames and the enemy. They gave orders to the Temple guard to withdraw to the upper town. Small detachments were to keep the separate gates of the Temple and cover the others' retreat.

Everybody knew that those who remained behind to defend the gates of the Temple were doomed, but nobody

hesitated to volunteer for the task.   Even the boy Ephraim
volunteered and was accepted.   When John of Gishala
left he laid his hand on Ephraim's head and said : " You
are worthy of the trust.   Help to spread our religion, my
son."   So the great doctors were accustomed to lay their
hands on their pupils' heads when they granted them the
privilege and authority to disseminate their religion.

The Romans soon overpowered the little bands that
defended the gates of the Temple.   They came to the
Temple stairs and descended into the court where the altar
for the burnt offerings stood with its immense platform and
its mighty horns fashioned out of unhewn stone as if for
eternity ; for iron had never been allowed to touch it.   A
party of some fifty Jewish soldiers had now set up a catapult
upon it.   " Makkabi ! " they shouted, and the Romans
shouted back ; " Hep !   Hep !   Down with Judaea ! "
and they tried to rush the altar.   The catapult flung rocks
and pieces of iron into their midst, but they pressed forward
on both sides of the altar and presently they had encircled it
and flung themselves upon the platform.   They were men
from the fifth legion, Pedanus's men.   A tremendous din
rose, but in a little a voice pierced it, a hoarse blatant voice
that sang the blatant song of the fifth legion.   More joined
in, and now all of them sang, one could no longer hear the
shout of " Makkabi," one could only hear the words :

> " Who can beat the good old Fifth ?
> A soldier's never at a loss.
> He can fight and he can wash,
> The good old Fifth can beat the lot."

And now they had forced the other gates of the Temple,
flung them wide and poured in from every side.   In double
file, shields advanced, their faces watchfully half-turned,

shoulder to shoulder, they marched on, keeping step and mowing down their enemies. From all sides they appeared, encircling all the Jews they encountered and driving them towards the great altar. On the right horn of the altar, where the head priest of the Temple service had been accustomed to give the signal to the officiating priests and Levites, Pedanus stood now, and all round him rose the song of the fifth legion. He too, sang, he swung his sword, and sometimes for the sake of variety he flourished his cudgel. The Jews were driven up on to the altar ; they shouted : " Hear, Israel," but on the horn of the altar stood Pedanus, and he shouted " Hep ! " and lifted the cudgel and smashed it down on their skulls. Swords flashed, blood flowed like a brook down the platform, and the heaps of dead rose higher round the altar.

24

TITUS had just lain down for a short rest. He sprang up and saw the maddened legions rushing towards the city. And then he saw the smoke and flames rising. He ran out of his tent as he was, unarmed and without any badge of his rank. He burst into the midst of the savage and exultant legionaries. Many of the men recognised him, but they did not stand on ceremony, they shouted feverishly and joyously : " Come on, comrade. Come with us and set fire to the Temple. Hep ! Hep ! " He tried to resist, to direct the wild confusion. But did he really want to ? " Hep ! Hep ! " he found himself shouting with the others. " Let's set fire to the Temple, comrades," he shouted.

The guards before his tent had heard the commander's outburst. His alarmed officers and bodyguard forced a way to him through the tumult. At last, when he had been swept through the gate of the Temple, they reached him. He had himself in control again. Had it been he who

had shouted with the others ? " Put out the fire ! " he
roared. " Water ! " And the officers shouted : " Water !
Water ! Put out the fire ! " They flung themselves
among the maddened soldiers, shouting : " Water ! Put
out the fire ! " The centurions beat their enraged men
with their cudgels.

But it was senseless to resist the maddened troops. The
whole army had been seized with an insane lust for slaughter.
They had waited for such an endless time ; for all those
unendurable hot summer months they had waited to trample
this thing under their hob-nailed boots. Now they were
resolved to revenge themselves for their torments ; they
rushed on, Roman legions, Syrian and Arabian troops sent
by the vassal states, all mingled in one confusion. Nobody
wanted to be left behind ; they rushed on, they grudged
their comrades the privilege of arriving before them. The
path to the wall that was to have been cleared had never
been finished. They leapt over the glowing debris, tramp-
ling one another down, butting one another into the smoking
ruins. Over a whole mound of corpses they rushed on.

When Titus saw that there was no use in resisting the
furious army he withdrew with his officers to the central
court of the Temple, which was divided from the burning
part by a thick wall. The sacred room rose lofty and
cool, cut off from the heat and the savage tumult outside.
The candelabra stood there, the table with the shew bread,
the altar where the incense was burnt. Slowly and hesitatingly Titus advanced to the veil behind which lay the
mystery, the Holy of Holies. Since Pompey no Roman
had set foot there. What was behind the veil ? Was it
perhaps only some silly idol, an ass's head, a monster half
animal and half human ? With his broad short-fingered
hand Titus seized the veil. Behind him the faces of his

officers grew intent and eager, especially one broad, ruddy face, that of Pedanus. What was behind the veil? Titus tore it aside. A shadowy room, square, not very large, revealed itself, and Titus entered. There was a smell of earth and very old wood. The bare hewn rock, the topmost peak of the hill on which the Temple stood, rose there; the room was filled with a great and oppressive isolation; and that was all. "Well, well," said Pedanus, shrugging his shoulders, " it's just silly."

Titus breathed freely when he was back again in the lighter hall adjoining the Holy of Holies. He recognised the noble simplicity and symmetry of the room, and eyed the austerely beautiful sacred vessels ranged against the walls. " We must save all this, gentlemen," he said, not loudly, but imperiously. " We daren't let all this be desstroyed." Pedanus grinned. Already tongues of fire were shooting in through the doors; at all the doors the soldiers had kindled fires. It was too late.

In great haste the soldiers bore out the sacred vessels. The vessels were heavy, of solid gold. Ten men panted under the weight of the candelabra; then they collapsed. The candelabra crashed to the ground, killing one of the bearers in its fall. Encouraged by the shouts of their commander and the cudgel blows of the centurions, the soldiers bowed their backs anew and bore the vessels out of the burning and falling shrine. They carried out the twelve golden shew bread loaves, the frankincense vessels, the silver trumpets of the priests, and folded up the magnificent Babylonian veil, on which was embroidered a chart of the heavens. Titus stood on the stairs of the Temple with the flames at his back and looked on while the candelabra and the table with the show bread rose and fell amidst the confused throng of soldiers, moving towards the Roman camp

over dead bodies and shields like a ship on a stormy
sea.

25

MEANWHILE the legionaries rushed through the Temple,
drunk with blood and triumph. They looted whatever
they could lay their hands upon, tore the golden and silver
garnitures from the doors and walls. They clambered
perilously up the outer walls to seize the trophies fixed
there, standards and arms of ancient Syrian kings, and the
eagle of the tenth legion which four years previously had
been captured from Cestius Gallus. They sacked the
chamber where the sacred robes were kept, the chambers
where were stored the spices and the musical instruments.
With their arms full of costly and bizarre plunder they
hastened through the Temple. This was the crown of
the campaign. To tear down and sack this house of the
invisible god they had died in tens of thousands and endured
extreme hardship and privation. Now they wanted to
drink their triumph to the lees. They screamed, butted
one another, laughed stupidly, danced with their hob-nailed
boots on the floor, whose marble and mosaic were covered
with corpses and blood-stained arm-bands bearing the
initials Makkabi.

The dark passages which led downwards to the treasure
chambers were packed with soldiers. These treasure
chambers were securely locked, but the impatient men did
not wait for the locks to be burst with levers or battering
engines ; they set fire to the metal-plated doors. But
the wealth inside began to melt before the doors could be
burst open, and now out from the treasure chambers ran a
slow, thick stream of molten metal. In that stream flowed
the sacramental gifts of Roman emperors and Parthian
kings, the savings of poor people in Galilee, the wealth of

rich men in Jerusalem and the seaports, and hundreds of thousands of gold, silver and copper coins minted by the Avengers of Israel and inscribed with the word Makkabi and with the date ; first, second, or third year of deliverance.

The great curtains were rent asunder with a tearing sound, and burning strips detached from them flew through the air. With a crash the beams of the Temple fell in, bringing with them pieces of the walls. Until suddenly a sound arose that was louder than the roaring of the flames, the crash of the beams, the hoarse singing of the soldiers, the shrieks of the dying ; a piercing, sobbing, lamenting sound which was re-echoed dreadfully from the hills around. It was the shawm with the hundred notes. The soldiers had started to carry away the strange looking thing, but then had left it lying as being of no value ; now the wind of the flames swept through the shawm and made it resound.

It was as though this sound awoke the upper town, which, after the Jewish soldiers had broken the bridges to the Temple, lay cut off on its hill. The starved and exhausted soldiers in the upper town had seen the smoke and the first flames, had seen the fire spreading until gradually the whole white Temple Mount seemed to glow from its roots to its summit. From their dry throats all that they could summon was a feeble moan. But now that the great blast of the shawm rose in the air there broke from their throats too all the power that was left in them, and out of the moaning of the multitudes in the upper town there grew a high, shrill, continuous shriek, and the mountains took it up and shrieked it back again.

On that day it chanced that many people from the upper town had gone to the Temple. Doctor Nittai had summoned them. He had seen a vision and heard a voice.

Stubborn though exhausted, he had walked through the streets of the upper town proclaiming to the crowds that they should go to the Temple, for that day Jehovah would manifest himself as their Saviour and Redeemer. The fanatical voice of the old man had sounded so imperious and assured that everybody who could drag his limbs along had followed him. Several hundred people had done this. Of these believers only a few had been able to save themselves when the Jewish troops withdrew ; for the bridges to the upper town were narrow, and the troops had requisitioned them for their own use and destroyed them once they had passed across. The Temple was in flames and in the hands of the Romans. There was nothing left for the faithful worshippers but to take refuge in the lowest floor of the Temple, in the great colonnade on the extreme south verge immediately overlooking the ravine.

In their task of driving out the Jews the Romans had now penetrated to the lowest floor of the Temple. They descended the stairs, they saw the crowd in the hall, men, women, children, rich and poor, a great crowd of them, a huge supply of living human flesh. Although the price of slaves had fallen extraordinarily because of the capture of so many prisoners of war, the huge crowd in the hall still represented considerable wealth. At worst they could be sold in dozens to the managers of public spectacles. But the soldiers were not now in a mood to calculate. They wanted to have their private amusement, they had paid dearly enough for it ; the men of the fifth legion locked the door. The Jews saw the Romans in front of them and the ravine behind. Officers appeared. Lepidus, the general of the tenth legion. They gave orders to wait until they had received instructions from the commander. But the men of the fifth legion had no intention of waiting. They had just retrieved the colours that the tenth legion had lost four years before, and now were they going to allow the general of the tenth legion to spoil their sport for them ? They did not even grumble ; they only laughed good-humouredly. Why, these generals could hardly themselves imagine that the army would allow itself to be robbed of this great prize of human flesh. In good order they formed up at one side of the colonnade in four ranks ; then they set fire to the cedar beams of the roof. It was great sport to see the Jews in the hall beginning to dance about, to see them rushing out to be cut down, or clambering up the walls, or leaping into the ravine, or hesitating whether they should be killed by the sword or by the fire or by flinging themselves to destruction. The soldiers looked on with tense excitement while their prisoners came to these difficult decisions. With amusement the legionaries listened to the old and familiar death cry of the Jews : " Hear, Israel, Jehovah is the only God." They had often heard it before, but never uttered by so many people at one time. " Jehovah ! Jehovah ! " they shouted in mockery, after the Jews. " Jeh ! Jeh ! " they brayed, imitating the braying of a donkey.

Among the trapped crowd were two members of the High Council who were known to the Roman officer Paulinus, Meir Bar Belgas and Joseph Bar Dalaeus. Paulinus commanded them to advance and surrender themselves to him. He gave them his word that he would protect them. But they remained until the colonnade crashed in ; they wanted to die with the others, a burnt offering to Jehovah.

The priests chosen for the day had gone through the ritual of their service as though nothing out of the common were happening round them. As on every other day they had put on their robes and performed the ceremony of purifying the altar and the sacred vessels. The first flames burst out, the first Romans were already there ; but the priests walked through the tumult as if they saw nothing.

At first the Romans did not touch anyone who wore the white robes and the blue sash of a priest. But soon they were cutting the priests down just like the others. With a certain satisfaction they saw that a man who wore the blue priestly sash of this god Jehovah died like anybody else if one rammed cold steel into him.

When he left the Temple with his troops John of Gishala had offered to take the High Priest Phanias with him. But Phanias had declined the offer. If he could only discover what Jehovah wanted him to do ! That was a very difficult question, for Jehovah had given him a simple understanding. If he could only have remained a builder's labourer ! Now he wandered about, helpless and lachrymose ; his sad brown eyes looked round for someone who could give him advice ; he listened intently lest Jehovah might have spoken to his inner ear ; but he could hear nothing. All these things had happened simply because he had yielded to the treasurer and allowed his sacramental robe with its eight pieces to be laid away in a secret and inaccessible place. If he were only wearing his vestments now and the sacred jewels the flames would sink to his feet like obedient dogs, and the Romans would fall down dead.

Along with some other priests he was made prisoner by the Romans. The soldiers set about cutting the priests down. They begged to be spared. They screamed that the High Priest himself was among them. The soldiers brought them to Titus.

Titus was in a great hurry ; his presence was demanded at the southern gate of the Temple. Among those standing round him was General Liternius. Titus saw that the general was looking at him attentively, with a faint smile on his face. This fellow Liternius could not understand why he had advocated at the council of war that the Temple should be spared ; no doubt he considered him an art-loving milksop. So that dolt there was the High Priest. " Look after him well," said Titus, " I want to lead him in my triumphal procession." Then he glanced at the other priests, twenty wretched emaciated forms tottering in solemn white robes which were far too big for them. His expression became wayward, spiteful, childish. He turned away. As he was going he said to the priests over his shoulder : " I might have granted you your lives, gentle-men, for the sake of your Temple. But seeing that your god is evidently not of a mind to preserve his Temple, it is only fitting that you, his priests, should perish with it. Am I not right, gentlemen ? " He went, and the officer who attended to the executions ordered the priests to be seized.

Like the other priests old Doctor Nittai had gravely and confidently set about the performance of his duties after he had led his faithful followers to the Temple. When the flames broke out a smile appeared on his morose old face. He had known that to-day a sign would come. When the Temple began to burn he did not flee like the others into the outer courts, but with the eight priests under his authority climbed the stairs of the Temple. It was good to climb ; as yet they were still in a house made with hands, but soon they would be up aloft under the sky and in the presence of Jehovah.

And now they were on the roof, on the highest ridge of the Temple ; beneath them were the flames and the Romans. The shrieks of the dying, the hoarse singing of the legions, came up to them ; from the upper town mounted a shrill long-drawn shriek. Then the spirit descended upon the priests standing on the roof, and their hunger made them see visions. Swaying rhythmically they recited in the prescribed sing-song battle songs and pæans of victory out of the Scripture. They tore out the golden spears which were fixed on the roof of the Temple to guard it against the birds, and flung them down at the Romans. They laughed, they were up above the flames, and up above them was Jehovah, and they could feel His breath. When the hour for intoning the blessing came they raised their hands and outstretched their fingers in accordance with the law, and shouted through the roaring flames the blessing and the proclamation of faith with which it ends ; they felt joyful and uplifted.

When they had finished Doctor Nittai took the heavy key of the great gate of the Temple, raised it on high, so that all the others could see it, and cried : " O Jehovah, Thou hast not found us worthy to keep Thy house. Take Thou the key back." And he flung the key high into the air. And he shouted : " Do you see, do you see the hand ? " And they all saw a hand coming out of the Heaven and accepting the key.

Then the beams crashed in, the roof collapsed, and the priests standing upon it died a glorious death.

26

PEDANUS had flung the first torch shortly before midday. At five o'clock in the afternoon the whole mount was blazing. The soldiers round the first of the signal fires that Titus had ordered to be prepared saw the flames, and as soon as dusk fell they gave their signal : " The Temple has fallen." And then the next fire flared out, and then the next, and in the course of an hour the news was known to all Judaea, to all Syria.

In Jabne the great doctor Jochanan Ben Sakkai was told the news : " The Temple has fallen." The little old man tore his garments and strewed ashes on his head. But he summoned a meeting for that very night.

" Until to-day," he announced, " the High Council of Jerusalem has had the power to interpret the Word of God, to lay down when times begin, when the moon is new, when it is full, what is right and what is wrong, what is holy and unholy ; the power to bind and to unloose. From to-day the Council of Jabne has this power.

" Our first task is to establish the boundaries of the Holy Scripture. The Temple is no more, the Scripture is all our Kingdom now. Its books are our provinces, its sentences our cities and villages. Until now Jehovah's Word has been intermixed with the words of man. Our essential task is to decide to the last comma what pertains to the Scripture and what does not.

" Our second task is to perpetuate the commentaries of the doctors for future ages. Until now a curse has been laid on the handing on of these holy commentaries in any form except by word of mouth. We annul that curse. We are resolved to transcribe the six hundred and thirteen commandments on good parchment, to show where they begin and where they cease, to hedge them about and shore them up, so that Israel may be able to take its stand upon them for ever.

" The seventy-one of us gathered here are all that is left of Jehovah's kingdom. Purify your hearts, that you may be a kingdom more enduring than Rome."

They said amen. That very night they came to the decision that twenty-four books were sacred. Forty books that had been considered sacred by many people they rejected. The debate was a stiff one, but they severely confined themselves to the Word of Jehovah as it had been handed down, and did not listen to their own vain wisdom. They had no desire for sleep, they felt possessed by Jehovah while they performed this task of acceptance and rejection which was to be binding for all time.

The sun had risen when they parted. Only now did they feel their exhaustion ; but in spite of their grief at the destruction of the holy shrine their weariness was not without comfort.

When the others had gone the great doctor Jochanan Ben Sakkai was reminded by his scholar Arach : "You haven't dictated the text for the day yet, my Doctor and Master." The great doctor reflected for a little while, then he dictated : "When a king invites you to his table rather put a dagger to your throat than cast longing eyes on his rich dishes ; for they are full of deceit." Arach looked into the great doctor's weary and bitter face ; he knew that Jochanan was grieved because of his favourite pupil Joseph Ben Matthias and feared for him in his heart.

27

THE destruction of the Temple took place on the 29th of August in the year 823 after the foundation of Rome, or the 9th of Ab in the year 3830 by the Jewish reckoning. It was also on a 9th of Ab that the first Temple had been destroyed by Nebuchadnezzar. The second Temple had stood for 639 years, 1 month and 17 days. During all that time the burnt offering in Jehovah's honour had been celebrated every morning and evening, and many thousands of priests had performed the rites as they are laid down in the third Book of Moses and elucidated to the smallest point by generations of doctors.

28

THE Temple burned for two days and nights. On the third day only two of its many gates remained standing. In the midst of the ruins, on the huge blocks of the altar for the burnt offerings, and just opposite the eastern gate which still rose meaningless and forlorn, the Romans now set up their eagle and performed before it their sacrifice for the victory. When any battlefield could show more than six thousand dead enemies the army was accustomed to proclaim their commander Imperator. So now, standing on the high altar, Titus accepted the homage of his troops.

The commander's staff in his hand, the red cloak over his shoulder, the golden eagle behind him, he stood where once the column of smoke had ascended to Jehovah; he, an idol of flesh and blood, on the shrine of the invisible god. The legions marched past; they clashed their shields together and shouted: " Greeting, Titus, Imperator." For hours Titus's ears were filled with the clash of arms and the exultant shouts of his soldiers.

He had longed for this hour ever since his father had entrusted him in Alexandria with the conduct of the campaign. Now it left him cold. Berenice was gone, had fled at the sight of the burning shrine, had fled from him who had broken his word. Had he broken his word? He had given clear instructions to spare the Temple. It was the gods who had decided otherwise, perhaps the Jewish god himself, angered by the blasphemy and stubbornness of his people. No, it was not he, Titus, who bore the guilt for the destruction of the shrine. He decided to publish all that had happened clearly so that the whole world must acknowledge it.

Several of the captured Jews had sworn that the fire
began in the chamber where the wood was kept. They
had tried to extinguish it. But the Roman soldiers had
always flung new firebrands in among the faggots of wood.
Only the troops sent out to clear a path to the walls could
have done that. Titus summoned Pedanus and his men
before a court martial at which he himself presided.

Shortly before the court martial was to take place he had a
talk with Tiberius Alexander. "Do you hate me," he
asked the general, "because the Temple of this Jehovah of
yours has been burned down?" "Was it *you* that burned
down the Temple, Caesar Titus?" asked Tiberius Alexander in his courteous voice. "I don't know," replied
Titus.

The accused were asked : "Did the first cohort fling
firebrands into the Temple?" "We don't know, Caesar
Titus," the soldiers declared in voices ringing with honest
loyalty. Nobody had seen Pedanus flinging firebrands
into the Temple. "It's possible," Pedanus explained,
"that we might have used firebrands to defend ourselves
against the Jews. 'The enemy is to be repulsed with
energy' it said in the order of the day. With energy, one
could take that to include firebrands, too, if one happened
to have a piece of burning wood handy." "Did you intend
to spare the building?" he was asked. Pedanus shrugged
his shoulders. An honest old soldier, he gazed frankly and
honestly at his judge. "The wall," he said, "was a thick
stone wall and none of the engines could shake it. There
were stone floors and stone stairs inside. Who would
have expected stone to take fire? It was clearly the work
of the gods."

"Have you," he was asked, "ever seen a plan of the
Temple? Did you know that the window with the golden

casement was the window of the wood store ? " Pedanus paused before replying. With his living eye he glanced at Titus, then at his judge, then at Titus again. He smiled slyly, he underlined his secret understanding with Titus until everyone could see it. And then he actually turned to Titus. In his hoarse voice he said casually and brazenly : " No, Caesar Titus, I didn't know there was any wood behind the window."

Tiberius Alexander saw quite clearly that this man Pedanus was lying, and he saw just as clearly that Pedanus believed himself to be perfectly secure, thinking he had carried out the unexpressed wish of his commander. Titus and this man, the general saw, different as they appeared, were at bottom alike ; they were barbarians. Titus had made a vow to everybody and to himself that he would spare the Temple ; probably his intentions had been honourable, but in his heart he had been just as resolved from the start as Pedanus to tear down the thing he hated so much and trample it underfoot.

All the other men stuck to what they said ; they had seen nothing. None of them could explain what could have started the fire. To all questions they had always the same loyal answer : " Caesar Titus, we don't know."

During the proceedings Titus was visibly uneasy. The insolent glance of understanding that that rascal Pedanus flung him had thrown him into confusion. The suspicion that had vaguely oppressed him, the doubt whether after all he might not have some share in the responsibility got this fellow's crime, he now violently rejected. Had not his orders been clear ? Had he not always insisted that he should be implicitly obeyed ? He waited in agitation for the verdict of the generals, firmly resolved to refuse pardon to the darling of the army if he should be condemned to death.

But obviously none of his generals intended to pass such a
sentence ; they vaguely talked round the subject.   Perhaps
some of the subordinate officers should be transferred to a
penal   regiment.   " And   Pedanus ? "   shouted   Titus
furiously, his voice breaking.

An uncomfortable silence followed.   No one wanted to
risk executing Pedanus, the bearer of the grass garland.
Cerealis, the general commanding the fifth legion, was on
the point of saying something to that effect, when Tiberius
Alexander began to speak.   This thing that Pedanus had
actually in all probability done, he said, or at least had
allowed to be done with his consent : this thing had been
the desire of the whole army.   It was not any single soldier
who was guilty of a shameful act that would stain the
Roman name for ever.   In his soft courteous voice he
proposed that all officers and men who had taken part in
the work of clearing the path to the walls should be commanded to line up, and that each tenth man should be
executed.

As none of the others could gainsay the logic of the
general's proposal, they exclaimed against it with all the
greater violence and unanimity.   It was insolence of this
man to vent his Jewish resentment on Roman legionaries.
The announcement of the sentence was postponed.

In the end nothing happened.   A feeble lecture was
read to the first cohort of the fifth legion expressing the
dissatisfaction of the commanders at their not having hindered
the fire from breaking out.

29

TITUS was deeply vexed at the outcome of the trial.   It
was hopeless for him to attempt to justify himself in that
woman's eyes now.   He shrank from making enquiries

where she had gone. He was afraid that she might have
been overcome by one of those wild moods which had already
thrice driven her into the wilderness, where by punishing
her flesh she hoped to hear the voice of her god.

Then he learned that she had gone to the little village of
Thekoa. It was only a few hours' journey away. But
the news did not make him any happier. What was she
doing there, in that half-ruined place ? Did she want to
gaze at the stumps of her grove, so as to keep in perpetual
memory that he had not even fulfilled that small request of
hers ?

Titus's broad face became sorrowful, his angular indented
chin jutted out more stubbornly than ever, his features
were distorted until they became those of a spiteful peasant
lad. What should he do ? He had no excuse that would
hold good in her eyes. Should he talk with rough joviality
about the rights of a soldier, and put on the master, the
Roman ? He would achieve no more by that than he had
done once before.

He told himself to think no more about Berenice. He
had work enough to distract him. The old town was still
standing, the upper town. It possessed thick and powerful
walls which could not be stormed without preparation ;
the battering engines must be set going again, the gates must
be undermined. He made an agreement with himself.
As soon as the upper town was taken he would present
himself before Berenice.

But first he gave orders that everything in the conquered
territory should be levelled to the ground. The walls
were to be pulled down ; not one stone was to be left on
another. A lust for destruction had seized him. The
pleasant villas on the edge of the Temple ravine, the houses
in the working class quarter of Ophla, the old massive

buildings in the lower town were laid low. The town hall and the archives, which had once been set on fire already at the beginning of the civil war, were now destroyed a second time. The legal agreements, the business contracts, the state treaties engraved in bronze, the records of long and passionate bargainings in the market and the exchange recorded on parchment; these were destroyed once and for all. The whole Temple quarter and neighbouring streets were left to the mercy of the looting soldiers. For weeks they raked fresh gold and treasure out of the debris. They even penetrated into the underground passages of the Temple hill, not without danger; for many got lost and never saw the light again, and some encountered death in fighting with refugees who remained concealed in this underworld. But the danger was worth it; the underworld was a gold mine. More and more new treasure was raised from its shafts; the hidden Temple treasures themselves were brought to light, among them the celebrated robe in eight pieces which the High Priest Phanias had missed so painfully. Jewels, noble metals, rare stuffs, piled themselves up in the Roman depot; the merchants became busy, the price of gold all over the East fell by twenty-seven per cent.

In the lower town there was a Jewish shrine, the mausoleum of King David and King Solomon. Eighty years before Herod had secretly opened the grave by night, allured by rumours of immense treasure. But when he tried to penetrate into the tomb where the bones of the ancient kings rested flames had burst out; his torches had ignited the poisonous gases. Titus knew no fear. With his officers he penetrated into the burial chamber itself. There lay the bodies of the two kings in golden armour, diadems on their heads, huge glittering rings hanging from their skeleton fingers. Lamps, vases, plates, vessels of all kinds had been

buried with them, also the ledger of the Temple, so that
they might be able to prove to Jehovah that they had lived
piously. Tiberius Alexander opened the books and regarded
the faded script. Titus took the huge diadem from one
of the kings' heads, planted it with his broad stubby hands
on his own, and turned to his officers. " The diadem does
not become you, Caesar Titus," said Tiberius Alexander
dryly.

30

JOSEPH had watched the burning of the Temple with
intense concentration, as a scientist watches a natural phenomenon. He had hardened his heart ; he wanted to be
nothing but an eye ; he wanted to see the whole thing,
beginning, middle, and end. Again and again he had
ventured to the very edge of the fire, had passed through
the burning building many hundred times, very tired and
yet over-wakeful. He looked, listened, smelt, noted ; his
true and faithful memory took note of everything.

On the 25th of September, a month after the fall of the
Temple, and five months after the beginning of the siege,
the upper town of Jerusalem also fell. While the cohorts
were casting lots for the separate quarters of the town,
dividing the looting among them street by street, Joseph
hastily made his way to Fort Phasael, for there the Jewish
leaders had kept their prisoners. He wanted to let his
father and brother out of their cells. But the fort was
empty, and he found only dead men and men almost dead
with starvation. The two that he sought were not among
them. Perhaps the Makkabi men had slain their prisoners
when the Romans burst through the walls ; perhaps some
of them had taken refuge in the underground passages.

Joseph penetrated further into the town, walking through
fire and slaughter incased in the cold tense objectivity of

the historian. Throughout the whole, long, hot summer day he wandered up and down the hilly streets, the stairways, the passages, from the Palace of Herod to the Gate of the Gardens, to the market place, to the Gate of the Essenes, and back again to the Palace of Herod Through these streets and lanes he had walked for thirty years, as a child, as a youth, as a man. He knew every stone. But he swallowed his grief, he wanted to be nothing but an eye and a pen.

He was unarmed ; but strangely enough the golden writing tablets hung from his belt. It was not very safe to wander about in this way in the doomed, falling city of Jerusalem, especially if one looked like a Jew. He could have secured himself by wearing the decoration that Titus had given him, the medal with the head of the Medusa. But he could not bring himself to do it.

For the third time he went to the Street of the Fishermen, to his brother's house. The house was empty, and all that was movable had been carried away. The soldiers had turned their attention to the house next door. They had looted it clean too ; and now they were on the point of setting fire to it. Joseph gazed through the open door into the courtyard. There, in the midst of the noise and looting, stood an old man with his praying mantle round his shoulders and his phylacteries round his brow and his arm. Joseph went nearer. The old man recited his prayer in a loud voice, rocking his body ; for it was the hour of the eighteen petitions. He prayed ardently, his whole body prayed as is commanded the Scripture, and when he came to the fourteenth head of the prayer he prayed in the old style, as people had prayed during the exile in Babylon : " Let our eyes behold Thee when Thou returnest to Jerusalem with mercy as of old." They were long lost words preserved only among the learned doctors ; they were history ; for six hundred and fifty years no one had prayed any longer in that way. But on this day they had once more acquired meaning, and the old man uttered them piously and confidently. His prayer moved Joseph more deeply than all the horrors of that day. Through the imposed calm of the contemplator there broke suddenly a fit of intense grief over the fall of his city, shaking him to the heart.

Busy with the burning house, the soldiers had not troubled about the old man. But now they gathered amusedly round him and imitated his speech, droning, " Jeh, Jeh." Then they seized him, tore the praying mantle from his shoulders and commanded him to say after them : " Je-hovah is an ass, and I am the servant of an ass." They tugged him by the beard and knocked him about. Then Joseph stepped into the midst of them. Imperiously he ordered the soldiers to leave the old man alone. They had no intention of doing so, they replied. Who was he, anyway, to give them orders ? Joseph explained that he was the commander's private secretary and acted with his authority. Had he not been given permission to free seventy prisoners ? Anybody could say that, the soldiers replied. They worked themselves up into a rage and flourished their swords. Very likely he was a Jew himself, seeing that he hadn't any sword and spoke Latin like a Jew. They had been drinking wine, and they wanted to see blood flowing. It had been a mad act of Joseph to inter-vene without having a written order to show. He had got out of Jotapat with his life and escaped from countless other dangers ; now he would die a ridiculous death here, a victim of a mistake made by drunken soldiers. Then he had an inspiration. " Look at me," he said to the soldiers. " If I were really one of the people in Jerusalem, wouldn't

I be much skinnier ? " They saw his point at once and let him go.

Joseph sought out Titus and found him in a bad temper. The respite that he had allowed himself was now over. Jerusalem had fallen ; to-morrow or at latest the day after he would have to ride to Thekoa. His interview with that woman would not be a pleasant one.

Joseph humbly begged for a written injunction empowering him to set free the seventy prisoners that had been promised him. Titus wrote it out glumly. As he wrote he flung at Joseph over his shoulder : " Why have you never asked me for permission to let Dorion come here ? " Joseph remained silent for a little while in pure astonishment. " I was afraid," he said at last, "that Dorion would disturb me and I wouldn't live through this war intensely enough to describe it afterwards." Titus said shortly : " You're disgustingly logical, you Jews."

Joseph was struck by these words. It had been his intention to ask for more than seventy prisoners ; but when he saw the commander's face he had given it up. Now he suddenly knew that everything depended upon Titus's allotting him more than seventy. Very humbly he pleaded : " Don't make it seventy, Caesar Titus, make it a hundred." " I have no intention of doing such a thing," said Titus. He looked at Joseph crossly, and his voice sounded as surly as his father's. " And I didn't intend to give you your seventy either," he said.

Ordinarily Joseph would never have dared to persist with his appeal. But something drove him on. He must persist. He would be shamed for ever if he did not persist now. " Give me seventy-seven, Caesar Titus," he implored. " Be silent," said Titus. " I've half a mind to take back the seventy after all."

Joseph accepted the little tablet handed to him, expressed his thanks, asked for an escort, and returned to the city.

With the life-giving tablet stuck in his belt he made his way through the streets. Slaughter everywhere. Whom should he save? He had little hope of finding his father or his brother alive. He had friends in Jerusalem, women, too, that he was fond of; but he knew that it was not for the sake of these that Jehovah had softened Titus's heart on that day when they both stood looking down into the ravine heaped with corpses. Nor was it for the sake of such people that he had urged his claim upon the commander with such discourteous persistence. It was a virtue, a great merit, to rescue human beings from death, but what were his wretched seventy compared with the multitudes who were dying? And though he refused to admit it, though with all his strength he tried to banish the image from his mind, one face kept rising up persistently before him. That was the face he must search for.

He sought for it. He must find it. There was no time to be lost, he dared not leave off; there were tens of thousands of faces, and he must find this one among them. It was not a question of seventy people picked out at a venture, but of the one right one. But all round him murder was going on, and he carried the life-giving tablet at his belt, and his heart beat loudly against his ribs. He must pass these people over; he had his task, he had to find that one face. But when one sees men being slaughtered, and one has the power to say " Live," it is difficult to go calmly on one's way and wait until the one face appears. And Joseph did not go on in silence; he said " Live," and picked out a victim here because he was touched by his terror, or a victim there because of his youth, or some other because of his looks. And he said " Live "; he said it five times,

ten times, twenty times. Then he summoned all his resolution again ; he had his task ; he restrained himself and
passed by human beings who would die because he passed
them by. But he could not keep this up for long, and to
the very next victim he said " Live," and then to the next,
and then to several one after another. Only when he had
rescued the fiftieth victim from the grumbling soldiers, who
punctiliously obeyed his commands, did the thought of his
task seize hold of him again, and he repressed his pity. He
had no right to indulge such cheap compassion ; otherwise
he would have nothing to show but empty hands when he
found the one he was searching for.

He fled from his own thoughts into the synagogue of the
Alexandrian pilgrims. He would take possession of the
seventy rolls of the Holy Scripture that Titus had made
over to him. The looters had been in the synagogue.
They had torn the holy books out of the chests where they
were kept, and stolen their precious embroidered coverings.
There they lay, these noble rolls covered with priceless
words, tattered, smeared with blood, trampled by the boots
of the soldiers. Joseph bent down and carefully lifted one
of the damaged sheets of parchment out of the dirt and
blood. Two pieces had been cut out. Joseph examined
the places and found that they were the shape of a man's
foot. He saw that the soldiers had found no better employ-
ment for the rolls than to slash them up to make soles for
their boots. He mechanically reconstructed the first of
the wanting passages : " Do not oppress the stranger in
your country, for ye too were strangers in the land of
Egypt." Joseph slowly assembled the tattered rolls, carefully lifted them, reverently put them to his brow and his
lips, as the usage commanded, and kissed them. He
could not entrust them to Roman hands. He went out

into the street to find some Jew who would carry them to
his tent and conceal them there. Then he saw a procession
moving towards the Mount of Olives, evidently prisoners
who had been seized with weapons in their hands. They
had been scourged and were carrying on their raw shoulders
beams joined in the form of a cross ; their outstretched
arms were bound to the cross-bars. So they were now
bearing to the place of execution the wooden crosses on
which they were to die. Joseph gazed at their lifeless
sagging faces. He forgot his task. He commanded the
procession to halt and showed his tablet to the officer who
was escorting it. He had still the power to save twenty
human lives, but there were twenty-three prisoners. The
crosses were lifted from twenty of them ; they gaped stupidly,
still half-dead with the scourging ; they did not understand
what was happening. Instead of crosses they were given
rolls of the Scripture to carry and commanded to follow
Joseph to his tent in the Roman camp instead of going to
the Mount of Olives. It was a strange procession, causing
much laughter among the soldiers, that Joseph led through
the city with his golden writing tablets at his belt and
carrying a roll of Scripture under each arm as tenderly as
if they were two very young children, behind him his twenty
blood-stained and exultant Jews, who bore the other rolls.

31

TITUS had ridden post haste as far as Bethlehem, but between
Bethlehem and Thekoa he slackened his pace. It was a
difficult task that lay before him. Its name was Berenice.
The worst was that he could not carry off the affair high-
handedly ; indeed there was nothing that he could do.
He could only present himself before her and wait for her
decision. She liked him, or else she did not like him. He

climbed a steep path. Bare and forsaken, Thekoa lay perched on a rocky hill, and behind it was the wilderness. The officer in charge of the place had drawn up his men. Titus listened to his report. So this was the Valens who had ordered the grove to be cut down. An honest and manly face, neither clever nor stupid. The man had received the command to spare the grove, and he had spared it. Then he had received the command to cut down the grove, and he had cut it down. It was strange that Titus seemed unable to keep his word with this woman.

He was now before her house. Small and weather-beaten, it lay on the very summit of the rocky hill; it had originally been built for Maccabaean princes whose destiny it was to sojourn in the wilderness. Yes, from here one looked straight out into the wilderness. After all Berenice must have fled into the wilderness.

A rough fellow, shabbily dressed and without livery, appeared before the house. Titus sent him to inform the Princess of his arrival. He had not told her beforehand of his coming, for perhaps she might have refused to see him. He waited, a malefactor, for his judge to appear. It was not because he had burnt the Temple that he felt guilty. It was not what he had done that demanded to be judged; it was his very nature. His bearing expressed at once a consciousness of guilt and of justification. There he stood, the master of a hundred thousand chosen soldiers and enormous fighting resources, a man with boundless power in all the East from Alexandria to the frontiers of India, and his future life depended on whether this woman said yes or no to him; and he was helpless; he could do nothing but wait.

The door at the top of the steps opened; she was coming. Of course it was natural that she should receive with every

mark of respect the military commander, the ruler of the
country ; yet it was a great relief to Titus to see her standing
up there, to know that she was there.   She was wearing a
simple robe made out of one square piece of cloth such as
the women in this country usually wore.   She was beautiful,
she was queenly, she was the woman for him.   Titus
stood and gazed up at her humbly and devoutly.   He
waited.

At that moment Berenice knew that for the last time she
held her fate in her hands.   She had foreseen that this
man would come some time, but she had not made any
preparations for his coming ;   she had relied on God, her
God Jehovah, to tell her what she should do.   She stood
at the top of the steps ;   she saw the man beneath her, his
desire, his devotion, his humility.   Again and again he had
broken his word ;   he had done violence to her, and he
would do violence to her again.   He had the best intentions,
but he was a barbarian, the son of barbarians, and that fact
was stronger than all his good intentions.   No tie held her
any longer to him ;   this man had destroyed all that had
united them ;   the past was dead.   She must decide anew ;
she could dare to do that now.   Hitherto she had been able
to tell herself that it was for the sake of the Temple that
she had yielded to Titus.   Now she had no longer any
excuse, for this man had burned the Temple to the ground.
To whom should she belong from now on, to the Jews or
the Romans ?   For the last time the choice was given her.
Where should she go ?   To this man, Titus ?   Or to
Jabne, to Jochanan Ben Sakkai, who was building the
Jewish kingdom anew by cunning and far-reaching strata-
gems, and making it more secret, more spiritual, more subtle,
and yet more firm than ever before ?   Or should she go to
her brother and lead the life of a great lady, full of busy

idleness ?   Or should she flee into the wilderness and wait there until a voice spoke to her ?

She stood at the top of the steps and looked down at the man beneath her.   She saw him standing there stained with Jewish blood ; she heard the horrible shout of " Hep, Hep," that she had heard in the camp and that had certainly been shouted in this man's heart too.   The wisest thing would be to turn and go back into the house.   Behind the house lay the wilderness, and there life was good.   She commanded herself to go back into the house.   But she did not go back, she remained standing with her left foot on the threshold and her right foot outside.   And now she advanced her left foot as well ; it pulled her forward ; she said to herself : " Back ! " but she did not go back.   Slowly, step by step, she descended the stairs.   She was lost, she knew it.   She accepted the fact, she wanted to be lost.   She descended the stairs.

The man standing below saw her coming.   She was coming down to him ; yes, it was the beautiful and beloved walk of Berenice that was carrying her to him.   He rushed forward and ran up the stairs ; he was radiant.   His face was young like that of a happy boy on whom all the gods have showered their blessings.   He outstretched his arm towards her in the Roman fashion, and rushed up the stairs shouting : " Berenice ! "

That night he remained in the small forlorn house. Next day he rode happily back to Jerusalem.   He happened to meet Joseph.   " Didn't you want seventy-seven prisoners, my dear Joseph ? " he asked.   " Take them."

32

WITH the tablet containing Titus's authorisation in his belt Joseph betook himself to the women's hall of the

Temple, which had been turned into a depot for prisoners of war. All these last days he had been dejected by the thought of having squandered so cheaply his power to save life. Now his hopeless and torturing search began anew.

Fronto, the Roman officer, was still in charge of the prisoners. For his services in Caesarea he had been promoted to a higher rank. He personally conducted Joseph through the place. He could not stand Jews, but he knew that this Josephus had been instructed to write a book on the war, and in that book he wanted to cut a good figure. He explained to Joseph the difficulties of administering a depot of such enormous size. The market for slaves was experiencing a hopeless slump. How was one even to feed the lot of them until one could find buyers? His dear charges were going to pot; they were nothing but skin and bone, and many of them were diseased. Eleven thousand had died on his hands that very week. But many had only themselves to blame. The Roman legionaries were good-humoured fellows and liked a joke, and often they offered the prisoners a share of their pork. But was it to be believed? These fellows preferred to say their last prayers rather than eat such stuff.

Prisoners who had borne arms he had not taken the trouble to feed at all, of course; he had had them immediately executed. As for the others, he had tried to hunt out relatives who might at least pay ransom money for them. Those that were not ransomed he hoped to get rid of in the course of the next six months by means of a few public auctions on a large scale. Prisoners without market value, elderly or feeble men, elderly women without any particular capability, he had set aside as material for lion fights and gladiatorial shows.

Slow footed and monosyllabic, Joseph walked along

beside the garrulous Fronto. The prisoners wore tablets containing their names and capabilities ; packed close together they squatted and lay about in the heat and stench ; they had seen death before their eyes for weeks ; they had drunk hope and despair so completely that they felt empty and apathetic.

The hall through which Joseph and Fronto were walking now contained the slaves reserved for lion fights and gladiatorial shows.

" Doctor Joseph," someone cried in a wretched voice that yet had a glad ring ; it came from an old fellow with a grey bristly face and in filthy rags. Joseph searched his memory but could not recognise the man. " I'm the glass-blower Alexas," said the man. What ! this fellow claimed that he was the worldly-wise merchant ? This was the stately, well-fed Alexas, who was the same age as Joseph himself ? " The last time I met you was at the fair in Caesarea, Doctor Joseph," the man reminded him. " I told you that anyone who stuck up for reason would have to suffer for it." Yes, Joseph remembered. This Alexas, cold and calculating as he was, had been the only one among the Jews then that had stood by him. Now he was sitting here waiting for the day when he would be led out into the arena to be devoured by wild beasts. " I'm certain this man was never mixed up with the rebels," said Joseph, turning to Fronto. " The interrogation commission have handed him over to me," replied Fronto, shrugging his shoulders. " Roman justice is not bad in its way." Alexas put in humbly, with a faint smile, " but for the time being it's being employed perhaps a little summarily." " This fellow isn't a bad sort," Fronto laughed, " but where would we be if we began to revise all our decisions ? And it's against my instructions. ' Better a violation of justice than

one of law and order.' That was what the commander
said to me when he put the depot under my charge." " Don't
worry about me, Doctor Joseph," said Alexas in a
resigned voice. " I'm so overwhelmed with misfortune
that no one's goodwill can do anything for me." " I ask
for the life of this man," said Joseph, showing his tablet.
" As you wish," said Fronto courteously. " Now you are
still six items to the good," he added, and made a note on
the tablet.

Joseph ordered the glass-blower Alexas to be taken to
his tent. He looked tenderly after the enfeebled and grief-
stricken man. Alexas told how when the Romans broke
into the city he had carried his father down into an underground passage in the hope of saving them both. Old
Nachum had resisted. If he were to die in his son's house
there would remain a faint hope that someone might find
him and bury him. But if he were to die down there in
the underworld he would remain unburied, denied the
covering of the good earth, and would not be able to give
his name on the resurrection day. Finally Alexas had
managed by persuasion and force to get him down into an
underground passage, but their torch had presently gone
out and they had lost each other. After a while he himself
had been discovered by two soldiers. They had tickled
him with their swords, and he had shown them some of his
hiding places. As he gave them to believe that he had
still more of these, they had kept him to themselves for a
while instead of delivering him at the depot. They were
droll circumstantial fellows, and besides one could treat
with two soldiers, and there was no treating with the depot
or the Roman army. They forced him to tell them funny
stories. If the stories did not please them they bound him
face downwards by his hands and feet to the branch of a

tree and swung him to and fro. That had been unpleasant. But usually his stories amused them. No, the two soldiers weren't so bad as they might have been, and he had got on tolerably well with them. They had gone about with him like this for over a week, making him go through his tricks and tell his stories for the benefit of their comrades. They and the other men had been greatly amused by his Jewish Latin. Finally they had decided that he would do excellently as a door-keeper, and had resolved to keep him by them until they could buy him and employ him for that purpose. The idea had suited him very well. It was better to be a door-keeper than to end one's life in some Egyptian mine or Syrian arena. But then his two masters had descended for a second time into the underworld and had never returned again, and their comrades had handed him over to the depot.

" All these things happened to me," Alexas said meditatively, " because I didn't follow my reason. If I'd fled from Jerusalem at the right time I would at least have had my wife and children still, but I wanted to have everything ; I wanted to have my father and brother as well. I have over-reached myself." He begged Joseph to accept a myrrhine vase as a present. Yes, that sharp fellow Alexas had still something in reserve. He had saved a great deal, he said bitterly ; only he had not been able to save what mattered most. His father Nachum, where was he now ? His wife Channa, his children, his charming, violent, foolish brother Ephraim, where were they ? As for himself, what he had suffered was beyond the endurance of one human being. He would go on making glasses and other beautiful things. But God was not gracious to him, and he would never dare to bring another child into this world.

Next day Joseph walked again through the prisoners' depot. He had now the fates of only six human beings in his hands, and he was resolved not to dispose of them until he had found the one face he was looking for. But how was he to find this one among the multitudes of dead and wounded and prisoners ? It was like looking for a fish in the sea.

When Joseph returned on the third day Fronto began to chaff him. He was charmed, he said ; Joseph showed more interest in his goods than any slave dealer did. Joseph refused to be ruffled. He searched during all that day. In vain.

Late that evening he learnt that as the result of a foray into the underworld eight hundred prisoners had been brought in and that Fronto intended to have them crucified at once. Joseph had already lain down in his tent ; he was utterly exhausted. Nevertheless he got up again.

It was the middle of the night when he reached the Mount of Olives, where the executions were taking place. The hill was studded thickly with crosses, many hundreds of them. Where the olive terraces had been, and the fine shop of the brothers Chanan, and the villas of aristocratic families, crosses now rose everywhere. Naked, with the marks of their whippings still on them, men hung in contorted postures on the crosses, their heads on their shoulders, their jaws fallen, their eyes leaden. Joseph and his escort raised their torches to light up the faces of the crucified ; they were all horribly disfigured with pain. When the light fell on their faces these men on the crosses began to speak. Some of them cursed, but the most of them stammered : " Hear, Israel." Joseph was on the point of falling with weariness. He was tempted, when he came to each of the crosses, to say : " Take him down ! Take him down ! " without counting the cost, so that he might bring his horrible search to an end. The little tablet that gave him the power of life and death grew heavier and heavier. If he could only get away from this place, if he could only go to sleep ! He longed to reach the seventy-seventh man and rid himself of the tablet. To be in his tent again, fling himself down and sleep.

And then he found the man that he sought. The man's yellow face was covered with a stubbly unkempt beard. But his face was no longer yellow ; it was a leaden grey, and a horrible furred tongue hung out of his gaping mouth. " Take him down ! " said Joseph ; he said it very softly ; it was an infinite labour to get the words out ; they seemed to choke him and he swallowed painfully. The executioner hesitated. He would have to summon his superior officer Fronto first. The delay was a torment to Joseph. He was afraid that the man up there would die while he was waiting below. That must not happen. The great reckoning between Justus and him was not yet ended. Justus must not die until then.

At last Fronto arrived, sleepy and ill-tempered ; he had had a tiring day. Nevertheless he listened to Joseph as courteously as ever and immediately gave orders to take the man down and give him into Joseph's care. " Now you're still five items to the good," he said, making a note on the tablet. " Take them down ! Take them down ! " Joseph cried, pointing to the next five men. " Now you've none left," said Fronto.

Justus had been nailed to the cross ; that was the milder form of crucifixion, but it proved to be very painful now that the crucified man was being released. He had been hanging for five hours ; that was not very long for a strong man ; but Justus was not strong. Joseph sent for physicians. The pain brought Justus to consciousness, then he fainted, then the pain once awakened him. The doctors arrived. It was a prophet of the Jews that they had to save, they had been told, and he had been taken down from the cross at Titus's instructions. Things of that kind did not often happen ; so the best doctors in the camp set off to look into it. Joseph pressed them for their opinion. They replied somewhat hesitatingly. They could not say for three days still whether the man would recover or not.

Joseph walked by the side of the litter in which Justus was being carried to the camp. Justus had not recognised him. Joseph was very tired, but he was filled with peace, and in his heart rose the words of the hymn of thanks which is sung when someone is rescued from a great peril. Sleep would not have refreshed him, food would not have given him any pleasure, nor books knowledge, nor success content-ment, if this Justus had been dead or had remained lost to him. He would have found no happiness in love ; he would have written his book without any sense of satis-faction. But now he had found this man to measure him-self against ; the only man who was his equal. " Your Doctor Joseph is a scoundrel." To listen to words like that was a very different matter from saying them ; the man should have thought of that. Joseph was filled with a sense of lightness, of peace and fulfilment. He slept long and deeply, almost till midday.

He went to the tent where Justus was lying. The doctors still maintained their silence. Joseph never left the tent. All day Justus lay unconscious. On the second day he began to rave ; he looked dreadful. The doctors shrugged their shoulders and no longer expected him to recover. Joseph sat in the tent. He neither ate nor changed his clothes, and a stubbly beard grew on his face. He pleaded with Jehovah ; why had He spared him through so many perilous vicissitudes, if He was to refuse him his great hour of reckoning with Justus ? Titus sent for him. Berenice sent for him, asking him to go to Thekoa. Joseph paid no heed. He sat in Justus's tent, stared at the sick man, and went over all the conversations he had had with him. The great discourse was not ended yet. Justus must not die.

On the fourth day the doctors amputated the man's left arm at the elbow. On the eighth they announced that he would live.

33

Now that he knew Justus was out of danger Joseph forsook the sick man's tent, leaving a supply of money for him, and troubled himself no longer about the man's fate. Much as he wanted his revenge, he had no desire to parade himself as the saviour of Justus's life. The great discourse with Justus would one day be taken up again, and that was enough.

About this time Titus begged Joseph to do him a service. Titus was elated by his success at Thekoa ; but he still felt uncertain in everything concerning the Jewish woman. He could not dare to take any further risks. What was to happen when he left the country ? He asked Joseph to sound Berenice and find out whether she would go with him to Rome.

In the forlorn house at Thekoa Joseph and Berenice now faced each other, one as empty as the other. As for her, had not her whole life, not to speak of her throwing herself away on the Roman, possessed a meaning only as an attempt to save the Temple ? The Temple was gone ; now the two of them were homeless. But they were both of the same metal, and they were not ashamed to show their

nakedness to each other.   Nakedly and coldly they regarded
their destitution.   Bereft of their nation, they would now
have to fashion with their own wills a new world to live in.
He had his book and his ambition ; she had Titus and her
ambition.   The future of both of them lay in Rome.

Yes, certainly she would go to Rome.

Berenice's assent reassured and elated Titus immensely.
He felt he must show Joseph some mark of gratitude.
" Don't you own some properties in the new town, Joseph ? "
he asked.   " And you must have inherited some landed
property from your father, too.   I am reserving all the
ground properties in Jerusalem for the legions that I intend
to leave behind as a garrison.   Give me an exact account of
what you lose by that arrangement.   I will give you in
exchange property to the same value from the other confiscated areas in the country."   Joseph was elated by this
present.   In a cold and matter-of-fact business spirit he
reckoned up the value of his properties in Judaea.   He
wanted everything to be definitely settled before he left
the country.

Titus rased Jerusalem completely to the ground, as in
earlier times victorious generals had done with the cities
of Carthage and Corinth.   Only the Phasael Tower, the
Mariamne Tower and the Hippicus Tower, as well as part
of the western wall, were allowed to remain standing as a
memorial showing how splendid and strong had been the
city that had had to bow to his star.

34

ON the 25th of October, to celebrate the birthday of his
brother Domitian, the ne'er-do-well, Titus held a great
spectacle in the arena of Caesarea, for which he employed
human material in unexampled profusion from the copious

supply of Jewish prisoners at his disposal. " Come and see ! " he said to Joseph.   Joseph went.

After the two thousand five hundred participants had marched through the arena, two troops of Jews were ordered to represent the storming of a city wall, the one troop as defenders, the other as attackers.   The wretched bearded actors slashed away at one another and leapt grotesquely into the air when they received the reluctant death thrust. The timid were driven into battle with whips and red hot bars.   Against those who simply could not be brought to the point of fighting accomplished gladiators were sent out. Theatre attendants in the masks of the god of the underworld took the fallen in charge and with pieces of burning wood experimented to see whether they were dead or only simulating death.   The arena was filled with shrieks : "Hear, Israel, Jehovah is the only God."   Many of the contestants died too insipidly for the taste of the spectators.   There were shouts of " Make a beginning ; don't stand about doing nothing.   You're only tickling with your swords, not fighting.   Go on, you with the beard, go on, old fellow ! Put a little more fire into it, if you please !   Die with a little more style, you rascals ! "   Joseph listened to the shouts. Well, these people sitting here knew that the Jews had died bravely in their fight against Rome, and now they were disappointed because the Jews were not pretending to die bravely.

It was not easy to banish monotony for long.   African lions, Indian elephants and German bisons were sent out against the prisoners.   Some of the doomed Jews had been dressed in festive raiment, and some in white praying vestments with black borders and blue tassels, and it was great sport to see how quickly these vestments were stained red. Many Jews, too, both men and women, were driven naked into the arena, so that the spectators might contemplate the play of their muscles during their dying struggles. A small number of powerful well-armed men were confronted with an elephant. The desperate band managed to wound the beast gravely, before, trumpeting with rage, it trampled them to death ; and the spectators felt sorry for the elephant.

The arrangers of the spectacle had a sense of humour. Many victims had to die in ridiculous masks. A number of old men had been shaven on one side of the head, while on the other side their long hair and their long white beards had been left untouched. Others had to run a race clothed in inflammable robes ; their clothes were set on fire by the wind of their movement, but two hundred yards away was a water tank, and if they reached it it was just possible for them to save their lives. It was screamingly funny to see them desperately flinging out their legs, panting in their haste, and plunging into the water even when they could not swim. Great amusement was caused also by a ladder that had been set up against a wall which had to be scaled. The doomed men, dressed up in tawdry finery, were forced to climb it, but the ladder had been smeared with grease, and they fell on the points of upright spears.

For two days the Jews died in such ways to the number of two thousand five hundred in the arena of Caesarea for the delectation of the uncircumcised. For two days Joseph saw and heard them dying. Often he fancied he could recognise faces he knew, but he must have been mistaken, for Fronto had chosen for the spectacle humble and unknown poeple, small peasants and workmen from the provinces. I have seen it, Joseph could add when later he described the spectacle. Mine eyes have seen it.

Things were now so far advanced that Joseph would soon be leaving Judaea, probably for ever. He considered for several weeks whether he should go and see Mara. He decided not to go. He allowed her an ample income and gave her instructions to live on an estate in the plain of Jezreel that Titus had given him.

The Jews had seen Joseph going to the spectacle. They now hated and despised him more than ever, and wherever he appeared kept a distance of seven paces. Nobody accompanied him to the ship that was to take him to Italy.

The harbour of Caesarea sank below the horizon ; then the colossal statues of the goddess of Rome and the Emperor Augustus. Then Fort Strathon disappeared, then the violet mountains of Judaea, and finally the green summit of Mount Carmel. Joseph was on his way to Rome. From Judaea he took with him nothing but the memory of what he had seen, seventy rolls of the Holy Scripture, and a little chest containing earth that he had scratched from beneath the debris of Jerusalem.

35

AT the top of the Appian Way, beside the monument to Cecilia Metella, the driver made the usual halt, and Joseph looked down on the great panorama of the city that opened out before him. It was a cool March day, the city lay clear in the bright sunshine, Rome, power, Gevurah ; it seemed still more powerful than it had been when he left it to go to Jerusalem. Now he had only to stretch out his hand to achieve what he had dreamt of then, on that day when he had gazed down at the city for the first time from the Capitol. The Emperor and Titus were waiting for his words, his words that would reveal the spirit of the East.

Joseph bitterly compressed his lips. The great doctor Jochanan Ben Sakkai had unfortunately been right. What had once seemed to him accomplished was only beginning.

The smelting together of eastern wisdom and western technique was a matter involving hard labour and little glory.

The carriage had gone on : it stopped at a gate. Joseph had not announced his arrival to Dorion. He loved Dorion, he had not forgotten her image as she stood with the cat in her arms the first time he had seen her ; nor had he forgotten her thin little girl's voice, nor the way in which she nestled close to him, nor her savage devotion. But by now there were so many faces between him and her, scenes from which she was shut out. He would wait, he would not awaken any hopes in her, he would see for himself and divine whether the old feelings between them still existed.

Dorion's house was small, stylish and modern. The doorkeeper, a slave, asked Joseph what his business was. Joseph gave his name, the doorkeeper bowed profoundly and disappeared. Joseph stood alone in the reception hall ; his face became overcast. The place was cluttered with pictures, statues and mosaics, all probably by that man Fabullus. What was he doing here ? He could not live here.

And then Dorion entered. Her long, thin head, her face with the great mouth rose from her straight, childish neck the same as ever. She stood and gazed at him with her sea-green eyes, which he could see visibly growing darker. She might well smile. She had waited for him so long, and now, thanks to all the gods, he was there. She had feared that that dreadful Judaea would swallow him up for ever, and now, thanks to all the gods, he had come. She slowly grew pale, until her pallor spread over all her face ; she stared at him and then stepped up to him, gave a tiny, shrill cry, and fell into his arms so that he had to support her. This was the golden brown girl that he

loved.   Her skin was sweet and smooth, but oh, how cold
it was, and that was because she loved him.

Minutes went past, and neither of them had yet uttered a
word.   All the sweetness of the world was in her, and he
loved her.   His knees had become weak when she fell into
his arms, deathly pale, fainting with agitation.   You
shouldn't have anything to do with him, Dorion.   He can
think only of his book, the waste landscape and the ravine
filled with corpses, the Temple mount fiercely glowing from
its root to its summit.   What was the meaning of these
silly mosaics round him, these stupid idyllic pictures of
peaceful houshold scenes ?   What was he doing here ?
What did the woman want ?

He felt like a stranger.

"You feel like a stranger here," she said ; it was the
first words that she had spoken to him for a year.   She
held him by the shoulders, her arms outstretched, and gazed
into his face.   She said : "You're like a stranger here."
She stated it as a fact, gravely, without accusing him.   She
loved him ; that was how she knew.

Petty comforts, petty lies, were no use here.   "Yes,"
he replied.   "I can't live here.   I can't live with you now,
Dorion."

Dorion did not utter a single word.   She felt that this
was no longer her Joseph, but another whose mind was
filled with pictures that she could not see.   But she belonged
to him even though he had changed ; she was stubborn and
brave ; she would win him over in spite of this new mask
he had taken on.   She let go his shoulders.   "If you want
me at any time send for me," she said.

Joseph went.   He felt very strange in Rome.   He made
his way through the streets and colonnades.   When he
saw faces that he knew he turned his head away ; he did

not want to speak to anybody. After some hesitation he summoned his resolution and called on Claudius Reginus.

The publisher looked tired ; his fleshy face was haggard. "Hail to him who comes," he grinned. "Well, my prophet, how is your book getting on ? Your prophecy has been fulfilled, though it must be admitted in a rather queer way. I fancy you can set about your work now. Or are you thinking of shirking it ? " "I haven't shirked anything," said Joseph bitterly. "You don't know how hard it was sometimes. But I haven't shirked it."

"I've met your wife once or twice, the beautiful Egyptian lady," said the publisher. "I don't intend to live with Dorion," said Joseph, "as long as I'm writing my book." Reginus looked up. "That's interesting," he said. "Yet in actual fact the lady was the cause of your book." "One of the causes perhaps," said Joseph reluctantly.

"If you want to stay with me, my house is at your disposal," said the publisher. Joseph hesitated. "I want to be alone," he said, "while I'm writing my book." "I fancy," said Claudius Reginus, "that the Emperor would let you have the house he used to live in. The house is a little bare, His Majesty was always somewhat stingy, as you know."

Joseph took the house. It was huge, dark and forlorn. He lived there with a single slave to attend to his wants. He took little care for himself, and ate only what he needed to keep him alive. He told nobody that he was in Rome. He wandered through the streets when he thought they would be empty, and looked at the preparations for the triumphal procession, of which the whole city was full. Already labourers were putting up platforms and tribunes. On the city walls and over the gates appeared huge portraits of Vespasian and Titus with inscriptions round them lauding the Imperators and taunting conquered Judaea. Huge and monstrous, the faces of the Emperor and Titus stared out at Joseph, empty, gross and distorted ; all that he had liked in them was gone ; these faces were like the face of Pedanus.

One day in the colonnades of the Campus Martius Joseph saw the litter of Marullus. He tried to slip by quickly, but the senator had caught sight of him. " You've made a career for yourself, young man," he said. " You have changed a lot. Yes, destiny changes our faces," he regarded Joseph through his jade lorgnette. " Do you remember the information about Rome I gave you that day in the Circus Maximus ? That was five years ago. I saw even then that it was worth while telling you things. You chose the right side at the right moment."

He refused to let Joseph go, took him into the litter, and began to talk. He was writing a farce that was to be produced in the Marcellus Theatre at the beginning of the triumphal week. The hero of the farce was to be the Jew Zachariah, a prisoner condemned to take part in the triumphal games ; the actor Demetrius Libanus was to play the part. Zachariah was to die in single combat with another man. The mortal fear of the Jew, his beseeching prayers, his confident expectation that in spite of everything he would be pardoned, his attempts at fighting and his refusals to fight ; all these would give an opportunity for a great many comic scenes, witticisms, dances, and satirical couplets. The only question was how the piece was to end. It was tempting, the idea of seeking out a double for Libanus— there was abundant choice now—a man so like Libanus that his own mother would not know the difference, and having him done to death by a professional gladiator. On the other hand the public was more than satiated at the

moment with crucifixions and dead Jews. Perhaps the
best thing would be to let Zachariah be pardoned after all ;
his joy at being granted his life would be a theme full of
possibilities, and at the end, driven by gratitude, he might
be made to bring out his hidden hoard of money and fling
it among the audience. Or perhaps one could manage
things so as to get him hung on the cross, and at the last
moment someone might come and take him down. "Didn't
you do something like that yourself, Flavius Josephus?"
And then he could fling his money down among the audience
from the cross, new minted coins celebrating the victory.

Joseph had to remain all that evening with Marullus.
The lean, clever senator was interested in various recondite
details of the campaign, and he questioned Joseph pretty
exhaustively. Also he was able to give Joseph some news.
It was now decided that of the three Jewish representatives
who were to be lead in the procession only Simon Bar Giora
was to be executed, as was customary, during the triumph.
The other two, John of Gishala and the High Priest
Phanias, were afterwards to be sold as slaves. There were
three bidders : Mucianus, the minister Talassos, and
himself. He had reason to believe that his chances were
good. Dame Caenis was a keen bargainer, but he would
not haggle over the price. Which of the two did Joseph
advise him to buy, the general or the High Priest?

Next day Joseph summoned his courage and sought out
Demetrius Libanus. He found him surprisingly aged and
irritable. "Oh, you're there!" he said to Joseph. "Of
course you were bound to come. Really I've been expecting you for a long time." He treated Joseph with an
irony filled with hatred. Slowly Joseph began to understand ; this man took to himself the blame for the destruction
of the Temple. He had taken Joseph to see Poppaea ;

it was he who had really got the three men pardoned ; and had not all these misfortunes begun with the pardoning of the three men ?　The amnesty, the edict of Caesarea, the revolt, the burning of the Temple to ashes ; all these were links in one chain.　And he himself was the first link. On him had depended the answer to the question : Would he play the Jew Apella or not ?　Jehovah had put in his hand the lots that were to decide whether his country was to live or perish, and his unlucky hand had produced the lot inscribed with the decree of destruction.

He got up.　He began to recite the tremendous curses in the fifth book of Moses.　He had certainly neither seen nor heard any of the prophets, both true and false, who had arisen in Jerusalem during the past decade ; but his gestures were the gestures of those prophets, and his voice sounded like theirs though he spoke in Greek.　The actor was not a dignified man, he was small of growth, but now he was like a tall, dark tree.　" In the morning thou shalt say, Would God it were even !　And at even thou shalt say, Would God it were morning !　For the fear of thine heart wherewith thou shalt fear."　The gloomy imprecations came with dreadful force from his lips, monotonous, heart-oppressing. " And so it has come," he would sometimes say matter-of-factly, but with savage and despairing satisfaction, in the middle of his curses.

After his meeting with Demetrius Libanus Joseph remained for two days alone in his great dark house.　On the third day he went across the Emilius Bridge to the other side of the Tiber, where the Jews lived.

As long as the war lasted the Jews of Rome had shown their loyalty in every way to the Roman government.　Even now they were loyal subjects, and held that the rebels themselves bore the guilt ; yet in spite of this they could not

refrain from openly showing their grief at the destruction
of their holy place.   Nor did they conceal their disgust at
the fact that Jews had assisted in its destruction.   As soon
as Joseph set foot on the right bank of the Tiber he could
feel a monstrous hatred meeting him in the face.   Everybody kept a distance of seven paces from him.   He walked
in an empty space which was walled in every side with
loathing.

He made his way towards the house of Caius Barzaarone.
The president of the Agrippine Ward, who had once been
eager to give him his daughter in marriage, confronted him
now and maintained the distance of seven paces.   The
man's sly, jolly face was darkened and distorted with hostility.
Caius Barzaarone now looked very like his father, the aged,
mumbling Aaron.   Joseph gazed at the man's stony face,
and all the courage oozed out of him.   " Forgive me," he
said, spreading his hands helplessly.   " It's no use."   He
turned back.   Through two rows of deadly enemies he
left the Jewish quarter and returned across the Emilius
Bridge.

When he was on the other bank and had turned a corner
where the Jews could no longer see him, he heard behind
him the steps of someone following him ;   he fancied that
he had heard it for some time.   He involuntarily laid his
hand on his heavy golden writing apparatus, meaning to
defend himself.   Then a voice behind him cried in Aramaic :
" Don't be afraid, it's me."   A quite young man stood in
front of him, his face seemed familiar.   " I used to know
you," said the youth, " on your first visit to Rome."   " Of
course, you're——? " Joseph said, searching his memory.
" I'm Cornelius, the son of Caius Barzaarone."   " What
do you want ? " asked Joseph.   " Why don't you keep your
distance of seven paces ? "   But young Cornelius came

nearer. "Forgive the others," he said imploringly, and his
voice sounded warm, trustful and bold. "The others don't
understand you, but I understand you. Please believe
what I say." He went up close to Joseph and gazed up at
him. "I've read your psalm. Often, when everything is
dark and I can't see my way, I repeat it to myself. Everything here is narrow and closed within stone walls; but
you have seen wide spaces. You're a great man in Israel,
Flavius Josephus; you're one of our prophets." A warm
stream of comfort ran to Joseph's heart. It was a great
tribute that this young man, who knew nothing about him
except the words he had written, should come to his support.
"I'm very grateful, Cornelius," he said, "I'm very grateful
for your words. I've brought earth with me from the
ruins of Jerusalem, I've brought the Scripture rolls with me
too; let me show you them. Come with me, Cornelius."
The youth was radiant.

36

MEANWHILE Titus had reached Italy. Many obstacles
had risen to keep him in the East after the fall of Jerusalem.
In the name of the fifth and fifteenth legions, which he had
ordered to remain behind in unpopular quarters on the lower
Danube, Pedanus had begged him to stay with them or
else take them to Rome with him. The commander had
immediately seized what was behind the naive cunning of
the blunt old soldier; namely an offer to appoint him
emperor in place of his father. The idea had tempted him,
but it was a very risky one, and he had not hesitated to
decline it in equally naive and jocular terms. But the
Orient had continued to feast him like an emperor, and
Titus had been unable to resist the temptation of having
the diadem of Egypt set on his brow in Memphis at the

consecration of the bull of Apis. That had been imprudent, it might have been misconstrued, and Titus had hastened to assure his father by letter that of course he had acted merely as the Emperor's deputy. Naturally he had taken it to mean that, Vespasian had replied by return ; nevertheless, in spite of his affection for his son, he had ten thousand men in readiness to march against the East.

So thereupon Titus, almost unattended, made post haste for Italy. If he wished to have his triumph ancient custom decreed that he should not set foot in Rome until the day that the procession entered it. So Vespasian went out to meet his son on the Appian Way. "Here I am, father, here I am," Titus loyally greeted him. "It wouldn't have been very good for you either, my lad," growled Vespasian, "if you had played about in the East much longer." And only then did he give Titus the kiss of greeting.

Immediately after they had eaten, the necessary explanation came between father and son in the presence of Mucianus and Dame Caenis. "You haven't given your father complete satisfaction, Titus," Caenis began resolutely. "Certain rumours reached us of your being crowned at the consecration of the bull of Apis, and they didn't give us unmixed joy." "I don't want to make an elephant out of a bull," said Vespasian good-humouredly. "It's another question that interests us more at the moment. Was it really impossible to save the Jewish Temple ? "

Father and son regarded each other with hard, keen eyes. "Do you wish it had been possible ? " Titus asked after a pause.

Vespasian nodded reflectively. "If this punitive expedition against Jerusalem," he said craftily, "had really to be worked up into a war, and had to end with a triumphal procession, which I will get the Senate to grant to the two of us—then perhaps it may have been impossible after all."

Titus got red in the face. " It was impossible," he said curtly.

" Let us accept that as a fact," the Emperor agreed with a grin. " It was impossible. Otherwise you would have spared the building for the sake of Dame Berenice if for nobody else's. And that brings me to the second point that concerns us all here. Dame Berenice is a lady who can't be left out of account. I can understand quite well your wanting to have her beside you during that long and boring punitive expedition. But must you have her beside you in Rome too ? " Titus made to speak. Breathing hard, his stern grey eyes fixed on Titus, Vespasian waved him aside. " Now look here," he went on as man to man, in the voice of a kindly adviser, " my friend Caenis is a simple woman—isn't it so, old girl ?—without any great claims on one, without any great title. She brought me a tidy sum of money ; and her eyes can see lots of things that my old eyes are too dim to see. All the same all Rome likes her, seeing that it hasn't to pay any subsidy to her. She's a Roman. But this Jewess of yours, this princess, is bound to attract attention because of her famous walk and all her eastern pother ; we're still a young dynasty, my son, I'm the first, and you're the second, and we can't afford this extravagant lady. I tell you this for your good, but in deadly seriousness. A Nero might have carried it off, a man of old stock. But if we were to do it the Romans would be annoyed. It'll annoy them, my lad. Tell him, Caenis, tell him, Mucianus. Will it annoy them, or won't it ? There, you can see for yourself, it will annoy them."

" I want to tell you something, father," Titus began,

and his voice rang out as sharply as when he gave his commands. " I could have had myself crowned in Alexandria. The legions wanted it, and I very nearly accepted. The Princess had only to say the word, and I would have done it. But the Princess didn't say the word."

Vespasian got up. Titus had been told that his father had aged greatly ; but that had all been talk ; now, at any rate, the old Sabine peasant seemed as vigorous as ever. He went up quite close to his son ; they faced each other, two savage powerful beasts prepared to spring. His face twitching violently, an agitated smile on his hard, thin lips, Mucianus looked on intently ; Caenis made to fling herself between the two of them. But the father regained his self-control. " What you've just told me," he said, " is very interesting. But in any case you're not in Alexandria now, and here in Rome you'll hardly entertain the idea of deposing me, even if your amiable friend should desire it. Well, then." He sat down, groaning softly, rubbed his gouty arm and continued. " You can't treat her like a little girl. This lady will want to be seen in public ; and she's quite right, she's a princess of a far older house than ours. But the Romans won't let you have this woman, believe me. Do you want to have jokes made at your expense in the theatre ? Do you want people to sing sarcastic verses about you and your lady during the triumph ? Or do you think you can prevent them ? Be reasonable, my boy. It won't do."

Titus sullenly nursed his anger. " You've never been able to stand me from the very start."

" True," said his father. " Nor you me. If you had your will we wouldn't be sitting here now. There's lots of very biting things that I could say. But I won't say them. You're in love with this woman. I have nothing against her. But I won't have her in Rome. Make her see that. It was a piece of madness to bring her here with you. She can do whatever she pleases otherwise, but she must disappear from Italy. Tell her that."

" I shan't do anything of the kind," declared Titus. · " I intend to keep this woman."

Vespasian gazed at his son ; in Titus's eyes was that dancing half-mad look which had once daunted the Emperor in the eyes of the mother, Domitilla. He laid his hands on his son's shoulder. " You're thirty now, my son," he said warningly. " Don't behave like a child."

" May I make a suggestion ? " Mucianus interposed smoothly. He advanced, holding his stick behind his back. Titus gazed mistrustfully at the man's lips. This fellow Mucianus, who pretended to be so shaky on his legs, evidently played the role of an infirm old man simply to provide a foil to Vespasian's vigorous health, and the Emperor was obviously flattered, even though he saw through the man quite well. " The relations between Caesar Titus and the Princess," Mucianus began, " are a source of annoyance. In saying that no doubt your Majesty is quite right. But that is simply because the Princess belongs to a rebellious race. We here know that she can be counted among our loyal Jewish subjects. But in their jokes the Roman populace made no distinction between one Jew and another. We must bring the Princess to the point of declaring herself clearly and unmistakably for us. I fancy it would be quite enough if she showed herself in the Imperial box during the triumphal procession."

They all considered the implications of this proposal. Vespasian decided that his adroit friend had manœuvred the Jewess into a position from which she would find it difficult to escape. His good son could hardly refuse

Mucianus's demand. What would Berenice do ? If she consented to be present at this triumph over her own people she would become contemptible in the eyes of the Romans. It would be impossible after that for Titus to think of making her his wife. Caenis, too, saw this at once. " If a woman loves a man," she said resolutely and flatly in support of Mucianus, " then she must have the pluck to stand by him."

In tense anxiety they all waited for Titus to speak. There was nothing he could advance against the argument of Dame Caenis. At bottom she was right, he thought. When he celebrated his triumph he had a right to expect that his mistress, whom he intended one day to make his wife, should be present. To put this to her would not be a pleasant business. But pleasanter, all the same, than to send her away. He growled something to the effect that one couldn't expect the Princess to do such a thing. The others declared that in that case the Romans couldn't be expected to stomach the Princess. He reflected despairingly ; she had those eastern notions of hers, those voices that she had heard in the wilderness. On the other hand she was a realist in her way of looking at things. After half an hour of confused discussion Titus agreed that either the Princess would be present in the Imperial box during the triumphal procession, or else she must leave Italy.

He asked Berenice to come and see him. He felt confident that he would settle the whole matter in five minutes. Standing in the reception hall waiting for her arrival, he decided once more to treat the whole matter lightly, as if it were the obvious thing for her to do.

Then Berenice appeared. She looked cheerful and yet grave ; she kept her beautiful keen face bowed in an expectant attitude, her deep voice answered his greeting, and all at once his plan seemed impossible. He plucked up his courage ; he must not prepare her for the shock ; he must spring it upon her. He felt like a man taking a deep breath before summoning the resolution to plunge into ice cold water. "The triumphal procession," he said, and his voice was tolerably clear, he didn't even have to clear his throat, "the triumphal procession will take place in ten days now. I'll see you in the Imperial box, won't I, Berenice ? " Really it had gone off quite smoothly, except that he had gazed into space while he spoke, without glancing at her. Nor did he look at her now that he had finished.

Berenice's face grew white. It was a good thing that she was seated ; otherwise she would have fallen. This man had cut down the grove of Thekoa ; then he had taken her by violence; then he had allowed the Temple to be burned to the ground. And she, she had never said no, always yes. She had swallowed every insult because she had been unable to tear herself away from this man, from his broad peasant face, his brutality, his childish cruel whims. She had breathed the smell of blood, the smell of burning ; she had renounced her days in the wilderness and the voice of her God. And now this man invited her to stand in the Imperial box and witness his triumph over Jehovah. Really he was acting quite logically, and for the Romans it would no doubt be a piquant adjunct to this triumph if she, a Maccabaean princess, were to look on. But she would not. It would be endurable to be led in the triumphal procession in fetters, as a prisoner. But to sit of one's own free will in the victor's box, and provide the sauce to his banquet, no. " I thank you," she said, and her voice was not loud, but it was very hoarse. " I shan't be in Rome on the day of the triumphal procession. I intend to go to my brother."

He looked up and saw that he had struck this woman to the heart.

He had not intended to do so ; he had not intended any of the wrongs he had done her. Every time he had been forced to act as he had acted. Just as now. His father had forced him on, and he had not been able to resist. Yet these other people were flabby and unstable, and he himself was strong ; but he never recognised that until it was too late. How could he have expected her to look on at this brutal triumph ? He would renounce his procession ; he would report that he was sick. He stammered a few hasty excuses. But he spoke to the empty air ; she was not there, she was gone.

His face twisted into a look of mad savagery. From his mouth poured obscene curses against the woman. Her simpering oriental affectation. Why couldn't she look on at the procession ? Hadn't other people, German princes, for instance, looked on at triumphs in which their own sons, brothers and grandsons were led in chains ? He shouldn't have let himself be bluffed ; he should have played the master. It would have been quite easy to accuse her of disloyalty, of some rebellious act, and declare her his prisoner, and lead her in the procession in chains, and then, when she was completely humbled, to raise her out of her shame with a mild, strong, benevolent hand, a man's hand. Then at last she would know her place, the haughty creature.

But while he was thinking all this he knew that it was only a puerile fantasy. For she was no barbarian ; she was not like that German tribal prince Segestus, she was a real princess, and in her veins was the ancient Eastern nobility and wisdom. All his rage turned against himself. Rome and his triumph were spoilt for him. One could really live only in the East ; here everything was stale and flat ; the Capitol was a wretched affair compared with the Temple of Jehovah. And he, idiot that he was, had burned that Temple and thrice driven from him this woman by his Roman brutality, and this time for ever.

37

NEXT day Joseph appeared to pay his respects to Titus. Titus was in the glitteringly genial mood that Joseph hated. This triumph, he said jokingly, was causing more work than the whole campaign. He would like to have it behind him ; he wanted to get back into his native city again, but, thanks to the stupid old custom, he had to wait until the day of the procession. Wasn't it a nuisance ? He couldn't even go to see Demetrius Libanus in the Marcellus Theatre. He gave Joseph instructions to see, during the rehearsals, that there was no error in the representation of Jewish customs. " I have now," he said, " myself taken charge of the arrangements for the triumph and everything connected with it. I'm curious to see what impression the procession will make on you. Of course you'll be seeing it from the Circus Maximus ? "

Joseph saw that Titus was waiting with tense anxiety for his answer. Really it should have been obvious to this Roman that he, the chronicler of the campaign, must be an eye-witness of its conclusion. Strangely enough he himself had never even considered whether he should go or not. It would have been a fine thing to say : " No, Caesar Titus, I'm not going, I intend to stay at home." It would have been a satisfaction to say that ; it would have been a gesture, magnificent, but meaningless. He said : " Yes, Caesar Titus, I'll watch the procession from the Circus Maximus."

Titus's face altered. His mask-like exaggerated politeness fell away from him. " I hope, my Jew," he said warmly, " that things have been made comfortable for you in Rome. I hope," he went on, " that you'll want to live in Rome. I'll do all that I can to make that possible, believe me."

As a preparation for the triumphal procession Joseph attended the performance of Marullus's farce in the Marcellus Theatre. Demetrius Lebanus was a great actor. He was the prisoner Zachariah to the life, very real and horribly funny. At the end he was given an absurd little clown's mask, such as was often put on condemned men in the arena, so that its absurdity might provide an effective contrast to the dying struggles of its wearer. Nobody knew that under the mask of the prisoner Zachariah the actor Libanus, was almost choking for lack of air ; nobody saw his heart fluttering and failing. He bore up to the end. They bound him on the cross. He cried, as the Scripture commanded : " Hear, Israel, Jehovah is our God," and the eleven clowns danced round him disguised as asses and parodied his shrieks : " Jeh ! Jeh ! " He endured it to the end, to the moment when he was taken down from the cross after flinging money among the audience. Then he collapsed. But no one noticed it ; everybody thought he was merely acting, and amid the glorious hubbub that broke out when the coins were scattered among the audience no one had much attention in any case for the actor. Joseph managed to secure a few of the coins, two silver and several copper ones. They had been issued that very day, and they showed on one side the Emperor's head, and on the other a fettered woman sitting under a palm with the inscription : " Captive Judaea." The woman—could that be the work of Dame Caenis ?—had the features of Princess Berenice.

Next day he received a visit from his publisher Claudius Reginus. "I have been instructed," Reginus said, "to give you this ticket for the Circus Maximus." It was for a seat on the row reserved for members of the second nobility. "You're being given a high honorarium for your book," said Reginus.

"One must see it," said Joseph stubbornly. Reginus smiled his all-knowing smile. "Of course, and as your publisher it's all to my interest that you should see it. I fancy, Flavius Josephus, that you'll be the only Jew to look on and see it. Don't get angry," he said a little wearily, when Joseph seemed on the point of breaking out. "I believe you when you say that it won't be easy for you. I, too, when I take part in the procession among the Emperor's officials, intend to lace my shoes very tightly and keep a stiff upper lip."

38

ON the morning of the 8th of April Joseph was in his place in the Circus Maximus. The new circus could hold three hundred and eighty three thousand spectators, and the stone seats were filled to the last inch. Joseph had brought it off; he was sitting there among the members of the second nobility; this was the place where he had dreamt of sitting five years before. Stiff and motionless he sat among the animated crowd, his fanatical arrogant face very easy to distinguish. The others seated in these select rows knew that the Emperor had given him the task of writing the history of the war. Books were highly esteemed in Rome. Eyes were curiously turned on this man who had the power to dispense good or bad fame to so many people. Joseph's face was calm and composed, but his heart was full of rebellion. He had walked through the rejoicing streets of

Rome, all of them filled with a hubbub of happy anticipation. All the houses in the colonnades were decorated, and everywhere, on scaffoldings, ledges, trees, roofs, people wearing garlands were to be seen. Here in the Circus Maximus, too, all the spectators were garlanded and had flowers in their laps and in their arms to fling at the soldiers marching past. Joseph alone dared to sit there without garland or flowers.

At the head of the procession the members of the Senate strode somewhat stiffly in their high-heeled red shoes. The majority of them were taking part in it reluctantly, and with many secret reserves. In their hearts they were filled with contempt for the upstart to whom they had to do honour. The forwarding agent and his son had seized the Empire, but even on the throne they remained peasants and plebeians. Joseph caught sight of the lean, sceptical face of Marullus, the finely-cut, exhausted, cruel features of Mucianus. Although he wore his gala robes, Mucianus carried his stick behind his back, and his face twitched every now and then. There had been a day when the two scales of the balance were dead level, and perhaps Joseph had only needed to throw in a word for the scale of Mucianus to outweigh tha: of Vespasian.

The ministers appeared. It was only with the greatest difficulty that the infirm old minister Talassos managed to drag himself along ; but this procession was his work, and the shrivelled old fellow did not intend to miss his day of greatness. Then, quite alone, an empty space round him, came Claudius Reginus, very grave and holding himself unusually erect. No, he really wasn't taking it easily. He gazed watchfully around him with stern and angry looks, and he disappointed the expectation of the spectators ; in vain they searched his third finger for the celebrated pearl, and his shoelaces were firmly tied.

Then the band came, an enormous band. To-day it
played military airs, in particular the march of the fifth
legion which had quickly become popular : " Who can
beat the good old Fifth ? "

And then at last came the plunder captured during the
campaign, of which everyone had heard such marvellous
things. The Roman populace was spoilt. But now that
they saw all those treasures, gold, silver and ivory, not
separate pieces merely, but a stream, the spectators could not
contain themselves. They craned their necks, staring over
the head of the people in front, and the women emitted
shrill little shrieks of admiration and envy. It flowed past
in an unending river, gold, silver, precious stuffs, robes, and
ever again gold in every conceivable shape, coins, bars,
vessels of all kinds. Then engines of war, weapons, arm-
bands with the initials Makkabi, clean bands, filthy and
bloodstained bands, in baskets, in carts, many thousands of
them. Standards, banners inscribed with squat Hebraic
and Syrian-Aramaic letters, banners once made to uplift
men's hearts and now adroitly displayed to please a blasé
crowd. Movable stages painted with bloodthirsty repre-
sentations of battle scenes, some of them consisting of
gigantic four-storied scaffoldings which made the spectators
start back in terror when they were borne past ; for if they
fell they might crush one to death. Battered ships from the
sea fight outside Joppa, boats captured at Magdala. And
again gold.

So it flowed past in an endless stream. Truly gold was
no longer a rarity. It was no wonder if the price of gold
was falling and falling ; already it was worth only half
what it had been worth before the war.

But now the crowd grew quiet, for now appeared the
officials of the Imperial treasury in gala uniform and bearing

laurel branches; they were the escort guarding the most valuable part of the plunder. Borne by soldiers there appeared the golden table for the show bread, the gigantic seven branched candlestick, the ninety-three sacred vessels of the Temple, the rolls of the law. The soldiers lifted the rolls high so that everyone could see them, could see the law of Jehovah captured by Jupiter the great god of the Romans.

Next came a grotesque band. It was composed of the Temple musical instruments, the cymbals of the Levites, the blaring ram's-horn blown at the feast of the New Year, the silver trumpets which at the end of every fifty years proclaimed that all property in land returned once more to the State. The Romans played on these instruments; they parodied the melodies they had heard in Jerusalem; a ludicrous and barbarous din arose. And suddenly a joker among the spectators had a happy inspiration. " Jeh! Jeh! " he brayed like an ass. Everybody started to bray, and the sacred instruments of the Jews provided the accompaniment. A tempest of laughter swept over the long rows of the circus.

Joseph sat where he was with his face turned to stone. Keep a stiff upper lip. Everybody is looking at you. The priests had to study for ten years before they were considered worthy of playing those refractory instruments. Keep a calm face, Joseph, you represent Israel here. Pour out your fury on the nations.

Now came the living part of the plunder; the prisoners of war. From the immense number of captives seven hundred had been selected and clothed in gay robes, which contrasted effectively with their gloomy faces and their chains. Priests, too, had been forced to march among them, wearing their priestly caps and sashes. With intense

interest the spectators in the circus contemplated their
conquered enemies. There they were going past. They
had been fed abundantly, so that they should have no pretext
to break down and deny the Romans a really deserved
spectacle. But after the show was over the conquered
would be transported as forced labourers to the mines and
the tread mills, or sent to the arenas to fight beasts and
perform as gladiators.

The people sitting in the circus had become silent, and
gazed with all their eyes. But now a savage shout, a shout
filled with hatred, broke out, a shout of " Hep ! Hep ! "
of " Dogs, sons of dogs, godless dogs ! " They pelted the
captives with rotten turnips and filth. They spat, although
their spittle could not reach those it was aimed at. There
the enemy leaders Simon Bar Giora and John of Gishala
were going past, men who had once spread such fear and
panic ; but they were in chains now and humbled by the
gods. It was a great joy to the Romans, the greatest joy
they knew, to see their enemies passing before them like
this, humbled from their insolence which had driven them
to rise against the divinely ordained and ever-increasing
power of the Empire.

They had set on Simon's head a crown of nettles and dry
thorns and hung round his neck a tablet with the words :
" Simon Bar Giora, King of the Jews."   " John, General
of the Jews," they had stuck into an absurd tin suit of
armour. Simon knew that before the procession ended
he was to be executed. Thus the Romans had treated
Vercingetorix and Jugurtha and many another who had
perished at the foot of the Capitoline Hill, while up aloft
his conqueror sacrificed to the gods. Curiously enough,
Simon Bar Giora was no longer the surly fellow his men had
known towards the last ; he had regained some of the

radiance of his earlier war days.   He walked along quietly
beside John of Gishala, his legs in fetters, and they talked
to each other.

"The sky in this country is lovely," said Simon, "but
how pale it is compared to the sky in Galilee.   It's good
that I should have a blue sky over me now that I'm going
to die."   "I don't know where I'll be sent," said John,
"but I think they'll let me live."   "It's a great consolation
to me, John," said Simon, "that you'll remain alive.   For
this war isn't finished yet.   It's strange that at one time I
should have wished to kill you.   Bad as things look now, it
was a good thing that we entered on this war.   It isn't
finished yet, and those who come after us will have learnt
a great deal.   Oh, John, they'll scourge me, and they'll
lead me where their people will spit at me and pelt me with
rotten turnips, and they'll put me to a shameful death.   But
all the same it was a good thing that we began this war.
The only thing I'm sorry for is that my body will lie about
unburied."   And as John of Gishala remained silent he
went on after a pause : "Do you know, John, we should
have laid that L mine more to the right.   Then their F
tower would have fallen and what could they have done
then ? "   John of Gishala was an accommodating man, but
on tactical questions he was immovable and impatient of
nonsense.   He knew that he had been quite right about the
L mine.   But he was going to live and Simon was going
to die, and he forced himself to reply : "Yes, Simon, we
should have laid the mine more to the right.   Those who
come after us will know better."   "If we had only stood
shoulder to shoulder from the start, John," said Simon,
"we would have beaten them.   I've had a look at Titus
close at hand now ; a good fellow, but no commander.'

Joseph saw the two leaders approaching.   They were

walking slowly, so that he could see them for a long while, could see the radiant look on Simon's face, the same radiance that had lain on it when Joseph first met him going to the Temple. And then Joseph could no longer restrain himself. He tried to keep the cry back, but he could not, and it escaped him, a muffled, despairing groan, so terrible to listen to that the man sitting next him, who had just been shouting like the others " Dogs ! Sons of dogs ! " broke off in terror and turned quite pale. Joseph stared at the prisoners ; he was afraid they might look across at him. He was a hardened man, he was prepared to vouch for his deeds, but if they had looked over at him he would have died of shame and humiliation. The knowledge that he was the only Jew watching the spectacle weighed terribly upon him ; he felt he was choking. He had endured hunger and extreme thirst, scourging and all manner of shame, and he had faced death many times. But this he could not endure ; this nobody would endure. It wasn't human, it was a harder punishment that he had deserved.

The two of them were quite near now.

He would build a synagogue. All the wealth he possessed, as well as all he earned by his book, he would devote to the building ; it would be a synagogue such as Rome had never seen before. The sacred Scripture rolls he had brought from Jerusalem would be kept in it. But the Jews would have nothing to do with a synagogue built by him. They had accepted gifts from the uncircumcised, but they would accept nothing from him, and they were right.

Now the two leaders were directly below him. They did not see him. He stood up. It was impossible that they could hear him in the wild tumult, but he opened his mouth and shouted across to them the confession of faith to cheer them on their way. With a burning passion such as he had never before felt in his life he cried in a choking voice : " Hear, Israel, Jehovah is our God, Jehovah is the only God."

All at once, as though they had heard him, the Jewish prisoners began to cry, at first only a few, then more, then all of them : " Hear, Israel, Jehovah is our God, Jehovah is the only God."   When the first cries rose the spectators laughed and brayed like asses : " Jeh ! Jeh ! " But then they became silent, and some began to doubt whether it could really be to an ass that the Jews were crying.

When the cry came up to him Joseph grew calmer.   In all the synagogues of the Jews he knew that that cry was now being upraised, that ancient cry : " Hear, Israel." Had he ever denied his faith ?   He had never denied it. He had done what he had done that everyone should be made to acknowledge it.   He would write his book, he would write it with a pious heart, Jehovah would be with him.   It would be misunderstood both by the Romans and by the Jews.   A long time would have to pass before it was understood.   But a time would come when it would be understood.

But who was that walking there behind the two Jewish leaders in all the glory of the famous Temple vestments ? It was the High Priest, the builder's labourer Phanias. He walked on dully, gazing straight in front of him, his eyes almost closed as if in an oppressive nightmare.   Marullus took a look at him.   There was not very much to choose between this Phanias and John of Gishala ; each would serve equally well as a slave.   John looked the more intelligent ; one would be able to have interesting conversations with him ; but it would be more piquant to have a High Priest as one's doorkeeper.

A band next appeared, then the sacrificial oxen, and then

the crown of the whole procession, the splendid chariots of the conquerors. First appeared the lictors with their fasces garlanded with laurel, and notaries bearing the proclamation of victory ; then a troop of clowns, impudently and good-humouredly taking off the better-known traits of the imperators ; Vespasian's niggardliness and Titus's pedantic precision and shorthand. Then came a burlesque of the conquered presented by the most popular actors, among them Demetrius Libanus, the first actor of the age. Yes, he had overcome his sickness and infirmity of body, had refused to listen to his complaining heart. His art and his ambition were at stake. The Emperor had summoned him ; he had pulled himself together ; he was at his post. He was the Jew Appella ; he leapt, danced, stroked his two-pointed beard, and carried with him his phylacteries and his invisible God. Torn between the claims of his art and his eternal salvation (for he had to sacrifice one or the other) he had decided for his art. Joseph saw the tortured man passing, a great actor, a wretched human being.

Then followed the generals of the legions and the officers and men who had won distinction on the field. One man in particular was received with tumultuous applause. Wherever Pedanus, the darling of the army, the wearer of the grass garland appeared, people began to sing the catchy song of the fifth legion and spirits rose high. Yes, that man was flesh of their flesh ; that man was Rome. Nobody would get the better of that self-satisfied, self-assured fellow ; the capitoline Jupiter was with him. Vague rumours had gone round that this time, too, it was he who had brought about the victory. What he had actually done it was inexpedient to divulge for certain reasons ; but that it was something extraordinary one could easily guess from the fact that he

had once more been granted a very high decoration. Joseph
looked at the man's ugly bare face with the one sound eye.
There he swaggered past, cunning, complacent, strong,
blatant, pleased with himself, a man. No, nobody could
do anything against such assured vulgarity. This soldier
who was never in doubt, who was always on the best terms
with himself : the world belonged to such men, and it
was for such as they that Jupiter had created it.

And now approached the glittering triumphal chariot,
high as a tower, garlanded with laurel, and drawn by four
white steeds. On it stood Vespasian, his face made up to
resemble Jupiter's, the laurel crown planted on his broad
bald peasant's skull, his elderly underset body clothed in the
purple robe embroidered with golden stars which had been
taken from the shoulders of the capitoline Jupiter for this
one occasion. With a somewhat bored expression he gazed
out on the rejoicing crowd. The procession would last
for another good three hours, the robe of Jupiter was heavy,
and the long stand in the bumping chariot was anything but
comfortable. He had really taken all this upon him simply
for his son's sake. To found a dynasty was a laborious
business. It was hot. Jupiter must have a pretty hot time
in summer, seeing that his robes made one sweat like this
even in April. One simply couldn't reckon up what this
triumph would cost. Reginus had suggested twelve millions,
but it would certainly work out to thirteen or fourteen.
There were lots of better ways of spending the money, but
these fools insisted on having their spectacles, and one could
do nothing. It was pleasant to think that the Temple was
no longer in existence. The boy had managed that very
cleverly. When a rascally act was necessary one had just
to do it and invent excuses afterwards. That was the only
way one could keep one's end up in life and against the gods.

The slave standing behind him holding the heavy golden crown of Jupiter over his head shouted in the prescribed phrase : " Look behind thee and forget not that thou art a mortal." Well, well, it was to be hoped that he would live a good long while yet before he had to become a god. He thought of the statues of the deified former emperors. One of the results of this triumph would be that he would become a god a week earlier than he would have done otherwise. The chariot bumped. With a groan Vespasian cast his eye on the sundial.

Standing on the second triumphal chariot, Titus often glanced at the amulet that he was wearing to preserve him from envy and the evil eye ; for his brother Domitian, the ne'er-do-well, was standing by his side. But his fear of the envy of his brother could not spoil the glory of this day. Coldly radiant, he stood on his chariot uplifted above all human weaknesses, the soldier who had gained the victory, Jupiter himself become flesh and blood. As he passed the Imperial box he became reflective for a little while, it was true. That woman was not there, the woman they had taken from him. To whom could he show himself in his glory ? What meaning had all this without that woman to see it ? His eyes searched the crowd, searched the place where sat the members of the second nobility. When he found Joseph he outstretched his arm towards him in greeting.

The chariots of the victors passed and came to a halt at the foot of the Capitol. Eye-witnesses reported that Simon Bar Giora had been scourged and then strangled. Heralds announced the news to the people. An immense shout of rejoicing arose ; the war was ended. Vespasian and his son descended from their chariots. They offered up swine, goats and oxen to expiate their own guilt and that of the army, in case some offence displeasing to one of the gods should have been committed during the campaign.

Meanwhile the army marched past the Circus Maximus. They passed, two cohorts from each legion, also all the engines of war, including the catapults and ballistas, and Big Julius, the battering ram. The colours were greeted with tempestuous applause, in particular the golden eagle of the twelfth legion which had been recaptured from the Jews, as the eagle that the German chieftain Hermann had treacherously seized had once before been recaptured. Joseph saw the army marching past, happy, peaceable, full of contained power. The guarantee of order in the Empire. But Joseph also knew the other face of that army. He knew that all these men were like Pedanus. He had heard them bawling : " Hep ! Hep ! " He had seen them dancing, drunken with blood, on the floor of the Temple whose marble slabs were buried beneath corpses.

The march past of the troops lasted for a long time. Many people, especially in the rows where the nobility sat, went away. Joseph stayed where he was. He waited until the last of the legions had passed whom he had once seen laying waste Jerusalem and the Temple.

39

ON the evening of that 8th of April a few Jews appeared before the overseer on duty at the Mamertine prison. They produced a document stamped with a seal. The overseer read it and led them to the cellar of the prison, which was jocularly called the cold baths, for it had originally been a well. In this forlorn dark room they found the body of Simon Bar Giora. According to ancient custom his corpse should have been flung that night into the refuse heap on the Esquiline. But the men had been given permission to take charge of his dead body and do with it what they pleased. It was Claudius Reginus who had obtained this privilege. He had obtained it in return for his pearl, which he had resigned to Dame Caenis in exchange.

So the men took charge of the scarred and blood-encrusted corpse of the Jewish commander, laid it on a bier, and covered it up. Then they bore it through the city, which was brilliantly lit with festive illuminations. They walked bare-foot. At the Capenian Gate several hundred more Jews awaited them, among them Caius Barzaarone. They, too were bare-footed, and their garments were rent. They carried the dead body, changing the bearers every fifty yards, along the Appian Way until they came to the second mile stone. There Claudius Reginus was waiting for them. They bore the dead Jewish leader down into the underground burial place of the Jews. They laid him in a coffin, bedded his blackened head in soil taken from Judaea, and poured scented water over it. Then they closed the tomb and fixed a tablet to it. On the tablet was scratched in clumsy Greek letters: "Simon Bar Giora, Soldier of Jehovah." Thereupon they washed their hands and left the burial place.

40

JOSEPH walked from the Circus Maximus to his house. He had fulfilled his task; he had not spared himself; he had witnessed the course of the Jewish war to the very end. But now he was at the limit of his strength. He collapsed and fell into a sleep that was like the sleep of death.

He was alone in the great, empty, forlorn house, with only an old slave to attend to him, and so he was not disturbed. He slept for twenty hours. Then he got up and knelt on the floor in the posture of a mourner.

A courier from the Imperial palace arrived with the auspicious laurel wreath. When the slave conducted him to this figure who crouched on the floor with unshaven face and rent garments, ashes sprinkled on his head, the messenger doubted whether this could really be the man to whom he was sent. Hesitatingly he handed Joseph the letter. It was in the handwriting of Vespasian saying that the secretary of the Imperial archives had been instructed to give Joseph access to all documents he might wish to examine for the purposes of his book. Moreover the Emperor was pleased to grant him the golden ring of the second nobility. It was the first time that the courier was not given a tip for appearing with the laurel wreath. Joseph contented himself with reading the chief heads of the letter. Then he relapsed into his former posture.

The youth Cornelius came. The slave did not dare to admit him to Joseph.

After seven days Joseph emerged from his mourning. He asked what had been happening in the meantime. He heard that Cornelius had called, and sent for him.

When Cornelius arrived the second time Joseph and he did not say very much to each other. Joseph announced that he needed a good and reliable secretary. Would Cornelius like to help him in the writing of his book? Cornelius beamed with happiness.

That very same day Joseph began his work.

"It is probable," he dictated, "that other writers will attempt to describe the war of the Jews against the Romans, writers who were not eye-witnesses of the actual events and who will have to rely on foolish and contradictory rumours. I, Joseph, the son of Matthias, priest of the first rank in Jerusalem, and an eye-witness of those happenings from the beginning, have therefore resolved to write the history of this war as it actually happened, that it may be a remembrance to my contemporaries and a warning to later generations."

The End

Lion Feuchtwanger, 1884–1958, was a prolific author of novels, plays, critical essays, and short fiction. Among his works are The Ugly Duchess *and* The Power. Josephus *is the first part of a trilogy which includes* The Jew of Rome *and* Josephus and the Emperor. *Feuchtwanger left Germany in 1933 and lived in Sanary-Sur-Mer, France. Feuchtwanger and his wife, Marta, escaped to the United States in October 1940 and settled in Los Angeles with a number of other refugee writers.*

Atheneum Paperbacks

Atheneum Paperbacks

LITERATURE AND THE ARTS

Atheneum Paperbacks

THE WORLDS OF NATURE AND MAN

LIFE SCIENCES AND ANTHROPOLOGY

Atheneum Paperbacks

PSYCHOLOGY AND SOCIOLOGY

STUDIES IN HUMAN BEHAVIOR

Alfred M. Freedman, M.D., and Harold I. Kaplan, M.D., General Editors

Atheneum Paperbacks

STUDIES IN AMERICAN NEGRO LIFE

Atheneum Paperbacks

HISTORY—AMERICAN—BEFORE 1900

Atheneum Paperbacks

HISTORY—AMERICAN—1900 TO THE PRESENT